TEE TIMES

On the Road with the Ladies
Professional Golf Tour

JIM BURNETT

A LISA DREW BOOK
SCRIBNER

A LISA DREW BOOK / SCRIBNER
1230 Avenue of the Americas
New York, NY 10020

Designed by Colin Joh
Set in Bembo

Manufactured in the United States of America

1 3 5 7 9 10 8 6 4 2

Library of Congress Cataloging-in-Publication Data is available.

ISBN 0-684-83128-7

For my father, who taught me the game of golf as well as
many other things of enduring value

Contents

Acknowledgements

This book was a team effort. Special thanks to two people who made it possible: agent extraordinaire Denise Marcil, who found the perfect home for a proposal lost in the labyrinths of the publishing world; Lisa Drew, a terrific person to work with as well as a wonderful editor whose guidance was invaluable.

Thanks to Kim Higgins, artist and friend, for the photos and the introduction to Japan.

Thanks to those who read the proposal, sample chapters, or manuscript pages at various stages: Dale Cockerill, Holly Towle, James Bartlett, April Henry, Joel Avina, Kim Higgins, George Kehoe, Nancy Warren, Judy Rankin.

For research assistance and/or advice, thanks to Christine Brennan, Geoff Russell, Liz Kahn, Guy Towle, Lewine Mair, Rhonda Glenn, Patricia Davies, Charlcie Hopkins, Lisa Mickey, Margaret Maves, Khristine Januzik, Rich Weinstein.

Thanks to the LPGA staff, in particular Elaine Scott and the communications department for research material, Jim Webb for travel arrangements in Japan, Ty Votaw for Solheim Cup travel arrangements, and Kathy Peterson for travel planning and reservations.

Thanks for the hospitality to Dick and Claire in Phoenix; Rich in Los Gatos; Kim in New York; Mike, Jennifer, and Monica at the 4th Street Cafe in Ocean City, N.J.; Bill and Paddy in Chepstow, Wales; Bill and Clara in Ocean City; Paul and Suzanne in Edmonton; Patricia in Wilmington; Joe Adams at British Airlines.

Finally, thanks to all the players, caddies, and LPGA officials and staff for treating a visitor to their world so decently. And, in particular, a very special thank you to Patty Sheehan, Juli Inkster, Caroline Pierce, and Leslie Spalding. I'll always be grateful for your time, generosity, and good spirits.

The 1996 LPGA Schedule

TOURNAMENT	DATE	PURSE
Chrysler-Plymouth Tournament of Champions, Orlando, FL	January 11–14	$725,000
HealthSouth Inaugural, Orlando, FL	January 19–21	450,000
Cup Noodles Hawaiian Ladies Open, Kapoleo, Oahu, HI	February 22–24	600,000
Ping/Welch's Championship, Tucson, AZ	March 14–17	450,000
Standard Register PING, Phoenix, AZ	March 21–24	700,000
Nabisco Dinah Shore, Rancho Mirage, CA	March 28–31	900,000
Twelve Bridges LPGA Classic, Lincoln, CA	April 4–7	500,000
Chick-fil-A Charity Championship, Stockbridge, GA	April 19–21	550,000
Sara Lee Classic, Old Hickory, TN	April 26–28	600,000
Sprint Titleholders Championship, Daytona Beach, FL	May 2–5	1,200,000
McDonald's LPGA Championship, Wilmington, DE	May 10–12	1,200,000
LPGA Corning Classic, Corning, NY	May 23–26	600,000
JCPenney/LPGA Skins Game, Frisco, TX	May 25–26	540,000
U.S. Women's Open, Southern Pines, NC	May 30–June 2	1,200,000
Oldsmobile Classic, East Lansing, MI	June 6–9	600,000
First Bank Presents Edina Realty LPGA Classic, Brooklyn Park, MN	June 14–16	550,000
Rochester International, Pittsford, NY	June 20–23	600,000
ShopRite LPGA Classic, Somers Point, NJ	June 28–30	750,000
Jamie Farr Kroger Classic, Sylvania, OH	July 5–7	575,000
Youngstown-Warren LPGA Classic, Warren, OH	July 12–14	600,000
Friendly's Classic, Agawam, MA	July 18–21	500,000
Michelob Light Heartland Classic, St. Louis, MO	July 25–28	550,000
du Maurier Classic, Edmonton, Alberta, Canada	August 1–4	1,000,000
Ping Welch's Championship, Canton, MA	August 8–11	500,000
Weetabix Women's British Open, Milton Keynes, England	August 15–18	850,000
Star Bank LPGA Classic, Dayton, OH	August 23–25	550,000
State Farm Rail Classic, Springfield, IL	Aug. 31–Sept. 2	575,000
The Safeway LPGA Golf Championship, Portland, OR	September 6–8	550,000
Safeco Classic, Kent, WA	Sept. 12–15	550,000
The Solheim Cup, Chepstow, Wales	Sept. 20–22	
Fieldcrest Cannon Classic, Charlotte, NC	Sept. 26–29	500,000
JAL Big Apple Classic, New Rochelle, NY	October 3–5	725,000
CoreStates Betsy King Classic, Reading, PA	October 10–13	600,000
Samsung World Championship of Women's Golf, Korea	October 17–20	500,000
Nichirei International, Ibaragi-ken, Japan	October 25–27	675,000
Toray Japan Queens Cup, Inashiki-gun, Japan	November 1–3	750,000
ITT LPGA Tour Championship, Las Vegas, NV	November 21–24	700,000

"That's all I've ever really been interested in: whatever happened to the American Dream."

—HUNTER THOMPSON

"Golf is like faith: It is the substance of things hoped for, the evidence of things not seen . . ."

—ARNOLD HAULTAIN, *The Mystery of Golf* (1908)

TEE TIMES

$\mathcal{P}$alm Springs: Prelude to a Golf Tournament

For a professional golfer, the practice range is a laboratory and an assembly line. Swings are analyzed and dissected, evaluated and corrected, repetitiously grooved, and occasionally even resurrected. But never perfected.

At the plush Mission Hills County Club in Rancho Mirage, California, on Tuesday, March 26, 1996, two days before the kickoff of the first major championship of the season, the $900,000 Nabisco Dinah Shore, the range is a beehive of sound and motion.

On a rectangular field about 300 yards long and 100 yards wide, the best women golfers in the world blast shots that rocket into the powder blue sky, arcing toward nearby sandhills and distant blue-black peaks of the Little San Bernadino mountain range before tumbling to the sunlit sea-green lawn.

It's a picture postcard spring day in the Coachella Valley: brilliant sunshine, temperature in the mid 70s, a hint of a breeze rustling the leaves of the spidery mesquite trees lining both sides of the range. Sparrows and doves flit through the branches, their chirps and trills mingling with the "THWACK, THWACK, THWACK" of irons slicing through the turf and the high-pitched "CLICK, CLICK, CLICK" of the ultimate oxymoron, metal woods.

Located in the basin of the valley, Mission Hills is ringed by sandhills and mountains—the Little San Bernadinos to the north and east, the Santa Rosas to the south, and, to the west, San Gorgonio Mountain and Mount San Jacinto, which looms over downtown Palm Springs like a black, craggy wall. San Jacinto Peak looks like it has been dusted with a sprinkling of powdered sugar, remnants of the near year-round snow atop its 10,804-foot summit.

Patty Sheehan, dressed in a white sleeveless sweater vest, tan shirt, and green shorts—a departure from her trademark knickers—is in the middle of the range, hitting irons with her classic, almost flawless swing. "Sheehan's swing," Tom Boswell once wrote in Golf magazine, "makes [PGA star] Mark Calcavecchia look like a driving range pro." Arrayed behind

Sheehan and the line of other players are small knots of instructors, equipment reps with bags of clubs (Callaway, Taylor Made, Rawlings, Carbite Golf), family members, agents, photographers, and camera crews.

Caddies, attired in white jumpsuits with the name of their boss stenciled on the back, also are at home on the range. They visit with their buddies, study the swing of their players, clean clubs, and fetch fresh buckets of balls.

No scuffed-up, black-striped range balls here! No nets or mats either! The pros practice with pristine Titleist Tour Balata 100s, donated, to the tune of 4,896 (408 dozen) new balls every week, by the premier golf ball manufacturer in the game. (They are later donated to junior golf programs. Caddies are warned that pilfering the choice orbs can result in banishment from the Tour.)

The range is packed. Nancy Lopez, waiting for a spot to open up, stands behind Sheehan, kibitzing with her caddie, Tom Thorpe, and Sheehan's looper, Carl "Caddie Machine" Laib.

Sheehan and Lopez, both 39, are two of only fourteen members of the LPGA Hall of Fame, the most exclusive club in sports. They have accounted for 81 career victories and official earnings of over $9 million, not bad for whacking a ball around a field with a stick. Despite the fiercely competitive nature of the game, they also constitute something of a mutual admiration society.

"We've always been good friends," says Lopez, "and we're probably better friends now because of the respect we've developed for each other through the years. She's always been one of my favorites to play with because of her attitude—she's a 'go out and get it' type player."

Sheehan says she has "always admired Nancy for her ability to be courteous and respectful of *everyone* she meets. She's certainly the master of any situation, the best. There was a lot of criticism and people jealous of her when she was a rookie—it didn't set well, her winning nine tournaments. She handled that like a real champion."

And despite the awesome influx of young talent from around the world, led by Sweden's Annika Sorenstam, 25, and Australia's Karrie Webb, 21, the old pros aren't ready to pull up their rocking chairs. Lopez, mother of three daughters, splits her time between the Tour and her home in Albany, Georgia. Yet she still managed to earn $210,862 and rank twenty-eighth on the money list in 1995. Lopez also had a grand opportunity to capture the Dinah Shore last year, before a balky putter betrayed her down the stretch.

Sheehan won in Rochester and Seattle last year, ranking fourteenth on the money list with $333,147, even though a new set of Callaway Big

Bertha irons gave her fits. After her victory in Seattle in September, a burned-out Sheehan took the longest break of her professional career. She tossed the clubs in the closet for three and a half months and relaxed at her new home in Reno, gardening, lounging by the pool, raising money for charity at her annual Silver Belle girls junior tournament, finishing up an instructional book, and dabbling in course design and even art. (Collaborating with painter Don Kettleborough, Sheehan smacked golf balls soaked in different colored paints into a canvas. The resulting work—abstract, to say the least—sold for $10,000.)

Now Sheehan is refreshed and eager. "She's jazzed to play," said her manager and best friend, Rebecca Gaston, early last week as we watched Sheehan practice her chipping in Phoenix. "You usually don't see her at the course on a Monday."

Sheehan posted a solid seventh in Tucson and a ninth in Phoenix in the past two weeks. But she's still missing the touch she used to have with Taylor Made blades, which fit her like an old, treasured baseball glove.

However, you won't hear Sheehan complain about Callaway, the strongest presence in women's golf, with 23 LPGA players in its stable. Sheehan left Taylor Made two years ago after the company offered the two-time U.S. Open champion a contract extension worth about $30,000 per year, which Gaston termed "insulting." Shopping for a new club deal, Gaston sent Callaway a proposal, asking for dollars at the top of the scale for women pros. She received a phone call from Ely Callaway, the CEO and founder of the company that sold $553 million worth of clubs last year.

"Rebecca, would it be okay with you if we added seventy-five K to your proposal? We'd like to pay Patty what we're paying our top PGA players."

Gaston allowed that it would, indeed, be okay.

Last week Sheehan switched shafts for the sixth time this season, changing from graphite to steel, which she abandoned two years ago because of tendinitis in her elbows. But the tendinitis is gone. Sheehan is hoping the return to steel, which is more stressful at impact on the arms and shoulders and elbows, will bring back her old pinpoint control.

Sheehan's goals for 1996 are simple—secure a spot on the U.S. Solheim Cup team and win the Dinah Shore, the only big prize in women's golf that has eluded her.

The Dinah Shore is extra special for Sheehan this year for very personal reasons. Patty's father and mother, Bobo and Leslie, live in Mission Hills. Several weeks ago, Bobo, 73, was hospitalized for five days with serious liver problems.

Like many little girls, Sheehan worshipped her father. "Sports was a man's world, and Patty wanted to be near Daddy," said Claire Shields, Sheehan's former publicist. "He's been the moving force in her life."

To some extent, Sheehan's success on Tour seems almost preordained. For an athlete, she has impeccable bloodlines. Father Bobo coached football, baseball, golf, and skiing at Middlebury College in Vermont. Mother Leslie, a nurse, was also a fine athlete. Patty's three older brothers were champion skiers.

In fact, Patty's name has been on the lips of sports announcers since birth. Sheehan was born during a Middlebury football game. The announcer told the cheering crowd, "Here's a final: Patricia Sheehan, seven pounds, fourteen ounces."

Although Bobo never pushed his children into athletics, the Sheehan house often resembled a gymnasium and locker room. The kids tried virtually every sport—baseball, basketball, golf, the trampoline, even pole vaulting. Jaw jutting out, Patty tried to match her big brothers step-for-step. When she was 4 years old, Patty was elbowing timid college students out of the way on the Middlebury College ski jump, fearlessly swooshing down the ramp and soaring into space.

Sheehan can't make her father well. But she can honor him with a gift, and the gift she most wants to give him, says Gaston, is simple: "A Dinah for Dad."

The arrival of Lopez, still the most popular figure in women's golf, lures a group of intrepid autograph seekers, who scurry under the yellow rope at the back of the range. Caddie Thorpe waits until the first batch of fans have an autograph on their programs or posters. But when a second wave approaches, the six-foot-four Thorpe says, in a friendly but commanding voice, "You're gonna have to wait until she's done practicing."

Lopez has one of the most unorthodox swings in the game. She raises her hands vertically just before takeaway, then brings the club back so slowly it's like watching the door of an old house with rusty hinges creak open. When she was a junior golfer—Lopez won the 1969 New Mexico Women's Amateur at the age of 12, defeating CBS and ESPN golf analyst Mary Bryan 10 and 8—people used to tell her, "Oh, you'll never get anywhere with that swing."

Fortunately, she ignored the critics. Years later, she would say, "My swing is no uglier than Arnold Palmer's, and it's the same ugly swing every time."

The "ugly" swing has been one of the most reliable the game has seen. Dee Darden, who caddied for Lopez for years before becoming a golf photographer, once told *Golf World*, "Lopez hits the ball flush almost one hundred percent of the time. After being with Nancy so long, I get frustrated watching our great male pros hitting it sideways. I don't understand why they can't hit the ball flush, too, most of the time."

Give Lopez the last word. "What happens just in front and after impact is the only thing that matters."

She's right, of course. Just ask Lee Trevino or Jim Furyk or Miller Barber or Moe Norman, or dozens of other pros who attack a golf ball with a swing that drives the purists nuts. You can send your backswing via Pony Express to Boise or Atlanta as long as you eventually arrive in the correct hitting position.

Golf swings are as distinctive as fingerprints, and the variety of swings on the range is quite remarkable. Jan Stephenson, 44, still as petite and shapely as in her *Playboy* pictorial days, swings almost as hard at a golf ball as José Canseco swings at a baseball, nearly wrapping the club around her neck with the force of her follow-through. Three-time U.S. Open winner Hollis Stacy, 42, recuperating from off-season knee surgery, cranks out irons with a simple, lovely, rhythmic tempo. Marta Figueras-Dotti, 38, a veteran from Spain, takes the club back in a low, flat arc and sweeps across the ball, finishing with the club resting on her left shoulder. Helen Alfredsson, 30, the tall, fiery Swede, tucks her hands close to her body, pulls the club to the inside at takeaway, loops it to the outside at the top, then explodes straight down the line, generating blinding clubhead speed. Schoolmarmish Shelley Hamlin, 45, who won the 1992 Phar-Mor at Inverrary just seven months after a modified radical mastectomy for breast cancer, her first victory in 14 years, hits the ball with an easy, graceful motion that doesn't seem to generate enough power to blow out a match. Short, stocky, Hall of Famer Sandra Haynie, 52, one of the former champions invited to compete in the Dinah Shore as part of its 25-year anniversary celebration, displays a silky smooth tempo and weight transfer as polished as the gears of a Mercedes. Annika Sorenstam, 25, begins to turn and lift her head before impact, which is considered one of golf's cardinal sins.

One of the appealing aspects about golf is that body type is not necessarily destiny. In golf, the little boy or girl, the chubby boy or girl, the frail boy or girl, still has a fighting chance. In golf, discipline, temperament, tenacity, guts, and hard work outweigh raw athletic ability.

That's how Sorenstam became the top woman golfer in the world last year. Sorenstam is a good athlete, but she never cracked the top ten as a junior tennis player in the city of Stockholm. So she turned to golf, a game she could practice on her own, and worked like a maniac. "When I do something, I want to do it one hundred percent," she says. "I want to do it right." That's why John Daly, blessed with as much raw talent as anyone in the world, wins an occasional major on courses conducive to big bombers, but usually loses, often in embarrassing, halfhearted efforts, to the Corey Pavins and the Mark O'Mearas of the world the rest of the time.

For LPGA players, the Dinah Shore is the women's equivalent of the Masters. It's the tournament that put the LPGA on the map and on TV screens across America. It was created by David Foster, CEO of the Colgate-Palmolive Company, who was searching for a marketing vehicle to reach women consumers. Seizing upon golf, Foster anted up a $110,000 purse for the inaugural 1972 event. Players were stunned: at the time the average LPGA purse was $30,000, and the highest $50,000. Sportscaster Heywood Hale Broun declared that Colgate (which also initiated several other big-money international women's events, and paid large salaries to 26 LPGA pros to sign with Colgate-owned Ram Golf Company) had pulled the LPGA out of "the sisterhood of the semisolvent." Foster used LPGA players extensively in his advertising. ABC commentator Judy Rankin, who won the Dinah Shore in 1976, made her TV debut in commercials for Colgate dental creme and Fab laundry soap.

Other companies followed the leader, upping purses and endorsement deals. By 1977, ten LPGA events boasted purses of at least $100,000, but the Dinah Shore still led the pack by a wide margin with prize money of $240,000, and outshone the U.S. Open in terms of viewing audience and prestige.

Foster retired in 1979; Nabisco became the tournament's title sponsor in 1981. Bolstered by the energetic, hands-on efforts of Dinah Shore, who initially assumed Foster was asking her to lend her name to a women's *tennis* tournament, the Dinah Shore retained its status among LPGA players, even as other tournaments, most notably the U.S. Open and the LPGA Championship (now the McDonald's LPGA Championship), ponied up fatter purses, and as other sporting events, most notably the NCAA College Basketball Tournament and the PGA Players Championship, relegated the Dinah Shore to also-ran status on the tube.

However, the death of Dinah Shore from cancer in 1994, just a month before the tournament, was a tremendous blow.

"Dinah was a really cool person, a tremendous friend," says Mike Galeski, who worked for the tournament committee from 1980 to 1993, serving as tournament director the last seven years.

"*Everybody* liked her," says the lanky, affable Galeski, now vice president in charge of the tour players division at Callaway. "She made them feel comfortable. She had the patience of a Southern lady while being totally genuine in the process. You were enriched by being around her."

"The year 1994 was a tough one," says tournament director Terry

Wilcox. "She didn't talk to *anyone* about her illness; then she was in the hospital and dying."

Shore, who lived near the 9th hole of the tournament course at Mission Hills, had immense regard and affection for the players and became a fairly decent golfer after taking up the game later in life. In many ways Shore was the best marketing person the LPGA has had in its 46-year history. Her description of LPGA players as "wind-blown all-American girls" outclasses almost anything LPGA image-makers have devised.

"The tournament," says Nancy Lopez, "is not quite the same now. Dinah is really missed by everybody." Sponsors, players, and total strangers were touched by her generosity. At the 1994 Dinah Shore, I met two women from Seattle who had been standing in the clubhouse at Mission Hills a few years earlier. Shore had strolled over and, out of the blue, invited them to a barbecue at her house.

Wilcox admits the 1995 Dinah Shore lacked its usual luster. A columnist in *Golfweek* speculated that the tournament itself was in jeopardy, theorizing that Kohlberg, Kravis, Roberts (KKR), the firm that acquired control of Nabisco after a bitter takeover battle in 1988 (later chronicled in the book and movie *Barbarians at the Gate*), might be fed up with the "other" events of tournament week: the annual invasion of 20,000 or so lesbians into Palm Springs from across the country. The party, known as Dinah Shore Week, links the golf tournament, in name if not in fact, with one of the largest gatherings of gay women in the world.

In the staid, conservative golf industry, such an association gives the LPGA and Nabisco the heebie-jeebies. And leads to some amusing questions from the golf media, far out of its comfort zone when it encounters hot-button social issues.

"To what do you attribute the migration of lesbians to the desert?" a reporter once asked Galeski.

"Unlike Canada geese," he replied dryly, "it's not a North-South issue."

Nabisco would breathe a sigh of relief if the gay hordes decided to descend someplace else for spring break. But it seems grudgingly resigned to the annual invasion.

"Nabisco's commitment as it stands today is one hundred ten percent," says Wilcox, noting that the company has a five-year deal with Mission Hills and that the Dinah Shore has become a prestigious event on the crowded convention calendar of the Food Manufacturers Association, a vehicle allowing Nabisco to wine and dine its prime suppliers and customers. Rumors about the demise of the Dinah Shore are old hat, says Galeski. "Did they think Nabisco was just being a good Samaritan? They spend all that money because it's an excellent sponsorship opportunity."

How much money? About $5 million each year, including the purse money and about $1 million to ABC for air-time and commercial spots.

So tournament officials try to ignore Dinah Shore Week. When asked about it, Wilcox, sitting in the conference room at the tournament office in Mission Hills, which features a large oil painting of Dinah Shore, stares out the window. In a flat, expressionless tone he says, "Whatever happens in that world, we try to stay away from. We don't condemn it, we don't promote it. We're not trying to move it forward or set it back. We don't want to start it or stop it. It's an issue in society wherever people are."

It's been quite a 25-year evolution. The Dinah Shore has, in the mid-1990s, grown into three separate, overlapping, but distinctly different events: a golf tournament, a major bash for the food industry, and an exuberant celebration for lesbians.

The 129 players who will tee it up Thursday could not, of course, care less about the latter two side shows.

Usually LPGA tournament fields consist of 144 golfers. Although the Dinah Shore is a regular-season event, technically it is an invitational with its own set of eligibility criteria. Those invited to tee it up include winners on the LPGA Tour from 1986 through 1995, the top 60 money winners from 1995, anyone finishing in the top three in an LPGA event in 1994 or 1993, and Hall of Fame members. Instead of the normal allotment of two sponsor's exemptions, the Dinah Shore gets up to fifteen, which it usually doles out to a number of amateur stars, and several standouts from the Japanese Tour.

For the contestants the Dinah Shore is the beginning of a front-loaded spring schedule of eight events to June 2 that includes the most important majors—the Dinah Shore, the McDonald's LPGA Championship in Wilmington, Delaware, and the U.S. Open in Southern Pines, North Carolina—as well as the women's version of the Players Championship, the $1.2 million Sprint Titleholders Championship in Daytona Beach.

(The Dinah Shore is the sixth event of the 1996 LPGA season. Two tournaments, the Tournament of Champions, won by Liselotte Neumann, and the HealthSouth Inaugural, won by Australian rookie sensation Karrie Webb, were played in January. Just one tournament, the Cup Noodles Hawaiian Ladies Open, won by Meg Mallon, was played in February. The concentrated week-to-week grind of the Tour kicked into gear two weeks ago with the Ping/Welch's Championship in Tucson, won by Neumann, and the Standard Register Ping in Phoenix, won for the third consecutive year by Laura Davies.)

If major titles and massive paychecks weren't enough, the next two months will go a long way to determine the 1996 Solheim Cup teams, pitting the U.S. versus Europe at the St. Pierre Golf and Country Club in Chepstow, Wales, on September 20–22. In its short five-year history, the Solheim Cup has become the biggest event in women's golf. When the Europeans upset the Americans to win the cup in 1992, it heralded an international boom in the women's game.

Two weeks ago in Tucson a reporter mentioned the Solheim Cup to England's Alison Nicholas, who teamed with Laura Davies to lead Europe to victory in 1992. In 1994, when America recaptured the cup, Nicholas and Davies lost to Dottie Pepper (formerly Mochrie—she reclaimed her maiden name after a divorce last year) and Brandie Burton, in a bitter match that drew howls of criticism from British reporters. They accused Burton, and especially Pepper, of Ugly American behavior, openly rooting against their opponents and refusing to concede putts of tap-in length.

As the diminutive Nicholas, who won twice last year on the LPGA Tour, walked away to practice her putting, she smiled broadly and uttered one word, drawing it out to make it reverberate in the air: "Revennnngee!"

With a major championship and $900,000 at stake, the players will leave the partying this week to the food company moguls and the gay tourists. For LPGA professionals, this week is strictly business.

At 8:40 on Wednesday morning Juli Inkster, winner of the Dinah Shore in 1984 and 1989, tees off in the pro-am. Her playing partners are Bob Piccinici, chairman and CEO of Save Mart Supermarkets, Martin Wingard, director of accounts development for Nabisco, Doug Carolan, executive vice president and CEO of Associated Wholesale Grocers, and Lyle Yates, president of the Kroger Company.

It's another gorgeous day in the valley, warm with a hint of a breeze. Birds twitter cheerfully in the trees; ducks float lazily on the ponds. Walking the golf course with Inkster and her teammates for the day is a particular treat. The greens are as smooth and slick as billiard tables. The fairways are cropped as close as a marine haircut. The rough is as thick and matted as an old hippie's beard. It's easy to understand why the tournament course at Mission Hills was named last fall as the number-one layout in the Coachella Valley by the *Desert Sun* newspaper.

For the executives from the food industry, the two-day pro-am is the highlight of a party that began when they arrived in town last Saturday and ends when they leave Palm Springs tonight or tomorrow, just as the tournament itself begins.

Guests of Nabisco pay their own travel expenses, but everything else is on the house, including a gift bag containing two watches, sweaters and shirts for the executive and his (or, in a few cases, her) spouse, a sterling silver hourglass, Bolle golf sunglasses, Footjoy shoes and accessories, Ralph Lauren luggage, a sterling silver photo album, and a Nabisco blanket to cuddle up with on the flight home. Estimated value: $3,500.

There's more: plush accommodations at the Palm Springs Hilton, tennis and exercise classes, practice rounds Sunday and Monday, dinners and hospitality suites, and the chance to rub elbows with celebrities ranging from Johnny Bench to Julius "Dr. J." Erving to soap stars Kimberlin Brown and John Callahan to Joanna Kerns, Joe Pesci, and Alan Thicke.

In previous years, Inkster has drawn some high-powered celebrity pro-am partners—Joe DiMaggio, Dr. J., John Havlicek. In 1985, as defending champion, she played with Gerald Ford, Bob Hope, former hockey star Bobby Orr, and F. Ross Johnson, who set new standards of extravagance as the head of Nabisco before initiating the ill-fated management-led takeover bid in 1988 that put Nabisco into play, drew KKR into the battle, and led *Time* magazine to portray Johnson as its cover-boy symbol of the greed of the 1980s.

(Johnson spent other people's money like it was confetti: billing Nabisco for his two dozen country club memberships; commanding a fleet of ten corporate jets; distributing authentic French bonbons twice a day at reception areas in the Atlanta headquarters; prowling New York night spots with the likes of Frank Gifford and Roone Arledge. He spread the wealth to friends and colleagues as well, paying jocks such as Dandy Don Meredith ($500,000 per year) and Gifford ($413,000 plus a New York apartment and office) to join Team Nabisco, his cadre of celebrity endorsers and glad-handers. Team Nabisco featured star golfers too: Ben Crenshaw ($400,000), Fuzzy Zoeller ($300,000), and Jack Nicklaus, who earned a cool $1 million for six appearances a year, according to *Barbarians at the Gate* authors Bryan Burrough and John Helyar. O. J. Simpson was a teammate ($250,000), "but he was a perennial no-show at Team Nabisco events."

Johnson spent $10 million to stage the Dinah Shore, twice as much as current management. Some of that money trickled down to the masses. Rick Aune, who caddies for LPGA player Caroline Pierce, once took home an entire case of Nabisco goodies. Jerry Potter, veteran golf writer for *USA Today*, says the media center was so stuffed with packages of Oreos and Ritz he "used to have to knock the stuff out of the way to go to work.")

Although a few Secret Service agents, comically dressed in an approximation of golf attire, hovered around Ford, the 200 or so spectators could get as close as a handshake from the ex-president on the tees.

Ex-presidents, at least this one, perhaps are best viewed at a distance. Ford handled requests for autographs and photos from well-behaved fans—mostly women and their children—with curt irritation. "Did I hear you say please?" he snapped at one fan with a camera.

Hope, on the other hand, was charming. His face an ashen gray, the then 81-year-old delighted the fans, humming a tune as he teed it up, and boyishly bouncing on his toes after smacking a drive down the heart of the fairway.

Inkster's view, from inside the ropes, was just the opposite. She found Ford to be "a nice guy, a real gentleman." As for Hope, Inkster shrugs, "He played to the galleries. That's his job. He called me Judy all day long. I corrected him after the first hole, then I gave up. I ran into him at the pro-am party that night, and he said to [wife] Dolores, 'This is Judy. I played with her today'!"

In the mid 1980s Johnson's social circle and Nabisco's lavish entertainment budget lured top-of-line entertainers such as Hope and Frank Sinatra to the Dinah Shore.

But in recent years the celebrity entertainers have tended to be a bit musty—Steve Lawrence and Edie Gorme topped the bill last year, with Toni Tennille on the undercard. So this year tournament organizers have punched it up, importing singers and avid golfers Amy Grant, Vince Gill, and even Alice Cooper, onetime bad boy of rock and roll. Cooper is now a spokesman for Callaway, along with the placid purveyor of jazz saxophone Muzak, Kenny G. (Golf, not politics, truly makes strange bedfellows.) Cooper, known for performing in Satanic makeup with a boa constrictor wrapped around his neck, was something of a gamble in the eyes of tournament director Wilcox. "I was reluctant when his name came up," says Wilcox with a wry smile, "me not being a hip music aficionado. We're gonna see how he acts here."

No need to worry. Cooper, lounging in the clubhouse two days ago, was wearing a red golf shirt, khaki pants, a Callaway visor and a long black ponytail, instead of a reptile, snaking down past his shoulders. Like many other musicians, golf has become Cooper's new drug of choice—and an addictive one at that. "I traded a bad habit for a very good one," Cooper told *Golfweek*. "I used to drink V.O. and Coke from seven in the morning until I couldn't walk. I'd throw up blood in the morning. So when I got out of the hospital, I substituted thirty-six holes of golf a day for drinking."

Juli Inkster knows doctors and hospitals too.

When her daughter Hayley, now 6, was younger and suffering frequent ear infections, Inkster searched out pediatricians at virtually every Tour stop. Her daughter Cori, who just turned 2 on Monday, was sick in Tucson two weeks ago. Last evening at six o'clock, Juli took Cori to the emergency room with an ear infection and fever.

"Then I had to go to that dinner"—the Friends of Dinah shindig at the Palm Springs Convention Center, where the former tournament champions were introduced.

And what a dinner! With the Convention Center gussied up to look like a ritzy supper club complete with dim lighting, squadrons of waiters, and a 40-piece orchestra on stage, Nabisco really strapped on the feedbag for some 800 guests. No Snackwells here! The menu included:

- Arrangement of Chilled Maine Lobster & Gulf Shrimp served on a Mango-Basil Coulis and Baby Red Oak
- Roasted Beef Tenderloin with Red Wine and Horseradish Sauce
- Dauphinoise Potatoes
- Steamed Baby Fresh Vegetables
- Multi-Chocolate Terrine served on Mixed Berry and Coffee Bean Sauce

The steak was tender enough to cut with a fork. And the dessert was to die for—or at least risk a heart attack.

A smorgasbord of entertainment followed, ranging from comedian Norm Crosby, who smarmily worked the names of Nabisco executives into his jokes, Susan Anton, who belted out two Broadway numbers, an all-too-short set from Vince Gill and Amy Grant, corny but funny jokes from Gary Mule Deer, and an egregious display of ego by Hal "Barney Miller" Linden, who worked every award garnered since his Boy Scout days into a routine about New York City.

By this time Inkster was long gone. She escaped the dinner about 10:00, went to sleep at 11:00, brought Cori into bed with her and husband Brian when Cori woke up crying at 1:30 ("I had feet in my face all night," she jokes), and got up at 6:30 to make breakfast for the kids and herself. To her relief, Cori seemed fine this morning, but Mom was a bit drained.

Still, the show must go on. Pro-ams are the lifeblood of the LPGA Tour. (The PGA, which receives millions from the networks for rights to telecast their tournaments and has major corporations clamoring to sign on as sponsors, is not as dependent on pro-ams.)

So Inkster, dressed in a shortsleeve white-knit jersey with black Izod Club logo, black-and-white houndstooth shorts, black-and-white two-toned shoes, and a white visor with Wilson stenciled in red on the bill, performs her duties as hostess with grace and skill, picking up divots and calling out encouragement.

"Okay, Lyle. Stuffarooni . . . Get up . . . Nice shot."

"Kay, Martin. Knock it in there."

"Left edge putt, guys, no more, no less."

Amidst the cheerleading, Inkster gets some work done. After the group putts out, she places a white cardboard circle, the same circumference as the cup, down at various locations on the green, getting a feel for the line and speed of different pin positions she's likely to encounter during the four days of the tournament. As with almost every animate and inanimate object at a golf tournament, the white cardboard circle is slapped with a logo—"Nothing else is a Pepsi."

The LPGA itself has over 30 promotional licensees, ranging from Rolex ("Official Timepiece of the LPGA") to Izod ("Official Apparel of the LPGA"), to Paul Arpin Van Lines ("Official Mover of the LPGA"), to Sunderland of Scotland ("Official Rainwear of the LPGA"), to Mead Corporation ("Official Trash Receptacle of the LPGA"). If the golf industry ever builds a theme park, it should be named "Logo Land." (The kids will love it.)

On the 6th tee Jan Stephenson suddenly appears, dressed in a yellow Guess? shirt and gray cord Guess? shorts. (Guess? which clothing company sponsors Stephenson.) "Look!" Inkster tells her pro-am partners. "Jan Stephenson came out to see you play." Stephenson has a glamorous reputation, but it can be almost impossible to watch *her* play. Often she's fretful and glum; it seems like a black rain cloud is hovering over her. Yardage book in hand, she compares notes with Inkster and caddie Greg Johnston. The 6th hole is one of the most beautiful and treacherous at Mission Hills. A lake runs down the entire left side of the fairway, which slopes gently downhill and doglegs toward the water. Two fat fingers of the lake invade the fairway, one about 150 yards from the tee, the other at 215 yards, creating a peninsula. The ideal drive is a draw between the fingers of the lake, leaving a short iron to the green. The bail-out shot is to the right, leaving a mid-to-long iron from a sidehill-downhill lie to a slick green. For Inkster, the appropriate club is a 5-wood, which she hits about 210 yards. But if the wind is blowing at her back, which it often does on the hole, she drops back to a 3-iron, which she hits about 200.

Preparation is critical. Inkster has been gearing up for this season for some time. Two months ago in late January she discussed it at her home in Los Altos, California, a woodsy, upscale community in the rolling hills southwest of San Francisco.

The rambling ranch house, with a big patio, pool, and long sloping backyard, is dominated by kids and sports. *Golfweek* magazine and a book called *Baby Animals* share space on an end table next to the couch in the living room. Floor-to-ceiling bookcases on either side of a stone fireplace feature family photos, toys, crystal, silver, and gold cups and trophies celebrating Juli's victories, and an assortment of sports memorabilia that would make a collector drool—footballs autographed by Jerry Rice and Joe Montana, a San Jose Sharks hockey stick (Inkster often attends their practices—"I'm fascinated by how other athletes practice and prepare for games"), a painting by LeRoy Neiman, old hickory-shafted golf clubs, and a coal-black Louisville Slugger with the name Ken Griffey, Jr., etched into the barrel. "He doesn't like giving his bats away," says Inkster, who met Griffey at a promotional event at the Kingdome, "but I told him I'd give it to my daughter."

The bat has actually been passed from one major league family to another. Jack Simpson, Juli's dad, played shortstop for the Cincinnati Redlegs in 1955–1956, before becoming a captain in the fire department. Inkster's brothers were jocks; so was she. Jack urged Juli to take up golf. For a while, she stubbornly refused. "Finally I realized that's where all the good-looking boys were."

Inkster played basketball in high school, and was good enough to attract some interest from college coaches. But by then her talent on the links was in full bloom.

And Inkster found that she loved to practice. She still does. "I play games with myself," she says. "Up and down to win a tournament or make the cut. The last ball usually turns out to be about a bucket. An hour of practice usually turns into two."

Inkster made All-American as a freshman, junior, and senior at San Jose State; she teamed one year with Patty Sheehan. She also started dating Brian, whom she met when she was 15 and he was a 24-year-old assistant pro at Inkster's home course, Pasatiempo. They married in 1980. Juli was 20. They honeymooned in Hutchinson, Kansas, at the 1980 U.S. Amateur. Juli won the first of her three straight amateur titles, the first person, male or female, to accomplish this feat since the 1930s.

As a rookie in 1983–1984, she was a sensation. Inkster won the 1983 Seattle Safeco Classic in just her fifth professional event, and two majors, the Dinah Shore and the du Maurier Classic, in 1984.

She's been a star ever since. At five feet seven, Inkster's not all that big, but her lanky frame and athleticism give her a rangy appearance. She has dark, bold, attractive features, most notably a wide, expressive mouth (friends might affectionately describe the playfully sarcastic Inkster as having a big mouth), and a thatch of thick black hair. With fiery intensity on the course, and a confident, friendly California casual manner off of it, she's been a crowd pleaser as well.

The game has been very, very good to her. Inkster has won over $2.2 million swinging a club. She also has had lucrative endorsement deals with Izod and Wilson Sporting Goods throughout her career. Last year she tallied $195,739 on the course and banked another $130,000 from Izod and Wilson, which pay an annual retainer plus bonuses based on performance. (The deals are worth over $200,000 if Inkster has a great season.) It costs plenty to play the Tour—Inkster's expenses were close to $100,000 in 1995 even though she often stays at private homes—but she's well ahead of the game.

And, in her mid-thirties, still excited about it. "I enjoy golf more now," says Inkster, watching Cori color with crayons in the den. Dressed in powder blue jeans, a purple and black turtleneck, a forest green sweatshirt, and Nike sneakers, Inkster, slouched on the couch with her legs slung over one end, adds, "It's more of a challenge [after the kids]. I appreciate it more."

She was particularly pumped about the 1996 season. For the first time in several years, Inkster believed her game was back on the right track.

From the beginning of her career Inkster had been taught by her husband Brian, the head professional at Los Altos Country Club, and Englishman Leslie King. But King died in 1993, the same year Inkster's game collapsed. (She earned just $116,583 after tallying $392,063 and losing the Dinah Shore and the U.S. Open in playoffs in 1992.)

"I thought I knew [King's] methods and Juli's swing well enough to keep her tuned," Brian told *Golf World*, "but I was wrong. We got sloppy."

So the Inksters hired Mike McGetrick, swing guru for U.S. Open winners Meg Mallon and Lauri Merten. McGetrick dropped Inkster's hand position a full six inches at the top of her backswing. He also moved her weight farther back on her heels. "I used to come through the ball on my toes and miss it right," says Inkster, who began "to play well with some feel," late in 1995, when she finished third at the du Maurier Classic in August and tied for third at the Fieldcrest Cannon Classic in October.

She's worked hard on her chipping and putting as well. Inkster agrees with Curtis Strange, who said, "You can count on one hand the number of days when the golf swing is perfect and the ball flight is perfect."

"That's why the short game is so important," says Inkster. "Players learn that in their late thirties and forties. There's more to golf than a perfect golf swing."

Inkster also began jogging last year, increasing her running time from 20 to 45 minutes, partly to improve her fitness, partly to be able "to eat that extra bowl of ice cream at night," and mostly as a way of rededicating herself to the game.

Actually, Inkster seems to be running about 18 hours a day, as she gets ready to carpool Hayley and some of her classmates to school, which she does three days a week when she's in town.

"You can have one nutritional snack and one that's junk," she tells Hayley. Hayley opts for carrots.

"That's your junk food," she kids her daughter, who eventually scampers into the backseat of a navy blue Chevy Suburban with carrots and Skittles.

The delicate, never-ending, at times impossible attempt to balance a professional golf career and family life is something Inkster has wrestled with for six years. Some things, such as naps and daily viewings of ESPN's *Sports-Center*, quickly fell by the wayside. But Inkster believes the dilemma is "more a mental than a physical thing. My mom was always at home with a snack for me when I got home from school. I wanted to be that kind of mom."

So when she started hauling Hayley around the country to golf tournaments in 1990, Inkster was wracked by doubts.

Am I doing the right thing?

Is it worth it?

How well adjusted will Hayley be?

How good will she be with other kids?

"It's a harsh thing," says Inkster, "to think I have to choose between letting my family down versus letting myself down by not being one hundred percent mentally ready to play golf. When other players ask about having kids, I tell them, 'If you're thinking about kids, be sure you're going to be committed, because it's a hundred times harder than you think it's going to be.' On the other hand, you can't imagine the joy that kids give back to you."

To her great relief, Inkster discovered that she was a good mom, regardless of the condition of her golf game. "She really loves her family," says fellow pro Caroline Pierce. "You can just *see* it."

And motherhood changed Inkster's attitude about her work. "I used to get angry at a bad round and stew all night. But kids don't care whether you shoot 66 or 76. It's a lot easier to leave golf at the golf course now."

Two months later the balancing act continues. "Everyone kinda takes it for granted that she just comes out here and plays," says caddie Greg Johnston, marveling at his boss's ability to juggle her myriad obligations.

Sometimes there are simply too many balls to keep in the air at once. Since Cori got sick and the season rolled into high gear two weeks ago in Tucson, Inkster hasn't found the time to jog. "I'm beat by the time I'm done playing. I'd rather spend time with the kids."

Tonight the Inkster clan—Juli's and Brian's parents are in town—will celebrate Cori's birthday, which actually was two days ago. But the grandparents hadn't arrived Monday, and Cori was sick yesterday, so tonight is the night. "It's the kind of thing you can get away with when they're two," smiles Inkster.

So after her postround practice session, Inkster will prepare for the festivities, which include a Barney cake, balloons, and presents, plus a pop-up Sesame Street book—"although she'd rather just play in my purse."

"Long day, huh," Inkster says at one point, out of the earshot of her playing partners. When a marshal on another tee asks her how she's doing, Inkster wearily replies, "Hanging in there."

Fortunately for Inkster, her playing partners are good sports, even though the team is doing miserably. Usually, in a scramble format, a team has to birdie practically every hole to be in contention. Inkster's team is barely under par.

But no one is tossing clubs or threatening to hang himself from the branches of a nearby eucalyptus tree. Pained expressions and sarcasm—"One in a row!" says Inkster after a rare birdie—is the order of the day.

It's not always so civilized.

Inkster can't stand macho pro-am partners. She saw enough chauvinistic preening to last a lifetime when she played on the boys' golf team at Pasatiempo High School. There wasn't any problem from her coach and teammates. "I'm still friends with many of them. They saw me as a jock—not a prissy little girl." But opposing teams hated playing against a girl. "The more they hated it, the more I liked to beat them," says Inkster.

The pro-am pet peeve of Nancy Lopez is similar in nature: males who hit a long drive under a tree, and say, "Let's use my ball," even though Lopez has split the fairway. "I *hate* that," she says.

Caroline Pierce dreads guys who walk up to the first tee and tell her about all the money they've bet against other teams. She's also not crazy about guys who not-so-subtly pry into her sex life or, to be more precise, her sexual orientation. "It happens all the time," says Pierce, who in terms of stereotypes, equates being a female professional golfer with being a male flight attendant or hairdresser. "You can suss them out real quick," says Pierce. "They'll say, 'Well, how's your boyfriend?'"

"Fine. How'd you know I had one?" she'll reply.

"It hurts your feelings sometimes. And sometimes you feel it necessary to tell people [you're not gay], which is sad."

Then there are the occasional out-and-out whackos. Some years ago Hollis Stacy played with a businessman who, midround, accused her of deliberately missing putts. He even followed her to the putting green after the round, attempting to confirm his paranoid delusions. Stacy later was surprised and amused to read the man had been indicted for fraud in the Silverado Savings and Loan scandal in the late 1980s.

Nothing so dramatic with this pro-am group. Just another long workday for professional golfer/mother/LPGA public relations agent Inkster.

But she's buoyed when her parents, Carole and Jack, come out to walk the back nine, as does a good friend, Gerry Plunkett, wife of former Stanford and Oakland Raiders quarterback Jim Plunkett. And relieved when Brian appears on the final holes and tells her Cori is feeling fine.

Inkster finishes at even par. Her short game, in particular, is razor sharp.

It better be. Tomorrow she'll tee it up with Laura Davies and Liselotte Neumann. "Yeah!" she says, when asked her about the pairing. "I can't get caught up in Laura's game. They're both playing well, maybe it will rub off on me," says Inkster, who finished twenty-eighth in Tucson and missed the cut in Phoenix, betrayed by mediocre putting.

The preliminaries are over. The Dinah Shore may throw the most extravagant pro-am party of the year, but the basic structure and buildup to the main event are similar at virtually every tournament. Tomorrow the Nabisco guests will be back in their offices. Tomorrow at seven o'clock in the morning Pearl Sinn from California and Lisa Walters from British Columbia will tee off on the 1st hole. Laurie Rinker-Graham from Florida and Carin Hj Koch from Sweden will tee off on the 10th hole. The serious business will begin.

$\mathcal{P}$alm Springs: A Dinah for Dad

Most of us would give up our wives, our firstborn
and our favorite putters just to finish in the top ten
in a major.

—*Lee Trevino*

Sandy, tumbleweed-laden desert terrain lies just outside the beige walls surrounding Mission Hills. But inside the walls is a garden oasis containing 1,250 homes and three golf courses, that is so lush and beautiful it shimmers like a mirage. Mesquite trees with spring bouquets of poppies and pansies ablaze at their base—purple, yellow, pink, white, orange—line the narrow roads that run like arteries through Mission Hills, transporting cars, golf carts, joggers, dog-walkers, baby carriages, Rollerbladers. Dark green shrubs frame the one-story beige and cream condos and houses, with their pink tiled roofs and swimming pools filled with aqua-blue water.

Fan palms and date palms abound throughout the community, some soaring hundreds of feet into the sky, their long green fronds swaying in the breeze like hula skirts. Broad, towering eucalyptus trees line the fairways of the golf courses, casting cool shadows. Snapdragons, petunias, and marigolds dot the magnificent clubhouse grounds; pink and purple bougainvilleas flow from flower beds. Ducks and swans float in the ponds and lakes; birds trill and chirp and flit through the trees. Rabbits, hawks, and even the occasional fox and coyote find a friendly habitat at Mission Hills.

The sunshine beams down like a smile. The mountains hover all around, fissures and peaks as sharply defined as the facets of a diamond.

If you can't feel happy here, better hope for paradise in the *next* lifetime, because this is about as good as it gets. "It's like being on vacation every day," Debbie Grindall, who moved to Mission Hills a year ago, told the *Desert Sun.*

With the local real estate market still suffering through the aftermath of the recession in the Golden State, plenty of homes are available. A booth at the tournament is hawking one-bedroom condos for $78,000–$119,000, and houses for $129,000–$459,000. The winner of the Dinah Shore could take her first-prize check of $135,000, sign on the dotted line, and never leave.

*   *   *

The grounds of the tournament course are quiet early Thursday morning. Scattered fans armed with lounge chairs and Thermos bottles amble out to secure choice viewing locations. About 75 people are following Patty Sheehan, Annika Sorenstam, and Karrie Webb—a big crowd for a Thursday. A flock of photographers march along too, betting that one or more of the trio will wind up among the leaders at the end of the day.

On the 16th hole—the group began on the back nine today—Sheehan hits a mediocre iron, whips off her black Callaway visor, and rips off her glove—the snap of the elastic is as audible as the crack of a rifle. Sheehan wears her emotions as visibly as most pros display their corporate logos, and you don't need to look at the scoreboard to know she's struggling, already two over par and in jeopardy of digging herself into a huge hole.

Maybe she needs someone to tell her she stinks. Two weeks ago in Tucson, Sheehan hit a lousy chip. "I heard some people snickering in the gallery. Stuff like, 'Well, at least she got it on the green, har har.' It just kind of set me off," said Sheehan, who wound up shooting 66. (Pros who best respond to positive reinforcement might consider hiring Rent-A-Fan Club, a Los Angeles business that supplies gushing, swooning, applauding, autograph-seeking groupies.)

But it's awfully quiet as the threesome waits for the green to clear at the 171-yard 17th hole. Sheehan is dressed in a yellow shirt and olive shorts. Her brown hair is streaked with silver. Or perhaps it's more accurate to say her gray hair still retains traces of brown. The gray hair is a legacy of her 16 grueling years on Tour, a legacy that can be denied—or at least dyed—but not forgotten. It's lunchtime, and Sheehan eats a sandwich and swigs from a plastic bottle filled with Shaklee Performance drink, an energy-replenishing amber liquid.

Sorenstam, 25, who became the best woman golfer in the world in 1995 when she won the U.S. Open and, in an unprecedented feat, topped the money list on *both* the LPGA and European Tours, is wearing a turquoise shirt, black shorts, black Callaway visor, and a big black bow in the ponytail of her sun-streaked honey-blonde hair. She stands by herself on one side of the tee box, practicing her backswing

Webb, the 21-year-old Australian sensation—and the youngest player on the LPGA Tour—is wearing a shirt with bold blue and white horizontal stripes, blue shorts, and a white baseball cap, her dishwater blonde hair in a ponytail. Webb, who has streaked to the hottest start by an LPGA rookie—a win, two seconds, a fifth, and a seventh in five starts—since Nancy Lopez won five straight tournaments in 1978, checks her yardage book with caddie and fiancé Todd Haller. She's at one under par, off to a solid start in her first major. So far, the youngsters are making Sheehan look like the old gray mare.

Actually, though, Sheehan has aged like fine wine.

An outstanding athlete—Sheehan was a potential Olympic skier until she gravitated toward golf at the age of 13—Sheehan burst onto the Tour in 1981 after a fine college career at San Jose State.

Small but strong, the five-foot-three Sheehan seemed to have a physique manufactured for golf—a slim, graceful upper body resting on ski-slope muscled thighs that a female middle linebacker would envy. With a swing reminiscent of Ben Hogan and the feisty energy and athleticism of a Gary Player, Sheehan attacked courses with the relentless persistence of a terrier.

Sheehan won early and often—the LPGA Championship in 1982 and 1983 and 18 other tournaments in the 1980s. But she seemed to lose some of her lust for battle as the decade wore on.

It took the mother of all wake-up calls, the San Francisco earthquake in the fall of 1989, to reignite her fire. The quake hit as Sheehan and good friend Juli Inkster were sitting in Candlestick Stadium waiting for the start of the World Series. When Sheehan made it back to San Jose, she walked into a house filled with rubble and a trophy room strewn with "billions of pieces of broken glass."

For the next few nights Sheehan slept on the lawn as aftershocks rumbled through the Bay Area. "That was probably the best part of it," says Sheehan, "watching the stars and satellites." The biggest aftershock was financial. Sheehan's house was not insured for earthquake damage, and her small financial empire was rocked to the foundations.

Low on dough and high on motivation, Sheehan sent her caddie at the time, John Killeen, a Christmas card with a bold message: "4 wins, 1 major." Lacking enough money in her checking account to pay Killeen or fly her new manager, Rebecca Gaston, to the first tournament of 1990, Sheehan solved her cash flow problem by winning the $500,000 Jamaica Classic and pocketing $75,000, plus another $80,000 in the Jamaica Series bonus pool.

After two more wins in the summer, Sheehan opened up a nine-stroke lead on the final day of the U.S. Open in Atlanta, only to collapse and hand the biggest trophy in golf to a disbelieving Betsy King. When ABC's Judy Rankin thrust a microphone in front of her face at greenside, a shell-shocked Sheehan burst into tears and cried like a rainstorm.

"Oh, I cried on national TV!" Sheehan said to Gaston in the locker room. A few minutes later, Sheehan was composed and philosophical as she met the media in the interview room. "No, I won't be able to forget this. Hopefully I'll learn from it. It's not the end of the world."

She and Killeen and Gaston went to dinner. "We had a couple of glasses of wine," says Killeen. "Patty was in good spirits."

Well, relatively good, at least, considering that Sheehan had just experienced the worst day of her career in front of millions of people. Relatively good, considering the prize she sought most in golf, the U.S. Open, had glittered in her hand, and then crumbled into dust. Relatively good, considering that many fans and sportswriters were labeling yesterday's best woman golfer in the world as today's choke. Relatively good, considering that she had broken down on national TV.

Actually, the tears weren't surprising.

Unlike other athletes, golfers can't relieve their frustrations or screw-ups by slamming a quarterback to the turf or jamming a basketball through the net.

So pro golfers, male and female, bottle up their emotions on the course like chemists cramming ingredients into aerosol cans.

When the round is over, the aerosol cans, overloaded with strain and fatigue, sometimes burst.

Curtis Strange, one of the iciest gunslingers on the PGA Tour, broke down in tears after winning the U.S. Open. Sometimes players fall apart before they even reach the clubhouse. Craig "The Walrus" Stadler once was spotted behind a tee at the Masters weeping in despair. He had been brought to his knees by the brutal holes at Amen Corner, where a golfer's prayers are rarely answered.

Sheehan won two more tournaments in the fall of 1990, running her earnings for the year to a career-best $732,618. But the U.S. Open debacle continued to overshadow all of her other accomplishments. Sheehan often refers to "golf demons"—spooky creatures that mess with a player's mind. The Atlanta Nightmare was the biggest, baddest demon Sheehan had ever seen.

For the next two years it haunted her days and nights. A horror movie played in her head, flashing scenes of her collapse on the screen.

"The dreams were pretty specific," says Sheehan. "They would wake me up." At other times, on the cusp of sleep, Sheehan wasn't sure whether she was awake or not, only that the demon was flicking the projector on and off. "My brain just didn't let me quit. I needed a frontal lobotomy."

"I believe in turning negatives into positives. But Atlanta was *so* disappointing, *so* devastating, that it just sort of kept grinding on me."

After a freak injury—Sheehan was accidentally kicked in the hand by fellow pro Pam Wright while reaching for a balloon at a birthday party—effectively ended her 1991 season, Sheehan gloomily spoke of cutting back her schedule or even quitting the Tour altogether.

Then, in 1992, Sheehan exorcised the Atlanta demon for good and secured her place as one of the finest female golfers ever to swing a club. In the U.S. Open at Oakmont, Sheehan, two strokes behind Inkster with two holes to play, birdied the 17th. She rifled a 5-iron to 18 feet on the final hole and lined up the putt to tie.

"Get it to the hole!" she told herself. When the perfectly stroked putt dropped into the center of the cup, Sheehan had Houdinied perhaps the greatest clutch finish in the history of the U.S. Open. A day later she outlasted Inkster in a playoff, with five up-and-down pars on the back nine.

"I was so patient, I can't even believe it was me," Sheehan said four months later. "I didn't have one ounce of nervousness on the golf course. I was never afraid or disappointed. I've been trying to train myself for years and years to get to the point where I could be that way."

Sheehan won another U.S. Open in 1994, outdueling Tammie Green down the stretch. And she did it without her "A" game. By her late thirties Sheehan had metamorphosed from a great professional *athlete* into a great professional *golfer*.

In sheer athletic terms, Sheehan no longer has an edge on her rivals— in fact, she's outgunned by the big, strong, new breed on Tour, players like Kelly Robbins, Karrie Webb, and Michelle McGann. To her surprise, Sheehan enjoys watching the kids. "I thought I'd be real upset seeing the youngsters come in and take our places. But it's been fun and interesting. I'm pleased and thrilled they're coming up."

On the 526-yard 18th hole, a narrow, beautiful, and brutal monster with a lake down the entire left side of the fairway that rings an island green, Sheehan rolls in a 15-foot birdie putt. Then she walks over and stands on the bridge linking the green to the fairway, peering into the waist-deep water in the pond. At the urging of the massive gallery that fills the grandstand overlooking the 18th on Sunday afternoon, the last few winners of the Dinah Shore have plunged into the aqua water, which looks pristine from a distance, but scummy and algae-ridden up close. Perhaps Sheehan is contemplating a victory dive.

Meanwhile Sorenstam is floating along—she slam-dunks a 20-foot birdie putt on the 504-yard 2nd hole and pumps her fist, a significant display of emotion from the robotic Swede, as she soars to the top of the leader board at four under par.

Last July, when the baby-faced second-year pro won the U.S. Open at The Broadmoor in Colorado Springs, her maiden victory on the LPGA Tour, casual golf watchers considered it a shocking upset.

Not her colleagues, however. "It's so like Annika to win a major as her first event," said Leta "Tiger" Lindley, Sorenstam's roommate and team-mate at the University of Arizona. "As a freshman [in 1991], she won the NCAA Championship like it was nothing. There's no end to her talent."

No kidding. Turning pro after her sophomore season, Sorenstam cap-tured Rookie of the Year honors in Europe in 1993, Rookie of the Year hon-ors on the LPGA Tour in 1994, and won two tournaments in Europe just prior to the 1995 U.S. Open. At The Broadmoor, she loomed as a strong contender.

At least in the eyes of others. Sorenstam thought only "Superwomen" won the Open. As an amateur, she declared she would quit if she ever did it. "Once you've reached Mt. Everest, what else is there?"

Controversy and criticism, as it turned out.

In the aftermath of her U.S. Open triumph, Sorenstam, suffering from the flu and overwhelmed by the sudden demands of fame, withdrew from the next LPGA event, the JAL Big Apple Classic. It promptly landed her in the LPGA's doghouse. Then-commissioner Charlie Mechem was furious—the Tour's bright, attractive new star was tentatively scheduled to appear on *The Late Show with David Letterman,* a publicity plum the LPGA had unsuccessfully sought for years.

Two months later in September, Sorenstam gave an interview at the Safeco Classic in Seattle. She had just flown in from Europe after finishing second to countrywoman Liselotte Neumann in front of thousands of adoring hometown fans in Stockholm at the Swedish Open. After failing to persuade an LPGA official to cancel the interview, Sorenstam showed up an hour late.

But when she pulled up her chair onto a shady hillside above the 18th green at Kent Meridian Country Club, she came across as a soft-spoken, charming, and highly perceptive young woman. Buffeted by a sea of demands from fans, sponsors, and the media—"They want part of you all the time"—Sorenstam wore the U.S. Open crown as tentatively as a kitten exploring a strange room. Like her fellow Swede, Greta Garbo, Sorenstam yearned to tell the world, "I want to be left alone."

During the interview Sorenstam was asked about Judy Rankin's descrip-tion of her—"sweet, shy, and a bit of a loner." Sipping from a can of Diet Pepsi, Sorenstam thought it over carefully and decided it was pretty much on target.

Afterward, Sorenstam sat under a piercing-hot Indian summer sun for over an hour while a photographer fussed and fretted and took endless pictures. Sorenstam was patient and polite, brightening when she was told she could keep a cap from the shoot. There was a plastic putting green floating on a nearby pond, used for a chipping contest for spectators, and it was suggested Sorenstam pose on the tiny island.

"Because I'm a loner?" Sorenstam asked.

"No. Because you're on top of the golf world."

"Oh," she said quietly.

The next day Sorenstam shot 76, one of her worst rounds of the season, with a four-putt on one hole and a missed one-foot tap-in on another. Yet she seemed mostly cheerful and utterly at home inside the ropes.

At one point Sorenstam went into a portable rest room, and when she emerged, her caddie, Colin Cann, had teed up an orange, a midround snack, on the fairway. Like a scene from a "Peanuts" cartoon, Sorenstam playfully ran up and pretended to boot it like a football.

"I love what I do," she said. "I don't get so down on myself as I used to. When I was twelve or thirteen, I was suspended at my club at home for throwing a club in a tree. When you're playing bad, you think, 'This is the only thing in the world that exists.' But there's always another day and another tournament."

After the round she spent two and a half hours on the putting green, working out the kinks in her stroke. ("I tend to get too quick and jerk putts.") Sorenstam finished 70-67-68 to tie for sixth. A week later she won the Heartland Classic in St. Louis by a staggering ten shots, kicking off a fall campaign that brought victories in South Korea and Australia, money titles in the U.S. ($666,533) and Europe (£130,324), and all of the LPGA's major awards for the year.

Exhausted after playing into December, Sorenstam vacationed in January and February, once again landing in the LPGA's doghouse when she withdrew from the first event of 1996, the Chrysler-Plymouth Tournament of Champions. New commissioner Jim Ritts pleaded with her to appear. NBC criticized her on the air. Chrysler was upset. Golf writers speculated that Sorenstam was being manipulated by her powerful agent, International Management Group (IMG), or by Callaway, which recognized her potential and signed Sorenstam when she was just a rookie.

But Sorenstam was simply refueling the tanks. She didn't touch a club for five weeks, the longest break she had ever taken from the game. She spent the time skiing at Lake Tahoe and visiting with fiancé David Esch, whom she met on the practice range at Moon Valley in Phoenix.

Esch used to work for Ping, but after the U.S. Open, when he appeared on NBC's telecast in a Ping visor, Callaway pirated him away. Now it's a match made in Heaven Woods. "My time with David is the most precious thing to me," says Sorenstam. Later this year, they expect to be married;

the date is a secret. "David knows the date, so hopefully he'll show up," Sorenstam jokes.

Sorenstam also spent some time reading, most notably a book called *How to Say No*. "I thought people would get mad if I said no. But I learned I can still be accepted as a person, and sometimes more respected. It's better to say, 'Thank you, but not this time,' than to commit and show up late."

When she returned to the Tour two weeks ago, in Tucson, some of her colleagues in the locker room had their claws out.

"Oh, you made it!"

"*You're* playing this week?"

But Sorenstam was in great spirits as she met the media. "Mentally, I was drained. Now I wake up and want to go to the golf course. . . . I'm still a very shy person, but I know I can't go and hide. I'm dealing with it. I have to stand up for what I do and what I say."

Later, Sorenstam said she was glad she had bucked the commissioner and refused to play in the Tournament of Champions. "I was proud of myself for sticking to my decision. I think it will pay off in the future, not just golf-wise but in living too." (Ritts, who pushed hard to change Sorenstam's mind, says he wasn't as sensitive as he should have been. "What she really said that I finally heard is, 'I truly love the game. I look forward to playing. But I won't go out and compete if I can't compete well.' ")

It was a decision strongly supported by Pia Nilsson, head coach of the Swedish National Golf Team, which consists of 150 golfers grouped into six teams—men and women pros, men and women amateurs, and boys and girls juniors. Nilsson, 38, has guided the careers of no less than six Swedes currently playing the LPGA Tour—Sorenstam, Neumann, Alfredsson, Carin Hj Koch (formerly Hjalmarsson), Catrin Nilsmark, and Eva Dahllof.

Six Swedes, from a country with a golf season so short you could blink and miss it! Now that Harvey Penick has passed away, the best coach in the world, hands down, is Pia Nilsson. What Nilsson and the rest of her coaches are creating in Sweden is something of a cultural revolution—golf's version of letting 150 flowers bloom.

"We don't believe in one model for everybody," says Nilsson. "We have to ask questions and find out who the people are that we are dealing with. Different ages, different genders, different tours, different schools, etc., all make us realize that we have to be more flexible in the way we structure what we are doing and how we communicate.

"We develop as human beings through the game of golf. We won't do anything that might lead to lower scores but might not be good to us in our lives as a whole. Who we are is, for us, always more important than what we do."

To those who view golf through a prism of swing planes or titanium technology, Nilsson's new age philosophy may sound a bit spacey. And Nilsson cheerfully admits to having a visionary's head in the clouds: "Human beings have unlimited potential" is one of the "chosen truths" that guide the SNGT. But her cleats are firmly anchored in the turf as well: Another chosen truth is that "Swedish golf players are good putters."

Nilsson began putting her ideas to work as a college student at Arizona State from 1979 to 1982. Intent on pursuing a pre-med degree—Nilsson's father is a doctor, and her mother is a nurse—she discovered that lab work conflicted with golf practice. So she opted for a major in physical education, but it was hardly a rocks-for-jocks curriculum. Nilsson took classes in everything from sports psychology to public speaking to economics, graduating summa cum laude. A voracious reader, she devoured books about communications, philosophy, and history, including the history of sports.

After playing the LPGA Tour with modest success from 1983 to 1987, Nilsson became a teaching professional, played part-time in Europe and Sweden, attended USGA workshops, served as a Swedish tour official, and helped the SNGT on an informal basis.

Her years on the LPGA Tour left the deepest impression. She discovered that success, for many players, "seemed kind of hollow. They seemed almost to forget to have a life outside the Tour."

All of the Swedish professionals have individual instructors, often in the United States. "I don't want responsibility for all the technical teaching," says Nilsson. "There's not enough time, and players like and need different theories. Besides, I don't want them too dependent on me."

That's something you aren't likely to hear from the big-name golf gurus, who often sell themselves and their theories as The Light, The Truth, and The Way. Nilsson shudders at the notion. "[Our program] is not a religious sect," she laughs.

Although it's an oversimplification, it could be said that the individual instructors work on the player's swings and Nilsson works on their minds and spirits. She spends hours observing her players in practice and in competition, "watching with open eyes and listening with open ears." She studies everything: body posture, pace of play, practice routines, relationships with caddies, media interviews.

"Annika is going to be fine," Nilsson, a friendly, soft-spoken woman, said last week in Phoenix. "The LPGA may be disappointed short-term but will be happy long-term. The American way of thinking is too rushed—do everything [to cash in] now when going so good. Annika is really stubborn and wants to make her own decisions. When that comes from the inside out, it's going to stick. That's true motivation and discipline. She's not going to be like other stars—she's going to be like 'Annika-Star' and do it the Annika way."

It's not surprising that Sorenstam chafed under the team conformity imposed at the University of Arizona and other U.S. college programs. "The [Swedish] philosophy is that people are like plants," says Sorenstam. "Some need space, some can grow close together. You need to find *your* way."

Last night Sorenstam, despite a case of laryngitis, closed the range at Mission Hills. As a glittery orange sun slid toward the peaks of Mount San Jacinto, Sorenstam, shades down, blasted fairway woods into a stiff westerly wind.

A small knot of fans paused to watch on their way to the parking lot.

"Marvelous, marvelous," said an older gentlemen.

"That's so lovely," said a woman to her friend. "It looks so effortless."

But Sorenstam wasn't happy. Sorenstam had been experimenting with a 7- and a 9-wood, but the trajectory of the two clubs was, to her dismay, virtually the same. Her caddie, Colin Cann, raced off to the parking lot. Callaway's on-tour rep, Todd Strible, was packing up the trunk of his car, his work, he thought, done for the day. Cann returned with a 9-wood with a stiffer shaft.

This shaft did the trick. Sorenstam began launching towering drives, the kind best designed to hold the firm, fast greens at Mission Hills, and decided to substitute the 9-wood for her 4-iron this week.

"She's very driven," says Leta Lindley. "Very focused about what she wants to accomplish—to be the best. She doesn't let anything stand in the way of that." Her tournament preparation complete, Sorenstam finally left the course. She's not Superwoman, but she's definitely a woman of steel.

As the trio heads off the 7th green, an older man, muttering out of the side of his mouth like a Mafia don, says, "Good putt, Patty." As they wait for the green to clear on the 166-yard 8th hole, Sheehan and Cann clown around, talking out of the sides of their mouths.

Cann, 28, a skinny, bespectacled English lad who looks like he took a wrong turn on the way from physics lab to chem class, has been caddying for six years. Trained as a mechanical engineer, he dreaded "being stuck indoors." A 4-handicapper at West Byfleet Golf Club, where Laura Davies is a member, Cann met Davies's older brother and business manager Tony. After caddying on the European circuit for several years, Cann, aided by a recommendation from Davies, hooked up with Sorenstam at the beginning of the 1994 season and headed for America.

"It was a goal to get here," says Cann. "You can't make a proper living on the ladies' tour in Europe." A calm, steady presence who knows Sorenstam's swing inside-out, Cann is a strong element of Team Sorenstam, which includes Pia Nilsson, fiancé David Esch, instructor Henri Reis, Mark Steinberg, her agent at IMG, and Callaway. (Cann is deceptively strong in a physical sense as well. Stuffed with clubs and gear, a touring pro's bag weighs at least 40 pounds. Slung over a shoulder, it feels like a bag full of large boulders.)

After the delay Sheehan and Webb hit glorious irons through a strong, swirling wind to within four feet of the cup. Both make birdie.

It's the kind of shot her colleagues already are coming to expect from Webb. "She's strong, she's long, and she's confident," says Jane Geddes, who lost a four-hole playoff to Webb at the HealthSouth Inaugural in January. "I've left the course late, and I know she's the last one to leave the practice green."

Webb is medium-sized, at five feet seven inches and about 130 pounds. She doesn't appear to be particularly athletic, until you see her walking with big strides down the fairway, arms swinging long and free. A self-described tomboy, Webb played lots of cricket, basketball, and soccer as a youth. She has a powerful, aggressive swing, dominated by a pistonlike lower body move reminiscent of a young Brandie Burton, the odds-on favorite to be the Generation X star of the 1990s just a few years ago.

Webb, who has been dreaming of a life on Tour since she was 11, now appears to be the pick of the litter. A native of Queensland, the northeastern Australian state that also produced Greg Norman, Webb took up golf at the age of 8, after watching her parents and grandparents play at the local course in Ayr from the time she was a toddler. When Webb was 11, her grandparents gave her a grand birthday/Christmas present—a plane trip to the Gold Coast, some 1,000 miles away, to watch Norman play. It was 1986, the year Norman won the British Open and a raft of tournaments in Australia.

Webb's excellent adventure was a seminal event. By the time she had watched Norman win and had queued up with hundreds of other fans to get his autograph, she knew she wanted to follow in his footsteps.

Five years later, as a reward for winning the Greg Norman Junior Golf Foundation Championship, the 16-year-old Webb flew from Ayr to Jupiter, Florida, to spend a week with Norman. "He was great," says Webb with a big smile. "Not many people get to meet their idol." During the week Webb hung out with Norman; they fished, toured Universal Studio, played golf, practiced, and worked out in the gym.

"If they came, they had to do everything I did," Norman told *USA Today*. "She stayed right with me during the workouts and during practice. That's when I knew she'd be a special player. I didn't have to help her much. She has a beautiful swing." But Webb credits Norman with improving her short game—in particular, correcting a tendency to move her head when putting.

So the idol became a mentor as well. When the 20-year-old Webb stunned a strong field of Americans and Europeans by winning the 1995 Weetabix Women's British Open, she received a congratulatory fax from Norman. When Webb was in Australia last fall, she taped a segment about her experiences with Norman for a "This Is Your Life" show about The Shark. If Webb finds the increasing demands of newfound fame to be a problem, she knows just where to turn for advice.

But she may not need any help.

So far the media, even the Australian media, which has brutalized Norman in the past—the build 'em up and tear 'em down treatment of celebrities is called the "tall poppy syndrome" in Australia—hasn't affected Webb. "I'm still an up-and-comer. They've been very good to me."

It helps that Webb has a calm, pleasant, straightforward, "throw another shrimp on the barby, mate" manner. Although she seemed a bit dazed (she constantly referred to the LPGA money list as the European "Order of Merit" early in the season), she also seemed right at home once she got between the ropes. "Ever since I turned pro, all I've wanted to do is compete," she told *Sports Illustrated.* "I just love it, I love the pressure and being in contention."

That's quite remarkable considering that just three years ago Webb was beating balls on a scruffy practice range and finishing high school in Ayr, a town of 8,600 known primarily for its sugarcane industry. (Webb's father owns a small construction company, her mother a fast-food business. Webb used to work there, flipping burgers and making sandwiches.) Although U.S. college golf programs were scouring the globe for talent, inexplicably they forgot to look Down Under, and Webb received nothing more than a form letter from the University of South Carolina.

So she hit the road with her boyfriend and now fiancé Todd Haller, who chucked a career in the insurance business and became her caddie. Haller is also from Ayr. His uncle, Kelvin Haller, an amateur golfer, has been Webb's teacher since she first picked up a club. (Kelvin Haller suffered a stroke six years ago that rendered him paraplegic but he continues to teach his protégé.) "Our families were friends, but Todd is four years older, so we didn't have much to do with each other until he came back from university."

Webb played five events in the U.S. on the minor league Futures Tour early in 1995, then traveled the European circuit. It was quite an education—different countries, languages and currencies every week. "You can get ripped off if you don't think quick enough." Webb particularly remembers an Austrian tournament played in the shadows of a glacier. "It was the first time I ever saw snow."

After a number of top-ten finishes, Webb broke through at the British Open. "I held it together on the last nine. Even since then I've had that little bit of extra confidence."

So it was on to America, where she found the LPGA to be more hospitable than she expected. "I was accepted well in Europe, which is a lot more laid back. I heard rumors that senior players on the LPGA Tour gave rookies a hard time, but it's not true. It's more serious here, but just as friendly."

When she's not playing or practicing—"Laura Davies and the other Europeans give me crap about practicing too much"—Webb enjoys working out, watching basketball, furnishing her new home, which she shares with Haller in Orlando, "vegging out in front of TV," and reading.

She has devoured books by comedians (Jerry Seinfeld, Tim Allen, Ellen DeGeneres), John Grisham thrillers, and *The Silence of the Lambs*. All were best-sellers, which seems appropriate as Webb continues her Shark-like assault toward the top of the charts in women's golf.

Webb bungles the 508-yard 9th hole. She hooks her second shot into the trees, angrily whacks the grip of her fairway wood off the toe of her shoe, tries to punch out, catches more branches, dumps her fourth shot into a greenside bunker, then raises her wedge with two hands over her head, as if to snap it in two. But she hits a great trap shot to save bogey and salvage an even par 72.

Webb's only weaknesses appear to be youth and inexperience. When Carl "Caddie Machine" Laib walks off the final green he gives Webb the insider's laconic accolade: "Girl's a player."

As the TV cameras beam first-round coverage to ESPN viewers, Sorenstam drains a 15-foot birdie putt and pumps a fist overhead, a major display of emotion. She's the first-round leader at 67. "Such a pure putting stroke," Laib says with admiration. "And the girl never gets in trouble."

"When she's on, she's just so on," says Sheehan. "Even when she's off, she looks like she's on. She's just that good."

Sheehan, the old pro, escapes with a 71. "We hit it all right," Laib says without enthusiasm, as Sheehan emerges from the scoring tent and is engulfed by autograph seekers. "I think Patty tries too hard here. She's trying to knock it in the hole every shot. Just play!"

The trio of Caroline Pierce, Terry-Jo Myers, and Florence Descampe make their way around Mission Hills later in the afternoon. No TV cameras. No crowds either. In fact, there are as many people inside the ropes—three golfers, three caddies, and a kid carrying the aluminum portable score-board—as there are outside the ropes. To be specific, the gallery consists of Pierce's father and mother, on a two-week visit from their home in Sussex, England, a family friend, Myers's father, Descampe's coach from Paris, and a reporter.

It's a throwback to Pierce's first seven years on Tour, when she labored as a dew sweeper in the early morning and a trash collector in the late afternoon.

Professional golfers can be sorted into four groups—Stars, Contenders, the Pack, and the Fringe. Most players back in the pack and clinging to the fringes of the Tour are "B" players, consigned to one predawn wake-up call and one twilight finish during the first two rounds of a 72-hole event. ("A" and "B" lists are somewhat fluid—a player on the cusp can bounce from "A" to "B" on a weekly basis. Generally, however, the "A" list consists of players who have won within the past two years, and players in the top 40 on the career money list. For a full field of 144 players, 60 players normally will be in the A bracket and 84 in the B group.)

Pierce, 32, spent 1988 to 1994 slowly working her way from the fringe into the pack. Her official earnings were as follows:

1988	$1,153	1992	$46,767
1989	$25,545	1993	$33,987
1990	$23,944	1994	$84,756
1991	$56,813		

In 1995, she broke into the ranks of the contenders, placing thirty-second on the money list with $196,722, including seven top-10 finishes. She also got a heavy dose of the pressure of being in contention. What did she learn from the experience?

"That I'm nervous as hell!" she says with a rueful smile. "The confidence is not there totally. But it's getting a little easier."

Her goal for 1996 is simple. "Win a tournament." She currently ranks thirty-first on the money list with $23,289. She also picked up another $7,500 in unofficial money at a big two-day pro-am in Hawaii. Last week in Phoenix she was "between swings," but when she came off the range a few days ago, she was hitting it better.

What was the answer?

"Not to worry so much about my swing," she says semiseriously. Pierce also spent time hitting balls with a golf glove under her right armpit; the glove is supposed to remain in place until impact and follow-through. "It keeps me connected," Pierce explains.

At five-foot-three, Pierce is one of the LPGA's smaller players, tipping the scales at barely 110 pounds. She averages about 220 yards off the tee with her Callaway War Bird, sacrificing miles of real estate to the Tour's long bombers.

She plays with a brisk energy, walks with a brisk stride, and produces as much power as her waifish frame can muster, driving through the ball with a strong, swooping acceleration of her arms and shoulders.

The LPGA boasts dozens of exceptional athletes: champion skier Patty Sheehan; Japanese professional softball pitcher Ayako Okamoto; a raft of standout basketball players, such as Michelle Estill, a member of the U.S. junior Olympic team, Betsy King, who played basketball and golf at Furman before a knee injury put an end to her hoop dreams, and high school stars Kelly Robbins, Tammie Green, and Juli Inkster; high school track star Vicki Fergon; bowler Barb Mucha, good enough to contemplate a future career on the lanes after she retires from the links.

Pierce, at first glance, doesn't fit the profile. In her long-billed black baseball cap, black shorts, pink Fila shirt with a dark pink collar, white socks, shoes, and glove, she looks a bit like a tomboyish refugee from a pickup softball game, a girl that the boys stuck out in right field.

Appearances, however, are deceiving. Pierce is a good athlete. She played field hockey, netball (English basketball), and table tennis; her father, Bill, played for the English national table tennis team. Pierce also ran cross-country. "I think it was more determination than talent. I didn't like people in front of me."

Although small in stature, Pierce stands tall among her peers. She's the vice president and one of six Tour players on the LPGA's Executive Committee, part of the 11-member LPGA Board of Directors. Pierce also served on the selection committee that recommended hiring new LPGA commissioner Jim Ritts, who took the reins of the LPGA in January of 1996.

"A hard worker, feisty, a great sense of humor" is how Juli Inkster describes Pierce.

"A great lady, period," says Missie Berteotti, who occasionally rooms with Pierce. "Very mature, handles herself with a lot of class in a lot of situations."

"Very intelligent," says Sheehan. "And a great sense of humor."

Pierce's sharp, dry wit and English accent are reminiscent of actress Emma Thompson, who recently won an Oscar for her screenplay adaptation of Jane Austen's *Sense and Sensibility*. It seems a fitting coincidence—Pierce is a big fan of Austen's works and has read most of her books and seen all of the recent film versions, including *Persuasion* and *Pride and Prej-*

udice. Her recent reading list includes books on Vietnam (caddie Rick Aune served in the war), novels by Patricia Kingsolver and Tim O'Brien, and *The Fountainhead* by Ayn Rand.

"That's a nice straight shot," she says archly after pushing her drive into the rough at the 2nd hole. The group started on the back nine today; Pierce is one under par after her first ten holes.

By this time, the tiny gallery is getting quite chummy, chattering behind the yellow gallery ropes lining the edge of the fairways and greens like railbirds at a racetrack.

"Sometimes I don't claim any relation," jokes Glenn Myers, after his daughter hits a poor iron. Myers, from Ft. Myers, Florida, gets to see Terry-Jo play about four times a year. Marveling at the luxurious Mission Hills lawns and gardens he says, "Bet the caretaker drives a Mercedes here."

Walking up a long, steep hill to the green at the 409-yard 3rd hole, Maureen Pierce discusses Descampe's game, which went to hell last year—she ranked 125th on the money list with $24,324.

It's quite a tumble from the 27-year-old Belgium native's rookie season in 1992, when she won $210,218, earned a spot on the European Solheim Cup team, and appeared on the verge of stardom.

A protégée of the technically oriented David Leadbetter, Descampe is suffering paralysis of overanalysis. "I don't need someone to tell me my clubface is one inch inside," Descampe told *Golf World.* "I still have a David Leadbetter swing, but I think I went a bit too far."

Perhaps her motivation isn't as strong as it used to be either. Descampe is three months pregnant.

"She married a diamond merchant," Maureen says, then adds, with a twinkle in her eye, "We're looking for one for Caroline."

Maureen ran the tote systems at 12 racecourses in England before her recent retirement. Bill Pierce, who formerly worked for Texas Instruments, leases computer systems. When Caroline came home from Houston Baptist College in the summertime, she worked at the racetracks, "taking bets in my little red dress." Laura Davies usually was around as well, hobnobbing with the bookmakers.

By the time the threesome reaches the 158-yard 5th hole, proceedings have ground to a halt, as the group up ahead, which includes 18-year-old amateur phenomenon Cristie Kerr, hacks it up on the green.

"So slow . . . ," sighs Pierce, sitting on her golf bag. Then she walks over to the ropes to make sure the proper amenities have been observed. "Have you met my mother?" Mother and daughter smile at Bill Pierce, the former table-tennis champion, who is nervously bouncing around like a Ping-Pong ball. "He can't sit still at home, either," says Caroline. Slow play agitates the father even more than the daughter. "He got mad once when I took a practice swing in college," says Caroline.

A few clouds filter over Mount San Jacinto, blocking the sun. The temperature drops some 20 degrees in minutes, and an LPGA official drives up in a green cart and offers Myers a windbreaker.

"They look out for her," says her father. "They know what she goes through." Myers, 33, has interstitial cystitis, an incurable bladder condition that affects mostly women. Victims may need to urinate 50–60 times a day and 15–20 times a night. Pelvic pain can be excruciating. Since winning the Mayflower Classic in 1988, Myers has struggled to remain on Tour.

In an interview with *Philadelphia Golfer* Myers, now a national spokesperson for the Interstitial Cystitis Association, explained how the disease affected her work.

"If the golf course is more than a mile or two from my motel, I may have to stop once or twice to go to the bathroom on the way. Once I get to the course I may need to go to the bathroom five more times before I can make it to the tee. Then after I tee off I must find a Porta-John every two or three holes so I can finish my round. I've had to withdraw from eight or ten tournaments because I couldn't make it to a bathroom . . . so it's an extremely debilitating disease."

About three years ago, Myers picked up a kitchen knife and contemplated suicide after another agonizing, sleepless night. But when she walked into her 6-year-old daughter's bedroom to say good-bye, she decided she couldn't leave her. Then she discovered that a urologist who suffers from IC had developed a treatment, including dietary changes and an experimental drug Elmiron. Myers started taking the drug in 1994. It only works for about 40 percent of IC sufferers, but Myers was one of the lucky ones. Within four or five months she was essentially symptom-free.

The winds are howling now. The middle holes of the front nine are on open, higher ground, unsheltered from the trees. Strong head winds and cross winds buffet the players. "Batten down the hatches," says a marshal.

The greatness of the pros is best illustrated in conditions such as these. They handle 25-mile-per-hour winds with aplomb. They have seen worse, much worse. Before the trees matured at Mission Hills, the wind used to rip through the course. Kathy Whitworth once walked backward from the tee to the green at the 18th hole, the only way she could get through the gale without blowing sand from the desert blinding her.

A few days ago Pierce was asked what specific shots she was working on for the Dinah Shore. "I'm practicing like hell out of the rough. You need an *aggressive* flop shot—one you can be aggressive with yet it lands soft." Pierce misses the green on the last three holes, but gets it up-and-down every time, with a dazzling array of flop shots, chips, and clutch putts.

When she rolls in a four-foot putt on the final hole for an even par 72, a superb score under the conditions, Bill Pierce thrusts his arm skyward in a gesture that seems to say, "Tally ho!"

The family recital is over. The small audience shakes hands and says, "See you tomorrow." The Pierces discuss dinner plans. Caroline heads to the practice range. Her parents head for their hotel.

"Now we can go home and you can make me a margarita," Maureen Pierce tells her husband.

Friday is a day of edginess on the course and a night of exuberance off it.

Under a warm and sunny sky, a big happy, holiday crowd checks out the action. Couples—male and female, female and female—stroll hand-in-hand, carrying bags of free merchandise from a booth sponsored by *Golf for Women* magazine and bags of pricey apparel from the Mission Hills pro shop. A large yellow plastic blimp, floating a couple of hundred yards in the air like a pinata, lends a festive touch. Much higher up, the real Goodyear blimp, symbol of major sporting events, hovers over the action, humming like a giant—and extremely annoying—outboard motor. Later in the afternoon a ghostly, white half-moon rests against the powder blue sky.

On the fairways are:

** **Juli Inkster,** after an opening-round 70, birdieing the 368-yard 10th hole and chipping in on the 506-yard 11th to go to four under par, her razor-sharp short game vaulting her up the leader board. The chip-in draws a roar from the crowd, and a delighted "Whooh!" from husband Brian, sitting at the back of the green. When Laura Davies rolls in a birdie putt, Inkster calls out, "Nice putt, mate," and Davies walks over and pats her on the back.

** **Liselotte Neumann,** rimming out a long chip shot and leaving a succession of birdie putts hanging on or rolling across the edge of the cup. Neumann, already a double winner in 1996, came to the desert several weeks ago to practice. She's always been baffled by the greens at Mission Hills, so different from those in her home base in Florida, and the mystery continues. Her game seems ideally suited for the Dinah Shore—Neumann is straight, longer than ever after the addition of a titanium Great Big Bertha driver to her bag several weeks ago, thrives on big crowds and major championships, and is a stoic, steady, relentless competitor who never quits. She is also, according to Davies, "the best fairway wood player in the world, man or woman." (Neumann carries five woods, eschewing a 3- and 4-iron in favor of a 7- and 9-wood, which she hits higher and stops more easily on hard, slick greens.)

Neumann, 29, also is in the best form of her career, gliding along the fairways with the aura of a magnificent lioness prowling the savannah. "She's mature in herself and as a golfer," says Pia Nilsson. "It's easy to see from the outside. Some people play a game they don't have. Lotta accepts herself for the shots she *can* hit. She's in harmony with the course somehow."

Still, so far at least, Mission Hills remains a riddle. On the last hole Neumann barely misses yet another birdie effort. Usually Neumann is as unemotional as fellow Swede Björn Borg—except when she hits a great shot and flashes a dazzling, incandescent smile at the gallery. But now she lowers her head and slumps with her hands on her knees for a long moment.

Neumann and Sorenstam are alike in many ways. Both are sweet and shy, loners off the course and ferocious competitors on it. Both have strong ties to the Swedish national team. Both won the U.S. Open as youngsters, and wilted under the spotlight of fame in the aftermath. Sorenstam, along with other Swedish players, regards Neumann, the first Swede to win a major in the United States, as something of an idol. She recalls staying up until the wee hours as a teenager in Stockholm to watch Neumann win the 1988 U.S. Open. "She's a role model for our younger players," says Nilsson of Neumann. "Her way of behavior, the way she carries herself. So classic."

Yet they rarely speak. Too shy, perhaps. When Sorenstam won the U.S. Open, Neumann left a note of congratulations in her locker, and urged her to carve out enough time for her family and friends, the biggest mistake Neumann believes she made in the wake of her difficult bout with stardom.

** **Cool Kelly Robbins,** three-putting the 148-yard 14th hole and disgustedly flipping her ball into the pond guarding the right side of the green. Robbins, 26, gets her nickname partly from her demeanor—she won her first two LPGA events in sudden-death playoffs and outdueled Laura Davies to win the 1995 McDonald's LPGA Championship last May, amidst the sideshow carnival of the Ben Wright controversy—and partly because she's a really cool person, immensely popular among her peers. "Great gal!" enthuses Inkster. "I love to see her win."

Fans love to see her hit the ball. Next to Laura Davies, who cranks it about 25 yards further than anyone else, Robbins and Michelle McGann are the LPGA's longest bombers, even though

Robbins is a relatively small five foot eight and 135 pounds. Her swing is fundamentally sound, relatively compact, and beautifully balanced. It was constructed by her father, Steve, who wrote his master's thesis on the mechanics of the golf swing before becoming a high school biology teacher and golf coach. The results speak for themselves. Robbins ranked third on the money list with $527,655 last year.

Everything about Robbins seems well balanced. She's personable, articulate, and low-key, blending a strong Christian faith with a nice sense of humor and a self-effacing unpretentiousness. She loves to fish and usually can be found on a boat on a lake in Florida or her native Michigan during off-weeks.

But Robbins isn't interested in escaping the fires of competition for long. "When I played high school basketball, it was everything," said Robbins, who earned All State honors and scored 1,200 points one season. "Being in contention now is kind of like that. You see your name up there, know you're playing well, and try not to get too caught up in it and just let your talent and ability take over. That's why we put in all the hours we put in—to get in contention and then handle the situation *nicely*."

But Robbins seems a bit out of sorts today, edgy and grumpy. On the 390-yard 16th hole, she yanks an eight-foot birdie putt to the left, ramming it four feet past the cup, and grinds like crazy to save par. A relieved Robbins takes a couple of mock stagger steps off the green; caddie Chuck Parisi coaxes a tiny smile by tugging on the bill of her khaki Titleist baseball cap.

After crushing a drive close to 300 yards on the 526-yard 18th hole, Robbins prepares to go for the green in two. It's a shaky, probably foolish decision, although a nearby fan seems to approve. "If she goes down, she goes down in a blaze of glory." But when the wind freshens, rattling the fronds high in the palm trees along the 18th fairway, Robbins puts the fairway wood back in the bag and lays up with a short iron, choosing wisdom over valor.

** **Laura Davies,** butchering the 18th, "my favorite hole in golf, even though it hasn't been very kind to me."

No lie. In 1994, Davies was nursing a one-stroke lead when she bogeyed 18 and lost to Donna Andrews's closing birdie. It was an utterly devastating defeat. "On a scale of one to ten, it's a ten," Davies quietly told the press as Andrews was diving into the green-side lake and soaking up the cheers of the crowd. Even when she hits the island green in two—a feat only Davies, Robbins, McGann, and a couple of other women can even contemplate—she always winds up three-putting.

Trying to mangle a drive, Davies rips a low hook into the lake, the force of the blast raising a waterspout. She slams the butt of her club against her Maruman bag, stalks off, drops a ball near the lake, and slashes an iron up the fairway. Still steaming over her drive, Davies throws the iron to the turf. After a wedge to the green backs up into the front fringe, Davies disgustedly tosses the club in the direction of her cousin and caddie, Matthew Adams. The 18th, Laura Davies's great green whale, continues to haunt her.

By Friday night the other massive party of the week is in full swing. As the *Los Angeles Times* put it, "While the golfers play under sunny skies at Mission Hills, thousands of other women have descended on Palm Springs for the country's—if not the world's—biggest lesbian bash."

Dinah Shore Week began in the 1970s as a series of small pool parties for gay LPGA players and their partners, friends, and fans.

The parties grew. So did the reputation of Palm Springs as a gay-friendly city. "We're accepted here," says Ann Bracken, a beauty salon owner from San Francisco and a visitor to Palm Springs for the last five years. (Tourist industry officials estimate that as many as one in eight Coachella Valley guests are gay. Next week 35,000 gay men are expected to invade the city for the annual "White Party.") More and more gay women began to make the scene. Many had little interest in golf and no desire to attend the tournament. Many didn't even realize there *was* a golf tournament in town.

Two years ago Dinah Shore Week came out of the closet and into the mainstream when *Buzz* magazine in Los Angeles published an article about the festivities, which are now choreographed by promoters in San Francisco and Los Angeles, who book entire hotels and import big-league entertainment. Sandra Bernhart, Fem 2 Fem, and Janis Ian are some of the headliners this year. The *Desert Sun* is running a series of articles on the positive impact of gay tourism. Civic boosters and businessmen, including many who used to view the gay market with fear and loathing, are jumping for joy as the cash registers jingle.

It makes sense, especially in a community with a long-running marriage—or perhaps an affair is a better description—between entertainment and commerce. In addition to the traditional obsessions in Palm Springs—food, fashion, and facelifts—the town has long been linked to Hollywood, with streets named in honor of Bob Hope, Frank Sinatra, Gene Autry, and Dinah Shore. Flamboyant celebrities such as Liberace and Truman Capote found a home in the valley, spreading a hedonistic frosting on top of the bedrock conservative Republican economic philosophy of the wealthy denizens of Palm Springs.

The morphing of conservative and libertarian strains in the valley is embodied in the form of ex–Palm Springs mayor (now U.S. congressman) Sonny "I Got You Babe" Bono, a Republican whose daughter recently declared she was a lesbian.

But it's not only gays packing the streets and sidewalks along Tahquitz Way in downtown Palm Springs on a balmy Friday night: a classic car convention is auctioning vintage autos for five-figure sums; packs of teenage boys are loitering on corners and checking out the babes; yuppie couples are dining alfresco at sidewalk tables.

A small media group, including Amy Nutt, a writer for *Sports Illustrated*, and Nancy Warren, a writer for *Golf Today*, head for the Wyndham Palm Springs Hotel to a National Organization for Women fund-raiser. Billed as a "party with a purpose," NOW is honoring LPGA player Muffin Spencer-Devlin with a prestigious "Woman of Courage" award.

Two weeks ago, in an article written by Nutt and John Garrity, Spencer-Devlin became the first player in the 46-year history of the LPGA to publicly come out of the closet.

The reaction has been a profound . . . yawn. When the story broke, *Pulse*, a TV tabloid, called Spencer-Devlin at the Ping/Welch's Championship in Tucson, and asked her to appear. She declined. And that was about it. Some of the secrecy, speculation, and suspicion about the LPGA and the gay issue, which had built up over the years until it hung over the Tour like a giant helium balloon, seemed to pop as easily as a soap bubble.

Most of the LPGA's sponsors and players took the announcement in stride. Mike Galeski of Callaway, Spencer-Devlin's main sponsor, says, "Her decision has nothing to do with golf equipment. We stand tall with Muffin, just as we always have."

Of course, the gay issue is still kicking. Prejudice, after all, is as tough to eradicate as bacteria, and the jokes and insults about the "Lesbian Professional Golf Association" will be with us well into the twenty-first century.

For example: The clubhouse lounge and restaurant at Mission Hills is a bright, airy, modern, room, with floor-to-ceiling picture windows looking toward the 18th green. Last Sunday it was a lovely place to relax and watch the final holes of ESPN's telecast of the LPGA event from Phoenix. At least until a short, balding baby-boomer, nicely turned out in expensive golf togs, sauntered up to the bar, grabbed a handful of pretzels and nuts, glanced up at the screen at Laura Davies, disdainfully muttered "Professional dyke golf," and walked away.

A day later, near the membership desk in the clubhouse, an older man tried to cadge tennis privileges.

"This is a busy week," said the receptionist.

"Oh, I know," said the man. "Spikes on dykes and all that."

So the response from the 500 or so lesbians gathered in the hotel ballroom, who understand Spencer-Devlin's bravery in emerging from the closet, is a loud standing ovation, punctuated with whistles and whoops of joy. "We honor you for being such a strong athlete, such a strong woman, and such a strong lesbian," says Patricia Ireland, president of NOW, as she presents Spencer-Devlin with her award.

Too bad no one from the LPGA is here. Last spring, when the Ben Wright controversy erupted, some NOW leaders chastised the LPGA for its neutrality. But Ireland, a former flight attendant who has become an extremely polished advocate for women's rights, is much more sympathetic. At a small press interview, she responds quickly to the question of how political she thinks the LPGA can afford to be without jeopardizing its sponsor base.

"I don't think the LPGA can be *partisan*," says Ireland. "But politics is much broader than just elections. Changing the social culture and changing opinions is political. Promoting women's sports and showing women athletes is very political. So is fighting for more prize money."

Ireland is 50. She grew up in the northwest corner of Indiana. In high school, her athletic options boiled down to a choice between girl's intramurals and cheerleading. In Ireland's book, women's athletics and the LPGA have come a long way, ladies.

But enough politics. How, inquiring minds want to know, is the party?

The comedy performance by Suzanne Westenhoefer, deftly mixing lesbian-oriented material and more universal themes, is a hoot.

"Muffin Spencer-Devlin asked me, 'Do you think I'll make it into your act?' Hmm. You're an open lesbian with the name *Muffin*. It's a gift from the comedy goddess!!" (Big laugh.)

It's a little weird, I must admit as a male reporter, to be in a room with 500 women who don't know that you're alive—including a few who would be happier if you weren't. But, to be perfectly honest, there are a lot of great looking women here.

But it's not that much weirder than being in a ballroom at the Dinah Shore dinner with 800 food-industry moguls. After exhausting the topic of golf, what else do you talk about with the captains of the food biz. Shelf space?

*   *   *

Big crowds flood Mission Hills on Saturday, another warm and sunny day. On the pathways in front of the clubhouse, near the booths hawking T-shirts and Bollé sunglasses, Nabisco products come to life. People encased in felt full-length Mr. Peanut and Oreo cookie outfits pass out samples to fans. Later they probably pass out themselves from heat stroke, but that's the way the cookie crumbles.

The next-to-last day of a golf tournament is known as Move Day, as players jockey for a contending position going into the final round. For those who miss the cut, Move Day has a more literal meaning: Players who shot 149 or higher in the first two rounds pack their bags and hit the road for next week's tournament in Sacramento.

Sheehan and Pierce are paired together after completing their first two rounds at one under par 143. Through the first five holes, they cruise along. But golf is a cruel sport. One bad swing, one lapse in concentration, and the world turns upside-down. On the 352-yard 6th hole, trying to find the peninsula with a fairway wood off the tee, Pierce hits a duffer's shot—so fat she even takes a divot—and watches in horror as the ball splashes into the first fat finger of the lake, after traveling only about 150 yards. She stands at the edge of the tee box, a thin smile on her face, more embarrassed than angry. Five strokes later Pierce walks off the green with a double-bogey and tumbles back into the pack.

Sheehan, on the other hand, is rifling her irons at the flag, but her putting reeks. After half-chunking an 18-foot birdie putt on the 378-yard 7th hole, Sheehan angrily tugs her visor over her eyes and loudly exclaims, "Oh, Patty! Come on!"

"She needs a new putter," whispers manager Rebecca Gaston at greenside. "Or," she jokes, "a new puttee."

On the back nine everything falls into place. Sheehan birdies 10, 11, 12, 14, and 15 and finishes the day tied for the lead at six under par after a no bogey 67. "That was a great round of golf," says Pierce's caddy, Rick Aune, as he comes off the 18th green. "It was almost flawless."

Pierce is not so fortunate. "She hung in there," says Aune. "It could have been worse. She hit the kind of putts where you're reaching to take the ball out of the hole." But they didn't drop; Pierce ends the day at two over par for the tournament after a 75.

Inkster and Sorenstam, paired at four under par at the start of the day, drift in opposite directions as well. Sorenstam takes the lead with a 15-foot birdie putt on the 7th hole, raises both arms overhead and pumps a fist, a *monstrous* display of emotion. She carries the lead to the final hole, when an ABC cameraman, moving around behind her on the fairway, spooks her. Sorenstam backs off and, just after ABC's Judy Rankin has told a nationwide TV audience that Sorenstam rarely makes a mistake, dumps her pitch shot in the drink.

The long week finally begins to take a toll on Inkster. Two late bogeys drop her to two under par for the tournament.

The day's best moment belongs to Davies, who finally puts a harpoon in the flesh of the great green whale. In her forthcoming autobiography, Davies writes of "the finish of my dreams—hearing the roar of the crowd as my second shot lands safely on the island," followed by a putt for eagle. Today the dream becomes reality. After belting a drive close to 300 yards, Davies blasts a 3-iron over the lake to within 12 feet of the cup and rolls the eagle putt home, unleashing a bellowing roar from the packed grandstand overlooking the green.

Red-faced from the sun, Davies's caddie (and cousin) Matthew Adams maneuvers his way through hundreds of fans thronging around the scorer's tent and stops for a chat with a few reporters. "It was 209 [yards] over the water and 215 to the pin. It had to be the perfect strike!"

After appearing on ABC, coleaders Sheehan and Burton meet the press in the media center, housed in a large white tent located between the clubhouse and the 10th tee. The media center is divided into three rooms. A large workroom is in the center, with long rows of blue-clothed tables, chairs for about 100 people, electrical outlets and phones, big scoreboards covering the front wall, and radio booths at the back. The lunchroom is at one end of the tent and the interview room at the other. Players sit on a raised platform at the front of the interview room while an LPGA media rep sits beside them taking notes.

Except for the U.S. Open, the Dinah Shore attracts the largest media contingent of the season. Credentials were issued to over 300 reporters, photographers, and TV crew members from around the globe. The Japanese media, a ubiquitous presence on the LPGA Tour since Ayako Okamoto started making waves on the links in America in the early 1980s, is out in force, dogging the footsteps of Okamoto, highly touted rookie Mayumi Hirase, Hiromi Kobayashi, and several other Japanese players in the field. The Swedes are here too—Sorenstam, along with NHL hockey star Peter Forsberg, is currently the hottest sports star in Sweden, and Neumann and Helen Alfredsson are not far behind. London papers are well represented, tracking Laura Davies and the rest of the British and European players. Even a Pulitzer Prize winner, Jim Murray of the *Los Angeles Times*, who is fond of the LPGA Tour, is here to chronicle the event.

The coverage of a golf tournament is a curious affair. Some reporters never leave the media center, which provides food, drinks, scoreboards,

TV sets, interviews, interview notes, and reams of background material and statistics. The rarest sight on a golf course, next to a double-eagle, may be a golf writer. Yesterday, a reporter was spotted sitting in the lunchroom with a tape recorder and a pairing sheet in his hand, watching the tournament on ESPN and taking notes.

As Ben Hogan, whose caustic wit was as crisp as his iron play, once noted, "If there was an atomic bomb dropped on the fifth hole, golf writers would wait for someone to come in and tell them about it."

Consider a 1987 front-page *Wall Street Journal* article with the title "Golf Is Nice Work, But for Real Leisure, Try Golf Writing. Reporters Get Many Perks, Don't Even Have to Stir to Go Out on the Course."

Reporter Walt Bogdanich, amused and appalled at the freebies available to golf writers—playing privileges at exclusive clubs, gifts of equipment and apparel—sarcastically noted that "the job can have its trying moments. For example, the free beer ran out one day during the tournament."

Don't tell a golf writer that there's no such thing as a free lunch. We bitch if the meal isn't catered. Last week in Phoenix, in addition to eating meals brought in by various local restaurants, I carted home a new straw hat, a slick vinyl briefcase from Ping, two sleeves of Ping golf balls, and a leather notebook holder.

Sloth and ignorance are as firmly linked to golf reporting as double-bogeys are to duffers. One of the week's big stories, reported in every paper, was a pretournament injury to first-round leader Tracy Kerdyk, who sprained a finger so badly when hitting a 7-iron on the range she thought she would have to withdraw. Yet when Kerdyk appeared in the interview room yesterday with an ice bag on her hand after firing a 72 to tie for the second-round lead, a reporter asked: "What's wrong with your hand?"

That's hardly the stupidest question golfers must endure. The classic Forrest Gumpism came last year at a PGA event when Jim Gallagher, Jr., was asked the following question:

"What's your father's name?"

Touted as a can't-miss superstar when she joined the Tour in 1991 at the age of 19, Burton lived up to her early press clippings, becoming the LPGA's youngest and quickest millionaire in just two and a half years and winning a major, the du Maurier Classic, in 1993.

She hasn't won since. Burton tumbled to twenty-seventh and thirty-fifth on the money list in 1994 and 1995, and was shoved into the background by the surge of other Generation X stars—Robbins, Sorenstam, and now Webb. A relentless practice-range workaholic, Burton burnt herself out, and then took to sitting on a bar stool into the wee hours. Her problem wasn't alcohol; it was frustration and self-pity. Last year Burton stonily signed a few autographs on the range, barely favoring her fans with so much as a glance.

Burton's dourness was somewhat understandable. Five feet seven and blocky, Burton looks indestructible. Her imperviousness to cold weather— Burton often amazes her colleagues by wearing shorts or short-sleeve shirts on days when they shiver in long underwear and jackets—adds to the image. But appearances can be deceiving; Burton has been plagued with injuries during her slide, including a broken rib in 1994 and a wrist problem in 1995, all this after three reconstructive knee surgeries as a teenager, which ended a promising future as a competitive swimmer.

Yet a relaxed and smiling Burton seems to have a whole new attitude. "I've changed everything from my shoes to my earrings," she said two weeks ago in Tucson. The changes include a rounder backswing with her left heel firmly planted on the turf, which has tightened up her swing, a new forward press on her putting stroke, the guidance of sports psychologist Deborah Graham, and some time away from the assembly line, fishing and relaxing. She's also been working with Senior Tour player Dave Stockton, one of the finest putters in golf, on her short game. Not even back spasms—Burton visibly winced after her drive on the final hole today—can dampen her spirits. Winning the Dinah Shore "would be the ultimate," says Burton, who hails from nearby Rialto. "It's been the biggest dream of my life since I was nine years old, when my mother took me out here to watch behind the ropes." At that tournament Nancy Lopez gave the youngster an autographed golf ball; it remains one of Burton's most precious possessions.

Sheehan also is in fine spirits as she follows Burton to the interview room. "I was very relaxed today, as relaxed as I can remember. I wish it could be like that all the time. I hit the ball as good as I have all year."

Why was she so relaxed?

Echoing the Caddie Machine's advice for her after the first round, Sheehan says it was the result of "don't try so hard. Don't be so hard on myself. Just go and play." Sheehan adds that she enjoyed the pairing today—"I always have a good time when I play with Caroline Pierce."

Not only is Sheehan one of the best players in the world, she's also one of the best playing *partners*, so gracious you'd think she was gambling for dime Nassaus rather than playing for major championships. When Sheehan outdueled Tammie Green at the 1994 U.S. Open, *Golfweek* editor Steve Ellis, who was married to Green (they divorced in 1995), wrote a column entitled, "Likable Sheehan Is a Considerate Competitor."

"I really enjoy playing with good players," says Sheehan, warming to the theme. "I respect them so much. It's a treat to beat them."

A reporter from *Golf World* asks Sheehan about her first- and second-round pairing with Sorenstam and Webb, noting that there wasn't much chatter among the players.

"It may have *seemed* not friendly," says Sheehan, quickly grasping the reporter's insinuation. "But to the contrary. I told them both how very enjoyable they were to play with. It was two of the nicest days of golf I've had in a long time."

Sheehan goes on to rave about their games, adding that she even sat down with Sorenstam for a big sisterly chat two weeks ago in Tucson. "Patty was very encouraging and supportive," says Sorenstam. "She was the only player who told me I did the right thing. I thank her a *lot* for doing that."

"Annika needs to be true to herself, needs to do what she needs to do," says Sheehan. "She's doing a wonderful job dealing with the pressure. She'll come out of her shell. Just give her some time."

After the press conferences, reporters tap away on laptop computers, filing their stories for the Sunday paper. ABC already has apologized to Sorenstam for disrupting her on the 18th hole. A reporter for the *Sacramento Bee,* who planned to feature Sorenstam in his story, is on the phone with his editor.

"Annika really reamed us by dumping one in the water on the last hole."

It hasn't been a great day for some of the boys in the tent. It has, however, been a fine week for the LPGA and Nabisco. Earlier this afternoon the LPGA announced a big new season-ending event. The $700,000 Tour Championship, sponsored by ITT, is slated for Las Vegas on November 21–24, a week before Thanksgiving.

And don't think the LPGA isn't grateful. Such a grand finale has been at the top of the LPGA's wish list for the last few years. "It's the period on the end of the sentence," says Jim Ritts.

Too true. For the last few years the LPGA has concluded its official schedule in Japan. Talk about a symbol of public indifference! The LPGA had to travel thousands of miles simply to play out the season at an event that drew about as much coverage in the United States as the national curling championships.

Now, instead of ending the year with a barely audible whimper, the LPGA acquires a prestigious sponsor (part of the LPGA's overall game plan to bolster its image by rubbing shoulders with big, well-known corporations), four days of coverage by ESPN and ABC, and the likelihood of a glorious shoot-out for leading money winner and Rolex Player of the Year honors. It's a feather in the visor of new commissioner Ritts, hired in the hopes he could seduce corporate bigwigs into the LPGA family.

Nabisco bigwigs are happy, too. About 80,000 people will flood Mission Hills this week, the lesbian link between the tournament and Dinah Shore Week doesn't seem to rankle as much, and Nabisco guests left town clutching expensive gift bags and fond memories.

If Ray Tarver is representative of other Nabisco guests, the shindig was a phenomenal success. Tarver is a senior vice president in charge of 257 Thrifty convenience stores, which are owned by the Thrifty Oil Company. Those stores, as you might imagine, move a lot of Oreos and Life Savers.

A few days ago he was in the clubhouse raving about his playing partners this year (Dawn Coe-Jones and Nancy Lopez) and last year (Liselotte Neumann and Patty Sheehan). "The ladies are so relaxed, so pleasant. They couldn't be nicer. More people need to get to know these folks."

How much did he enjoy the Dinah Shore?

Enough to give up a trip to the Masters. No, that's not a misprint. Tarver gave his Masters tickets to a colleague in order to play golf with the ladies in Palm Springs. "And I'll do it again."

Before the final round, the practice range offers players a last chance to lasso the butterflies doing loop-de-loops in their guts. Or at least, in the words of Julie Piers (formerly Larson), a strong contender at the 1995 U.S. Open, "to get them flying in the same formation."

Sheehan and Martha Nause, paired with Brandie Burton, are the last two golfers on the range. Dressed in vibrant, TV-friendly colors, Sheehan is wearing black shorts, a pink blouse with tiny black dots and black trim, black visor and socks, and white shoes.

Her body coiled with nervous energy, Sheehan alternates hitting warm-up shots and mopping off her face with a white towel as a brilliant, yellow-white, late-morning sun beats down.

Team Sheehan is gathered around her—Laib, manager Gaston, and instructor Ed Jones, who drove down from Reno on Tuesday.

Nause, in a sleeveless ivory blouse, black-and-white shorts, and a snazzy Ping straw boater, finishes her warm-up and greets a handful of friends and fans at the back of the range. "Warm today," she says cheerfully. "Good morning."

Four years ago Nause, now 41, contracted Ramsay Hunt syndrome, a stress-related virus that caused nerve damage in her ear and destroyed her equilibrium to an extent where Nause couldn't stand and walk without assistance. She couldn't drive a car. Doctors advised her to look for a new career. "It was like feeling really drunk," Nause told *USA Today*. The right side of her face became paralyzed, and Nause lost much of the hearing in her right ear. She spent most of 1993 trying, literally, to get back on her feet. "It took a year of exercising, therapy, and work to relearn how to do everything."

Now, despite some ringing in her right ear, Nause is fit and tan, gleaming with good health and brimming with good cheer. In 1994 she won a major, the du Maurier, and earned $212,130, her best year as a professional. Last year she slumped to $49,525, perplexed by putting woes. During the off-season she discovered the problem: the lenses of her glasses were distorting her vision when she stood over putts, just enough to alter her aim and alignment. The spectacles came off, the putts began to drop. Nause is off to a great start in 1996, after losing out in a playoff against Karrie Webb and Jane Geddes at the HealthSouth Inaugural.

When Sheehan leaves the range, she's followed by about 20 fans and autograph seekers. Pros talk about being "on stage" at tournament sites. For the next five hours she'll be on center stage, her every move and gesture scrutinized by spectators, cameramen, and TV commentators.

Jones, the architect of one of the finest swings ever seen on a golf course, ambles along in the wake of the crowd. Many swing gurus have become as slick and as publicity-conscious as televangelists, hawking books, instructional videos, golf schools, and training gadgets while festooned with as many corporate logos as their pupils.

Jones, wearing a brown short-sleeve shirt, old khaki pants, and a tan fedora and carrying a walking stick, looks like the smart brother in those old TV ads for Boone's Farm wine coolers. You picture him whittling in an old rocking chair on a shady porch.

"How often do you see Patty?" Jones is asked.

"Whenever she's home and hits balls," he shrugs.

"What do you look for?"

"I just watch her. Check her balance, setup. Good fundamentals. Sometimes I miss things."

But Jones knows exactly what's going on. He's been working with Sheehan since Patty was 13, burned out on skiing and searching for a new outlet for her competitive drive.

"She's making awfully good contact on the ball," says Jones. "Playing about as good as she can play. She's in a good frame of mind—she'd like to win this tournament so bad she can taste it."

A vast, boisterous river of fans follow the trio. Three youngsters selling lemonade in the shade of a fairway condo clear $70 from the perspiring mob. The mountains sparkle, every craggy fissure outlined as sharply as a razor's edge, looming so closely that it looks like you could take a giant spoon, scoop up some snow from the summit of San Jacinto Peak, and eat it like vanilla ice cream.

Sheehan hooks her drive into a fairway trap on the 504-yard 2nd hole, and the Sunday galleries ooh and aah and applaud. Thursday and Friday tournament crowds, more knowledgeable and fewer in number, tend to sit on their hands, as difficult to please as the haughtiest Broadway critics. The weekend masses, in comparison, are as undiscriminating as *Beavis and Butt-head* fans. Often oblivious too, tramping about as players are about to tee off or putt. "Stand, please! Stand, please! Stand, please!" yell the marshals.

Sheehan, striking the ball beautifully, three-putts two of the first five holes. "That flat stick," says Ed Jones, shaking his head. "Whoo! A little scary."

It promises to be a long and winding road to the clubhouse. It is, after all, the final round of a major, a five-hour journey through the Fun House of the Psyche, filled with mirrors of distortion, mazes, pitch-black passageways, ghostly voices, unearthly screams, demons and clowns, daggers and banana peels. No refund. No exit.

Especially for Nause. She's all over the course, her game suddenly in tatters. Already four over par for the day, her chances, so bright a short time ago, have crumbled to dust in the desert.

Earlier in her career, Nause worked with two different sports psychologists trying to get a grip on the anger that often afflicted her work. One suggested Nause imagine filling a black bag with her rage and tossing the bag in the ocean. After a double-bogey at the 158-yard 5th hole and a poor drive at number 6, Nause walks up the fairway shaking her head from side to side, her preround serenity shattered, the black bag already stuffed with dark thoughts.

Despite her three-putts, Sheehan seems calm and collected as she walks up the 6th fairway, chatting with Burton, eating a few orange slices and flipping the rinds into the lake for the ducks to feast upon. After another superb iron, she lines up a nasty, downhill, sliding six-foot birdie putt, taps it as carefully as a sculptor, and buckles at the knees in relief as the ball tumbles over the edge and into the cup.

After nine holes the leader board is logjammed with no fewer than six golfers at six under par: Sheehan, Burton, Robbins, Sorenstam, Mallon, and Amy Fruhwirth. A dozen other players nip at their heels.

By the time Sheehan regains a tie for the lead with Robbins after birdies at the 506-yard 11th and the 379-yard 12th holes, the atmosphere has changed completely. The huge, festive, party-hearty crowds have dispersed, some tracking Robbins, or Mallon, or Sorenstam, many staking out strategic viewing positions on the last two holes to watch the leaders jockey down the stretch.

Several hundred fans are still with Sheehan, Burton, and Nause, a group of excited but nervous followers, including many of their friends and family members.

Sheehan walks about 100 yards amidst the crowd from the 12th green to the 13th tee. ("We're the only sport that plays in the audience," says Lee Trevino.) Leslie and Bobo Sheehan, who looks thin and fragile, walk slowly along the edges of the gallery as they root for their daughter. Eleven years ago during the 1985 Dinah Shore, a hale and robust father, walking almost the identical path, cheerfully stopped to tell a reporter why he was so proud of her. Patty often has been portrayed as a natural athlete, seemingly born with a glorious golf swing. And with the pride of a star athlete who likes to make her craft look effortless, she rarely bothered to set the record straight.

But Bobo knew, better than anyone else, exactly how hard Sheehan worked to reach the top of her profession, spending six or seven hours a day on the range as a teenager. "It was a lonely life, hitting ball after ball after ball."

Burton, who has been spraying shots all over the course, is now three behind Sheehan, and fading fast, after finding a fairway bunker on the 386-yard 13th hole. Her back is killing her. ("It was bad enough to inhibit me," Burton confessed later. "I compensated for it on some shots.") But she gamely battles on, sinking a clutch 12-footer to save par.

"Good putt!" Laib tells her, appreciating her display of heart.

Sheehan studies her two-and-a-half-foot par putt, which is no gimme. The hole is cut on a slight crown, and it's as slick as ice around the cup. Sheehan pushes the putt just a hair, it curls around the lip. Sheehan walks off the green with a wry little smile on her face, as if to say, "Do you *believe* that?"

Under a broiling sun—the temperature has crested at 90 degrees—Sheehan waits on a narrow tee box at the 148-yard 14th hole. An ABC cameraman, a tall guy in a blue golf shirt, stands on the tee no more than two paces from Sheehan, a hand-held camera perched on his shoulder and trained on Sheehan's face as she wipes off perspiration with a white towel.

Between ABC's on-course cameramen, soundmen carrying cylindrical boom mikes, and roving commentators wearing headphones, with antennas sticking up like exclamation points out of each ear hole, the scene resembles some sort of alien space invasion. With the cameraman right in her face, never leaving her alone for a second, Sheehan must feel like she's undergoing some sort of excruciating psychological probe.

Sheehan hits her first bad iron of the day, a hook into the front trap, and then bolts for a nearby Porta-John, the only place she can escape prying eyes and lenses. (The networks will probably wire up the toilets before too long.)

The middle holes of the back nine are the most remote at Mission Hills. Usually, on the final day of a tournament, distant roars erupt like thunderclaps from around the course.

But it's eerily silent out here. No noise. No roars. Only the droning of the Goodyear blimp overhead. And behind us, nothing but empty fairways and greens.

"This is wearing me out!" says one of Sheehan's friends from Reno, drained from the heat and the tension. Actually, Sheehan seems to be the freshest person out here, a small forcefield of concentration, energy radiating off her in waves. And her emotions, usually so volatile, have leveled out, as they did when she won the U.S. Open at Oakmont. As Sheehan walks to the tee at the 390-yard 16th hole, fans applaud loudly and yell, "Go, Patty!" Sheehan responds with a small, determined smile.

When she tees up her ball, a plastic bag suddenly blows into the fairway, near a gaggle of photographers just inside the ropes, about 20 yards in front of the markers.

"Someone want to grab that for me, please?" says Sheehan. A photographer dashes out and scoops up the bag.

"You're a good man, Charlie Brown," Sheehan says pleasantly, as the gallery laughs. But Sheehan now trails both Sorenstam and Robbins, and some of the air goes out of the gallery as we pass a scoreboard.

Sheehan pars the 390-yard 16th hole to remain six under par and waits on the tee on the 171-yard 17th hole. One shot behind Robbins and Sorenstam, who are playing the 18th, a potential birdie hole, Sheehan figures she probably needs to birdie the last two holes to force a playoff.

The 17th is a beautiful, tree-lined par three to a slightly elevated two-tier green, set in the base of a steep hillside, a natural amphitheater for hundreds of spectators. It's been the scene of many cruel disappointments over the years, as well as a few glorious moments—most notably Betsy King holing a bunker shot in her march to victory in 1990.

Sheehan and Laib conduct a critical business meeting: 5-iron or 6-iron? A choked-down 5-iron is the choice. As Sheehan prepares to play, ABC's on-course reporter, Bob Rosburg, tells the viewing audience, "She desperately needs to get it close."

Athletes live for fleeting moments of perfection. Once a year, or once a decade, the thousands of hours of practice and long years of discipline fuse, the tumblers click into alignment, and the lock springs open. Inside the vault is a priceless treasure, a moment of exquisite grace that will be preserved in the trophy room of an athlete's heart.

For an instant, just for an instant, an athlete shrugs off the limits of the body, the limits of the mind, the limits of gravity itself, and flashes across the sky like a rainbow.

The ball screams off Sheehan's clubface, arcing in a tight draw toward the flagstick. As it reaches its apex, the crowd begins to buzz. And when it rolls up three feet from the cup, the fans on the hillside explode with whoops and screams. Sheehan pumps a fist in exultation.

Sheehan crouches and studies the birdie putt, her hands cupped over the sides of her visor. But even now, facing one of the most important putts of her career, she remains a considerate playing partner. Nause, who found her game for a little while, has lost it again. When Nause's par putt lips out, Sheehan raises her hands in a gesture of disbelief and sympathy.

Then she takes care of business, rolling in the putt, exhaling in a huge sigh of relief, and briefly clasping hands with Laib.

The five-minute delay on the tee at 18 is excruciating. With the cameraman in her face again, Sheehan towels off, stretches her neck from side to side, stretches out her quad muscles, waits, and waits some more.

Professional golfers who have played other sports pinpoint the wait between shots as the key element that makes golf so agonizing. In the mirrors of the Fun House, time is distorted into slow motion: seconds drip down like an exquisite Chinese water torture, playing havoc with the mind. The Fun House is more than a metaphor. A *Golf Digest* article in 1994 detailed the physiological effects of nervousness, the times when "your body can turn into a stranger." The effects include soaring blood pressure, accelerated heartbeat and respiratory rate; blood flowing from the extremities to the brain and torso, resulting in cold, stiff hands and fingers; the digestive system shutting down, resulting in stomach, bowels, and bladder trying to empty; secretion of endorphins that can result in numbness; blood, oxygen and nutrients pouring to the brain, which at first enhances thinking but soon, when the brain can no longer process the nutrients, produces confusion.

In her amateur days, Lopez used to "throw up in the morning, throw up on the way to the course, and throw up at the golf club." Bobby Jones lost up to 18 pounds in a single tournament, concentrating so deeply he burned calories like a marathon runner. Afterward his hands often shook so badly he could only remove his necktie by cutting it off.

Ellsworth Vines, the top U.S. tennis player in the 1930s before becoming a fine professional golfer, once said, "In tennis you seldom have a chance, once things get going, to get shaky. You're too busy running around like a racehorse. But in golf—hell, it makes me nervous just to talk about it. That little white ball just sits there. A man can beat himself before he ever swings at it."

Up ahead, the great green whale continues to wreak havoc. "Nobody wants it," says Dee Darden, photographing from the 18th fairway. Robbins, whose second shot lands in deep rough, has to lay up short of the pond, then misses a beautifully struck par putt that curls around the high side of the cup. Sorenstam, in perfect position in two, boldly attacks the flag, located in the back right corner of the huge green, but can't hold the slick putting surface with a wedge. Her four-foot par putt spins around and out of the cup. Mallon, who knocked the pin down on the closing holes but couldn't buy a putt, misses a six-foot birdie effort. All three finish at six under par. Although Sheehan doesn't yet know it, she's back in the lead.

No one wins a major championship without a break or two along the way. Sheehan pulls her drive toward the lake and stares in agony as the ball descends to earth.

"Oh, don't go in the water," she prays aloud.

"Is it wet?" yells a fan.

"Oh, it's fine!" says another.

Barely. Sheehan gets lucky, the ball coming to rest a few yards away from a watery grave. Maybe the golfing gods, high up in their viewing box— maybe Dinah herself, who once nicknamed Sheehan "Mighty Mite"— used a bit of celestial body English.

As Sheehan prepares to hit her second shot, the Caddie Machine, who has caught a glimpse of the scoreboard back by the 17th tee, decides it's time for a conference.

"Patty, can I tell you something?"

"What?"

"You're leading."

"I *know* I'm leading," says Sheehan, thinking she's tied for the top spot.

"No," says Laib. "You're *leading*."

Meanwhile Nause is playing her second shot from the right rough. She pushes a fairway wood, and with a huge gallery gathered around her, Nause yells at the top of her lungs.

"Hook!!! Damn it!!!"

What a game golf is! Five hours ago Nause was as confident, collected, and composed as a news anchor on a good hair day. Now she's a raw nerve ending, her overstuffed black bag of anger splitting at the seams. Maybe she can get a sports psychologist referral from Burton, who has retained her equanimity despite her ball-striking struggles and back pains.

Sheehan pushes her second shot into a fairway bunker. She has 116 yards over the lake to a pin tucked in the back right corner of the green, a shot that would terrify most golfers. But for Sheehan, it's a comfortable 9-iron.

It comes out dead left, however. Sheehan is left with a monstrous putt of about 120 feet over a big ridge.

Robbins and Mallon sit on their golf bags just across the island green, on an incline underneath the scorer's tent, joking and readying themselves for a playoff. Sorenstam sits nearby with fiancé David Esch. Webb, who finished at five under par, after rimming out a 20-foot birdie try at the 18th, hangs around to soak in the drama.

It couldn't be a tougher two-putt. As is her wont in such situations, Sheehan gives herself a little pep talk. "C'mon! You're a good player! Don't let this slip away!" From a vantage point at the back of the green, Sheehan is so far away, and the ridge bisecting the green is so steep, it's impossible to see the lower part of her body.

With the whole golf world watching, and the crowd as hushed as church mice, Sheehan raps the putt over the ridge and watches as it funnels down to within six feet of the cup, a brilliant effort. Still, none of the contenders have made a putt from this distance all day. If she misses—and Burton sinks her 15-foot birdie putt—a five-way playoff will ensue.

Burton's brave bid slides by the cup.

Sheehan paces the green and studies the putt from every angle. Then she crouches down, hands cupped around her visor, and takes a big breath. "You've done this thousands of times before," she tells herself. "So go ahead and do it again."

Curtis Strange once called Nancy Lopez "the best putter in the world from eight feet in, man, woman, or child." The best clutch putter in golf, in recent years, has been Patty Sheehan. And she's performed seeming miracles—such as finishing birdie, birdie at the 1992 U.S. Open—with the same weapon she's carried since she turned pro, a Wilson 8802 model with a silver blade as nicked-up as the putters handed out at a miniature golf course.

As she takes her stance, Sheehan's cool concentration is palpable. Sorenstam can feel it as well. "It's going in," she whispers to fiancé Esch.

The putt is struck so purely that Sheehan begins to straighten and shout and jump for joy before the ball rolls into the heart of the cup. A mighty roar erupts from the grandstand, flooding over Sheehan like a tsunami. Sheehan once turned a somersault after winning a tournament in Japan. A few days ago, in a practice round, she tried a cartwheel. Now, at her mother's request, she performs a nifty one on the edge of the green as the crowd continues to stand and cheer.

ABC, almost out of airtime, collars her for a quick interview. "I'd like to dedicate this to my dad," says Sheehan. "He's not been feeling that well lately."

"Water! Water! Water!" the fans yell, and a reluctant Sheehan, clutching a huge, silver four-foot trophy and a bouquet of roses, finally obliges, wading back and forth across the waist-high water, the great green monster vanquished.

Eventually Sheehan arrives in the pressroom after signing hundreds of autographs, hugging Bobo and Leslie, and receiving congratulatory hugs from Mallon, Robbins, Amy Alcott, Helen Alfredsson, and other players.

"Are you disappointed you didn't get the first putt closer?" Jim Murray asks her.

"Not now," Sheehan says with a grin.

The sun slips through the turquoise sky and slides behind the blue-black mountains. The desert begins to cool. Sheehan, surrounded by family, friends, and well-wishers, holds court at a raucous clubhouse party. Bobo and Leslie walk down the clubhouse steps, heading home. The big, silver championship trophy will remain on display at Mission Hills, a gift of love and gratitude from their daughter.

A replica of the trophy will rest at Sheehan's home, in Reno, and when Patty sees it, she'll think about the day she dreamed a dream and made it come true and remember, with love and gratitude, the gifts her father gave to her.

CHAPTER 3

Nashville: Golf at the Country Club

Sometimes the life of a professional golfer is as glamorous as a Hollywood premiere starring Arnold or Demi.

On Tuesday afternoon, April 23, at the Hermitage Golf Course in Old Hickory, a suburb just east of Nashville, Nancy Lopez, Michelle McGann, Kelly Robbins, and Tammie Green tee it up in the Vince Gill $30,000 Skins Game, a prelude to the 54-hole $600,000 Sara Lee Classic, which begins on Friday.

Lopez and Green (who just rejoined the Tour after emergency surgery in January to remove an ovarian cyst and her appendix) have endorsement contracts with Sara Lee. McGann won last year's tournament; Robbins tied for second.

The LPGA stars are paired with pop and Christian music star Amy Grant, Canadian songbird Anne Murray, Grand Ole Opry veteran Jan Howard, and Martha Sundquist, wife of Tennessee governor Don Sundquist.

Gill is tall, handsome, and as affable and relaxed as an old hound dog. In fact, he looks like he could sleep standing up. Today he's emceeing the action and also teamed with Samantha Fox, 15, the precocious Tennessee state women's amateur champion.

It's a raw, blustery day. But the crowd following the tensome looks larger than the entire first-round gallery at last week's star-crossed tournament in Atlanta, won by Barb Mucha. Nashville has embraced the LPGA. *The Tennessean*, one of the tournament sponsors, runs a story or picture on the front page of the paper every day, in addition to exhaustive coverage in the sports section.

Players and caddies rate Nashville close to the top among Tour stops. For players, private housing and transportation are available for the asking. Stars cruise the route from the golf course to the official tournament hotel, the Sheraton Music City, in big black Cadillacs. Even the five-foot-eleven Michelle "The Hat Lady" McGann can leave her hat on behind the wheel of a 1996 Seville. The Skins Game purse of $30,000 is gigantic, a sweet bonus for the four LPGA stars chosen to participate. (Usually the prize money for such pretournament exhibitions runs about $15,000 and is divvied up among as many as 16 players.)

Tomorrow's Sara Lee gala dinner at the Sheraton features entertainment by Amy Grant. Usually a few LPGA players are lured onto the stage for a duet or as backup singers. Caddies as well as players get invitations to a Thursday evening picnic at the nearby Hermitage Mansion, former home of Andrew Jackson; Tracy Byrd will sing for the masses this year.

Entertainment abounds every night at the numerous clubs that dot Nashville, featuring everything from country to blues to rock to alternative sounds. Venues range from the foot-stompin' Wildhorse Saloon to the legendary Bluebird Cafe, a small, low-ceilinged, acoustically pure room with a bar in the back and pictures of all of the stars who have played there over the years—everyone from Garth Brooks to Loretta Lynn—covering the walls.

Last week Nashville hosted Tin Pan Alley, a well-known gathering of top-notch writers and musicians. In addition to conferences and concerts, the artists found time for a little recreation—a golf tournament at Hermitage Golf Course.

They probably enjoyed the outing. Hermitage is a decent layout, located near the banks of the Cumberland River. It's generally flat, and the trees lining the outskirts of the course seldom are a factor. But water, in the form of streams, ponds, and lakes, comes into play on the majority of the holes; the rough is nasty; and the greens are slick, with plenty of undulations. Open to the public, Hermitage charges $33–$38, a relative bargain these days for a pleasant, daily-fee course.

Amy Grant, wearing a black sweater and black pants, armed with Big Bertha clubs and a floral print Callaway bag, dribbles a drive about 20 yards off the first tee.

"Don't even *think* about clapping," Gill tells the crowd, as he trots out to retrieve the ball.

Gill, who recently picked up two Grammys for his gospel song "Go Rest High on That Mountain," a tribute to his late brother, has been heavily involved in the Sara Lee Classic since he played in the pro-am for the inaugural event in 1988. A single-digit handicapper with a quick, powerful swing, Gill has been rounding up his golfing buddies, such as Diamond Rio and Wynonna Judd, for the celebrity kickoff to tournament week for the last three years. He also has raised over $700,000 for junior golf programs in Tennessee at a charity golf tournament called "The Vinnie."

Grant, a good pal, took up golf just two years ago. The second round of her life was played in the 1994 Sara Lee Skins Game, a terrifying experience. "I was so afraid I was going to kill someone." But soon she was hooked. "It's nice to get outside," she told *Golf World*. "And it's a great thing to do on tour—especially in cities I've visited so many times I know the animals at the zoo by their first names."

Playing in celebrity events, she also gets a lot of tips from pros, caddies, and instructors. The best tip? "A great swing is muscle memory," Grant says. "The idea is to get a good feeling and recreate it. If you're *thinking* about your swing, you're on the wrong track."

Locked in fierce concentration, Grant, long wavy auburn tresses curling around her beautiful face, stands over the golf ball for a frozen moment before taking the club back with a forceful athletic lunge. Just by watching her swing a club, it's easy to see the determination that drove the aspiring singer and songwriter to pound on the doors of Nashville's Music Row at the age of 15. And to overcome Christian critics who accused her of selling her soul when she crossed over to pop music in 1991 with the album *Heart in Motion*, which sold 4 million copies.

On the 2nd hole, Grant raps a drive about 160 yards. Clowning around as they walk up the fairway on the soggy course, which has been battered by violent spring storms, Gill begins singing "Baby, Baby," Grant's smash single from *Heart in Motion*. The video from the song, which featured Grant playfully flirting with a male model, was the last straw for some Christian radio stations, which banned her from their play lists.

"This is the hillbilly version," says Gill, and he starts singing, "Bubba, Bubba, let's go get some bar-be-que." The crowd laughs. Grant breaks up, a big grin on her face, and puts her arm around Gill's waist as they continue up the fairway together.

None of the celebs, except for Gill, are good golfers. Martha Sundquist grounds a shot into a large pond guarding the green of the 2nd hole. In a gesture of bemused resignation, she raises her hands as if to signal a touchdown. In politics, she's seen much uglier things than a topped fairway wood.

Golf, in many ways, is still an elitist sport, a security-gated enclave of posh clubs, $50,000 membership fees, and $600 titanium drivers, manufactured by designers who once devised weapons systems for Lockheed or the Defense Department.

But it is also a great leveler, reducing the mightiest of celebrities to human dimensions. As Kassie Wesley, who stars in the TV soap opera *One Life to Live* and plays in the Dinah Shore pro-am, puts it, "I always say that golf doesn't build character; it reveals it. You get a good idea of what a person is like during a round of golf." At the least, you get a few clues. Kevin

Costner, at a celeb event prior to the AT&T Classic at Pebble Beach in January, cheerfully signed autographs for kids, and went out of his way to acknowledge his fans—even the dolts who shrieked and pointed at him like he was a baboon in a monkey cage at the zoo. He also shrugged off his terrible shots with good grace. (Costner, a relative beginner, plays like Amy Grant, exhibiting a strong, athletic swing and producing a combination of terrific shots and embarrassing dubs.) Clint Eastwood, on the other hand, was as disdainful of the gallery as Dirty Harry.

Celebrity events are something of a goof for the pros. LPGA player Kris Tschetter even comes along to caddie for Gill today, toting his lightweight black carry bag. When Jan Howard rolls a shot onto a green that winds up closer to the pin than her teammate, Nancy Lopez, Tschetter razzes the queen of women's golf.

"Good thing you got a partner."

"Caddies aren't supposed to talk," shoots back Lopez.

For the celebs, however, playing with the pros in front of hundreds or thousands of fans is a nerve-wracking affair. "There are times in the hotel when I don't want to go out there," says Costner, who hit the pro-am circuit in earnest to promote his film *Tin Cup*. "I know I'm going to hit some bad shots," he told *Golf World*. "It's not a good feeling. You say to yourself, 'You're not a pro. You know you're going to be a little humiliated. You're going to hit shots that are just bad.'

"But I come from a world where people think I'm supposed to save everybody. I play heroes, guys who get it done. Then everybody looks up—and my ball has gone only forty yards."

Rambo lives in terror as well. "I thought marriage was tough," Stallone told interviewer Ann Liquori on The Golf Channel. "That's a walk in the park. Believe me, golf is like going over Niagara Falls in a barrel."

Through the magic of Hollywood—including endless retakes and the tutoring of CBS commentator Gary McCord—Costner looks like a pro in *Tin Cup*, which Warner Brothers expects to be a huge hit.

And why not?

"Golf is as big as rock and roll," John Sykes, president of VH-1, told *Golf Digest*. "Golf is now cool, hip, fun," says Rob Goulet of Cornerstone Sports, which represents, among others, Phil Mickelson, Corey Pavin, Steve Jones, and LPGA rookie Jill McGill. Cornerstone put together Fairway to Heaven, a music-oriented golf celebrity event that airs annually on VH-1.

Not long ago, golf was plaid pants, fat cats, and Amana hats. Golf celebs were squares like Joe Garagiola, Andy Williams, Danny Thomas, and Bing Crosby. In his rock idol days, Alice Cooper used to hide his golf clubs and sneak away to play; golf, it was feared, would destroy his bad-boy image.

But it's not your father's country club anymore. Golf is everywhere. Rock stars from bands such as the Black Crowes, Gin Blossoms, Bon Jovi, Soul Asylum, R.E.M., Dinosaur Jr., and Stone Temple Pilots tee it up. So do Meat Loaf and Neil Young. *The Source*, a hip-hop magazine, ran a cover photo of rapper Luther Campbell on the links. Hootie and the Blowfish featured Gary McCord and PGA players Fred Couples and Jay Haas in their video for the smash hit "Only Want to Be with You." On the day after he won the Masters, Nick Faldo played in a celebrity pro-am organized by Hootie and his fishy friends. As R.E.M.'s Mike Mills told *Details* magazine, "I know it has a certain amount of baggage because it's played by rich people with terrible taste in trousers who are racist snobs, and I'm sorry about that. But golf is very meditational."

Kramer babbles about his golf game on *Seinfeld*. *GQ* and *Men's Journal* run cover stories on golf. The movie *Happy Gilmore*, described by *Sports Illustrated* as "inane and embarrassing," proved a minor hit at the box office. Golf has been the backdrop for recent commercials for Ford, Budweiser, Miller Lite, Perrier, and Dockers. Golf equipment companies hire Alice Cooper, Michael Bolton, Michael Jordan, and Larry Bird to pitch their new clubs. The Golf Channel brings hard-core junkies 24 hours of golf 365 days of the year. (Catch live action from the first round of the Nike Tour's Wichita Open!)

Michael Jordan and Charles Barkley practically live on the links. The richest man in the world, Bill Gates, brags about breaking 100 and, displaying the same type of ruthlessness on the links he is accused of in business, sandbags to win a tournament. (He told officials at a charity outing in Seattle he was a 30 handicap before shooting 87.) The most powerful man in the world, Bill Clinton, fights his slice every chance he gets, refuting critics who believe he always veers to the left. JFK's woods are auctioned off to Arnold Schwartzenegger for $772,500; a set of head covers fetch $34,500. "Pulling a Norman," a reference to Greg Norman's final-round collapse at the Masters, has already entered the lexicon—Clinton used the phrase to warn aides not to become complacent about his big lead over Bob Dole in the polls. O. J. asserts he was chipping with a 3-wood in the dark at the time of the murders, a claim as implausible as the rest of his defense.

"Golf is the only participant sport that crosses so many segments of the population," Budweiser marketer Bob Lachky told *Golf Digest* in 1994. "It's really become more of a common man's recreation. When you look at hot buttons in the 21–35 age group, golf is definitely up there."

Certainly the LPGA is seeing its share of hipper celebrities. Bill Murray teamed with Sherri Steinhauer in a pro-am before the Chrysler-Plymouth

Tournament of Champions in Orlando in January. Charles Barkley teamed with Lauri Merten at the Jamie Farr Toledo Classic in 1994 and 1995. "He seems like such a brute on the court," says Merten. "But he's a very nice person." And as uptight as most amateurs who tee it up with the pros. When they played in 1994, Barkley leaned down and quietly told her, "I'm so nervous, you couldn't get a stickpin between my cheeks."

If the Bulls were not otherwise engaged in the NBA playoffs the biggest celebrity-athlete in the world, Michael Jordan, probably would be in the pro-am field in Nashville this week, since Jordan shills for Hanes, a Sara Lee company.

Usually LPGA players, who are huge sports fans, and often movie and music buffs, enjoy rubbing elbows with the stars. Inkster cherished her round with longtime idol Julius Erving. "He was even more my idol after I met him—such a class guy." Meg Mallon relished playing with Joe DiMaggio. "He was very businesslike and serious about his golf game. You could tell he thinks the way people behave toward celebrities is foolish."

In 1994 Dottie Pepper became neighbors with Michael Jordan when he rented a house during spring training in Sarasota. Pepper thought Jordan was a great guy, remarkably down-to-earth, "very, very normal." Nevertheless before their one golf outing, Pepper, concerned about Jordan's history as a high-stakes gambler, withdrew $500 from an ATM machine. She and Jordan, who were partners, lost, but the damage was a paltry $60.

But celebs sometimes have feet of clay. An LPGA veteran once played with former congressman Dan Rostenkowski, who subsequently pled guilty to felonies for misappropriation of funds while in office.

"He had slime written all over him," says the player, curling her lip in disdain. "Not an honest guy, you could just tell."

The LPGA is trying to find a formula to ride the wave of golf's surging popularity. So far it's mainly been watching from the sidelines, more cheerleader than participant. Cadillac runs TV and print ads with male stars Fred Couples, Tom Kite, and Lee Trevino. The ladies, in comparison, are stranded by the freeway, trying to hitch a ride. Name a corporation—other than a golf equipment manufacturer—that features an LPGA player in a major national TV or print campaign outside of golf magazines.

Don't strain yourself. There isn't one.

Actually, Inkster, to her everlasting chagrin, was one of the latest, pitching Kaopectate on TV a few years ago. When her agent, IMG, brought her the deal, Inkster turned it down. When Kaopectate shoveled more money at her, she turned it down again. When the company upped the ante a third time, Brian urged her to accept. "God, it's so easy," he told her.

How much money was she paid? Inkster won't say.

Would she do it again? "Probably not."

Did her peers give her a lot of crap? No shit, Sherlock. Sheehan probably got off the best line. Asked if she had been approached by Kaopectate, Sheehan said no, then dead-panned, "I guess I wasn't in the running."

Fortunately for the LPGA, Gill and Grant are helping push women golfers into the celebrity spotlight, a vital factor in attracting media attention and corporate sponsors. It's a great fit too.

Gill and Grant are wildly popular and squeaky clean, with images that blend the traditional values of the Old South and the progressive values of the New South. And both country stars and LPGA players believe in the personal touch; reaching out to fans with their likable approachability is a primary selling point.

Gill's attachment to the LPGA runs deep. He met Heather Farr, who represented Sara Lee, at the first Nashville tournament in 1988, and the tiny but tough five-foot bundle of energy knocked his socks off. "I made a fast friend," says Gill. "She had great charisma, a great aura. Always had a smile on her face. And to see that little thing just rip that golf ball!"

Farr, who joined the Tour in 1985, flirted with stardom until she was diagnosed with an advanced stage of breast cancer in 1989 at the age of 24. After an excruciating battle with the disease, including a mastectomy and a bone marrow transplant, she succumbed in late 1993. Gill, who had dedicated an album to Farr, sang at her funeral, as did Wynonna Judd.

"LPGA players are kinda special," says Gill in his soft, laid-back, high-lonesome drawl. "I'm always impressed with how nice they are to other people. They're not getting the respect they deserve. I grew up as a player and a golf fan. I didn't care whether it was [Kathy] Whitworth or Jack or Arnie. If somebody shoots 65, they shoot 65." Gill describes himself as a hillbilly, and he does sometimes chew gum with his mouth open. But this good ole boy has shucked all traces of redneck. "I never thought there was a lesser ability because of gender."

Gill sees parallels between LPGA players and women in the music business. "I think there are similar double standards. Women [in the music business] had to be pretty first, which made no sense at all. Music isn't visual. You listen to it, you don't watch it. I never cared what a singer *looked* like. People are getting older, getting wiser. That stuff doesn't matter."

Both Gill and Grant have little patience for those who gay-bait the LPGA or anyone else. Grant is exceptionally warm and friendly, but the criticism from religious groups over her conversion from Christian to pop music left a scar and makes her wary of political and social issues. When asked about the involvement by Christian groups in ballot initiatives to deny civil rights protection for homosexuals, Grant literally backs up a step. But she makes her beliefs clear. "I wouldn't want to be allied with anybody who judges anybody else."

How sold is Nashville on the LPGA?

Tournament officials boldly predict the Sara Lee may someday become a major, with steadily increasing purses and the likelihood of a move to more favorable dates in May. Such talk represents delusions of grandeur—the same delusions that have some Nashville civic officials portraying Nashville as the new Atlanta—but it indicates how deeply entrenched the LPGA has become in the city.

Even the sportswriters, normally the most cynical of folks, are jumping on the LPGA bandwagon. David Climer, who is coordinating *The Tennessean*'s superlative coverage of the tournament, predicts the Senior Tour, which left the LPGA in the dust in the 1980s, and holds an event in Nashville in May, is ripe for a stall, if not a fall. After Nicklaus, Palmer, and Trevino leave the stage, he reasons, who will fans flock to see? Jim Albus? Tom Wargo? Especially since many of the forty-something stars, such as Tom Watson, Curtis Strange, and Tom Kite, are filthy rich and unlikely to play the geezer circuit on a regular basis when they turn 50.

Climer also believes the Southern-style hospitality of LPGA players gives them a bright future. "The toughest person to deal with out here [at the Sara Lee] is better than the easiest person on the PGA Tour. And you can quote me on that."

Nancy Lopez cleans up in the Skins Game, pocketing $14,000. Contestants receive framed platinum sales awards (highly valued collectibles) from Gill's album *Souvenirs* and fancy bathrobes from Sara Lee, which particularly pleases Grant. "I'm a robe fanatic," she says as the fans descend with pens and cameras.

The Sara Lee Classic is the third event since the conclusion of the Nabisco Dinah Shore. After Sheehan's dramatic victory, the LPGA Tour traveled to Sacramento the first week of April for the inaugural $500,000 Twelve Bridges Classic, won by Kelly Robbins after a marathon five-hole playoff with Val Skinner. Then it took a break during the week of the Masters. (Karrie Webb and fiancé Todd Haller were in Augusta, rooting for Norman. Webb left in tears after Norman dumped his tee shot into the pond on the par-3 16th hole. "I was just gutted," Webb said later. "I felt like *I* had lost. Even with the experience he's had, Greg's whole routine was eight, nine seconds slower. He looked scared to take it away, which is understandable. I don't think I could have finished that round.")

It was a grim day for Norman, and it's been a grim period for the sports world in general. In the past year "America's Team," the Dallas Cowboys, has been almost as prominent on the police blotter as in the sports pages. Cowboy Michael Irvin was busted for cocaine possession, after pretty much telling the nation to go screw itself on TV after the NFL Championship game. The litany of offenses by other Cowboys, ranging from sexual assault to substance abuse to weapons charges, may earn the team a spot on *America's Most Wanted* as well as on *Monday Night Football*. The Cowboys, who once stood for style and excellence, are led—so to speak—by owner Jerry Jones, a well-known party animal who gleefully thumbed his nose at NFL rules when Nike came calling with a Brinks truckload of endorsement money, and coach Barry Switzer, who had an affair with the wife of his defensive coordinator when he ran the football factory at Oklahoma.

But the Cowboys are a drop in the polluted bucket of modern big-time sports. "The sports world has created Frankenstein's monsters in the form of players," said NBA legend Bob Cousy, who vows never to coach again. "We say 'yes' to everything these man-children want."

The sports pages used to be an escape. Now they're a through-the-looking-glass descent into a twisted wasteland of jurisprudence, social pathology, and skewed values. All-American running back Lawrence Phillips drags a former girlfriend by her hair down three flights of stairs as she screams for help. He gets reinstated by Nebraska coach Tom Osborne after a month-long probation and drafted by the pros, where he will earn millions. The ex-girlfriend, a basketball player, loses her scholarship. Convicted rapist Mike Tyson whines about the inadequacies of his multimillion-dollar paydays after his release from prison. Albert Belle assaults fans and photographers, chases kids who come near his house, taunts female sportswriters—and gets standing O's from the Cleveland Indian fans who are willing to overlook anything for a few W's. Marge Schott insults blacks, Jews, and Asians; she praises Hitler but says he "went too far." It takes major league baseball about five years to conclude she may not be fit to own a piece of our national pastime.

Coaches such as Rick Pitino, Mike Ditka, and Pat Riley, the ringmasters of the pro and college sports circuses, earn $20,000–$40,000 a pop for "motivational" speeches to businessmen. Tanya Harding, the luckiest unjailed athlete next to O. J., remains a media darling.

In the cesspool of modern professional sports, covering the LPGA is like diving into a pristine mountain spring. Bad behavior on the LPGA Tour usually is limited to griping and whining about course conditions, a few naughty words uttered in the heat of battle, and the occasional tossed club. The biggest scandal in recent years was Lori Garbacz's on-camera tirade at an ESPN cameraman who got in her face during a bad round (she said, "Get that fucking camera out of my face," which earned her a $5,000 fine).

LPGA players don't bitch about multimillion-dollar salaries. They don't go on strike at midseason. They don't get arrested for dealing cocaine. They don't beat up their spouses. They don't hire thugs to shatter the kneecaps of their rivals. They don't throw firecrackers at kids or wade into the crowd to punch out hecklers. (Although Dottie Pepper came close. On the 71st hole at the 1992 Nabisco Dinah Shore, Pepper missed a birdie putt which would have tied her for the lead. Suddenly a voice boomed out from the massive gallery sitting on the hillside behind the green: "Choker!" Pepper whirled, pinned the cretin with a glare that could have melted steel, and took a half step in his direction, putter in hand. But she channeled her rage, birdied the final hole, and beat Juli Inkster in a playoff.)

Instead the LPGA takes its tone from most of its top players—Lopez, Sheehan, Davies, Mallon, Robbins—who try to destroy each other with as much consideration as possible.

IMG's Jay Burton says the best thing about representing LPGA athletes is the players themselves. "I've never met a nicer bunch of people." A few years ago, Patty Sheehan said that the difference between the LPGA and PGA Tours is that "we treat each other like human beings." Kay Cockerill, who has struggled to succeed on Tour after winning back-to-back U.S. Amateur Championships, says, "We all treat the LPGA as a big team, a big team effort."

It's not because women, particularly women athletes, always are a kinder sex. As Heather Farr said in *Golf for Women* in 1992, "The LPGA is very special. I don't think it's necessarily because there's more camaraderie among women; I'm not sure the women's tennis tour has it. Golf is an individual sport and we have hundreds of different personalities on Tour, yet everybody pulls for each other. Every player wants to compete against the best golfers in the world at their best. If you win then, you've accomplished a lot." When Laura Davies won in Phoenix this year after Kristal Parker-Gregory choked on a two-foot par putt on the final hole, Davies could barely enjoy the victory.

Nice is nice. Yet it doesn't win tournaments or pay the bills. And there's no injured reserved list for the sick or the hurt. In professional golf at the highest level, an essential truth remains: it's a Darwinian jungle out there. According to Patty Sheehan, "No one knows how competitive we really are." You can be the seventy-fifth best golfer in the world every week, miss every cut, and starve to death. The seventy-fifth best female doctor or attorney or businesswoman in the world is assured of a much more secure position on the food chain.

Consider the *Education of a Golfer*, an autobiography written by Lopez after her phenomenal rookie season in 1978. Lopez proudly highlights a quote from her caddie Roscoe Jones: "There she is, all sweet and smiling, kissing her daddy before the final round, then it's all business. She's got that ruthlessness."

Last week, after the conclusion of the Masters, the Tour invaded Atlanta for the Chick-fil-A LPGA Charity Championship, a well-run but desultory affair at Eagle's Landing, a private club in Stockbridge, a suburban community south of the city.

Crowds? Almost nonexistent.

Weather? Horrendous, featuring fast-moving thick pillows of over-stuffed black clouds, ready to burst at the slightest tickle. Burst they did on Saturday, when late afternoon torrents of rain, lightning, and a tornado warning washed out part of the round.

The field? Dismal. Only four of the top ten money winners showed up. After the tournaments in Atlanta and Nashville come two of the three richest tournaments of the year, the $1,200,000 Sprint Titleholders Championship in Daytona Beach, and the $1,200,000 McDonald's LPGA Championship in Wilmington, Delaware. Since few of the top players want to play four straight weeks, Atlanta was the logical event to skip. Even Albany, Georgia, resident Nancy Lopez was a no-show.

Course conditions? Brown fairways, painted green fringes, and putting surfaces spotty from the harsh spring, "You've got to be lucky," said Kelly Robbins, one of the few stars who teed it up.

The timing? Unfortunate. Last weekend was Freaknik, an annual invasion of black college students from all over the South and Midwest. City officials, leery of incidents that might tarnish Atlanta's image a few months before the Olympics, clamped down tight on the party. Traffic was a nightmare; residents stayed home or, in some cases, fled the city altogether.

The jokes? What do you call an LPGA player whose game has fallen apart at the seams? Chick-fil-A-ed.

One redeeming note. Chick-fil-A extended its sponsorship deal from one to three years after the tournament raised $170,000 for company founder Truett Cathy's Winshape Foster Care, a collection of nine homes which provide some 100 children with foster parents, a positive family environment, and scholarships for college.

Cathy is some piece of work. A 75-year-old with a high school education, Cathy tools around on a Harley with a Baptist biker group, the Holy Rollers. Fifty years ago he opened his first restaurant, called Dwarf House. As *The New York Times* put it in a recent profile, "Mr. Cathy personifies capitalism with a human face. Deeply Christian, he draws his management credo from the Bible—to a point where no Chick-fil-A is open on Sundays."

Cathy doesn't know a lob wedge from a bubble shaft. But tournament organizers believe the Atlanta event can produce $1 million annually for charity and offer a $1 million purse by the year 2000, so Truett has revved up his engines in anticipation of the millennium.

On the day before the start of the Sara Lee Classic, Juli Inkster is revved up as well, after skipping the Chick-fil-A and spending the last two weeks at home. Inkster visited with friends, parents, and grandparents, took Hayley and a friend to Great America amusement park, saw a George Strait concert, played golf at Stanford and Pasatiempo, and practiced.

Caddie Greg Johnston thinks Inkster was "friends-and-familied out," during the final two rounds of the Dinah Shore. Inkster agrees it was "a long week," but believes the real problem was that she started pressing the last two rounds. "I feel like a rookie," she says, sitting in a golf cart near the Hermitage clubhouse after her pro-am round on Thursday. "I need to learn how to win again. I've been working on my swing for two years, and I don't trust it as much as I should. Sometimes I don't feel comfortable over the ball. I'm thinking too much instead of just letting it rip."

Sacramento was much more encouraging. "I hit the ball as well as I've hit it in five years." Inkster's putter was cool, however, and she finished tied for thirteenth.

Yesterday Inkster did something else she hasn't done in a long time—slept in until 9:30, got the paper, and went back to bed. The kids are home in Los Altos this week, and Inkster says, "I don't know what to do with myself." Last night she attended the Sara Lee dinner and enjoyed Amy Grant's performance. Later this afternoon, after she practices, she's planning to catch a movie for the first time in about six months.

"It's been great the last few days," says Inkster, "but it's a catch-22. I really miss 'em." Next week Juli will meet the kids, nanny Tina England, and her parents in Daytona Beach. Then Cori and her nanny will accompany Juli to Wilmington. Hayley and Carole and Jack will fly home so Hayley can return to school.

Caroline Pierce has been busy too. Earlier this week she spent two hours at an Executive Committee meeting with LPGA commissioner Jim Ritts. Next Monday she'll attend an all-day Board of Directors meeting in Daytona Beach. Scheduling is a major issue—sponsors in Atlanta and Nashville want to move from April to May. But CBS, which televises the Daytona Beach and Wilmington tournaments in May, likes the present schedule just fine.

Before the Sacramento event, Pierce played a practice round with Shee-han, and confessed to Patty that she felt intimidated by what she perceives as Sheehan's superior athletic ability. Sheehan got mad. So did caddie Rick Aune. "I reject the premise," Aune told her.

It's been an up-and-down April for Pierce. In Sacramento she fired a second-round 66. Paired with Sorenstam in the final group on Move Day, Pierce hit two good shots on the first hole, narrowly missed a downhill birdie putt, and then missed again coming back. Bogey. "That set the tone for the day. When you miss a few putts, it puts pressure on everything else." Pierce finished 75-75 to tie for thirty-first.

The day after the tournament Pierce traveled with 24 other players from Sacramento to Los Angeles for a clinic for the LPGA Urban Youth Golf Program, which introduces mostly minority youngsters to the game. Pierce visited with her pen pal Tish, 12, a participant in the program. One of the kids praised John Morrison, who runs the LA program, and his staff for having the guts to venture into their crime- and drug-ravaged neigh-borhood to pick them up and take them to the golf course.

The Chick-fil-A last week in Atlanta was an exercise in frustration. "Goofy things happened," says Pierce. "Balls would *bounce* into bunkers and be plugged. You could see it getting to people. I think that's why there were a lot of high scores from good players."

Pierce herself skied to a 77 on Saturday after opening with a 71.

"I was very impatient. The winds were gusty and I hit it over the first green and doubled the hole. I was very annoyed."

"Why were you so impatient?" Pierce is asked.

Pierce hesitates. She looks over at caddie Aune, who is sitting nearby, and smiles. 'It happens every month. I've warned Rick."

While the players tee off in the first round of the Sara Lee Classic on Friday morning, the unique problems of women in sports is the topic of discussion at Vanderbilt University in downtown Nashville. Robin Roberts of ABC and ESPN moderates a "town meeting" with 15 female business, sports, media, and advocacy leaders from around the country. Brought to the Freedom Forum First Amendment Center by Sara Lee and *The Tennessean*, they address the question: "A Level Playing Field for Women in Sports: Whose Responsibility Is It?"

It's the third annual Sara Lee Corporation Women's Round Table, cre-ated two years ago to provide a forum for women leaders to analyze current sociological trends and practices. Perhaps the Round Table might at a future session consider the way corporations peddle unrealistic body images to women. After all, one of Sara Lee's hottest-selling products is the Wonderbra. (Soon to be "the official undergarment of the LPGA Tour"?)

I'm not sure if Sara Lee is sending out mixed messages, but the "town meeting" turns out to be something of a tease, lasting just two hours.

Too bad. The panel is terrific. It includes Linda Alvarado, president of Alvarado Construction Company and owner of the Colorado Rockies; Marcia Greenberger, copresident of the National Women's Law Center; Donna Lopiano, executive director of the Women's Sports Foundation; Julie Ward, managing sports editor at *USA Today;* and Debbie Miller-Palmore, general manager for the Atlanta franchise in the new American Basketball League. The LPGA is represented by Kathy Whitworth, winner of 88 tournaments in her storied career, and vice-president Cindy Davis, 34, one of the rising young executives in the sports business. (Asked what the LPGA can do to enhance its visibility, Dottie Pepper, who played on the golf team at Furman University with Davis, says, "Let Cindy do everything. She's fantastic.")

Lopiano pointedly notes that 80 percent of female executives at Fortune 500 companies identify themselves as former tomboys. The petite Alvarado, who grew up with five brothers, went to law school, and succeeded in the chauvinistic construction business, says women in America's workforce need attributes that can be derived from athletics: risk-taking, competitiveness, a comfort level around men. Roberts, an effortlessly charismatic class act, relates how she negotiated her contract with ABC on a golf course. "I didn't know how to play the game," says Roberts, a relative beginner at golf, "but I knew how to play the *game.*"

"Little girls need big girls to look up to," says Miller-Palmore, a former All-American. "I don't want my daughter wearing a Michael Jordan jersey. Or a Shaq jersey." (Big laugh from the audience.) "I want her in a Lisa Leslie jersey."

Ward recounts her experience as sports editor on the day the Dinah Shore was concluded. With space at a premium, she gave the event top billing over the PGA Players Championship. "I heard from the PGA so fast the next day, my phone lines were burning. I had to defend that decision."

Greenberger emphasizes that sex discrimination in sports, unlike business, is easy to prove, since the statistical disparities in college scholarships, facilities, coach salaries, etc., are so blatant. "Women are struggling in every area for power. Men do have to make way and make room for women. And that is a very threatening thing."

As for the LPGA, Cindy Davis points out that the Tour is evolving along with society as a whole. "Why aren't our purses the same as the men's?

Why aren't women as represented or as well paid in business or politics? The notion that the LPGA can achieve equality before women do in the rest of society is, says Davis, "absolutely nuts."

Yet that same rationale can foster an attitude that encourages passivity. In January the popular sitcom *Mad About You* took a cheap and easy shot at the LPGA. Discovering that his sister is a lesbian, Paul Reiser jokes: "I've just got to sit down awhile. I feel like I want to have some soup. And for some reason I want to watch women's golf."

LPGA staffers who watched the show were shocked. "Nice statement," fumed Dottie Pepper, noting that NBC was broadcasting the first LPGA event of the season, the Tournament of Champions, on the very next weekend. But the LPGA chose not to complain. Or, better yet, to suggest an episode featuring an LPGA player—Helen Alfredsson, perhaps—who could debunk a lot of stereotypes while giving Reiser a good butt- and ego-kicking on the links at the same time. (The producers probably wouldn't have listened. I called the show twice, only to be informed that no one was available to comment about "one joke.")

Nancy Lopez can't putt.

Ten years ago that would have been like saying Sugar Ray Leonard couldn't box or Chris Evert couldn't volley from the baseline. In her prime Lopez was the queen of the greens.

But that was then and this is now. Yesterday, in the first round of the Sara Lee, Lopez hit the ball decently and still shot 78. In frustration she even changed her putting grip during the round, switching from an interlock to something close to a baseball grip. She birdied two of the final four holes to avoid a dreaded snowman. (Scores of 80 or above are called snowmen, because of the shape of the 8 and, perhaps, because they leave the player out in the cold.) Caddie Thorpe says the grip adjustment "keeps her stroke from breaking down as much. It's a little more solid, not as wristy. She just needs to practice. She took three weeks off and played about three times."

About 150 people are following Lopez on a lovely spring Saturday with just a hint of a breeze, after near gale force winds the last few days. She is paired with tall, slender Susie Redman, 30, also a mother of three, and Page Dunlap, a dark-haired 30-year-old touted for possible stardom a couple years ago but struggling to keep up with the pack lately.

Lopez has virtually no chance of making the cut. She's playing for pride today. In Lopez's book, that means she's playing for the most important thing of all. In fact, the word pride pops up repeatedly in Lopez's two books and almost all her press conferences. Example: "Competitors take bad breaks and use them to drive themselves just that much harder. Quitters take bad breaks and use them as reasons to give up. It's all a matter of pride."

Several years ago Lopez said, "I think my problem is that I want too much. I want to be a great golfer. I want to be a great mother. I want to be a great wife. I don't know if I'm good enough to be all three."

She's close.

Lopez has juggled her roles quite adroitly since marrying baseball star Ray Knight in 1982, and giving birth to Ashley Marie in 1983, Erinn Shea in 1986, and Torri Heather in 1991. (Torri's middle name honors Heather Farr. When a three-month pregnant Lopez won the Sara Lee in 1991, she dedicated the victory to Farr, who was undergoing chemotherapy treatment.)

In many respects Lopez revels in her role as a traditional mom, cooking and shopping and raising the kids at home in the sleepy town of Albany, Georgia, and hunting and fishing with Ray on their woodsy 600-acre farm.

Yet she and Ray are enmeshed in jet-setting careers—Knight recently took the reins as manager of the Cincinnati Reds—that would tax the constitution of the highest-flying businessperson. Lopez plans to take weeks off when the Reds play at home in the summer; when Knight hits the road, Lopez will pack up the kids, the nanny, 15 pieces of luggage, and rejoin the Tour. ("I'm a professional packer," says Lopez. "I know how to pack any truck that exists. I give airport employees tips.")

Can Lopez play world-class golf with such a schedule? Obviously. She placed 14th, 25th, and 28th on the money list in 1993, 1994, and 1995, despite a limited schedule of fewer than 20 tournaments per year.

But that's not nearly good enough to suit her, especially since Lopez hasn't hit the winner's circle since 1993. "Forget accepting a slump," Lopez wrote in *The Complete Golfer*. "No golfer worth his or her salt will do that."

In an attempt to regain her top form, Lopez has lost 30 pounds since January. She looks and feels marvelous. She also talks fat grams with the zeal of a missionary.

In March during Dinah Shore week, after Lopez finished a practice round and a two-hour workout in the LPGA fitness van, a large trailer that travels with the Tour, she talked about her transformation.

Still dressed in her workout clothes—pink T-shirt and white shorts over black tights—Lopez walked into the Mission Hills clubhouse with a white towel draped around her neck and a plate of honeydew melon in her hand. She ordered ice water with lemon.

"I got tired of not feeling really good or healthy," said Lopez. "I'm going to be forty this year—and that really bothers me!" she added with a laugh.

"I'm feeling real strong, real confident, and I haven't felt that way for a long time. My endurance is so much better. Last year I worked hard on my game, but I was kind of sluggish, kind of tired—no get up and go."

Lopez always has had a sweet tooth—when she left Nabisco and signed an endorsement deal with Sara Lee, it may have been partly for the desserts. ("The pound cake is really good. It doesn't *feel* like you're eating a lot of calories. And you can just throw it in your bag.") In 1993, after huffing and puffing her way up and down the hills of the Stratton Mountain course in Vermont, Lopez said bluntly, "I'm fat. I admit it. I know I need to lose weight."

Diets and exercise regimes followed, but not for long, and Lopez yo-yoed up and down the scale. Finally in January, her pride overcame her fondness for McDonald's quarter-pound cheeseburgers and the five-pound restaurant-style cheesecakes Sara Lee sent her. ("Eat one of those and you *gain* five pounds.") Lopez hired an Albany aerobics teacher as a private fitness instructor; she gave Lopez the drill:

1. Two-hour workouts six days per week, including an hour on the StairMaster, treadmill, or bike, 200 sit-ups, and lots of stretching
2. A stringent limit of 20–25 fat grams per day

Nibbling on the lemon slices from her ice water, Lopez explained what foods were okay: bagels with jelly, cereal with fruit, no-fat waffles and syrup, an occasional egg, pasta, vegetables, pizza without cheese, sandwiches with mustard but not mayonnaise. Her addiction to cheeseburgers slowly has been replaced by a craving for fruit.

Lopez also was feeling better about her putting. Gardner Dickinson, a fine PGA player and instructor who is married to LPGA player Judy Dickinson, told Lopez her tempo had speeded up. "You could almost count out my putting tempo," said Lopez, as she finished chewing the lemon slices down to the rinds. "It was one . . . two going back and one . . . two forward. Gardner said I was putting like everyone else—a fast stroke."

Husband Knight helped too. Bothered by kidney stones, Knight has trouble sleeping, and when he does, he often pulls out golf videotapes of LPGA tournaments. "He'll wake me up at three in the morning and say, 'Nancy, you've got to look at this!' So I get out of bed and go watch my putting stroke."

In her first book, *Education of a Golfer*, written after her rookie season in 1978, Lopez stated that she could make any five-foot putt "99 times out of 100."

When asked if she meant that literally, she nodded. "Even standing over the ten-footers, I knew I was going to make it. I wasn't afraid to ram it by, because I knew I would make the one coming back—and a ball that's rolling hot has a much better chance of going in than a ball rolling soft and being so much more affected by the line."

You might get an argument about that theory from Ben Crenshaw or any other great die-them-at-the-cup putters. But the critical point is that Lopez believed it and it worked.

No longer. Lopez is wrestling with the same bugaboo as Tom Watson, the other great, boldly aggressive putter of the 1980s. It's easy to blast putts at the cup when the comebackers seem as easy as tap-ins. But when you stand up to the three-, four-, and five-foot comebackers and jangling nerves make you feel like you're putting on the rolling deck of an ocean liner, the game begins to cramp your mind like a vise.

"I've got my tempo back," said Lopez as she carefully fished a few pretzels from a glass bottle containing nuts and other bar snacks. "Now it's a matter of practicing and practicing and practicing to build confidence to make the five- and six-footers, the ones you have to make."

Lopez was a natural talent of extraordinary dimensions as a child, the equivalent of a once-in-a-generation chess prodigy or math whiz. The first time she set foot on a golf course, the 4-year-old tot astounded her parents by hitting the ball square on the nose and lofting it over their heads and down the fairway. She won a 27-hole junior tournament by 110 strokes.

But her genius was honed through blindingly hard work. "I used to putt for hours," said Lopez. "Sometimes I putted so long I couldn't stand up straight when I left the course."

Lopez looks marvelous. The gallery comments on her sleek, healthy appearance. But all those sit-ups haven't reduced her putting woes, and Lopez misses birdie putts of four and five feet on the first few holes. Rarely do you see steam coming out of Lopez's ears—too much pride—but you can often sense it percolating below the surface. Finally she rolls in a nice five-foot birdie putt on the 147-yard 5th hole, and her fans have a chance to cheer.

They don't need much encouragement. Consider Jennifer McCormack, 30, who works as a mortgage lender for the Bank of Mississippi in Tupelo. McCormack endured "the roughest flight of my life," bouncing around the sky in the fierce winds earlier this week, in order to see Lopez in person for the first time.

Yesterday McCormack, a 10–12 handicapper who plays nine holes almost every night after work, and local tournaments on the weekends, got an autograph from her idol, whom she admired even as a child. "It's just a pleasure to watch her play. To me she makes golf what it is. She did the same thing for the women that Arnold Palmer did for the men."

Lopez finishes with a mediocre 73. When she emerges from the scorer's tent two reporters collar her for quick interviews. Then she's surrounded by a crowd of about 100 autograph seekers. Lopez signs everything from caps to lounge chairs. The fans say, "Thank you." Lopez says, "Thank you." When Lopez was 15, she stood in line for an autograph from one of the biggest stars on the PGA Tour (Lopez has never revealed his name). But when she got almost to the front of the line, the pro said, "I don't have time for this. I have to go."

"I felt like a piece of trash," says Lopez. "It really bothered me and hurt me." When Lopez began signing autographs herself, she vowed never to stiff anyone, especially a child.

Ellen Hunter, 13, an eighth-grader from Memphis, excitedly tells Lopez, "I did a book report on you for English class!"

"What grade did you get?" asks Lopez.

"A hundred!" says Hunter.

Hunter happily brings her signed poster over to her parents, watching from the outskirts of the crowd.

When Lopez took the Tour by storm in 1978, the response from her colleagues was a frosty jealousy and resentment. "The first and second year I was winning so much I was never in the locker room," says Lopez. "I'd play, do interviews, practice. When I got back to the locker room, everyone was gone. People never saw me, so they'd say, 'Nancy's a snob.' It was a tough time for me."

A snob? Don't tell that to Jennifer McCormack or Ellen Hunter or any of the thousands of fans who have met her. "Nancy Lopez has the patience of a saint," LPGA communications director Elaine Scott once said. "She never says no to anyone."

One story that exemplifies Lopez came earlier this year in the first round at Tucson. The event was simply a warm-up exercise, a chance to try out a new set of Tommy Armour 855 irons, featuring a wider flange at the bottom, and tune up her game before the Dinah Shore.

Lopez played miserably. "Lots of skulled shots," caddie Thorpe said later. Lots of lousy chips and putts too. An embarrassing performance, regardless of the circumstances. Then, on the last hole, Lopez hit a sensational iron to within a foot of the cup. A small gallery along the ropes near Lopez cheered. Lopez turned toward the fans. A beaming smile, a smile that rivals Magic Johnson's as the best in sports, a smile as warm as the sun, lit up her face. Her eyes danced with pleasure. Lopez has loved the game since she was captivated by the crunching sounds of spikes on cement when she was a toddler. She still does. As casually as one weekend golfer would remark to another, she said, "That one shot always keeps us coming back, doesn't it."

Lopez takes a step and signs an autograph, takes another step and signs, takes another step and poses for a picture with a fan, doing the Superstar Shuffle.

The crowd finally satiated, Lopez walks toward the clubhouse where Torri is waiting with her nanny. When Torri sees Mom, she runs over and buries her head against Lopez's waist. "Hey, baby," says Nancy, kissing her daughter and hoisting her in her arms.

With a couple of holes left to play late on Saturday afternoon, Caroline Pierce, playing along steadily at four under par, casually glances up at a scoreboard, sees her name at the top, and smiles a smile of surprise and delight. Last year the pros ripped up Hermitage. Winner Michelle McGann was 14 under par. But the winds and wet conditions have taken their toll so far. After narrowly missing beautifully struck long birdie putts on the final three holes, Pierce finishes with a 69 for a two-day total of 140, one stroke in front of six other players. No less than 28 golfers are within four strokes of the lead.

When she emerges from the scorer's tent next to the 18th green, Pierce signs a few autographs and answers a few questions from reporters. One holds a tape recorder near the side of her face, but presses the reverse instead of the record button, and the machine starts screeching. Pierce, startled, whirls around, spots the source of the noise, and instantly quips, "I thought someone stepped on a cat." Everybody laughs.

Time to meet the rest of the press in the media center.

Pierce was a political science and history major at Houston Baptist College, which offered her a better scholarship deal than any other school. (European star Colin Montgomerie attended Houston Baptist at the same time; Pierce dated his Australian roommate, Glenn Joyner, who plays on the Australian Tour.)

Until her senior year, Pierce seemed destined for law school. But she played well enough to earn All-American honors in 1983 and 1984, and decided, "If I don't try the Tour, I might regret it." Pierce can still picture herself as a lawyer or lobbyist, or, best of all, a presidential adviser, a behind-the-scenes decision-maker and power broker. (That's actually a fairly good description of her role on the LPGA's Executive Committee.)

It's easy to envision Pierce in all of those roles. But she'd never make it as a candidate. Much too honest. During the press conference Pierce blurts out an astonishing confession. "I don't like people staring at me. I'm not comfortable when I'm playing and people stare."

The reporters perk up; the thrill of the unexpected sweeps the small room. "Now *this* could be good!" think the scribes. A golfer who admits she doesn't like people looking at her? In a profession where pros talk about being "on stage" when they arrive at a tournament site? Pierce tries to explain that no one likes being stared at by strangers. The reporters aren't buying it.

Afterward the reporters from *The Tennessean* discuss possible leads for the Sunday morning edition.

"All Eyes on Caroline," one suggests.

Instead *The Tennessean* runs an article with the headline, "Pierce to Face Her Fear Today."

Caroline Pierce's worst golf nightmare is about to come true. A lot of people, perhaps as many as 20,000, will be staring at her today at Hermitage Golf Course where she will attempt to win her first LPGA Championship.

On a sultry Sunday, waiting for her 1:00 P.M. tee time, Pierce sits in a cart near the 1st tee, sipping from a bottle of water. "People have been coming up to me all morning," Pierce says with a frown. "They say, 'I just want to be the first one to stare at you.'"

It's already been a tough week on-stage for her. At the Sara Lee gala dinner, Pierce and several other players were cajoled into singing a Carpenters song. "We couldn't remember the words," says Pierce, who performed gamely but left the stage thoroughly embarrassed.

Dressed in a pale yellow shirt, red Madras shorts, a black Top Flite baseball cap, white shoes, and silver tear-drop earrings, Pierce seems fairly relaxed. "The wind's come up," she notes. "That's good."

Under benign conditions earlier this morning, a number of players back in the pack scorched the course—Mayumi Hirase with a 67, Barb Mucha and Stephania Croce with 68. But the flags and tree branches are whipping back and forth as Pierce and playing partner Shirley Furlong tee off. It's an advantage for players accustomed to wind and bad weather—Pierce, Scotland's Pam Wright, and Meg Mallon, who won in hellacious 40 mph gales in Hawaii in February.

Hundreds of fans follow the final twosome. On the 515-yard 2nd hole, Pierce blasts an eight-foot birdie putt well past the cup, misses coming back, and walks off the green glassy-eyed.

Furlong, dressed in a navy shirt and khaki shorts, is amazed to be here. As the first alternate for a tournament slot, she got into the field at the last moment when Kim Shipman dropped out with a back injury on Friday morning.

"It's a Cinderella story," she joked to the press in her best Bill Murray-playing-Carl-the-Groundskeeper-in-*Caddyshack* voice after firing a 68 yesterday. A country music buff, Furlong "was chomping at the bit to get in this tournament because I just love Nashville." And because her parents, Pat and Francis, spent two days driving from San Antonio in the hopes of seeing their daughter play for the first time since 1993. And because she's trying to play her way out of a horrendous slump that began in 1992 and plunged Furlong from the ranks of the contenders in the late 1980s all the way down to the fringes of the Tour. Last year Furlong earned $4,104 in 22 events. She's clinging to the Tour by her fingernails.

By 2:00, the clock has already struck midnight for this Cinderella. After a 5-iron to ten feet on the 147-yard 5th hole, Furlong three-putts and tumbles off the leader board.

Despite the rains earlier in the week, the greens are slick and putts from above the hole are treacherous. On the 365-yard 6th hole Pierce hits a lovely long iron into a stiff crosswind to within 18 feet. Anxious to get back a stroke, she charges the putt, bashing it six feet past the cup. Pierce is muttering to herself as she marks her ball. Trying to coax in the par putt with body English, she almost goes to her knees. But the ball, like a petulant teenager, refuses to obey. Pierce's shoulders slump. She sighs and walks off the green, already three over par for the day and a fat four shots behind leader Meg Mallon.

It's getting ugly out here. The gallery steadily dwindles as the carnage mounts. "Come on, ball!" pleads Furlong's father, but Shirley three-putts again at the 369-yard 7th hole. On the 485-yard 8th hole the machinery totally breaks down. Furlong needs a new ball on the tee, but her caddie is at the back of the tee box, tossing away some trash. When he finally sees Furlong, waiting impatiently, he hustles back to scramble through the bag and flip Furlong a ball. Close to the green in two, Furlong scuffs a chip from near a trap guarding the left side of the green, then blasts her next shot 20 feet past the hole. Steaming, she yanks the flagstick out of the cup herself and glares at her caddie.

Are we having fun yet?

Pierce, after finding the rough with a poor second shot, blades her third over the green. With 90 feet to the pin and the green sloping away from her, Pierce delicately executes a fabulous shot that stops three feet away. Then she comes off the putt, pushing it well right for another gruesome bogey.

It's silent as a cemetery. It's like staring at the wreckage of a ten-car pileup on the freeway. Or watching an actor repeatedly forget her lines. Or a lawyer botch a closing argument. Almost all of the fans following the twosome have fled. No one is staring at Pierce anymore; they can't bare to look.

*   *   *

Pierce and Furlong play the back nine to the accompaniment of workers pulling up stakes, taking down gallery ropes, and dismantling concession stands. Up ahead they hear distant cheers for Meg Mallon, who shoots 69 to defeat Stephanie Farwig and Pam Wright by two shots. Mallon picks up her second victory of the year, a trophy, a $90,000 check from Vince Gill and Amy Grant, and a custom-designed Gibson guitar valued at $30,000. (A picture of the guitar is later printed in *Billboard* magazine.)

Furlong shoots 81 with 41 putts, finishes tied for sixty-sixth, and earns $729 for the week, almost enough to pay her expenses. Pierce angrily fights to the finish, birdies two holes on the back nine, shoots 77, finishes tied for twenty-second, and collects $5,313.

After the round she races back to the house she stayed in, grabs her suitcases, and scrambles to the airport to catch a flight from Nashville to Atlanta to Orlando.

Pierce rarely drinks, but she mopes in a beer on the plane, wallowing in self-pity, ashamed at losing her temper on the course and yelling at caddie Aune, who is like a brother, questioning if she has the talent and the toughness and the nerve to win.

Somewhere over the skies of Nashville, the faint strains of Waylon Jennings singing "Momma, Don't Let Your Babies Grow Up to Be Golf Pros" can be heard. Sometimes, the life of a professional golfer is as glamorous as that of a postal clerk.

$\mathcal{D}$aytona Beach: Sprinting for Gold

A number of players, LPGA officials, and others hustle from Hermitage Golf Course to the Nashville airport for a seven o'clock flight to Atlanta and on to Daytona Beach.

We sit on the tarmac for about 40 minutes. Some of the players are getting antsy. Dina Ammaccapane, due in Daytona Beach to play in an 8:00 A.M. Monday qualifier, confers with sister and traveling partner Danielle. This is the last flight of the evening to Daytona Beach; the sisters discuss the possibility of chartering a plane.

Finally the flight is scrubbed. Juli Inkster is first in line at the ticket counter. "It's a good thing I don't have the kids," she says, as she rebooks for tomorrow morning.

But the Ammaccapanes, Denise Killeen, and Kim Saiki, who also have trudged off the plane, don't have the luxury of staying overnight. Either they figure out another way to get to Daytona Beach, or they forfeit a chance at one of the final two slots available in the Sprint Titleholders Championship, a $1,200,000 event with $180,000 to the winner. In short, a "double-coupon week," as some of the players—generally the less prosperous ones—like to call it.

For the stars, this truly is the fat part of the season. Last week Davies, Neumann, and Sorenstam skipped Nashville and played in Japan for appearance fees in the neighborhood of $30,000–$50,000. This week Sheehan is off to Japan for a tournament that will pay her $100,000 to tee it up. (Tournament officials initially offered $80,000. Sheehan and manager Gaston bargained them up to six figures, plus expenses and first-class airfare.) She would have to finish first or second at the Sprint to do as well. So it was easy to reject commissioner Jim Ritts's argument that the Dinah Shore champion should be in the field in Daytona instead of overseas. "I didn't see any correlation," says Sheehan, "or feel any loyalty to the tournament." Last year Sheehan was relegated to an alternate's spot in the pro-am. Alternates almost always are the Tour's lesser lights. They are required to hang around for several hours in case a pro who suffers illness or injury must be replaced. "I was a Hall of Famer at a tournament at the

LPGA headquarters," says Sheehan. "It was kind of a slap in the face."

Saiki and Killeen joke about a lousy end to a lousy day. In addition to four 3-putts, Saiki's water bottle broke in her bag.

Soon they realize their only option besides throwing in the towel is to catch a flight on Southwest Airlines to Orlando, rent a car, drive to Daytona, and hope for a couple of hours of sleep. And off they go, scrambling down the corridor.

(Saiki, Killeen, and Ammaccapane make it on time. But Killeen's clubs do not. She has to borrow clubs from other players and the pro shop. "Everything was okay except the driver," she says later. "It was too whippy— I hit everything left. It was a bummer because I'd been playing well." None of the intrepid trio makes the final field. Life on the fringe of the Tour often is an unplayable lie. You take a drop, accept the penalty, suck it up, and soldier on.)

Those who managed to fly are greeted by signs at the luggage carousels reading "Welcome to Daytona Beach: Home of NASCAR and the LPGA." The LPGA moved its headquarters from Sugar Land, Texas, to Daytona Beach in 1989, part of an ambitious 4,500-acre plan "to create a first-class destination resort, residential, and commercial property to showcase the LPGA's National Headquarters and related golf facilities."

In short, the LPGA negotiated a juicy deal: The state kicked in grant money for the new, modern, spacious 20,000-square-foot headquarters, which opened just last week (the LPGA staff has been stacked up like cordwood in temporary digs for the last few years); Indigo Development, Inc., owned by timber and citrus giant Consolidated–Tomoka Land Co., donated the land the headquarters rests upon; the city built a new $10 million interchange at LPGA Boulevard and Interstate 95 to facilitate access to the complex, and also built the Rees Jones–designed tournament course, the LPGA International, a public facility which opened in 1994.

What a complex they envision! Two 18-hole championship golf courses. A luxury Radisson Resort. A 750-home gated enclave called Lion's Paw, portrayed as something approaching Nirvana in slick, full-color brochures touring the $100,000 to $2 million homes and lots. And all on a parcel of land that, just two and a half years ago, was nothing more than swampy, sultry, marshy, junglelike forest.

There are great scenes of beauty at LPGA International. On a warm, sunny, calm evening early in the week, in a small reed-filled marsh near the practice range, a long-billed egret, with its storklike legs, fishes for dinner, plunging its syringelike beak into the water. Just up the road, Kelly Robbins stands on a bank next to the new LPGA headquarters, casting a line into a shimmering golden lake.

But mostly it's a primitive, almost primordial beauty. The future site of Lion's Paw contains no lions—but almost every other form of tropical, hot-weather bird and animal roams the natural preserves, habitats, and oozy marshes in and around LPGA International. Sticklike tree stumps, which look fire-damaged, poke up through malevolent brackish green swamp water, which is ringed with ferns and reeds and bushes and small blue flowers. Sturdy, cart-bearing bridges carry golfers and fans over some of the marshes. If a bridge ever breaks and a golf cart plunges into the ooze, divers will fish out little more than a metal chassis, skeletons, and some gripless Pings and Big Berthas.

Two of the pros in the pro shop reel off a list of the creatures that have been spotted on or near the links: spoonbills, egrets, herons, sandhill cranes, eagles, hawks, turkey buzzards, wild boar, bobcats, alligators. "There's a ten-foot alligator in the lake on number seventeen," says one of the pros.

"Any type of snake," says the other pro. "We found a coral snake in the cart barn." One visitor swore he spotted a panther prowling through the woods surrounding the course, but the presence of the legendary and endangered beast, so far from the Everglades and so close to civilization, is discounted by the pros.

Even without lion's paws or panthers, Sprint and the LPGA expect the 1996 tournament to be extra special.

It usually is anyway. Sprint hosts the only lucrative event for women players over 50, the $200,000 Sprint Senior Challenge, in conjunction with the main event. In 1994 and 1995 the Senior Challenge lured Mickey Wright out of a reclusive retirement to compete, the equivalent of the return to the concert stage of a Streisand.

Last fall it was announced that the Sprint Championship would merge with the Titleholders Invitational, essentially defunct since 1972. The Titleholders for decades was the most prestigious venue in women's golf. Held at the Augusta Country Club, right next door to Augusta National, home of the Masters, the Titleholders was a tony affair, featuring tea dances and card parties. Players often would gather to sing, dance, and play the piano in the evenings. The roster of winners constitutes a roll call of champions—Babe Zaharias, Mickey Wright, Louise Suggs, Patty Berg, Kathy Whitworth. As part of the merger, a number of top young amateurs have been invited to compete in the Sprint, in an attempt to showcase the past, present, and future of women's golf on the same stage.

Sprint seems to have gotten its wires crossed. On Wednesday, the day before tournament play is to begin, Louise Suggs runs into Judy Rankin near the clubhouse, which at this point is little more than a small pro shop and snack bar.

"I've been disinvited!" exclaims Suggs. "I don't know what I'm supposed to do!"

Suggs won the Titleholders in 1954, 1956, and 1959. Small, lithe, and slender, Suggs was known for her beautifully fluid swing, often compared with that of Ben Hogan. She won 50 LPGA events, including 8 majors. Bob Hope nicknamed her "Miss Sluggs" after watching her blast a drive close to 300 yards. "I'm going back to the clubhouse to get me a skirt," he joked.

Her fans cross generations. One of the biggest is PGA star Paul Azinger, who learned to play the game as a youngster with a set of Louise Suggs model Wilson clubs.

Suggs, who served as LPGA president from 1955 to 1957, has donated much of her memorabilia to the organization, a generous gesture given the lucrative market for golf collectibles. She's befriended LPGA staffers as well, who cherish the times when she takes them out for drinks and regales them with stories of her battles with Babe Zaharias (whom she disliked for her publicity-seeking flamboyance) and Patty Berg, the Big Three of women's golf during its formative years in the 1950s. Known as the Georgia Peach, Suggs tended to take offense at perceived slights. When she was assessed the standard $25 fine for failing to show up for a tournament she had entered in 1962, she quit the Tour in a huff, and never played full-time again.

At the age of 73, the years have eroded her great skills. Last year she shot 87-87 in the Senior Challenge. But lots of fans would like to see her tee it up, to marvel at her glorious swing, even if it's only a shadow of its former greatness.

And to get a glimpse of the old competitive fire. Suggs was outwardly unemotional in competition. But, like all great champions, she played the game full-out. "Whenever I pick up a club and put a tee in the ground," said Suggs, "if there's five bucks [on the line], look out!"

However, Suggs has been excluded from the field of starters in the Senior Challenge. Instead, she's slated to serve as an "honorary starter" along with Marilynn Smith, 67, another Hall of Fame member, who won the Titleholders in 1963 and 1964.

Rankin is upset with tournament organizers too. She's frantically searching for a phone number for former LPGA player and current ABC golf reporter Sandra Post. Post is supposed to be in the field for the Senior Challenge—only no one bothered to tell her. So she's home in Canada. Rankin finally tracks down a phone number, but it's too late—Post can't make it to Daytona Beach on such short notice. She loses out on a chance to tee it up with her contemporaries one more time, as well as a juicy payday; the last place finisher in the Senior Challenge receives $7,700.

Which is just about the amount of money 27-year-old rookie Leslie Spalding has earned in her four-month career on the LPGA Tour. Spalding has made four cuts in the seven events she has played in; a thirty-fifth in Atlanta is her top finish. Her 1996 earnings total $8,260 and she ranks ninety-ninth on the money list.

That's a pretty good start for an unheralded, unknown rookie.

How unknown? When Spalding arrives for her 1:10 P.M. first-round tee time on Thursday, an older woman in a nearly empty grandstand says, "Good luck, Lorrie."

"Thanks," says Spalding, not bothering to correct her.

"Lorrie," an amused playing partner Tina Barrett whispers to her.

How unheralded?

The starter on the tee introduces Spalding as "the 1990 and 1991 Montana State Women's Amateur champion,"—actually it was 1991 and 1992—to date her greatest claim to fame.

You don't see a lot of Montana-breds on the Tour. And it's a true rarity to discover a golf pro from a family of nongolfers and nonathletes. Father Richard, a broker for Merrill Lynch, dabbled at golf, but joined a country club in Billings primarily as a place to entertain business clients. Neither of her two sisters play the game, nor does her mother, Marcia, a choir director. For a while Spalding didn't either; her club activities were limited to swimming and watching TV.

But when her mother signed her up for golf lessons in addition to ballet and piano classes, she found her game. What hooked her? "The challenge," she says. "And it's a fun game to practice. I like to practice a lot. You can do different things every day."

It's a beautiful day for golf, warm and humid with moderate breezes. A few soft, fleecy, white clouds, as well as planes from the nearby Daytona Beach airport float across the blue skies. A huge white sandhill crane, wings akimbo, languidly skims over a small lake near the fairway.

After a bogey on the 388-yard 1st hole, Spalding bounces back immediately, draining a 30-foot birdie putt on the 408-yard 2nd hole.

"Nice *putt!*" says a surprised Vicki Fergon, third member of the trio as well as current president of the LPGA players organization.

Spalding has been surprising a number of people lately.

There are LPGA rookies, such as Wendy Ward (1994 U.S. Amateur champ, third in the 1995 Standard Register Ping as an amateur) and Jill McGill (1993 U.S. Amateur champ, second in the 1995 Weetabix British Open), who advance to the Tour with agents and writers touting their praises. There are other rookies, such as Karrie Webb in 1996 and Annika Sorenstam in 1994, who are so talented their phenomenal skills transcend any youthful inexperience.

But Spalding is a true green-as-grass neophyte. No press clippings. No endorsement deals. Elandale was planning to give her clothes—but no money—until it decided to sign Wendy Ward. (Perhaps the company just had one set of outfits.) Her Sun Mountain golf bag was a gift from a Montana sporting goods company. She bought her own Callaway Big Bertha driver, 3-wood, 4-wood, and Heaven Wood, Tommy Armour 855 irons, Ping Anser II putter, and Cleveland Hogan sand wedge. As an exempt rookie, Footjoy gives her six pairs of golf shoes for the season, and Titleist gives her two dozen golf balls each week, as well as caps and visors.

So her ability to make cuts in most of her early starts is impressing other players and caddies. As is her friendly demeanor. "She's adorable," says Amador Padilla, who caddied for Spalding in Atlanta. "She's one of the people I'd work for again in a second."

Spalding has worked on her attitude almost as much as her ball-striking. About a year ago, she and her teacher, Paul Enright, set up a daily five-minute visualization routine. Spalding imagines doing something great in golf: winning the U.S. Open or hitting a spectacular shot and feeling the roar of the crowd wash over her.

That's not all. Every morning and every evening Spalding recites prayerlike affirmations to herself. At night she writes down "five really good things about the day."

"I think it helps a lot. I believe in myself a lot more than I did three years ago."

So after Spalding awoke at 8:15 this morning, after breakfast and some sit-ups, after ironing her outfit, after a little TV channel surfing—Spalding recited her affirmations

"I commit to every shot."

"I'm the best putter in the world."

"I'm cool, calm, and collected."

On the 473-yard 5th hole, a par five with several new homes under construction behind the green, Spalding rolls a 20-footer into the cup for a birdie.

"Great stroke," says Fergon. Spalding is dressed in a navy shirt and khaki shorts, blue and white shoes, and dangling gold earrings. Her honey blonde hair is affixed with a big gold barrette. It flows in a thick ponytail out from the back loop of her navy Titleist baseball cap. She looks cool, calm, and collected as her pale blue eyes flash with pleasure. She smiles and lifts an open palm to acknowledge the applause from the handful of people around the green.

Spalding has been hoping to hear such applause since she moved from Montana to Tampa three and a half years ago. "I knew I wanted to play golf, but I didn't have any money."

So she took a job as an assistant pro at a new public course, Westchase, on the day it opened, and spent the next two and a half years working, practicing, and earning her PGA Class A membership, which consists of 36 credit hours of study.

"It's kind of like getting a masters' in the golf business," explains Spalding. It's also an insurance policy—if she bombs out as a player, the PGA membership gives her an edge in securing a decent job as a club pro.

One day after she picked up her PGA membership, Spalding quit her job. From last April to October she played on the Gold Coast Tour, a minor league circuit that is the equivalent of a high-stakes poker game. Spalding and the other players anted up $15,000 apiece; essentially they played for their own money. Spalding raised $17,000 from friends and acquaintances. After a slow start she finished 16th on the money list with earnings of $22,400.

Then it was on to the annual LPGA Qualifying Tournament, known as Q-School, the golfer's equivalent of the bar exam or medical boards.

But much more selective. Q-School doles out only 20–25 fully exempt Tour cards and another 20–25 conditional Tour cards every year to hordes of desperate applicants from around the globe. Many of the best players on the European Tour join hopefuls from minor league circuits (the Gold Coast and Futures Tours in the U.S.), hotshot college stars, and pros from the LPGA Tour itself who have slipped to the fringe and lost their exempt status. Over 200 golfers paid the $2,000 entry fee and signed up for the sectional tournaments leading up to Q-School last year. Sixty of them made it to the finals on October 17–20 right here at LPGA International, where they joined 61 fringe dwellers.

Karrie Webb was here too. She finished second, after falling down some stairs just weeks before the finals and cracking a bone in her forearm; miraculously, it stopped hurting two days before the tournament. For the prodigiously talented Webb, Q-School was a breeze. Right?

Wrong. "It's the worst week of your life. Everyone's on edge. You're with your friends, and you want to see everyone make it."

Kris Tschetter can barely remember Q-School week. Except in her dreams. For several years after she survived Q-School to earn her card in 1988, Tschetter would wake up from a nightmare which found her confronting the 72 holes of Hell Week all over again.

"I had the dry heaves," said Kristal Parker-Gregory, who failed Q-School eight times and exiled herself to the Asian and European tours before surviving in 1994.

Spalding entered Q-School in 1992; she flunked out, missing the cut in sectional qualifying. In 1993 she made it to the finals, but shot 80-73-76 to miss the cut. Going through swing changes, she missed the cut again in 1994. When asked about Q-School, the normally articulate, upbeat Spalding can do little more than shake her head. "It's awful," she says quietly "It's awful."

Last fall she stared down a three-foot par putt on the final hole, after shooting rounds of 76-72-73. Sink it and finish 16th with a final round 74, and earn an exempt card, with the right to compete in every regular season, full-field tournament in 1996. Miss it and tee it up with eight other golfers in a playoff for the final exemption. The playoff losers would settle for conditional cards, likely getting into the field in only about one-third of the 1996 events.

(Conditional status leaves a golfer in limbo, hoping to sneak into next week's event when enough fully exempt players decline their reserved spots, due to fatigue or injury or the flu. To make it worse, conditional players from Q-School rank well down the priority list for admission into tournament fields. Those placing 90–125 on the money list from the previous season, and winners on the LPGA Tour, whether the victory came in 1995 or 1965, have priority over conditional Q-School survivors. Conditional players left on the sidelines have one last remaining option: to tee it up in a Monday qualifier, the razor's edge of the Tour's Darwinian blade. Early in the season, as many as 40 players were dueling for the last two spots in the field. Given the limited number of tournament opportunities, playing your way from Q-School conditional status into the top 90, and earning an automatic exemption for next season, is like climbing Mt. Everest without rope or boots. Annika Sorenstam did it in 1994, and the pressure of playing superbly in numerous Monday qualifiers strengthened her game and her psyche. Just earning your way from Q-School conditional status into the top 125 and thereby keeping your card is an impressive feat. Rookies who fall out of the top 125 and then bomb out at the next Q-School forfeit their cards altogether, and are exiled from the Tour for at least one season. In professional terms, players who lose their cards cease to exist, becoming nonpersons in the eyes of the LPGA Tour.)

"I'd been putting unbelievably well," says Spalding. "I knew if I just did what I had been doing it would go in." It did. Spalding had her card and a one-year exemption.

What she didn't have, however, was almost as essential: the money to hit the road.

From last October until March, just two months ago, Spalding scrambled to put together a bankroll. Essentially, she sold stock in herself, sending packets of information to prospective sponsors "and waiting by the mailbox every day for replies. I learned how to take rejection."

About 30 family friends and people from Tampa eventually came on board, investing a total of about $40,000 in shares ranging from $1,000 to $5,000. Investors receive 100 percent of Spalding's earnings up to the $40,000 break-even point. After that Spalding and her backers split earnings up to $100,000 on a 50-50 basis.

The market is bullish. On the 145-yard 6th hole, Spalding strokes a 20-footer down a ridge. It dives into the cup like a gopher. Perhaps she *is* the best putter in the world.

She's not the best ball-striker, however, at least not yet. Spalding sets up nicely to the ball, then wiggles back and forth from foot to foot a few times before pulling the trigger. Unlike most small or medium-sized players—Spalding is five foot six and medium-framed—she generally hits a fade rather than a draw.

Today her irons are all over the lot. After pushing one into the greenside bunker on the 377-yard 7th hole she whacks the club angrily off the turf.

But that's as much of a display of temper as you're likely to see from Spalding. The angriest she says she's ever gotten was in a regular Tuesday game with the guys at Westchase. "You could lose up to $100, which is a lot to me. I got in a slump and lost every week. I was so upset and furious. They'd tell me, 'You have the worst temper we've ever seen!'"

Not on Tour. Actually the LPGA's president could take a few pointers from the rookie. "Big Vic," as she's known, gets high marks from her peers for her work as leader of the players association. A champion hurdler in high school, the five-foot-nine Fergon, now 40, is in her twentieth season on Tour. It's been a solid career—Fergon has earned over $1.2 million. But she hasn't won since 1984, missed the cut last week in Nashville, and seems totally frustrated.

Fergon sees and hears everything, and everything she hears and sees irritates her. She chews out a volunteer on the first tee after her caddie receives a vest with a big mud spot on it from the volunteer, who claims "it's not my job" to replace it, gestures angrily at a cart that drives up when the group is putting on No. 2, shoots a dirty look at a greenside marshal who exclaims "ooh" on No. 8 when Spalding pushes a six-foot par putt to the right, uses her putter to mash a bug that disturbs her on No. 9, smashes the sand with her club after hitting a fat fairway bunker shot on No. 11, and yells, "Stop! Stop! Please!" at a convoy of CBS production staffers who motor up in carts as the trio tees off at No. 13.

Fergon's caddie lights up a cigarette. He's been chatting and joking all day long with her, valiantly trying to lighten the mood. It's like trying to charm the biggest grouch at the DMV. You might as well just take a number and shut your mouth.

I'm getting a bit grouchy myself. Following Spalding is a gas. Barrett, a quiet, shy 29-year-old who is playing with a wrist injury that may require surgery after the season, is easy to root for. Fergon's raging volcano-about-to-erupt antics are amusing.

But the course itself is a walking nightmare. Distances between greens and tees are so vast that players are shuttled on half-a-dozen holes. Carts from CBS and Sprint also whiz about, irritating players and fans alike. The handfuls of spectators on the course trudge along in the dusty wake of the carts under a hot, humid sun without a trace of shade other than the CBS towers erected behind some of the greens. Almost all of the water containers on the course are empty, a cruel mirage. There are only two concession stands on the entire course. Rest rooms are reserved for the players and closed to the public. Gallery ropes are set up in a fashion that prevents spectators from getting anywhere near the golfers on a number of the tees and greens. It's the golf spectator's equivalent of paying for box seats and winding up in the third deck of the right-field bleachers.

A big part of the problem is the layout itself, which is as bland as Velveeta. LPGA International features wide fairways and big three-tiered greens. The rough, soaked by recent thunderstorms, is thick and snarled.

LPGA players are loath to criticize any tournament venue, and particularly their home course, but a few brave voices can be heard crying in the swampy wilderness. Juli Inkster, who calls LPGA International one of her least favorite stops on Tour, describes it as follows: "Every hole's the same. Two bunkers right, one left in the fairway, one left and one right at the green."

That's a slight—very slight—exaggeration. Only the 172-yard 17th hole, with a big lake (containing a big alligator) in front and to the left of the green, and the 452-yard 18th hole, a short par five with a drive across a marshy waste area (containing various critters) have any real character. If LPGA International represents the LPGA, then the LPGA is everything its worst critics believe it to be: colorless, unimaginative, and devoid of distinguishing features. (To my amazement, some people actually like LPGA International. *Golf* magazine, its reviewers perhaps suffering from heatstroke, named it one of its top-ten new public courses in 1994.) This isn't even cart golf. It's bulldozer golf, a triumph of big machinery, land speculators, real estate developers, and marketing hype meisters.

If it gets any hotter by the weekend, fans in peach and turquoise and canary and chartreuse polo shirts will be crawling across the fairways, dizzy with heat prostration, collapsing facedown on the green grass under the cruel, merciless sun to become easy pickings for the gators and the wild boars and the turkey buzzards. (Which, come to think of it, could provide great TV ratings.)

Ah, maybe it's just the heat that's got me so irritated. Or maybe Fergon's black mood is contagious. Spalding seems chipper enough. When she comes off the tee at the 383-yard 16th hole, she sees a spectator dressed in slacks, white shirt, and tie. Amazingly enough, he's still upright.

"A little dressed up for golf," Spalding says with a smile.

"I'm just getting off work," says the businessman. "You caught me."

Spalding is slowly adjusting to her own work environment. So far she's held up nicely to the week-to-week grind of life on Tour. "Mentally I feel good. I feel stable. I don't get tired." But her workout routine from last summer, which included weight training and lots of time on the bike, treadmill, and StairMaster, already has slackened. "I try to work out, but I'm not very fit now, and I think I need to be my best. I brought my workout clothes today, but there's always something that comes up. And I don't want to be sore the next day once the tournament starts."

Those words are no surprise to Keith Kennedy, who runs the LPGA's traveling fitness van. "It's a rare rookie who can make it through a season of regular workouts," says Kennedy. "It's the first thing that takes a beating."

Free from serious injuries, Spalding suffers from occasional bouts of tendinitis in her shoulder and wrist, which is bothering her after four pain-free years.

"I've got to find a good-looking copper bracelet," she said a few days ago, as she sat in the media center.

"Do those help?"

"They're supposed to."

So does a good diet. Just ask Nancy Lopez. Spalding says she "grew up on junk food—I'm a big-time candyholic." But she's trying to cut down on fats, which, among other things, means substituting no-fat Gummy Bears and licorice for chocolate.

She's also trying to keep her expenses under control, and earn a few extra bucks in Monday pro-ams in the hope of buying a car. Spalding has picked up checks of $1,000, $700, and $900 at three Monday outings. Private housing, available at most sites for players who sign up a week or two in advance, helps immensely.

Usually private housing is a wonderful deal—free room and often board as well as the company of golf fans. (Pierce and Inkster have stayed with the same families at some sites for years and developed close friendships.)

But it's not always a sweet setup. In Nashville, Spalding stayed at the home of a woman whose dog used Spalding's room as a bathroom. "I woke up gagging at five in the morning, the smell was so bad."

Caddie expenses are unavoidable, though the use of a caddie isn't mandatory. (Lenore Rittenhouse shocked her fellow pros by toting her own lightweight bag at the U.S. Open in 1995.) Spalding pays her caddie $375–$400 per week, plus the standard portion of her winnings—5 percent if she makes the cut and earns a paycheck, 7 percent for a top-ten finish, and 10 percent for a win. She's been testing different loopers—"That's what I heard you should do." And since she's made the majority of the cuts, she's become a much more attractive employer to caddies without a permanent bag, who study promising young rookies like talent scouts scoping out Hollywood starlets. (Currently Scott Turner is on the bag, Spalding's seventh caddie of the season. Turner looped last year for his sister, Jenny, who lost her card. He's a fine golfer himself who has played the mini-tours.)

Club and clothing companies also are looking for long-term relationships. After being jilted by Elandale, Spalding is talking to another apparel maker, Bobby Jones.

"I'm sick of having to buy clothes, because I'm sick of my clothes," says Spalding. So far she has shelled out several hundred dollars for new duds. Her best investment to date, however, may be a high-quality travel iron. "I iron every day."

The most appropriate equipment company for Spalding?

Spalding, of course. The company paid her $5,000 to test equipment and consider switching to its Top-Flite brand. But she's playing too well to risk messing up her game with new tools.

Scheduling is another rookie dilemma. Veterans largely plan their season on the basis on their past performances at different events. Rookies have no data to evaluate. Spalding's plan is to take an occasional week, in addition to occasional days, off. "It can become a grind practicing and playing every day."

When she's not playing, Spalding likes to read, go to movies, and watch TV. (She majored in telecommunications and film at the University of Alabama.) A music fan, Spalding brings her CD player on the road, stocked with discs by Vince Gill, Hal Ketchum, Tracy Lawrence, Wynonna, Brooks and Dunn, U2, and Alanis Morissette.

Some sightseeing is also on the agenda on her journey across America. When Spalding and fellow rookie Susan Veasey missed the cut in Phoenix, they drove to the Grand Canyon with Veasey's boyfriend. And even rookies get a taste of glamour. Last week at the Sara Lee dinner in Nashville, Spalding sat in the front row and met Vince Gill and Amy Grant.

Spalding felt like singing the blues last month in Sacramento, however, after a rookie faux pas. Playing a practice round with Veasey and Emilee Klein, they briefly held up a pro-am group. Later, in the locker room, veteran Laurie Brower teed off on Spalding.

"She said to me, 'What's your name? You can't do that anymore. Those people are paying a lot of money.' She kept going on and on about how she should turn me in and how I should be fined. I heard other players talking about it at lunch. I hated that."

Another veteran, Missie Berteotti, told Spalding to forget it. Spalding appreciated the kind words. And she was impressed at the speed of the gossip mill. "Out here everything filters to everybody. Everybody knew about it by the end of the day."

The gossip mill on the college golf and Futures Tour circuits is pretty swift, too. Before she joined the Tour, Spalding heard tales of gay LPGA players harassing and hitting on fresh new faces. And of a player who was pursued so relentlessly she finally "turned." A PGA player told Spalding she should wear a wedding or engagement ring to fend off advances.

But the rumors of intimidation and seduction, of chicken hawks and their naive prey, now seem bogus to Spalding. "I've had no problems like that with the players."

Caroline Pierce agrees. In her nine-year career, "I've never had a problem with any of the [gay] players out here." (She's had trouble with rumors, however. A few years ago, some players in Europe, including college friend Colin Montgomerie, heard she had "turned gay." When the gossip spread to Glenn Joyner, her boyfriend at Houston Baptist, he rang her up and asked, "You haven't, have you?")

In general, Spalding feels quite comfortable in the enclosed, insular, cloistered world of the Tour.

"I had always heard people were mean," says Spalding. "But it's better than I heard it was. A few people I try to stay away from, but for the most part they're really nice."

Spalding bogeys the 383-yard 16th hole to fall back to one under par. Scores are extremely low today. The course is ripe for big hitters, in particular, who can blast tee shots over the fairway bunkers on many holes.

But even short hitters can score if they target the correct tier on their approach shots. One of the main traits that distinguish the pros from weekend hackers is their ability to hit the ball pin high, or close to it, most of the time. The reasons? (1) Consistent ball-striking. (2) Exact yardages—pros and their caddies know that they have, for instance, 171, not 170 or 172 yards to the flagstick. (3) Precise knowledge of their own capabilities. (Do you *really* know how far you hit a 5-wood or 5-iron?)

With 175 yards to a pin tucked into the back shelf of the green at 17, Spalding flags a 5-iron, the ball fading gently toward the stick. But instead of biting in birdie range, the ball hits a hard spot, jumps just over the green, and rolls down a steep slope. "I really got screwed," a fuming Spalding says to herself as she registers another bogey.

But she shakes it off, crushing a drive on the 452-yard 18th and ripping a 4-wood to the front edge of the green, just 20 feet from the cup.

"I deserve this!" Spalding tells herself, and drills the putt in the center of the cup for an eagle and a two under par 70. The 20 or so people rattling around in the huge kelly-green grandstand that surrounds the final green applaud. With three perfect shots, Spalding turns the day inside out and right side up. (And earns a small perk—eagles are worth a free upgrade from Budget, "The official rental car company of the LPGA.")

Emerging from the scorer's tent, Spalding pops open a can of Diet 7-Up. "What a good way to finish. What an up-and-down day," she says, before she heads to the practice range for a session of bunker shots and putting.

There weren't any Budget car rental upgrades or Budget cars or, for that matter, cars when women first picked up a club.

"I thank God to be busy with the Golfe . . . my heart is very good to it." Those words were written by Catherine of Aragon, first wife of Henry VIII, in 1513.

Perhaps the most famous woman golfer, other than Babe Zaharias or Nancy Lopez, was Mary, Queen of Scots, who took the throne in 1559 and also took up a game that previously had been declared illegal in Scotland. An advocate of free love in the '60s—the 1560s—Mary had four husbands, numerous affairs, and a courtier of pages, the sons of French noblemen, known as cadets. (The word *caddie* is said to derive from *cadet*. Although few modern caddies claim royal patronage, most know what it is like to incur the wrath of an imperious mistress.)

In 1567 Mary was forced to abdicate the throne. Later she was brought to trial for treason after being linked to the murder of her third husband, Lord Darnley. Evidence was introduced that Mary played golf shortly after Lord Darnley's death, an indication of her cold-heartedness. In 1587 she was executed. The last words she ever heard? "Keep your head down." As Rhonda Glenn, author of the superlative *History of Women's Golf,* drolly wrote: "Women's golf went into something of a decline after that."

Fast forward a few centuries. In 1855 at St. Andrews, Mrs. Wolfe-Murray became the first woman to play the regular links. Previously, women had been confined to the putting course; they were counseled not to raise a club above the waist. A Scottish paper reported that Wolfe-Murray "appeared regularly on St. Andrews links with two clubs and was apparently indifferent to the unflattering opinions expressed by the townspeople. She enjoyed her game, but attracted a great deal of adverse criticism, and was looked upon with horror by all the men and some of the women."

In 1893 the first women's golf championship was organized by the Ladies Golf Union in England, 15 years before women were allowed to compete in the Olympics. A male British golf official stated, "constitutionally and physically women are unfitted for golf." It would be more accurate to say they were sartorially unfitted for golf: players wore a heavy corset, two petticoats, a long-sleeved blouse with puffy sleeves, long skirt, necktie, boater-style straw hat, and chamois gloves. A good gust of wind could billow skirts like sails and topple players like dominoes. Two years later in 1895, at the first U.S. Women's Amateur, a similarly shrouded Mrs. Charles S. Brown (her first name apparently shrouded in the mists of history) shot 132 to capture the title.

At the end of the nineteenth century, an era of American millionaires, economist Thorstein Veblen defined a lady as "one whose function it was to display her husband's wealth by spending." The leisured lady was a status symbol; trophy wives were urged by *The Ladies Home Journal* to take up golf.

The first women to break 80 in a national competition was Glenna Collett Vare, who fired a 79 in a 1924 U.S. Amateur qualifying round. Vare was the prototype of the modern female athlete/golfer. A fine tennis player, swimmer, and diver, who dreamed of playing baseball, the five-foot-six and 128-pound Vare hit a drive 307 yards when she was 18.

Considered the Bobby Jones of women's golf, Vare won six U.S. Amateurs. Later she reflected on her days in the limelight. Champions must become, said Vare, "a bit of an actress, creating a professional manner. That's the insidious thing about being a champion, you change inside, or outside. But you change, anyhow."

Most women golfers in the Jazz Age were members of the American elite, introduced to the game at posh private clubs. F. Scott Fitzgerald modeled Jordan Baker, a character in *The Great Gatsby*, after Edith Cummins, who won the 1923 U.S. Amateur. A reporter wrote, "No handsomer girl ever graced an athletic contest. . . . She looked like a bewitching blonde."

When women had the temerity to turn professional, however, the press and public were less enraptured. As Rhonda Glenn writes, "Most fine players were making their reputations as amateurs, and the women's professional golf tour was not widely accepted. A requisite of women pros, or 'proettes,' as they were sometimes called, was thick-skinned immunity to public disapproval. To play the tour, one had to be something of a renegade."

The LPGA was founded in 1950, primarily as a marketing vehicle for Wilson Sporting Goods representatives Babe Zaharias, Patty Berg, and Northwestern's Louise Suggs. Fred Corcoran, a well-known sports promoter and manager, was hired as its director. In his book *Unplayable Lies*, Corcoran wrote, "The announcement that we had formed the Ladies PGA touched off a national storm of indifference. Potential sponsors were polite when I called them, but you could hear them stifling a yawn at the other end."

In 1955 the total prize money for the *season* was $175,000. Leading money winner Patty Berg raked in a grand total of $16,492. The LPGA announced it had purchased a new tape recorder and a portable aluminum scoreboard. Mary Katherine Wright was a rookie. *Golf World* wrote: "The prognosis is that Mickey, as she is generally known, will do much better than some recent additions."

"Throughout the 1950's and well into the 1960's," wrote Sarah Ballard in *A Gentleman's—and Lady's—Game*, "women's professional golf remained a hand-to-mouth business. Players supplemented their prize money with clinics and exhibitions, those of them who could, and as the scattered tournaments that make up the schedule grew into a tour, they traveled from place to place by car, sharing expenses and living out of a trunk."

Saturday dawns as humid as a steam bath. Crowds are still scarce, which means slim pickings for the companies that have set up outdoor booths near the clubhouse to hawk their wares—Sprint, Olympus cameras, Gayfer department stores, Power Bar, the Daytona Breakers hockey team, Discover, MasterCard, Bell South, Golf Collectibles, which sells photos of past and present stars, and Pevonia, a cosmetics company. Phillipe Hennessey, president of Pevonia, isn't selling much product, but he says he has found a new corporate spokesperson, Leslie Spalding. Hennessey, based in Daytona Beach, met Spalding several years ago. He plans to offer her a contract to endorse and use his line of skin care products.

Hennessey may have a rising star. Spalding makes the turn in four under par 32, after a nerve-jangling second-round 74 yesterday that brought her in right at the cut line of even par 144 for 36 holes. "I thought about the cut quite a bit," Spalding said after narrowly escaping the ranks of the weekend rejects, turned away from the big $1.2 million dance. "I was in and out of trouble the whole way. I tried to stay aggressive, tried to make birdies instead of trying to protect my position. That's when you make bogeys."

LPGA commissioner Jim Ritts is out spectating near the 10th green, dressed for an afternoon TV appearance in a yellow tie, long-sleeved blue shirt, and slacks. Ritts, thick mane of reddish blond hair swept off his wire-rimmed glasses, looks as fresh as if he were standing in a refrigerator.

He's cheerful, too. So far his new job has been a blast, a whirlwind of pro-ams and sales pitches and interviews. "There are a lot of great spirits out here," says Ritts, referring to the players. "I wouldn't have taken the job if I didn't think so, but it's double what I expected."

It's Kentucky Derby day, and for Ritts everything is coming up roses. (Ritts and some buddies used to breed racehorses as a hobby, and he's carrying around a piece of paper in his pocket with his Derby bet—Grindstone, who will rally to victory later this afternoon at 7-1.)

Ritts even likes LPGA International and thinks the mounds that have been bulldozed up along the edges of many fairways and the backs of greens to give spectators a bird's-eye view of the action constitute "manufactured uniqueness." In the mind of an advertising wizard that's a good thing. (Ritts, 43, made his mark as the youngest senior vice president at Dancer Fitzgerald Sample, Inc., in New York, before rising through the ranks at Whittle Communications to become president of Channel One Communications, a news program sold, complete with controversial commercials, to high schools across America.)

He's not as happy about the changes in the format for the Senior Challenge. In addition to eliminating Louise Suggs and Marilynn Smith from the field, Sprint increased play for the 50 and older set from 36 to 54 holes, threatening to drive out a number of other would-be competitors who aren't as young and frisky as they used to be.

The idea, says Ritts, was to make the Senior Challenge more competitive. "So they devised a ceremonial role [for Suggs and Smith], which didn't work. I think fans want to see the legends play."

He's right.

But that's what happens when corporate geniuses—whose idea of exercise is their weekly pedicure, and whose idea of entertainment is to downsize their workforce—get their hands on the controls. The idiotic decision to downsize the Senior Challenge and increase the workload for the chosen survivors could have, under slightly different circumstances, kept the greatest woman golfer in history, Mickey Wright, from teeing it up.

Wright, recently ill, isn't playing this week. But even if she were in the pink, hitting balls every morning from her backyard bordering a fairway at her home in Port St. Lucie, Florida, before settling down to study her extensive and successful ventures in the stock market, Wright might have found the move from 36 to 54 holes to be an undue burden for a 61-year-old.

When the reclusive Wright played in the Senior Challenge in 1994, it created a sensation among LPGA players. Wright had the most mundane of reasons for playing. She needed a new roof for her house, and figured she could pick up some easy money; easier, at least, than figuring out the cryptic pronouncements of the Federal Reserve Board.

But it was closer to a religious experience for dozens of LPGA players tagging along the fairways, who got up bright and early to see a legend in the flesh.

Using the same set of clubs that accounted for 82—that's right, 82—wins from 1956 to 1973, Wright shot 78-74 in her first competitive outing since 1985, tying for fifth with her old pal Kathy Whitworth. Booming 270-yard drives down the fairway, Wright astounded players and fans who came out to watch a swing that Ben Hogan described as the best he ever saw, regardless of gender. Jane Crafter's reaction was typical. "It was just awesome. Awesome! Awesome!"

Wright also transfixed the normally blasé press with her trademark blend of iron integrity. ("I have no interest in translating my name into $1 million, or any amount. To me, golf means one thing and always has: the pure pleasure I get from swinging a golf club.") Of unvarnished honesty. ("If you're talking about making it easier to get in the [LPGA Hall of Fame], absolutely not. If you're going to do that, let's don't call it the Hall of Fame, let's call it the Make Everybody Happy Club.") And of humility: Wright said she was flattered and surprised current LPGA players would turn out to watch "someone who's just a couple pops short of 60 years old." Elaine Scott, the LPGA's whip-smart director of communications, says that Wright's intelligence was so commanding, it was intimidating.

Spalding isn't playing with a legend today. She is, however, playing with her first real star, Donna Andrews as well as veteran Kathy Postlewait. Andrews burst to the top in 1994, when she won the Dinah Shore, placed fifth on the money list with $429,015, and was selected by JoAnne "Big Momma" Carner to anchor the U.S. Solheim Cup team against Liselotte Neumann and the Europeans.

But Andrews, whose career sailed smoothly and steadily upward after joining the Tour in 1990, when she was runner-up for Rookie of the Year honors, found out just how precarious a golf career could be in 1995.

Last year, plagued by back problems, she fell from stardom to the fringes of the Tour, earning just $25,345 and finishing 123rd on the money list. It was a sudden and shocking jolt. And a humbling one. When Andrews ascended to stardom, her cheerful confidence turned into something closer to a grating cockiness. After she beat Neumann in her Solheim Cup singles match, Andrews, interviewed by NBC, gushingly extolled her ability to handle pressure. In the eyes of her peers, she became something of a prima donna.

"She got the big head," says Juli Inkster. "But she handled herself last year like a champion."

Andrews and Spalding could pass for sisters. Both have similar builds, thick ponytails, steady demeanors, and mannerisms—Spalding has the same palms-up acknowledgment of applause that is a signature of Andrews's. "I've always liked Donna Andrews," says Spalding. "She has a good image and she's really a good player."

Spalding's flashy early run isn't enough to get her into contention—the leader, Catrin Nilsmark, begins play today at 13 under par. There's almost as much red on the leader board as on the faces of the spectators, who are beginning to resemble boiled lobsters. But Spalding's on target for a fat paycheck, which would be a major boost toward securing her card for 1997—that is, until she bogeys the 363-yard 12th and the easy 533-yard 13th hole. Spalding bounces the ball off her putter several times in anger. When she pulls an iron to the left of the green on the 167-yard 14th hole, it appears her ship is about to capsize. But faced with a delicate chip off a downward-sloping mound, she cozies it up to tap-in distance.

In at least one respect, Spalding appears to be a veteran—her ability to shrug off bad shots and bogeys. It's another thing that distinguishes the pros from the rest of us; we obsess over our shanks and skulls, carrying around the memory like a grudge.

Spalding birdies the 452-yard 18th hole to finish with a 69, her best round of the year.

When she leaves the scorer's tent she's met by two reporters who ask how she's handling life on Tour.

"I thought I'd be more nervous than I am," says Spalding. "I'm realizing I can make it out here—and win."

"Did you learn anything from the veterans today?" Spalding is asked.

"To stay more mentally even," says Spalding. "I got a little tense when I was four under par."

"Do you think this is a stepping-stone?"

"Sure I do."

A big step at a critical time. Next week is another double-coupon offering at the LPGA Championship in Wilmington. And on the following Monday she'll join dozens of other pros and attempt to qualify for the U.S. Open at Hartefeld National in Philadelphia.

Just around the time Spalding is finishing her round, the amazing JoAnne Carner defeats the remarkable Sandra Palmer by four strokes to win the Senior Challenge. In the 1960s and 1970s, Carner hit the ball almost as far as Laura Davies, talked to the ball like Dottie Pepper, and responded to fans as if they were old neighbors. "Carner is as tangy and sassy as Lee Trevino," wrote Tom Boswell.

Carner, 57, has played in only two LPGA events this season. She's been home in Palm Beach, Florida, caring for her husband, Don, 80, suffering from Parkinson's disease and felled last August by a stroke.

Extremely thin and fragile, Don has been JoAnne's designated caddie this week, sitting in the cart while Carner drove, cleaned and toted her own clubs, and paced off her own yardages.

The tiny five-foot-one-and-a-half-inch Palmer and the husky five-foot-seven Carner are the only players in the Senior Challenge who still play the Tour on a regular basis. In 1976 they finished one-two in four tournaments, with two victories apiece. Twenty years later and they're at it again.

Palmer, 55, a winner of 21 LPGA tournaments, including the last Title-holders in 1972 and the U.S. Open and Dinah Shore in 1975, finished eleventh in the Dinah Shore last year. She hasn't missed the cut at Mission Hills for 24 straight years.

Although Carner didn't turn pro until the age of 30—the purse money was pitiful, and Carner was having too much fun cleaning up in the amateur ranks, winning five U.S. Amateur titles—she has won 42 LPGA titles, including U.S. Opens in 1971 and 1976.

Big Momma used to have a body like a tree trunk. Now some of the limbs are creaky. But she can still play. In 1993 she almost achieved her final career goal, to become the oldest golfer to win a regular tour event (the mark is held by Sam Snead, who won at the age of 52), tying for first at the HealthSouth Palm Beach Classic before losing in a playoff to good friend Tammie Green. Last year she played in just nine events and still earned a healthy $38,033.

She married Don 33 years ago. They used to travel the Tour in a motorhome, fishing along the way. Later they bought a 42-foot boat and split time between the Bahamas and their home in Palm Beach, Florida. Now she's his full-time caregiver. She could have hired help, left Don at home, and played a full schedule this season. For Carner, it wasn't an option.

"I don't operate that way," she told the Daytona Beach *News Journal.* "Some people do, but I don't."

Why has she lasted so long as a player?

"I never had a bad attitude," Carner said a few years ago. "That's why I lasted so long. I never needed a sports psychologist. I may three-putt, but I always think I'm a good putter."

And she loves the game. Some pros talk about a "love-hate" relationship with the sport. Translation? Ninety percent of the time golf is as enjoyable for them as pulling out their fingernails with a pair of pliers.

But Carner relishes her days on the links, always has and always will. "I can go out and play all by myself at my home club and be thoroughly entertained."

The small but appreciative gallery certainly is entertained as the two old pros complete their rounds. Carner cans a 40-foot par putt on the 172-yard 17th hole to virtually clinch the victory. Palmer, who won the previous five Sprint Challenges, threatens to toss Carner's Odyssey putter to the gator in the lake. Carner walks off the green laughing, a deep whiskey-and cigarette-soaked "Huh, huh, huh, huh," gets in the cart, pats Don on the knee, and says, "All right! One to go."

"We'll see you in an hour for lessons," a fan in the grandstand calls out after Carner wraps up her victory on the final hole, shooting rounds of 66-69-70, on a course set up shorter for the Seniors than for the main event.

Looking up into the stands, Carner waves her putter back and forth and declares, "I can teach you to putt."

A few minutes later, in a presentation ceremony taped for broadcast by CBS, Carner receives her goodies—white roses, a silver cup, and a slick, Olympic-style medallion. She poses for photos and hoists a check for $40,000, one of the biggest paydays in her entire career. (Carner's victories in the 1976 and 1971 U.S. Open were worth $9,054 and $5,000.)

Carner gets a big hug from Louise Suggs, who is wearing a blue-knit shirt untucked over baggy blue and white pants. A military-style camouflage cap is perched on her head. She looks like someone's rural grandma, a woman more likely to have a fishing rod or shotgun in her hand than a brassie.

Suggs now knows her role—to hold Carner's partly finished can of Diet Coke. A good soldier, Suggs, who labored in the shadow cast by Babe Zaharias during her playing days, now stands in the shadows of the grandstand. In this helter-skelter age, when image is everything—at least if you choose to believe the image-makers—Suggs isn't young or hip or cool enough for prime time. Or even Saturday afternoon. Fortunately history, and her peers, know better.

At the Golf Collectibles booth, a chip shot from the 18th green, you can buy a photo of a slender, pretty 22-year-old amateur named Louise Suggs winning the 1946 Western Open against the pros. Three years later she defeated Zaharias by 14 strokes in the U.S. Open, a record that may never be broken.

In their rush to "honor the past, present, and future of women's golf,"

Sprint executives and tournament officials might want to pause for a moment to take a look.

"I'm exhausted," says Carol Mann shortly after she places seventh in the Senior Challenge with rounds of 75-75-77. She earns $10,500 for her labors. "It's so hard. I've always enjoyed the preparation more than doing it."

Mann doesn't look exhausted. In fact, the 55-year-old looks marvelous, dressed in a vivid canary yellow dress topped by a snazzy red hat resting on her long thick, blonde hair. Remember Sally Kellerman in the movie M*A*S*H? Mann is almost a dead-ringer, a six-foot-three-inch tall woman with a deep, throaty laugh, high intelligence, and charming warmth.

Mann mentions the article about Betty Jameson in the current issue of Sports Illustrated. Jameson, 76, a founding member of the LPGA and a member of the Hall of Fame, was the glamour girl of her time, a slender beauty who could play—she became the first woman to break 300 in a 72-hole tournament when she won the 1947 U.S. Open. She also came up with the idea of honoring the player with the lowest yearly scoring average, and donated a trophy in the name of Glenna Collett Vare to the LPGA. The Vare Trophy became one of the LPGA's three major awards, along with Player of the Year and leading money winner, and the original Vare Trophy is now in the temporary possession of last year's winner, Annika Sorenstam.

Jameson's longtime companion and fellow pro, Lena Faulk, recently died of lung cancer. Faulk's will failed to bequeath the house they shared for over 30 years to Jameson. So Jameson, a poetic, romantic spirit completely unprepared to deal with the situation, may be evicted.

It's a fate that won't befall Mann, who has flourished since leaving the Tour in 1981. The Hall of Famer, who won 38 tournaments, owns two thriving enterprises: a customer hospitality business for the PGA Tour and a course design firm. She also teaches golf at The Woodlands, a country club near Houston, and focuses on turning new women golfers into regulars. (Although over 40 percent of new golfers are women, more women than men are early dropouts from the game.) She's also popped up a few times on The Golf Channel. "I'm still a work in progress," Mann says cheerfully.

Mann joined the Tour in 1961. Her glory years were in the late 1960s, when the Tour was something of a low-rent traveling carnival.

Everyone was invited. No cuts. No Q-School. Today's young players hone their games in sleek, sophisticated college golf programs. Yesterday's young players, often rough stones, polished their games by rubbing up against the best of the best.

"It was more like a family or a big sorority," recalls Mann. "We kind of adopted or mentored rookies. There weren't that many of them. I got adopted by everybody."

If you're conjuring up visions of a big gay sorority at this point, don't. Even though a sizable percentage of players were lesbians, Mann was never hustled, at least not to the point of discomfort.

Mann has heard that some of today's college coaches discourage players from turning pro. "They tell kids that the Tour is tough, supercompetitive, those pros will eat your lunch. There are perimeters of falsehoods. For a young player that must be very scary. They tell the players they better be engaged or buy an engagement ring. It's so negative and homophobic."

It's been so for women athletes for decades, which explains why the LPGA has had a relatively high percentage of gay players.

In her 1994 book *Coming on Strong*, history professor Susan Cahn writes:

> . . . the apparently high percentage of lesbians in sport was proba-
> bly equally a product of positive appeals to lesbians and negative stig-
> mas that caused nonlesbians to opt out, especially after high school,
> when the proportion of women in sport has tended to decline. In
> sports like softball, basketball, field hockey, and golf, athletic culture
> functioned as a sexual force field—a magnet drawing lesbians in and
> repelling women who were uninterested in or threatened by the
> physicality, intimacy, and "masculinity" of sport.

As sports have slowly become more welcoming to women and girls, and a career as a professional athlete more acceptable, the percentage of gays on the LPGA Tour has gradually, but steadily decreased to an estimated 20–30 percent. And as purse money continues to rise, the lure of the Tour increases.

Mann marvels at the money that is up for grabs—$26 million in 1996. "We were so poor," says Mann, whose top year was 1969, when she won eight—eight!—tournaments and led the money list with a grand total of $49,152.

"There were very dire financial constraints"—in the years 1961–1964, Mann earned $2,145, $5,329, $6,789, and $6,672. "I went broke probably fifteen times in my first five or six years. It's tough to tee it up in the final round with thirty-five dollars to your name and you've got to pay your cad-die and hotel bill."

It wasn't uncommon for a down and almost-out LPGA player to find an envelope with travel money in her locker, an anonymous donation from her fellow competitors. LPGA players even voted to redistribute purse money in the late 1960s, taking dollars off the top, and out of the pockets of such stars as Mickey Wright (who supported the proposal), to help their struggling sisters at the bottom of the heap.

When asked if she ever thought about quitting, Mann responds, "Oh, no. I couldn't do anything else. I quit college after two years." (Mann attended what now is known as UNC Greensboro. She says she was discouraged from pursuing her main academic interest—a study of the physiological abilities of women athletes.) "I just played my little butt off not to be broke."

And traveled her little butt off to reach far-flung tournament sites, mostly in small towns such as Visalia, Muskogee, Beaumont, St. Petersburg, Waterloo, and Spokane, which as a general rule proved more hospitable to the women than sports fans in blasé big-league cities.

"Oh. Oh," says Mann, shaking her head, as she remembers riding in one of the four to eight cars comprising the caravans that crisscrossed the country as many as three times a year, rolling up around 60,000 miles. "It was drive, drive, drive, drive."

Mostly on two-lane roads, since interstate highways were, at the time, next to nonexistent. The caravans left after the final round on Sunday evenings, headlights arcing a path through the inky blackness, the stars and the moon, on a good night, illuminating the way.

Things that today's pros take for granted—courtesy cars, private housing, fitness vans—didn't exist even in the dreams of yesterday's road warriors. "There were no trainers," says Mann. "No focus on physical conditioning. We thought people who worked out were nuts."

Twelve-dollar motel rooms were standard. "They were really bad sometimes." At a dump in Shreveport, well back from the lights on the highway, Mann wincingly recalls "a big old guy looking in all the windows. We were petrified."

Courses sometimes resembled cow pastures. Conditions often were abysmal—bunkers without sand, fairways without drainage systems. Greens ranged "from slow to fast to bumpy to *Poa annua* to chickweed. If you couldn't adjust from week to week, you couldn't play."

Sometimes club members, fearful that the ladies would rip up their home turf, set tee markers at the tips. Courses averaged 6,400 yards: a few were over 6,900, a similar length to layouts the men professionals played. (Most of the 1996 LPGA courses are set up at about 6,300 yards.) Usually members were allowed to play all week. The pros endured practice rounds surrounded by duffers; after competition had begun, members teed it up on the heels of the contestants.

Horror stories abounded. A sniper opened fire at a tournament in

Florida. Golfers and caddies dove for cover; no one was injured. An Oklahoma event, which promised a percentage of the gate as the purse, was played in a dust storm. No crowds. No gate. No prize money.

The ultimate freak show? The 1967 Babe Zaharias Open in Beaumont, Texas, at the Bayou Den Country Club, a course surrounded by rice fields. Rain washed out the final round of the 54-hole tournament for ten days. The players stuck around, prepared to fulfill their obligation and finish the show. Wooden planks were laid on saturated fairways to provide a path to the greens, which proved to be a fortuitous move: water moccasins, lured out of the marshes to sun themselves when the weather finally broke, were more prevalent than fans.

"We had a snake rescue squad on every tee," says Mann, who served as tournament director at the event. Caddies dipping clubs into the casual water on the fairways, lifted them out with baby snakes curled around the shaft. Marilynn Smith, who won the tournament, found a snake wiggling in a ball washer. LPGA player Mary Lou Crocker described the week as "degrading and somewhat frightening." But no one bad-mouthed the tournament, at least not in public.

"At the end of the final round," says Mann, "I thanked every single player for putting up with the conditions and being professional enough to carry on."

"Hot Boiled or Roasted Peanuts" reads the sign at a roadside stand off LPGA International Boulevard on Sunday morning. Yesterday's temperature crested at 92 degrees. Today is even hotter: The air is stifling and still as the inside of a tomb.

Play is as hot as the weather and there are big Sunday crowds. Tina Barrett, six under par today through eight holes, is at 13 under par for the tournament, locked in a tie with defending champ Val Skinner, Catrin Nilsmark, and Kelly Robbins.

Colleen Walker, four months pregnant, walks down the fairway under a Cool Max umbrella, designed to reflect the rays of the sun. Massachusetts native Pat Bradley, her face New England lobster-red, gulps down Powerade as she, Michelle Estill, and Kelly Robbins wait on the 9th tee. Robbins, not nearly as cool as usual, slumps on a black plastic chair beside the tee box, her forearms resting on her thighs, and takes deep breaths through her mouth. She looks like an on-the-ropes boxer in the corner between rounds.

(A week later in Wilmington, Robbins will mention that she was feeling "under the weather" during the final round at Daytona Beach.

"Cold?" she's asked. "Flu?"

Robbins hesitates, then smiles and says good-naturedly, "It was the woman thing, all right?"

When a reporter starts writing in his notebook, Robbins laughs and says, "You don't need to write that, do you? 'Under the weather' should cover it.")

Spalding, who teed off on the back nine today with Donna Andrews and Martha Nause, is completing her final few holes. She's at even par today; the round could eventually spell the difference between keeping her card and enduring a miserable return trip to LPGA International for Q-School in October. On the tee of the 377-yard 7th hole, Andrews is mopping her face with a white towel like a basketball player during a time-out. Yesterday her back began to hurt; today she's playing miserably; and she seems giddy, almost slap-happy in the heat.

Nause, a wet towel wrapped around her neck, shows no sign of the angst and anger she displayed during the final round of the Dinah Shore. She does, however, seem cooked with fatigue. But she scrambles for a par on the 369-yard 8th hole and flashes a thin, exhausted smile at Andrews's looper, Chris Fitzpatrick.

Yesterday there wasn't much chatter between the rookie and the veterans, Andrews and Postlewait. But today Andrews and Spalding act like long-lost sorority sisters. As they walk up the final fairway on the 527-yard 9th hole, Andrews asks Spalding, "Who are you going out with?"

"No one," says Spalding.

"Donna has a husband and a boyfriend," says Fitzpatrick.

"Yeah, but they're the same person," says Andrews, who married club professional John Reeves in 1993.

Spalding narrowly misses a seven-foot birdie putt and flips her putter at her bag in disgust. The miss costs her about $1,500, big money for a rookie trying to pay the bills and edge her way up the money list. Still, it's the best tournament of Spalding's young career, a three under par 285, good enough for a tie for thirty-seventh with, among others, Nancy Lopez. Spalding earns $6,730 for her work, the largest payday of her career.

Andrews, who finishes with a 79—"We'll just take this day and throw it away," says Fitzpatrick—walks over to shake hands, a big smile on her face.

"Enjoyed it, young lady," she tells Spalding. "You've got a good golf game."

Spalding greets her biggest sponsors, Dick and Renee Bottini, who have invested $5,000 in Spalding, Inc.

"You played super," says Bottini, as he hands her a gift, a copy of Liz Kahn's fine new book, *The LPGA: The Unauthorized Version.*

"How are you doing for dollars?"

"Okay," says Spalding.

The caddies peel off their sweat-soaked colored vests. Even for veteran loopers, today was a long slog.

"Some of those holes it was smoking," says Chris Fitzpatrick.

"Brutal," says Scott Turner. "No wind—it was like a sauna out there."

(They could have benefited from a tip from Francis Ouimet, who wore an Indian topee, a type of pith helmet, in the 1925 U.S. Open. On the advice of a friend who had spent time in the Suez, Ouimet placed a large lettuce leaf on top of his head under the topee which helped him beat the heat.)

Turner's workday isn't over, either. Not by a long shot. In a while he'll be on the road to Wilmington, a rugged 16-hour drive. "I'm not looking forward to it," says Scott. "But we're doing a little three-car caravan." Carol Mann would understand.

After visiting with her sponsors, a drained but cheerful Spalding evaluates her performance in her first $1 million event.

"It was a good solid round," she says. "I was frustrated because nothing would go in the hole. I was nervous at the beginning [of the round], but I stayed aggressive all day."

Spalding now ranks 95th on the money list, with $14,990. Her ultimate goal—top 90 and another one-year exemption in 1997—is within reach. Her essential goal—top 125 to keep her card—appears likely.

Tomorrow Spalding flies to Philadelphia, where she'll rent a car (free bonus upgrade!) and drive to Wilmington to prepare for another double-coupon week and the first major championship of her career. For a rookie on the LPGA Tour, one way or another, the heat is always on.

Later in the afternoon a few reporters, including Lisa Mickey and Melissa Yow, editors at *Golf for Women* magazine, walk out to catch the finish. According to Mickey, a dead baby diamondback rattlesnake was found near the tee on the 4th hole. And at the 172-yard 17th hole, fans buzz about a two-foot-long loglike object floating through the water. With binoculars you can clearly see the top of the beast's scaly head, unblinking black eyes just above the surface.

Mickey offers a few alligator survival tips. Seems that gators, on dry land, are speedy, but they can only run in a straight line. So if a gator chases you, zigzag back and forth. All this information gives new meaning to the word "hazard."

After rapping a knee-knocking three-foot par putt into the back of the cup at the 383-yard 16th hole, Karrie Webb comes to the last two holes clinging to a two-shot lead.

There are no fewer than 13 people crowded around the tee box at 17— three golf pros, three caddies, and seven CBS employees—cameramen, sound people holding Frisbee-like microphones, technicians, and on-course reporter Jerry Pate.

A long delay ensues. While she's waiting for the green to clear—and perhaps to avoid the camera in her face, transmitting every flicker of emotion—Webb walks to the back of the tee to talk to some Aussie friends who are cheering her on, including LPGA player Alison Munt.

"Ready for a beer?" asks Munt.

Webb smiles and nods.

When the green is empty, Webb takes her stance. One of the caddies signals her club selection to Pate. Feeling uncomfortable over the ball, Webb nervously backs away. Setting up to the ball again, Webb executes her trademark preshot move—pantomiming the first couple of feet of her backswing, a reminder to get the club moving back on the correct plane—then launches a solid iron over the dangerous, gator-filled lake onto the front of the green. Webb nods okay. Caddie Haller nods back. But the ball is 50 feet short of the cup, treacherous two-putt territory.

"Big putt right now, obviously," Pate tell a nationwide viewing audience, as he walks off the side of the green so as not to be overheard by the golfers.

Webb lags it beautifully to tap-in distance. Two-stroke lead. One hole to play. A check for $180,000 just 452 yards away.

The crowd surges around the tee box. Haller stands behind Webb. "Nice and smooth," he says. "Pick a spot."

Eyes locked on the ball, Webb takes the club away. At the very apex of her backswing, at the instant just before she unleashes all of her power, Webb's face holds a look of such concentrated, focused, laser-beamed intensity that it could pulverize sugarcane into granules so fine they could go directly into a box of C&H.

The ball screams over the marshy wasteland toward the fairway lined with fans, toward the distant, green grandstand, toward the CBS tower. Time to break out the beer—or champagne—and start the celebration.

Or so it seems, until Webb, walking up the fairway, is startled by a roar from greenside, sudden and loud as a thunderclap. She looks up to see Kelly Robbins thrust both arms skyward as she marches toward the flagstick.

The eagle has landed. Battling through her fatigue and her, uh, "woman thing," Robbins rolls in a 15-foot eagle three to finish with a 66 for the day and a 15 under par 273 for the tournament.

In the blink of an eye, Webb's two-shot lead vanishes. She's facing a shot of precisely 200 yards to the flag, cut at the back of the narrow green. Miss it right and she's in a bunker or heavy rough. Miss it left and she's in a bunker. Either way, par and a playoff will be the most likely result. Miss it *way* left, and Webb's ball will sleep with the fishes and the gators, and she'll join her mentor Norman as the choke of the year.

Professional athletes prepare all their lives for precisely such moments. Champions revel in them. Webb pulls out a 3-iron and scorches it. The shot is a frozen rope, streaking toward the flagstick. It lands just short of the green, bounces straight toward the pin and rolls right by it, finally coming to rest just in the back fringe some 35 feet from the cup.

As chips go, it's an easy one. Unless you have to get up-and-down to win $180,000. Then 35 feet begins to look like 350 feet, and tension attacks the limbs like rigor mortis.

Robbins waits under the CBS tower in the shade at the back of the green, eating a few bites of ice cream. Webb lines up her chip, encircled by spectators in the grandstand. The CBS eye of the camera peers down from the tower. The white-yellow sun beats down from the heavens, waves of heat as heavy as anvils resting on Webb's 21-year-old shoulders. It's a silent, jaw-clinched, endless, frozen moment.

Until Webb, flicking a sand wedge with the cool precision of a heart surgeon wielding a scalpel, delicately rolls the chip a foot from the cup. When she taps the winning birdie putt into the cup, completing a final round 66, Webb raises both fists straight overhead and pumps them up and down in triumph as the crowd explodes, rising to their feet, cheering and shouting for the young woman. As she walks to the scorer's tent, she runs into Robbins. They slap hands. Robbins congratulates her.

"Thanks. You made an eagle on the last hole," says Webb, admiration in her voice.

After signing her card, Webb stands in the shade beneath the tower, waiting for the awards ceremony and her moment in the sun. She catches Haller's eye, and they smile. Webb receives a trophy, an Olympic-style medallion which she promptly slips around her neck, a big, cardboard, made-for-TV-size check for $180,000—she gives a little amazed laugh when presented with the check—and a green jacket, a symbol of the Title-holders tradition. About 40 photographers click away.

A few minutes later Webb is in the press room talking about her glorious 3-iron on the 18th hole.

"I couldn't believe it," says Webb. Her hazel eyes sparkle like chandeliers in an elegant ballroom. "That was just a great shot. It's always good to be put under that kind of pressure and produce. That's why I play this game."

A reporter notes that Webb is the first Australian to win a green jacket this year, a reference to Norman's collapse at the Masters three weeks ago. Everyone laughs; the writers have their themes. "The Australian who doesn't gag on Sunday" (*Golf World*). "This blonde Australian did what that other one couldn't: win a green jacket" (*Sports Illustrated*).

Asked about caddie and fiancé Haller, Webb says they try to keep their on-course business and off-course romance separate. "It's too hard to be having a fight about something else and play golf."

Haller, standing toward the back of the interview room, raises his eyes and smiles an ironic smile. In a few minutes he'll be telling a reporter, "Oh, God, it's the hardest thing I've ever done. Twenty-four hours a day, every day. . . . There's an incredible strain on the relationship. We try to leave the game on the golf course, but she's got to let off steam at someone."

But Haller, a fine golfer himself who shudders at the notion of beating balls for four hours, a typical practice session for Webb, is filled with admiration. "Today, under the circumstances, was the best I've ever seen her play. She didn't miss a green. She missed two fairways and both times it was by one yard."

For at least an hour after the main press interview is over, Webb is peppered by inquiries from a handful of reporters with additional questions, and shuttled around the media tent for radio interviews, both by reporters on the scene and by phone, answering the same questions over and over and over. "Did you expect to do this well in your rookie season?" is the chart topper.

While Webb occupies center stage, Haller sits in a chair near the back of the media tent.

"Want a beer?" asks a volunteer.

"I'd love a beer," says Haller, as the volunteer hands him a Michelob Light.

A few writers drift over to chat. Not long ago caddies were regarded as little more than beasts of burden, humping their loads across the fairways. To an extent, it's still true. Ask a pro golfer what she looks for in a caddie, and you'll often hear some variation of the following:

"Someone who shows up on time, gives correct yardages, and keeps his mouth shut." And the fact that pros have won tournaments with absolute beginners or, horror of horrors, sportswriters on their bag (Meg Mallon won a tournament with *Sports Illustrated*'s Sonja Steptoe looping for her in 1991) gives credence to the notion that caddies are little more than, in the words of former LPGA caddie Chuck Heath, "glorified rickshaw drivers."

But the popularity and stratospheric purse levels of professional golf have elevated the status of caddies as well and lured everyone from lawyers to accountants, club pros, and mini-tour dropouts into the profession. Loopers on the PGA and Senior Tour are featured on ads on ESPN. Freebies in the form of clothes and playing privileges abound. With the tours awash in prize money, caddies are no longer simply itinerant labor. Even on the less lucrative LPGA Tour, caddies with the top bags can earn over $100,000 a year. The Caddie Machine owns a condo in Phoenix. He hopes to buy another place in Montana before he hangs up his caddie vest, as long as his knees hold out. (Laib underwent operations on both knees in the fall of 1995. The reason? Simple wear and tear from hauling a 40-pound bag of clubs and gear six miles a day six days a week up and down steep hills and soggy fairways. Back and neck and shoulder and knee problems are almost as common to caddies as they are to players.)

It's a far cry from Haller's former job—after graduating from the university, Haller sold insurance in Australia for three years.

"How'd you like it?" he's asked.

"*Hated* it," smiles Haller, an intelligent, good-natured lad with a sweet disposition.

"What about the money?" a writer asks Haller. Today's victory boosts Webb's 1996 earnings over $460,000.

"It's just amazing how much money it is," says Haller. After Webb's hot start, she and Haller, who planned to rent a house in Orlando, traded up, buying a house in Bay Hill, the exclusive residential area containing the country club owned by Arnold Palmer. Conservative by nature, the couple still doesn't own a car—although they're eyeing a brand-new BMW.

Welcome to life in the fast lane. After the McDonald's LPGA Championship next week in Wilmington, Webb jets to a tournament in Japan, where she'll pick up a check for $10,000 to tee it up. Then she flies back to North Carolina for the U.S. Open. By that time the endorsement offers should be piling up; Webb currently represents Titleist clubs, Oakley sunglasses and Izod Club, giving her agent, IMG, plenty of space on her body to sell to the highest bidder.

The phone messages should be piling up as well. Webb and Haller recently obtained an unlisted number after an Australian journalist rang them up at three in the morning. Time for simple pleasures—the couple enjoy shooting hoops in their driveway, movies, and Bulls games on the tube, featuring fellow Australian Luc Longley, as well as a guy named Jordan—will be scarce.

"It comes to a point where we have to start saying no to people," says Haller. "She's not very good at doing that."

So it begins: Webb's dance with the bitch goddess of fame and the devil temptress of fortune, two dazzling charmers who have tripped up many a partner unprepared to tango. The heat under the spotlight is as withering as a Daytona Beach summer and it stays on 24 hours a day. The great Swedes wilted under it, Neumann for years and Sorenstam, learning by example, for months.

Great PGA pros are no more immune; under even bigger and hotter spotlights, such talents as Fred Couples and Nick Price have buckled and fled. The demands from the media and fans and sponsors, the unrealistic expectations, the microscopic scrutiny, the barbaric invasion of privacy—who needs it? In an era where athletes have replaced rock stars as demigods, how many people *really* want to Be Like Mike. Take it from Arnold Palmer, who is Just Like Mike. "I think there are guys playing below their abilities because they don't want the hassles," Palmer told *Golf* magazine.

But if anyone can handle the hype, the hoopla, the hysteria, and the hustle, I'd bet on Webb. So far, at least, she has her feet planted firmly in the turf, as well as a nice sense of herself. Asked earlier in the week if she considers herself a typical Australian woman, Webb replied, "I don't think there *is* a typical Australian woman."

Asked if her rookie season compares with that of Nancy Lopez, Webb emphatically says, "There's never going to be another Nancy Lopez. She made the Tour what it is, as did the other Hall of Famers."

As Webb answers questions inside the media tent, a few kids patiently wait for autographs outside. Tom Vincent, 14, who carried a portable aluminum scoreboard in the tournament, also carried Kris Tschetter's shiny Walter Genuin golf shoes to the 18th green yesterday after Tschetter, from the edge of the lake, played a shot barefoot.

Vincent wanted the shoes, which sell for $250–$300 a pair. He got a glove instead. And a cap and glove from Sorenstam. And a signed glove from McGann that, says Vincent, "an older guy offered me fifty dollars for."

"Did you think about selling?" he's asked.

"Nah," says Vincent. "I can sell it for more later when she retires."

Vincent got a glove from Webb as well. He's waiting for her to sign it. He may wind up with quite a valuable item. Time will tell, of course, but Webb just may be "one of the ones."

Someday she may join Carol Mann and the other Hall of Famers, winners of at least thirty LPGA tournaments. Someday she may even dislodge one of Rhonda Glenn's selections of the five greatest women golfers in the history of the game: Mickey Wright, Kathy Whitworth, Patty Berg, JoAnne Carner, and Louise Suggs.

CHAPTER 5

Wilmington: Reversal of Fortunes

As Karrie Webb deals with the media, the fans, and her newfound fame, other players dash to the airport to catch flights to Philadelphia.

Nancy Lopez wheels a carry-on suitcase to the gate as her row is called. Clutched to her chest is a jumbo-sized green carton of Corn Chex.

"Dinner?" Lopez is asked.

"Breakfast," smiles Lopez. "I couldn't fit it in here," she says, nodding at her suitcase, "and there's too much left to leave it behind."

Hurtling off the runway, we soar past Daytona Speedway into the deep blue evening sky and out over the blue-black water of the Atlantic, then turn north and head into a gradually thickening bank of clouds, arriving in Atlanta in plenty of time for the final leg to Philadelphia.

As we wait in the crowded gate area, a thirty-something man in a T-shirt approaches Davies, who is eating chocolate frozen yogurt and reading an English tabloid.

"Are you Laura Davies?"

Davies nods.

"I told my wife you're the best woman golfer in the world," says the man, as his spouse joins him and nods hello. "And you are."

That's enough to coax a little smile and a "thank you" from Davies.

A few minutes later Davies, who usually flies coach—"I hate spending money with the airlines; it's a pet peeve of mine"—wrestles a bag into the overhead bin. Lopez, also flying coach tonight, draws a mid-plane seat.

"I wish I hadn't gotten a window seat," Lopez says quietly.

"Why?"

"Because I'm claustrophobic," she says, plaintively laying her forehead against the seat back in front of her.

Then she laughs. "I guess I'll just go to the bathroom a lot."

Other passengers buzz as they board the plane. "That's Beth Daniel," says one traveler, pointing at Vicki Fergon.

Fergon, for her part, is as disgruntled outside the ropes as she was inside the ropes during the first round of the Sprint Championship.

"I can't get to my seat," she complains, when a herd of passengers block her way. "I can't get a drink," she says. Eventually she gets both.

"That's Laura Davies sitting up front!" says a slender, hawkish-looking thirty-something doctor named Randy with a cropped George Clooney haircut and a New York accent, returning with a handful of his pals from a golfing excursion near Atlanta.

When he spots Lopez, he makes a beeline for her row. Lopez is sitting next to her best friend and fellow pro Kim Bauer. The man leans over and asks Lopez a question she's never been asked in an interview room.

"You ever watch *Star Trek?*"

Then he takes Lopez's hand and presses it, fingers spread, against his face for about 15 seconds, explaining that he's getting a Vulcan Mind Meld—transferring Lopez's golf prowess into his body.

Lopez, Bauer, and everyone else in the nearby rows burst out laughing. Randy finally returns Lopez's hand, straightens up, and says to no one in particular, "I needed that. Otherwise I wouldn't have interrupted her."

Lopez and Bauer joke that they will signal "hello" to the boys on TV by putting a hand over their face.

For the next 40 minutes or so we sit on the runway delayed by a traffic jam of Sunday evening flights. Randy and his buddies, mostly doctors and lawyers, lean over their seats and clog the aisle chatting with Bauer and Lopez, who is truly trapped now.

Travel is a great leveler, especially on the LPGA Tour. Top PGA and Senior Tour stars—Norman, Price, Palmer, Nicklaus, Floyd—own private jets. Except for an occasional ride on a charter or a sponsor's corporate plane, LPGA players mingle with the hoi polloi at ticket counters, baggage check-ins, terminal gates, and rental car lots. Even first class offers, at best, only a brief respite from the cattle car conditions of airports and planes, from the delays and tedium and aggravation, and, for the stars, from the stares and finger-pointing and comments from fans and voyeurs.

Inkster used to tell seatmates she was a professional golfer. But she grew weary of the same old questions:

"Do you know Nancy Lopez?"

"Have you ever won a tournament?"

"So what do you *do?*"

"Do you make money at that?"

Now she tells people she's on her way to visit relatives, and uses air time as a quiet time to read or sleep.

Caroline Pierce can relate. When she tells strangers she's a professional golfer, "they get this strange look on their face. Then they comment on my size. Or ask, 'Where are you on the money list?' Or say, 'I've never heard of you.'"

It's a bumpy flight through black skies and thunderstorms. By the time we touch down on solid ground, it's almost midnight. Sheets of fat raindrops bounce off the tarmac like Ping-Pong balls. The temperature is 53 degrees, about 40 degrees cooler than it was in Daytona Beach when we left.

It takes about an hour to get our luggage. The locals shrug—the Philly baggage operation is notorious for its sluggishness. Too bad there's no penalty for slow play in the real world.

Players, caddies, and LPGA staffers who traveled on another flight from Daytona Beach to Cincinnati to Philadelphia also mill about. Despite their fatigue, you can still pick the golf pros out of the crowd. They're the tan, fit, and energetic ones, at least in comparison to the rest of the bedraggled passengers.

Some of the players are signed up for a Monday pro-am at eight o'clock tomorrow morning. The notion of staggering out of bed about five o'clock, after just a few hours of sleep, to tee it up in a cold rain and chitchat with strangers is, at the moment, about as appealing as breaking boulders with a pickax.

The weather at Du Pont Country Club on Monday afternoon is gray, drizzly, chilly, and dark. (But not quite bad enough to cancel the pro-am earlier this morning.) Saturated by spring storms, the Du Pont course, a lovely layout that rolls gently through fairways lined with tall maple and oak trees, is a boggy mess.

"You can't even practice," says caddie John Killeen.

Yet a few players are on the assembly line anyway, bundled up against the cold and hitting balls off uphill or sidehill lies, the only areas on the range dry enough to support them.

One is Judy Dickinson, who raps an iron against her mud-caked white shoes, trying to dislodge the mud on her club. Dickinson, like JoAnne Carner, has missed part of the 1996 season, staying home in Tequesta, Florida, to care for her ailing husband, Gardner, as well as their twin 6-year-old boys, Barron and Spencer.

Dickinson, 46, is one of the LPGA's unsung heroines. As LPGA president from 1990 to 1992, she spearheaded the creation of an on-site day-care center, sponsored by Smuckers. Previously LPGA moms not only shelled out hundreds of dollars a week for day care, they had to schlep their kids to and from a different facility in a strange town each week. For the 34 LPGA moms, with a total of 58 kids, it's a godsend.

She also orchestrated the ousting of former LPGA commissioner William Blue in 1990, after Blue reportedly had bungled relations with three tournament sponsors to such an extent that the companies were prepared to jettison the LPGA in favor of Senior or celebrity events, or simply abandon golf altogether.

At the same time Dickinson completed a Triple Crown of accomplishments by coaxing Charles Mechem, former head of Taft Broadcasting, out of retirement to replace Blue. The dapper, distinguished, well-connected Mechem, known to everyone from sponsors to caddies as Charlie, put out the fires and restored the confidence of a staff and group of players that walked around on eggshells. ("The biggest problem was our own institutional inferiority complex," said Mechem.) And he began hitting up his boardroom buddies for support and sponsorships.

It wasn't easy. A lifelong conservative Midwestern Republican, and a Yale-educated attorney, Mechem glided like butter through the corridors of corporate and political power throughout his career. But when he took the reins of the LPGA and started selling women's golf, he was often given the bum's rush. "So long, Charlie."

"I've had more doors closed in my face in the last four years than in the last thirty-plus years in the legal and broadcast fields combined," Mechem told *Golf World* at the end of 1994.

Eventually, Mechem saw the light. He still described himself as a conservative Midwestern Republican. But he also began describing himself as a "middle-aged male feminist." In 1994 Mechem told *Golfweek*, "When I see great women golfers who literally can't go into certain clubs today and play, or when I see tee time restrictions at clubs that are based on nothing other than the desire of male chauvinists to protect their turf, I just find that unconscionable. I must confess that when I took this job I had no idea of the degree to which women athletes have been discriminated against over the years."

Tiptoeing a tightrope through gusty winds with the agility of a Wallenda, Mechem soothed and stroked and softened the antagonism of the corporate world and the media toward women's golf, at the same time he was condemning sexism and discrimination from the very same groups. Mechem's message, boiled down to its essence and delivered in the most ingratiating manner, was simple: "Do the right thing."

IMG's Jay Burton, who represents 14 LPGA players, says Mechem's approach was almost magical. "I honestly have never heard anyone say anything bad about this man. I'm a huge fan. He's been the best ambassador for women in sports, not just golf."

By the time Mechem's five-year term was up, he had poured a foundation of solid steel for the LPGA. The new sponsors and events that have been announced or are in the works for 1996 and 1997—Kroger, Safeway, the ITT Tour Championship, and tournaments in Los Angeles, Myrtle Beach, and West Palm Beach—are part of Mechem's legacy, although "the new guy," as Mechem refers to his successor, Jim Ritts, is reaping much of the glory.

The LPGA's bright new fortunes are part of Judy Dickinson's legacy, too. But it seems like ancient history right now. "It's been hard," says Dickinson, describing her last two years. That's an understatement. From 1991 to 1994, Dickinson won over $1 million on Tour. In 1995, limited to 16 events because of her husband's poor health—Gardner has suffered three strokes—she earned just $23,602. Her play has been only slightly better so far in 1996.

It's a sad chapter in what has been a storybook romance and partnership.

Once described as a "dyed-in-the-wool child of the 1960s," Dickinson spent her college years demonstrating against the Vietnam War and for civil rights. She graduated with a history degree from Glassboro State College in New Jersey. Afterward she worked briefly, unsuccessfully and unhappily, as a schoolteacher, mail carrier, and waitress. Then, in a lucky twist of fate, she took a job mowing the golf course at a country club where her first husband worked as a mechanic.

It was the initial step in a long and winding road to the Tour. After mowing the course, Dickinson was allowed playing privileges. A childhood interest in golf was rekindled; soon Dickinson was shooting in the mid-70s.

After her marriage broke up, Judy began to fantasize about playing on the LPGA Tour. She ventured to Florida for a series of lessons from former PGA player Gardner Dickinson.

Gardner, a generation older than Judy, is a gruff, no-nonsense teacher. During his years on Tour, he was best known for his solid game and his habit of aping the wardrobe and mannerisms of his idol, the gruff, no-nonsense Ben Hogan.

When Judy told Gardner she wanted to qualify for the Tour, he thought she was joking. But she was determined, ambitious, a quick study, and an exceptional athlete. She earned her LPGA card in her first attempt at Q-School in 1978.

Improving steadily every season, Judy broke into the elite circles of the Tour in 1985. She won her first tournament. She placed ninth on the money list. And she married her teacher.

In 1989 Judy gave birth to twins. The next year Gardner underwent triple bypass surgery. Dickinson nursed him back to health, raised her rambunctious twin boys, led the players' organization, orchestrated the ousting of Bill Blue and the hiring of Charlie Mechem, won $80,784 on the course—and leaped tall buildings at a single bound.

At least it seemed that way. Four great years followed for Judy and Gardner and the kids. But now Gardner, dressed in a light blue jacket and a black fedora, sits slumped on a folding chair behind Judy, still teaching his wife and student but usually confined to a wheelchair.

At the other end of the range, Karen Weiss is hitting irons from an uphill lie as two Canada geese squackingly descend on an adjacent fairway. She hits a fat wedge and spends the next 30 seconds digging mud out from around her eyes and shaking it off her clothes. Weiss, 30, has risen from the fringe to the pack, after graduating from the University of Minnesota and taking a job as a display designer with Target Stores. But the Tour beckoned, and she quit her job and spent several years in the minors—the Player's West Tour, Futures Tour, Central Florida Challenge, and Asian Tour, where she won ten events, including the Republic of China Open—honing her game.

Now, in a nice twist of fate, she represents Target, as well as extralong Killer Bee driver, which is almost as tall (50 inches) as the slender five-foot-three Weiss. (Weiss smacks it a ton, averaging about 240 yards off the tee.)

A few intrepid fans brave the drizzle, including Fred Carter, 67, from Long Island. For the last few years Carter has journeyed from his home to Wilmington to visit his niece and see the tournament.

"I used to think it was a sissy game," says Carter. "But these girls are professionals. There's no horsing around. These girls are the best—and the friendliest."

They even exchange gifts.

"I've got a nice paperweight for you," Melissa McNamara says to Callaway rep Todd Strible, as she hands him the head of a Big Bertha driver which is attached to about six inches or so of a jagged-edged shaft. "It snapped at the airport," she explains.

"With golf bags the baggage people just lift and throw," says Strible. "They don't want to hurt their backs. Suzanne Strudwick had a driver broken last week." Strible leaves to rummage through his stock of clubs and returns with four possible replacements for McNamara to field-test.

Caddies trudge through the muddy pathways to the range wearing rubber boots and carrying hand warmers in their pockets. Vicki Goetze, who went to Georgia State University and lives in Florida, tiptoes through the mire and arrives at the range hunched over and shivering. In the chilly drizzle, muscles are stiffening and contracting by the second.

Pierce slogs to the range after playing nine holes. "I didn't hit an iron until the par three," she says.

After her final-round meltdown in Nashville, Pierce missed the cut—the first cut she's missed all season—in Daytona Beach. Perhaps her confidence, which often seems shaky, has been shattered.

Perhaps not. Pierce shrugs off her performance in Daytona Beach. "I don't think I've ever made the cut there." In fact, she's quite encouraged about her game, after discovering a flaw in her setup: Pierce had her hands behind the ball at address, which tilted her shoulders to the right and caused her to cut across the ball.

"It will be better this week," she promises. She also praises the Du Pont layout. "It's fair golf."

Perhaps so, but big bombers have an advantage here. Laura Davies has placed second, first, and first the past three years; Kelly Robbins outdueled her last year. The course is set up at almost 6,400 yards, a stout test under dry conditions, but in the muck, it seems more like 7,400 yards. Short, low-ball hitters can only pray for a freak heat wave. Short, low-ball hitter Jan Stephenson is more realistic. She withdrew.

Hard to blame her. It's pretty grim on the range. Instead of the crisp, pleasing THWACK of irons carving through sod, you hear a lot of Ross Perots—giant sucking sounds, as blades dully dig into the ooze. Near the clubhouse, a volunteer marshal rubs his hands over an imaginary barrel and says, "We need a fire."

Instead, Wilmington gets more rain, buckets of it. Three inches, to be precise. On a gray, gloomy, windy, wet, weather-you-wouldn't-take-your-dog-out-in Thursday, the first round of the tournament is delayed for hours and finally scrubbed. In an unprecedented decision at a major championship, the event is shortened from 72 to 54 holes.

The culprit?

"The Great God Television," says Patricia Davies, covering the tournament for *The Times* of London, the sarcasm in her voice dripping like acid rain.

Aided and abetted by the LPGA and by McDonald's tournament officials. "We wanted the tournament to end on national television," says tournament director and LPGA Hall of Famer Betsy Rawls. "And I look at it from the spectator's standpoint. We could have 30,000 people out here on Sunday. We hate to have players finish [Monday] without anyone being out here."

Players scatter. It's been a long day for Leslie Spalding, who awoke in the dark at four o'clock this morning, too keyed up to sleep, arrived at the course at six o'clock for her 7:30 tee time, hung around until nine o'clock, went back to her hotel for a quick nap ("I have allergy problems here"), returned to the practice range at eleven o'clock, and was preparing to hit her first ball when an LPGA official told her play was canceled. She and a number of other players spend the afternoon at a movie.

Wilmington is a conservative corporate town. And Du Pont, which employs 105,000 people worldwide, is the straw that sedately stirs the city's drink.

Built in 1920, the Du Pont Country Club is dedicated solely for the use and enjoyment of its employees and their families. After repeated expansion, the grounds now contain three golf courses, fifteen tennis courts, and a magnificent three-story tan brick Georgian colonial clubhouse.

The McDonald's LPGA Championship is the event of the year in Delaware. Daily attendance is stupendous, hovering around 30,000 on Saturday and Sunday. About 2,000 volunteers, ranging from civic officials to scout troops, staff ticket booths, sell programs, serve as gallery marshals, and drive shuttle buses from off-site parking lots to the course.

The buses run on time in Wilmington. The McDonald's LPGA Championship is the smoothest operation of the season, a tribute to Betsy Rawls, who turned 68 last week.

Quietly and modestly and brilliantly, Rawls has fashioned one of the most remarkable golf careers of the twentieth century. Last year she was honored by the USGA with its prestigious Bob Jones Award, which recognizes distinguished lifetime achievements in the sport.

The honor was well deserved. As a player Rawls won 55 tournaments, including 4 U.S. Opens, even though she never picked up a club until she was 17. The diminutive Rawls was known as a master shotmaker and a short-game virtuoso.

In 1975 she began a six-year term as the LPGA's tournament director. Then she took her management skills to McDonald's, becoming executive director of the McDonald's Kids Classic, which evolved into the McDonald's Championship in 1986 and the McDonald's LPGA Championship in 1993 after slumping auto sales forced Mazda to terminate its sponsorship of the LPGA Championship.

"How do you do it?" Rawls is asked on Thursday afternoon, as the small, gray-haired woman, dressed in a windbreaker and jeans, sits in her spartan office tucked away in the bowels of the clubhouse. After all, the tournament purse is $1.2 million, tops, along with the U.S. Open and Sprint

Titleholders Championship, on Tour. McDonald's also pays CBS about $1 million for air time. Yet the event produces a huge profit, all of which is earmarked for the Ronald McDonald Children's Charities (RMCC), which includes not only Ronald McDonald Houses for families of seriously ill children, but other organizations such as the Easter Seals. The 1995 tournament raised $2.1 million for RMCC; over the past 15 years the total is a staggering $23.8 million. It is the largest sum raised for children's charities by any single sporting event in the world.

Even for Rawls, a Phi Beta Kappa math and physics whiz at the University of Texas, the resulting bottom line seems near impossible.

But she makes it sound like child's play. Much of the money for RMCC is raised through the pro-am, which prices entry fees about four times higher than at other LPGA tournaments. It costs $10,000 for a pro-am spot (or four for $32,000) and they sell like Big Macs to golden arches franchise operators and food suppliers from around the country. Contestants fly in and are treated to two days of golf and three parties. "We have a very supportive McDonald's family," says Rawls in a typical understatement.

With the energy of a woman half her age, Rawls and a small staff and an army of volunteers do the rest. One of Rawls's tasks this afternoon is to devise a new bus schedule to take into account the closure of some parking lots due to rain and mud. For a woman called a "brainiac" by no less than Callaway vice president of business development Jan Thompson (whose last two jobs with Mazda and Wilson Sporting Goods made her the highest-ranking female auto executive and highest-ranking female golf executive in history), it's a cinch. "This is the easiest afternoon I've had in the last three weeks," says Rawls.

Like the raising of a curtain on a theater stage, gray skies slowly lift on Friday morning, and as temperatures rise, earmuffs and umbrellas are replaced by polo shirts and shorts.

Dottie Pepper, who teed off on No. 10 at 9:00 A.M. with Juli Inkster and Meg Mallon, already is hot. Her two-foot par putt on the 399-yard 18th hole pirouettes around the cup in almost a complete 360-degree circle, and spins out, laughing at her. Pepper stomps off the green, her face a frozen granite mask, and slams the ball into a cardboard trash bin near the scorer's tent.

A volunteer fishes out the Titleist Tour Balata 100. Players always mark their ball in some distinctive way to distinguish it from those of a competitor who may be playing an identical brand and number. Pepper's mark is particularly clever: •t (Dot-T) in green marker.

But another volunteer isn't impressed, telling nearby fans that Pepper ignored autograph seekers when she came to the 10th tee to begin her round. "She's been a pain in the ass all day."

It's been a much better morning for Leslie Spalding, who teed off in the first group at 7:30 A.M. Splashing through the mud and the casual water, she fires a fabulous one under par 70. An LPGA media rep is waiting with a cart near the scorer's tent; when Spalding emerges she is whisked away on her maiden voyage to the interview room.

Seven writers amble in and take a seat. Standard procedure is birdies ("Drive, 6-iron to 10 feet," for example) and bogeys ("Three-putted from 40 feet," for example), followed by general questions. The inquiries are brief and desultory, primarily dealing with course conditions. If any of the writers are interested in Spalding's game or background, they disguise it brilliantly.

Patty Sheehan, back from her lucrative tournament appearance in Japan, tees off at noon and shoots a solid 72. Late in the afternoon, in a booth by an entrance to the clubhouse, she sits down next to writer Betty Hicks and spends about two hours signing copies of her new book, penned with Hicks, called *Patty Sheehan on Golf*. (Hicks, a 76-year-old journalist, pilot, gourmet cook, and musician, was one of the early pioneers on the LPGA Tour.)

"Twenty bucks," Sheehan says cheerfully when a fan picks up a book and checks out the cover. Sheehan, in a chipper mood, autographs crates of books, visits with fans, and poses for pictures.

Caroline Pierce, off at 12:20, hits every fairway, misses every putt, and fires an extremely disappointing no-birdie 75 on an extremely weird day.

On the 381-yard 6th hole, as Pierce sets up to hit her second shot, she looks up to see a man parading back and forth on a CBS camera platform behind the green.

It is, of all things, an old boyfriend, a sportscaster from Pennsylvania that Pierce dated several years ago. "What are you doing tonight?" he asks when the group reaches the green. Unwilling to vacate the stage, the former beau struts around on the towers behind the next few greens.

Pierce is not the only one who is annoyed. A distracted Maggie Will, catching sight of the yahoo as she prepares to hit on the 192-yard 8th hole, backs off the shot, turns to Pierce, and says, "Your asshole's up in the tower again."

Ah, yes. There's always, it seems, an asshole in the CBS tower at Wilmington.

It took the club manager, summoned by Pierce's group after the 9th hole, only a few minutes to give the ex-boyfriend the boot. It took almost a year to get rid of Ben Wright.

Exactly one year ago the Wilmington *News Journal* printed an article by veteran writer Valerie Helmbreck, based on an interview with Wright, that ignited a media firestorm and permanently changed the lives of Wright, Helmbreck, CBS executives, and the LPGA. The brouhaha splashed women's golf over the front pages and airwaves of newspapers and TV stations across America for the first time in decades.

The story included the following quotes attributed to John Bentley Wright, an urbane 67-year-old who had been a fixture on CBS telecasts for 23 years.

"Let's face facts here. Lesbians in the sport hurt women's golf.

"They're going to a butch game and that furthers the bad image of the game.

Lesbianism on the Tour "is not reticent. It's paraded. There's a defiance in them in the last decade."

"The men's pro game is in a class by itself. The [professional] women's game equates to the male club golfer.

"Women are handicapped by having boobs. It's not easy for them to keep their left arm straight, and that's one of the tenets of the game. Their boobs get in the way."

In addition, according to the story: "Wright thinks Davies's long-hitting game is an example of the wrong direction of LPGA players. 'The woman's built like a tank. She's superwoman. She just beats the hell out of the ball.'

"Wright thinks it's a mistake for women to play a power-hitting game. The feminine game with its graceful, fluid strokes and impeccable timing is what LPGA golfers should strive for instead of, as Wright said, 'beating the damn golf course to a pulp.'

"Wright says the top names in the game now don't fire up the crowds. Michelle McGann, with her flamboyant hats, 'won't do it,' he said. As for Laura Davies, says Wright, 'Just being a casino rat doesn't make you a character.'"

The reaction from Wright was swift and apoplectic. On the same morning the story broke—it was front-page news in papers ranging from *The Washington Post* to the *New York Post* (with its memorable headline, "The Boob on the Tube")—Wright distributed a memo which was posted in the players' locker room. It read in part:

"I am disgusted at the pack of lies and distortion that was attributed to me in the newspapers this morning.

"I have been a supporter and friend of women's golf for more than 40 years as a writer and broadcaster. . . .

"It is regrettable that the *News Journal*'s dishonest tactics have resulted in this terrible, scandalous incident. As a result, I currently am exploring my legal options."

Summoned to CBS headquarters in New York on Friday afternoon by David Kenin, president of CBS Sports, Wright pled innocence. After a six-hour meeting, which Kenin dubbed a "thorough investigation," Kenin released a statement exonerating Wright and, by implication, excoriating Helmbreck as a lying, falsifying, malicious woman unfit to call herself a journalist.

The heart of Kenin's statement read as follows: "I am convinced that the offensive statements attributed to Mr. Wright were not made. . . . This man, as well as CBS Sports, has been done a grave injustice in this matter."

So began the golf world's version of the Clarence Thomas–Anita Hill affair. Ugly remarks attributed to an influential public figure by a relatively unknown woman. Outraged denials by the man and his supporters. Vicious attacks on the credibility of the woman. A relentless probe into her background and possible motives. Powerful forces much more interested in exonerating the man than discovering the truth.

Clarence Thomas and his backers got away with it, and so did Ben Wright.

At least for a while. Cleared by Kenin and immediately returned to his post, Wright was the focus of a two-day mea culpa orchestrated by CBS golf producer Frank "The Ayatollah" Chirkinian. On the Saturday telecast of the McDonald's LPGA Championship a nervous, perspiring Wright denied his reputed remarks in categorical terms. "Those remarks were totally untrue." He concluded his statement by angrily saying, "Let's get on with the golf!" Wright was featured with Nancy Lopez, asked by CBS to come to the booth to do commentary. The picture of Lopez and Wright, sitting side-by-side and chatting amicably, was a public relations masterstroke.

Jim Nantz, host of the telecast, jumped into the fray, stating, "All of us at CBS are deeply disturbed by the inaccurate and distorted [story]." (Nantz, in an interview with *Sports Illustrated* this week, says that remark was scripted by CBS executives. A source at CBS, however, says Nantz's on-air comments did not come from Kenin or any other CBS honcho in New York.) Other CBS staffers, whether out of malice or conviction or both, were telling reporters that Helmbreck was pushing some sort of gay rights agenda. Their evidence? That Helmbreck once wrote a story on gay tourism and that a gay reporter from the *News Journal*, whom they incorrectly assumed to be Helmbreck, was using the Internet to seek out sources for another gay-related story. "TV Dyke" (Helmbreck, at the time, was a media reporter) was the label some Wright supporters tried to pin on her.

On Sunday Nantz introduced an interview by The Golf Channel with

JoAnne Carner which, he claimed, "confirmed Ben Wright's position that much of the interview [with Helmbreck] was misreported."

Hardly. Carner said she had once told Wright a story using the word "boobs." Carner added that, in her opinion "[Helmbreck] just blew everything out of proportion to begin with, so I wouldn't believe what she says." What was Carner's opinion based on? Her friendship with Wright. Period.

All in all it was quite a show of force orchestrated by Chirkinian (using air time paid for by McDonald's), who told a reporter from CBS's Philadelphia station that Helmbreck's article was "a figment of one woman's imagination." There was just one problem. Chirkinian and Wright and Nantz had smeared Helmbreck in front of a live audience of viewers. CBS executives, particularly Kenin, were left holding a bag that slowly was beginning to stink to high heaven.

Two days ago David Kenin played in the pro-am at Wilmington with Juli Inkster. Kenin brought her a snazzy CBS Final Four jacket, a present for Inkster's caddie, Greg Johnston.

"Nice guy," says Inkster.

It's the latest of Kenin's fence-mending gestures toward the LPGA. Last week he appeared at a players' meeting in Daytona Beach and expressed his regrets.

"Nice guy," thought Caroline Pierce.

When I called Kenin in his office in New York this morning he answered the phone himself.

"Nice guy," I thought.

But also a defensive and stressed-out guy.

"I've been living with this for a year," says Kenin. "It's been so injurious to us."

No lie. Tonight *Dateline* is airing a segment with Valerie Helmbreck, making her first TV appearance since the story broke a year ago. (The segment has been in the can for weeks; NBC delayed its broadcast until the anniversary of the story, to ensure maximum publicity.) *Dateline* is expected to flay CBS (and Kenin) for the network's staunch defense of Wright and its vilification of Helmbreck, currently deciding whether to sue CBS and Wright. Numerous attorneys have contacted Helmbreck. They believe her defamation and injury-to-professional-reputation suit is worth millions.

That's not even the worst of it. The CBS golf crew, tops in the sport for decades, is unraveling at the seams. Chirkinian is slowly being eased out. Pro- and anti-Wright factions within CBS tear at each other's throats; his supporters want Wright, who just emerged from the Betty Ford Center in Rancho Mirage, California, where he recently was treated for alcohol addiction, back in the saddle. Earlier this week an embarrassed Kenin was forced to publicly state that CBS has no plans to return Wright to the tube.

Kenin, polite but agitated, refuses to answer the only two questions asked of him before he says adios.

1. Did you try to talk to Helmbreck during your investigation?
2. Was Jim Nantz's on-air editorial on the Saturday telecast—"All of us at CBS are deeply disturbed by the inaccurate and distorted [story]"—cleared by Kenin or by CBS attorneys? (The answers, it seems clear, are no and no.)

(A CBS staffer later says one of the sad legacies of the controversy is that Kenin—a nice guy and a golf nut with a reputation of supporting and promoting women at CBS—will carry around the Ben Wright fiasco like a leg iron the rest of his career. In October he will lose his job as CBS Sports president and be replaced by Sean McManus, a veteran TV executive and son of sportscaster Jim McKay.)

Lots of people assume CBS and Kenin backed Wright out of the most cynical of motives: the interview wasn't taped, so CBS was free to brazen and bluff its way through a "he said, she said" controversy that would soon be forgotten. In other words, the truth be damned, as long as the ratings points hold up. "They could easily stomp on her, so they did," *New York Times* sportswriter Richard Sandomir told *Sports Illustrated*. "Had it been a reporter they knew, Ben would have been gone."

And CBS has had plenty of experience at damage control in recent years, when other loose-cannon commentators wandered off the reservation—Jimmy "The Greek" Snyder's derogatory remarks about blacks, Andy Rooney's dopey remarks about gays and blacks, basketball analyst Bill Packer's assertion that high ratings for the 1995 Women's Final Four and for women's figure skating were inaccurate since women's sports couldn't possibly outdraw men's college hoops. (Snyder, unpopular at CBS, was canned. Rooney, one of the boys, was suspended and quickly reinstated. Packer's remarks were ridiculed.)

But Kenin genuinely seems to have believed Wright. Which, if true, raises a host of questions:

1. How could he clear Wright and put him back on the air so quickly after an "investigation" so cursory it looked at best like a whitewash?
2. How could he allow the golf crew—Chirkinian, Wright, and Nantz—to turn the CBS telecast into a pep rally for Wright?
3. And the biggest mystery of all, how could he ignore a pattern of crude and sexist remarks toward women and minorities by Wright

and Chirkinian, which, in one instance, led Chirkinian to deny statements that he had, in fact, uttered?

- 1991—Chirkinian tells *USA Today* women golf analysts aren't qualified to analyze or announce PGA events. "I don't understand what
perspective they bring. Are they in awe of the power of PGA players?
[Using them] is just a way for other networks to be different."
- 1991—Wright calls Jumbo Ozaki a "Jap" during the telecast of the
Masters.
- 1990—Wright tells *The Oregonian* newspaper in Portland, "The
women are very good at pro-ams, but I don't think the general public
knows them at all well. They're not great personalities. The last one
was probably JoAnne Carner. I love her because she'll have a cocktail
with you."
- 1989—When Chirkinian is asked by Memphis reporter Phil Stukenborg why CBS was dropping all of its LPGA telecasts in 1990, Chirkinian said:

> The last few years they have some dynamite-looking girls out
> there playing golf. And that's what the sport really needs . . . some
> striking female to take over and become a superstar. It would have
> been Nancy Lopez but Nancy turned to motherhood and so has her
> body. Nothing against Lopez or Lopez's body, but let's face it, guys
> like looking at good-looking females.

When Neal Pilson, then president of CBS Sports, questioned Chirkinian about the statement, Chirkinian told him he didn't remember talking
to Stukenborg. In fact, the interview had been conducted in a CBS trailer.
CBS, which takes to heart the old football adage that the best defense is a
good offense, attacked Stukenborg, bizarrely accusing him of using off-the-
record material overheard at a cocktail party.

One little problem: Stukenborg taped the interview.

Kenin, who took the reins of CBS Sports in 1994, was eager to believe
Wright's fervent denials. Under siege from NBC, which was gobbling up
rights to many of the glamour sports, including the Olympics, CBS Sports
was sinking almost as fast as the CBS prime-time lineup. The LPGA,
which craves air time, particularly network air time, was eager to believe
Wright as well. In addition, Charlie Mechem had used his relationship
with Chirkinian—Mechem calls him "a good friend"—to help lure CBS
back to women's golf in 1992.

When the controversy broke, vultures from *A Current Affair* and *Hard*

Copy raced to Wilmington. *Inside Edition* set up a boom mike on the putting green. The gay issue, locked in the closet for so many years, finally had burst loose.

It was the LPGA, not the U.S. military, that first adopted a tacit "don't ask, don't tell, don't pursue" policy. Fans, the media, and the general public gossiped about the LPGA for decades. The "Lesbians' Professional Golf Association" was one of the gentler insults. In her book *Are We Winning Yet?*, Mariah Nelson Burton devoted a chapter to closeted gay LPGA players. The LPGA, contended Burton, maintained "a silence so loud it screamed."

The LPGA was tone deaf. At least it pretended to be. In March 1995, two months before Ben Wright's fateful encounter with Valerie Helmbreck, in an interview in Phoenix, Mechem refused to discuss questions about the gay issue.

But in a follow-up interview a week later in Palm Springs, he cautiously addressed the subject. The words "gay" and "lesbian" never crossed his lips—instead, Mechem referred to "lifestyle." He claimed the gay issue, to his knowledge, had never cost the LPGA sponsorships; asserted that the private lives of players should indeed be private; condemned the locker room gossip about lesbians and the LPGA ("Most often from men, and often said, I think, with a smirk and in a spirit that suggests they really hope there is a problem"); and asked that the players be respected "in the same fundamental way as talented, hard-working people who have made it to the top of their profession and should be judged *only* by that standard."

Eloquent words. Words that he repeated at a jam-packed press conference last year at Wilmington on Saturday on the day after Helmbreck's story was published. But they were undercut by Chirkinian's picture-is-worth-a-thousand-words pairing of Wright and Lopez, sitting side-by-side on national TV.

Subsequently the LPGA was castigated for allowing Lopez to go on the air with Wright. Recently John Feinstein (author of *A Good Walk Spoiled*) wrote a column for *Golf* magazine stating that the LPGA "folded completely, taking the position that Wright was their buddy." Both the LPGA and Lopez claim their intent was to maintain a position of neutrality until the facts were clear. When Lopez was asked by CBS to come up to the booth to do commentary, she thought it was a routine request. The fact that CBS used her to prop up Wright irks her to no end. But so does the whole affair. Lopez got bad vibes from Helmbreck, who pounced on her for a comment about Wright's remarks when she emerged from the scorer's tent after her first round. And bad advice, she thinks, from Mechem and LPGA staffers, who okayed her appearance in the booth. LPGA staffers, for their part, claim CBS simply outfoxed and surprised them by putting Lopez on the air with Wright.

(As for Chirkinian's 1989 insults, Lopez, astonishingly, had never heard them until the 1996 Dinah Shore in Palm Springs. Lopez doesn't read critical articles. "It boggles your mind with negativeness, it really intimidates you. I read good articles to pump up my mind, to feel good and feel proud. [Husband] Ray reads everything. When he played for the Mets, I told him not to. I'd tell him, "You're going to say to yourself, 'I'm going to show them!' and then strike out four times."

As she pondered Chirkinian's words, Lopez did a slow boil. Proud of her heritage—she describes herself as Mexican American—Lopez said, "It doesn't matter what color you are, how you look, even though men put so much emphasis on looks, how much you weigh. What matters is whether you're a good person, with a good heart. I only live my life for God, for nothing else. If I live my life right, I'm going to be happy and be a good example for my kids.")

The LPGA further damaged its credibility by announcing its own investigation into the controversy. The two-week probe by LPGA general counsel Ty Votaw drew a blank. Votaw never talked to either Wright or Helmbreck. Subsequently *Golf World*'s Geoff Russell wrote, "The Tour promised to launch a probe into the issue, then investigated with the same vigor as O. J.'s search for the true killer of his ex-wife." There are still high-level LPGA officials who believe that both Wright and Helmbreck "came to the table with less than clean hands." The evidence? Lopez and Deborah Vidal, also interviewed by Helmbreck, got bad vibes from her. And some industry executives, quoted in a sidebar story which was written by a different *News Journal* staffer, told the LPGA their quotes were taken out of context. Two very slim reeds to conclude that Helmbreck had "less than clean hands."

Others in the cloistered world of golf, one of the last bastions of out-and-out sexism, still defend Wright. Columnists at *Golfweek*, a weekly magazine headquartered in Florida, continue to wring their hands over the wrongs done to Wright. And they don't let facts stand in the way of their beliefs. Media columnist Dave Shedloski claimed that the LPGA received phone calls from "witnesses" who contradicted Helmbreck's version of events. Shedloski used those "witnesses" as a hook to conclude that Wright and Helmbreck were both at fault for the controversy.

False premise. The LPGA received calls attacking both Wright and Helmbreck. They were not "witnesses" in any sense of the word, as Votaw confirms.

Dick Taylor wrote a *Golfweek* column claiming that Wright was the victim of "agenda-driven yellow journalism." His column constitutes sloppy journalism. Taylor writes that Helmbreck, according to Wright, didn't take notes when she interviewed him. Yet numerous reporters and editors at the *News Journal* saw those notes, which Taylor easily could have confirmed.

(Taylor's column, awash in homophobia, makes for fascinating reading. He fulminates about the Tour's long-standing lesbian problem, praises Lennie Wirtz, LPGA executive director in the 1960s, for convincing players to shave their legs, and reveals that he was "compelled" to counsel gay players about their lifestyle. Taylor is a member of the LPGA's Advisory Committee—the LPGA can't seem to resist sleeping, or at least fraternizing, with the enemy.)

During the Sara Lee Classic in Nashville last month, Helmbreck came to town to be honored by the First Amendment Freedom Foundation, and be interviewed for a program about the media by the local PBS station.

During a four-hour interview, Helmbreck, an animated 43-year-old, talked—and talked—and talked about her year. (One of the small ironies about the controversy is that both Helmbreck and Wright are world-class talkers.) Until recently Helmbreck was gagged by the *News Journal,* which feared Wright's threat of legal action.

In convincing detail, Helmbreck shreds Wright's defenses:

1. That he was speaking off-the-record. Helmbreck not only sat right in front of Wright in a small office furiously taking notes, she honored his midinterview request to go off-the-record when Wright told her that lesbians on the Tour have short fingernails and straight players have long fingernails.

2. That Helmbreck was pursuing a gay agenda. Actually, Helmbreck went to Du Pont Country Club to write an innocuous article about the release of a new golf fitness instructional video by a local company featuring LPGA players Lauri Merten and Cindy Rarick.

   But another *News Journal* reporter, Tom Tomashek, had the same plan. So after tossing around some other possibilities, Helmbreck was assigned to find out why the PGA was on the tube so much more than the LPGA.

3. That she was an unreliable reporter. In her 12 years with the *News Journal* Helmbreck has never been sued. Respected *News Journal* golf writer Tom Tomashek, who is quick to state he dislikes Helmbreck, never doubted her Ben Wright story. When Tomashek saw Helmbreck's notes, he thought "it sounded just like Ben." Tomashek's

description of Helmbreck? "A solid investigative reporter and a good writer." (She *is* controversial. Helmbreck is on the cover of the April issue of *Delaware Today,* her picture above the caption "Hell Raiser." She wrote a series of provocative articles about the Miss America pageants in the late 1980s and early 1990s. She was called catty, rude, and worse after an article about actress Kathleen Turner. She also won a national Best of Gannett feature award for a story about the effects of a fatal drunk-driving accident on the families of the victim and the driver.)

4. That Helmbreck set out to break a big story to advance her career. Helmbreck, totally ignorant about golf, didn't realize she *had* such a big, combustible story until other *News Journal* writers and editors got a gander at her notes.

She learned. The hate mail flowed.

Dear Ms. Helmbreck,

Congratulations. You really nailed Ben Wright. I figured the old man had it coming. Anybody in the sports limelight who's stupid enough to grant an interview with a female sports reporter deserves everybit of what he gets.

I'm looking forward to who your next victim will be. Might be sparse pickings though if they find out who you are and notice the hourglass markings on your belly. . . . At least you didn't eat him afterwards. You didn't, did you?

The attacks on her professional and personal integrity were splashed across TV screens and newspapers across America. Her parents, who live in Wilmington, watched as their daughter was branded a liar by CBS. So did her husband of 17 years, Al Mascitti, whom Helmbreck met at the University of Delaware, where they worked together on the student newspaper. So did their kids, Alexis, 14, Matt, 12, and Ben, 3, who saw their mother's name in the papers and heard the questions and whispers from their friends. Helmbreck says the ordeal left her physically ill for a year.

The bully boys almost won. But unlike Clarence Thomas, Wright's job didn't include lifetime tenure.

Wright went back to the booth. But the world-class talker couldn't keep his mouth shut. In June *Golf World* reported that Wright told dinner companions on two different occasions that he had made the remarks attributed to him, but claimed the interview was off-the-record. Wright denied the report and lived to pontificate another day. In November Kenin blessed him with a new four-year contract worth, according to reports, a bit over $1 million.

Then *Sports Illustrated*'s Michael Bamberger, tape recorder rolling, called Wright one night in late November. To Bamberger's astonishment, Wright explained the real reason why Helmbreck had smeared him: He said she was a lesbian sympathizer, possibly a lesbian herself, a divorced woman involved in a nasty custody battle who was unable to see her kids on Mother's Day—all of which was completely untrue.

Was Wright drunk?

Was he subconsciously trying to get caught?

Was he a pompous, powerful son of a bitch who thought he was untouchable despite the most outrageous lies?

Who knows? The *Sports Illustrated* story broke December 4. On January 9 Wright was suspended—not fired—by Kenin. CBS continues to pay him, although the network says it has no plans to return him to the tower.

In an ambiguous written statement, Wright declared, "Despite the fact that I have been widely misquoted, there is no doubt that I have been guilty of making some insensitive remarks." He apologized to Helmbreck "for any hurt she may have experienced."

So much for the ugly aftermath of the controversy. But what, you may ask, about the *substance* of Wright's remarks. Does the lesbian image of the LPGA Tour impair its sponsorship opportunities with corporate America?

Tom Watson thinks so. In an interview in 1993 with *Golf Digest*, Watson said, "I think there is some great talent out there, but I think the LPGA has a real problem because of the lesbian issue. I think the bottom line is, *that* hurts their ability to get good corporate sponsors. I think corporate sponsors have a very difficult time dealing with that. Whether it is right or wrong, I don't know."

Golf World's Geoff Russell disagrees. "The problem isn't that corporations don't want to spend money on lesbians. It's that they don't want to spend money on *women*."

Jim Ritts and Charlie Mechem also disagree, citing the robust health of the LPGA Tour, the cadre of loyal, long-term tournament sponsors who are completely sold on women's golf, and the addition of prestigious companies as new sponsors and licensees. If the LPGA Tour was somehow tainted, why would ITT, Safeway, Kroger, and Texas Instruments be joining the LPGA family?

On the other hand, when Mechem became LPGA commissioner, he initially met with a very chilly reception. Was the LPGA's perceived image a factor in the minds of *some* corporate and ad agency CEOs? It's a fair assumption.

Wright's crude remarks about breasts affecting a woman's swing weren't particularly newsworthy to editors at *Golf for Women,* which ran an article entitled "Bosom Buddies," about the subject in 1994. In fact, 20 years ago Jane Blalock wrote an article for *Golf Digest* that discussed lesbianism, menstrual cycles, and the swing changes necessary for women who, in Blalock's words, "are generously endowed."

So some of Wright's remarks have at least a grain of reasonableness to them. And Wright's hard-core defenders argue that his comments about lesbianism hurting women's golf and the difficulties of swinging with "boobs" were not sufficient to throw him to the wolves.

Maybe not. But his other remarks—the malarky about lesbianism being "paraded," the rubbish about a "butch" game, and the nastiness about Laura Davies—are more than sufficient to ban him from the airwaves.

Lesbianism paraded?

Until Muffin Spencer-Devlin emerged in March, every gay player in the history of the LPGA had remained locked in the closet. Except for a few gold bands on the ring fingers of players who are single (at least in the eyes of the law), gay players zealously hide their relationships from the general public.

Wright seems flummoxed and discombobulated by the very notion that some LPGA players are gay, and that, within the close-mouthed, protective world of the LPGA, such players are honest about their sexual orientation.

A "butch" game?

The exciting, high-powered, big-hitting games of Davies, Robbins, and McGann—none of whom, by the way, are gay—are no more "butch" than the in-your-face, baseline-to-baseline excitement of the U.S. women's basketball team. Wright seems utterly undone by the notion that there are women who are physically strong and powerful.

As Deb Price, a nationally syndicated columnist on gay and lesbian issues, wrote, "What you're seeing here is a kind of intimidation of all women that if they don't look and behave a certain way, in that sort of weak Barbie doll way that pleases some men, there will be punishment."

A casino rat who is built like a tank?

A fairly harsh description of the most popular woman athlete in Britain.

Although Davies publicly shrugged off the remarks—"If I'm a tank, he's a blimp"—the words cut like a rapier. Davies used to be ultrasensitive to her appearance—she wore sweaters or jackets in sweltering weather in an attempt to disguise her size. Now she's merely sensitive about it. In addition, she considered Wright to be a friend. They played together in a pro-am in Hawaii and got along famously. "I thought he was a nice guy," says Davies. "I certainly don't like him now."

Perhaps people who live in glass houses shouldn't throw clubs. Taken as a whole, Wright's remarks reek of arrogance, sexism, and all-around nastiness. As did Chirkinian's remarks about Nancy Lopez.

Still, there may be a place in golf for Wright and Chirkinian after all. A place where they can hang out with the boys during the day and ogle the girls, courtesy of the tour's sponsor, at night.

It's called the Hooters Tour.

Funny how the golf ball bounces. One year after the *News Journal* story was published, Ben Wright is at home after his stint at the Betty Ford Clinic, a diminished figure in every sense. Frank Chirkinian, "The Ayatollah," has lost grip on power, and soon will be forced from his producer's chair at CBS and into retirement. NBC is rubbing CBS's nose in its own mess on *Date-line.* Valerie Helmbreck is explaining to the nation how she was wronged.

And very convincingly too, although to date neither CBS nor the LPGA has apologized to Helmbreck. (Kenin issued a blanket apology after his pro-am round on Wednesday, saying, "We feel terrible about any harm that was done to anybody." But CBS has never directly apologized to Helmbreck. So it appears the network is still, to some extent, blaming the victim for its own disgraceful behavior.)

Helmbreck is neither an angel nor a saint. She's simply an excellent reporter who did her job and was vilified and slandered for doing it. An editorial from, of all places, the *Columbus* (Georgia) *Ledger-Enquirer* may have best summed up the whole sad episode: "Wright Makes Two-Footer."

That's Wright—*both* feet in his mouth.

After an overnight thunderstorm and a 30-minute fog delay, Saturday's second round opens under muggy, breezy blue skies. But the forecasters warn of more storms, perhaps even tornadoes, approaching Delaware.

"We ought to get the Weather Channel to broadcast this tournament next year," says media director Jim Murray. "In fact, maybe we ought to get the Weather Channel to sponsor it."

It's a lovely morning, however, with sunlight dancing through the golden-tinged apple-green leaves of the soaring maple trees lining the fairways. Robins chirp; ducks feed by the edges of streams. Terra firma, however, isn't. Fans slip and slide through fetid, muddy paths near many of the yellow gallery ropes. *Golf World*'s John Hawkins writes that it's "like walking on a birthday cake." Still, the course is packed like a sardine tin, every green ringed with fans. Yesterday's attendance of 22,900 was more than the final-round attendance at most LPGA events. Today's estimate is a whopping 30,600.

Fortunes rise and fall like the barometer:

Caroline Pierce sees her name on the leader board under "Hot Rounds" as she and playing partner Kris Tschetter get to three under par for the day. Yesterday Pierce hit the ball superbly, never made a putt, and appeared likely to miss the cut. Today she's hitting the ball decently, rolling in the putts, and en route to a 69, one of the best rounds of the day.

So is Kris Tschetter until she knocks a little wedge into a greenside bunker on the 465-yard 16th hole. Thinking birdie, she leaves the green with bogey.

It's been that kind of year for Tschetter, a vivacious 31-year-old perhaps best known for her friendship with Ben Hogan, who met her when she was a teenager hitting balls on the range at Shady Oaks in Houston. Hogan, who truly turned the range into an assembly line, manufacturing, hour after hour, a swing for the ages, liked what he saw. Although normally aloof, Hogan and his wife struck up a strong friendship with the aspiring youngster, who turned to golf after once dreaming of a career as a ballet dancer. ("I tried out for the School of American Ballet when I was 16," says Tschetter. "I was too old—it was awful to be 16 and be told you were too old! They didn't accept me so I said, 'Well, all right, I'll be a golfer instead.'")

With a few tips from Hogan and lots of work with teacher, caddie, and fiancé Kirk Lucas, Tschetter has become one of the best ball-strikers on Tour. In 1995 she vied for stardom, ranking twelfth on the money list with earnings of $363,202.

In 1996 it's been more of a struggle, although Tschetter's lone top-ten finish came in a major, the Dinah Shore. Two weeks ago in Atlanta, Tschetter opened the tournament 7, 6, 8—eight over par—then played the next 33 holes in four under par and eventually finished, remarkably enough, in a tie for twenty-eighth.

Tschetter has a penchant for fashionable, sexy outfits. She wore a little black dress at the JAL Big Apple Classic last year and signed a major endorsement deal with Liz Claiborne. But she's much more substance than style, a player at her best in big events.

On the 156-yard 17th hole, Tschetter smacks it all over the green, barely managing to three-putt. In two holes she's kicked away a fine round, and appears unlikely to make the cut. She seems more stunned than angry as she walks back to her white Ping bag, where Kirk gently grasps her elbow in silent sympathy.

*   *   *

Leslie Spalding tees off at 2:00 P.M. in the third-to-last group of the day—her 70 yesterday leaves her just three shots back of the leader, Sweden's Catrin Nilsmark. She's playing with Annika Sorenstam and Tina Barrett, and the crowd following the group is enormous.

This is the biggest test of Spalding's career. First major, first time in contention, first superstar pairing. In her plain navy blue jersey and khaki shorts, she looks a bit out of place next to Sorenstam, impeccably attired in her expensive Callaway golf togs.

Pierce, Tschetter, and the other players with morning tee times finish just in time. The wind is howling now, furiously whipping the cloth of the flagsticks back and forth.

Sorenstam, who has quietly become a sneakily long hitter, blows her drive 25 yards past Spalding and Barrett. Spalding hits an iron to the fringe and then stands over a relatively easy chip for endless seconds. From a distance, she looks calm and composed, but up close you can see her, almost imperceptibly, shaking. And it isn't cold out.

Her weak chip stops five feet short. She pulls her par putt badly to the left. It's a start that does nothing to calm her jangling nerves. On the 400-yard 2nd hole, Spalding leaves a long fairway bunker shot well short of the green and kicks at the sand. On the 372-yard 3rd hole, after a magnificent, aggressive drive over the corner of a pond guarding the left side of the fairway, she comes up short of the green on her second shot and pulls a four-foot par putt. She walks off the green plucking at her shirt. She's ready to dive into the pond and escape from the eyes of the crowd, sympathetic, but judging her a failure.

Encircled by fans crowding around the tee box at the 370-yard 4th hole, Spalding keeps fighting, crushing a drive down the fairway. "There you go," says caddie Scott Turner. The crowd cheers. Spalding gives them a nice smile and that little Donna Andrews–like palms up acknowledgment of appreciation. After a great iron to 12 feet, trying to stem the tide of black numbers on the scoreboard, signifying bogeys, Spalding charges the putt. Turner stretches out a leg trying to coax it in with body English, but to no avail, and Spalding barely curls in a nasty four-foot comebacker to save par.

Black clouds begin rolling across the sky. The flags are absolutely stiff now, as spectators anxiously scan the horizon. Spalding blocks an iron badly to the right on the 167-yard 5th hole. With a yawning bunker between her and the pin, and little green to work with, she hits a brave, high, soft flop shot that checks up six feet from the cup.

"Great shot!" Sorenstam calls out, although the wind is making too much of a racket for Spalding to hear the compliment.

Great shot. Terrible putt. Overcompensating for her nervousness, Spalding smashes the ball over the edge of the cup for her fourth bogey in five holes. She walks off the green looking pale and ill, and flips her putter at her bag.

An hour ago, she was a contender. Now she's fighting what appears to be a losing battle to make the cut. Casual fans might say Spalding choked today. But choking is an overused, simplistic notion. As Johnny Miller puts it, "Everyone has their own choking level, a level at which he fails to play his normal game. As you get more experienced, your choking level rises."

Nancy Lopez supplies an early jolt of electricity, birdieing four of her first six holes to burst into a two-stroke lead at six under par. Lopez is playing with Helen Alfredsson and Emilee Klein. The group is slow as molasses.

On the 192-yard 8th hole, while the wind swirls and howls, Alfredsson twice changes clubs, then fidgets over the ball for a good 60 seconds. Alfredsson is in a slump, obsessed with technical flaws in her swing.

"Is She Crazy or What?" blared the title of a feature story about Alfredsson in *Golf Digest* in 1994. Well, sort of. Alfredsson has packed lots of living into her 30 years, showing up for high school classes after all-night escapades, traipsing off to Paris to become a model, creating a sensation as a student at the U.S. International University in San Diego by having an affair with former Mexican World Cup soccer player Leo Cuellar (who at the time was the school's soccer coach and a still-married father), cursing at golf balls like a drunken Swedish sailor, and driving cars and motorcycles with the pedal to the metal—at a drag-racing school in Florida earlier in the year, Alfredsson topped out at 164.05, smoking PGA pros Davis Love, Bruce Lietzke, Kenny Perry, and Jay Don Blake.

"She's a lunatic," says Laura Davies.

"She's nuts," says Meg Mallon.

"She's probably my favorite playing partner," says Juli Inkster. "She's fiery, like me."

Perhaps too fiery.

"She just wants to get the ball in the hole so badly," says Pia Nilsson. "Her problem is staying patient and calm."

Especially on the greens, where Alfredsson probably moves her head more than anyone in the game, looking for the ball to disappear into the cup almost before she completes her backswing. When she blew a seven-stroke lead at the 1994 U.S. Open, she twitched and fidgited so much it was almost as painful for the viewers as for her.

"A lot of people think, 'Oh, she's gone,'" says Nilsson, referring to Alfredsson's mediocre play so far in 1996. "But she's such a fighter. I think she will be better than before. She's a natural talent, but she got lost. Lots of people are giving her advice. You have to decide who you want to listen to."

Right now, she's locked in a straitjacket of swing theories, unable to take the club back. As Alfie tries to figure out what it's all about, you can almost hear the huge gallery silently shouting one specific piece of advice—"Just hit the damn ball!"

A few minutes later Alfredsson misses a par putt, stalks off the green in a blind fury, and slams her putter into her Taylor-Made bag with such force it almost breaks through the bottom. Leo Cuellar, Alfredsson's long-time fiancé, is caddying for her this week. Standing next to his raging Swedish volcano, Cuellar is as stoic as a stone.

Lopez bogeys but retains her lead as she makes the turn. "Naannceeee!!" booms a voice as Lopez walks through the throng on her way to the 10th tee. "Go get 'em!!"

She never has a chance. By the time Lopez completes No. 11, bruised-looking purple and black clouds settle over Du Pont Country Club. A siren sounds. Play is suspended. Rain falls in buckets. Hail pings off cars in the parking lot. Tornado watches are posted.

The second round will resume tomorrow morning at 7:30 for the 69 players chased in by the storm. The third and final round will follow. It promises to be a long, long day.

But the media demands to be fed, including CBS, confronted with the unappetizing choice between: (1) broadcasting rain-saturated empty fairways and greens; (2) replaying last year's event (not bloody likely!); or (3) conducting a bunch of interviews.

A stream of players troop in to face the cameras and the notepads. Laura Davies sings the praises of Nancy Lopez. "I played with her last week at Daytona. She was hitting everything at the stick."

Davies also sings the praises of the Tour in general. "It doesn't matter who you're paired with now. You can just stand back and watch the great golf. If you go to sleep at all, everyone is going to go by you. You've got to get better, and that's magnificent for everyone."

Her one complaint? The pace of play, much slower on the LPGA Tour than in Europe. "On a weekly basis, it's terrifically slow," says Davies.

Shirley Furlong, rebounding nicely after her disastrous final round in Nashville, gets her bearings. "Oh gosh. I haven't been here [the interview room] for so long. . . ." Furlong took a four-shot lead over Betsy King into the final round of the McDonald's in 1989 and promptly birdied the first two holes. "Walking from the second to the third hole, it hit me that I had a six-stroke lead on Betsy King, and I thought 'Wow!'" By No. 10 they were tied; King eventually won and Furlong tied for second. "It was a learning experience for me," says Furlong. "I learned how easy it is for your mind to go off on another tangent."

Nancy Lopez enthralls the media with a detailed description of her new exercise routine and diet. Major revelation—Lopez weighed 129 when she married Ray in 1982. The 30 pounds she has shed since January hasn't quite reduced her to her wedding day weight, but she's in the ball park.

The changes in her physique have been matched by the changes in her attitude. "Things don't bother me as much. I don't gripe at Ray as much. It's just changed my whole life."

But she's not as sanguine about reporters who suggest that Karrie Webb's sensational rookie year matches or even outshines her own in 1978. That's a direct hit at her most vulnerable area, her pride. "When I [turned pro], I didn't care what it took. I wanted to win. I know how hard I worked to accomplish that."

"The players that played then are just as good as the players now," Lopez says forcefully. "I had total respect for them. I was in awe of them."

With good reason. Lopez, who turned pro after her sophomore season at the University of Tulsa—and after tying for third at the U.S. Open as a teenager in 1975—was facing heavyweights, not cream puffs: JoAnne Carner, Jane Blalock, Sandra Palmer, Sally Little, Hollis Stacy, Amy Alcott, Pat Bradley, Kathy Whitworth, Donna Caponi. A murderer's row of champions and future Hall of Famers.

They went down like dominoes. Lopez set a new LPGA record for earnings ($189,813), became the first LPGA player in history to average fewer than 72 strokes per round (71.76), won a record five consecutive events and a total of nine for the season, and carted home enough trophies to fill a museum.

Lopez subtly reminds the scribes at Wilmington that no one has handled the pressure of sudden stardom—both on and off the course—as well as she did. "Lots of players can win one or two, but they don't feel comfortable there. Karrie seems to feel comfortable there."

Was *she* comfortable there? asks a writer.

"Heck, yeah," Lopez says, the trademark smile lighting up the room. "I liked the attention. People were really good to me. I enjoyed everything about it."

And while you can argue that Webb's smashing debut, achieved against fields much deeper that Lopez faced, puts her in the same league on the links, as a cultural phenomenon the two were operating on different planets.

Webb's play has been a big story in the golf world. But as far as the general public is concerned, the word Webb conjures up visions of computers and arachnids. Although the media in Australia have gone wild over the young star, she's rarely if ever recognized in the U.S. when she leaves the golf course. Lopez, on the other hand, transcended golf, and even the sports world, as a celebrity. During her winning streak she appeared on *Good Morning, America*. *The New York Times Magazine* made her their cover girl. Cabbies rolled down their windows to yell encouragement as she walked down the streets of Manhattan.

Asked if Alfredsson's slow play had distracted her, Lopez, notoriously slow herself, shakes her head. "Nothing bothers me but that stinking hole in the ground." Lamenting two birdie putts in the six-foot range that she had missed, Lopez says, "The old Nancy wouldn't have missed those putts. That's the only thing that aggravates me. Tonight, when I lay down by myself, I'll think about those putts."

The news on Mother's Day, Sunday morning, is grim. A Valujet airplane carrying 110 passengers plunges into the swamps of the Everglades and is swallowed up.

Yesterday the temperature crested at a muggy 83 degrees before the storm blew in. It was a monster—roofs were ripped off houses and 24,000 homes lost electricity. It even brought snowflakes to higher terrain.

The wind-chill is in the 30s this morning. It feels a lot colder, with gusts up to 33 mph. A local news anchor sums it up, accurately, if not very scientifically: "Weird weather!"

Players stumble into the frigid, howling early morning winds, wearing earmuffs and mittens. Fortunes are blown asunder. First-round leader Catrin Nilsmark, last off Saturday, has to finish the final eight holes of her washed-out second round. She winds up shooting 82, including a stretch of scores that she probably hasn't shot since she was a youngster—6, 5, 6, 5, 5, 5, 5, 5. Nilsmark misses the cut, one of the few first-round leaders on any tour to achieve such a dubious distinction. In the coldest weather she's played in since a snowy round in a high school match in Montana, Leslie Spalding shoots 41 on the back nine—and actually plays quite well—for an 81. Nancy Lopez, five over par on her final six holes, shoots 41 and tumbles off the leader board. (Tomorrow morning *USA Today* will run a picture of an agonized Lopez with her hand spread over her face. She appears to be trying to Vulcan Mind Meld herself to infuse the putting prowess of the 20-year-old Lopez. She and Bauer dissolve in laughter when they see it.)

The cut, projected at 146, four over par, rises to 148 when all the damage is toted up. Tracy Kerdyk, who drove to Washington, D.C., after shooting 148, races back to Wilmington after casually calling in to check on scores.

The Sunday sermon for the day?

And the last shall be first.

Well, it's not *quite* that dramatic. But the second round concludes with 39 players within five strokes of the lead. Everyone, it seems, is back in the hunt. Caroline Pierce left the course yesterday buried in the pack. She returns this morning to find she's moved up about two dozen places without swinging a club. Sweet dreams, indeed.

Not to mention a huge break for her and everyone else who completed their rounds yesterday. At the Dinah Shore, Pierce got shafted by "the flip," as the players call it, the early first round followed by a late second round (or vice versa) tee time. But sooner or later, the breaks even out.

Patty Sheehan is back in the hunt too, gunning for her second straight major. Sheehan is at one over par after two rounds, just three strokes back of the leader Kelly Robbins. But then—disaster. She misses her tee time, arriving at the 10th tee at 11:35 for her 11:33 appointment, and is promptly assessed a two-stroke penalty. Sheehan is livid. For all her impishness, Sheehan is the consummate professional. She's never missed a tee time in her 17-year career.

The Caddie Machine is stunned. To his horror, he discovers his watch is 10 minutes slow. As keeper of the timepiece, the blunder, as inexcusable as an attorney strolling in late for an argument before the Supreme Court, is on his head.

Team Sheehan suspects foul play. Laib leaves his watch in plain view on Sheehan's golf bag. The watch has always been right on the money. How did it suddenly lose 10 minutes? (The suspicion deepens when Laib later tests the watch and finds it to be working flawlessly.)

In a cold fury Sheehan scorches the back nine in 33, an almost superhuman score in these playing conditions, at one point climbing to second on the leader board. She finishes with an even par 71. It would have been the only score of the day in the 60s without the penalty strokes. Instead of a tie for third, she ties for tenth, a difference of over $40,000. Sheehan endorses Rolex, but, as it turns out, Laib's is the most expensive timepiece she's ever seen.

The trio of Inkster, Pierce, and Deb Richard complete the front nine and walk down the 10th fairway.

Giant red flags with the McDonald's logo decorating walkways along the fairway whip so furiously that the WHAP, WHAP, WHAP sound of the cloth snapping back and forth sounds like whirling helicopter blades.

"It's not golf weather," says a fan. "It's football weather." Yeah, *lousy* football weather, the kind that leaves you shivering under a thick woolen blanket, slurping a Thermos of hot coffee while your nose drips and your teeth chatter. There are 19,200 hardy—or foolhardy—souls trudging along the muddy edges of the fairways, a remarkable turnout given the inhospitable conditions.

The greens, soft from the rain and pockmarked from the golfers' spikes, are spotted with *Poa annua,* a weedlike plant that is the acne of greenskeepers. Players confronted with putts over the scraggly blades of the weed can only rap them with authority and hope they stay on line. On these greens—and with this wind, which plays havoc with balance and touch—even foot-long tap-ins can turn into an adventure.

Inkster is coming off a tie for ninth at the Sprint last week after closing with a final round 66. "It was nice to play well on Sunday." She's dressed in a dark pink sweater and black slacks. Her black thatch of hair is blown sideways in the wind, like the flags on the flagsticks. She misses a beautifully struck birdie putt that curls around the cup, leaving her three over par for the tournament. She stands at the edge of the green, shoulders hunched against the cold, shivering. Later Inkster will say, "It was a survival test out there." Only once in her 14-year career has Inkster played in worse conditions—a round in Seattle in 1983, when she fought through temperatures in the 40s, wind, rain, and hail to reach the winner's circle.

Pierce, in a cream jersey and blue rain pants, lines up a short slippery five-foot birdie putt that will bring her back to two over par for the tournament, solidly in contention. She leaves the putt short, looks at caddie Rick Aune, and almost giggles in disbelief.

On the 528-yard 11th hole Deb Richard, a star from 1990 to 1994 before back problems and eventual back surgery in 1995 compromised her form and threatened her career, lines up her pitch shot. She backs off when a straw hat begins rolling across the fairway, and a little girl, on a Mother's Day outing with her mother and grandmother, races out to retrieve it. "Next time you need to wear an elastic band," says Mom. It's not a great day for hats: if a good gust of wind hits Pierce's long-beaked black baseball cap at the right angle, it could flatten her. On the 357-yard 12th hole Richard backs off a putt when wind blows a piece of debris into her eye.

But it's a group with great spirit and lots of jokes and mutual encouragement, despite the weather, despite the fact that all three are still in contention, despite the fact that they're grinding their hearts out.

Inkster blocks an iron well to the right on the 184-yard 13th hole, then hits a fabulous wedge over a gaping bunker to eight feet of the cup. Inkster studies a nearby leader board. The leaders are at one over par. Judy Dickinson, playing brilliantly, is at two over par through 17 holes. Under these conditions, two over par would be a very sweet score to take into the warmth of the clubhouse. Inkster knows a bogey will all but doom her chances.

It's times like these that test a golfer's skill and nerve and heart and courage in ways that other athletes, usually caught up in the headlong rush of action and movement, find horrifying. As George Plimpton wrote in *The Bogey Man,*

> There was not an athlete I had talked to from other sports—the roughest of them: football, hockey, basketball—who did not hold the professional golfer in complete awe, with thanksgiving that golf was not *their* profession. The idea of standing over a putt with thousands of dollars in the balance was enough to make them flap their fingers as if singed. They would have none of it.

When Inkster rolls the putt into the cup she raises her hands overhead in a kind of exaggerated shrug, as if to say, "How'd I do that?" Pierce and Aune, standing at the edge of the green, smile in appreciation.

The 390-yard 14th hole is a monstrous beast today, playing into a howling wind. It simply overpowers Pierce, who hits a solid drive and solid 3-wood, which dives into a fairway bunker about 20 yards directly in front of the green. Pierce barely scrapes her long bunker shot onto the front of the green and then, battling like crazy, almost sinks her 50-foot par putt, the ball hitting the cup and spinning out. She's four over par now, and her chances are almost gone.

Not Inkster's. She rifles a sensational iron to ten feet on the 392-yard 15th hole, gets a good read from Pierce's longer putt, which is on the same line, and drains the birdie to get back to two over par. Inkster pumps a fist softly as the ball disappears.

"Great bird," says a fan.

"Great bird," says caddie Johnston.

It's a kick to watch Inkster. You know exactly how she stands, from moment to moment, just by watching her face. Smiles, frowns, grimaces, sighs—the whole wide world of emotion, agony and ecstasy, victory and defeat. CBS likes her chances too—on-course cameramen and a gray-haired woman with a conical-shaped microphone have been tracking her down the last few fairways.

The tee box at the 465-yard 16th hole, the last good birdie opportunity, is tucked away in a grove of maple trees. It's a challenging driving hole, a tight dogleg right. You can see Inkster's confidence surging the last few holes, and she absolutely crushes her drive, the ball soaring over the corner of the dogleg.

"Nice shot" rings out from Pierce and Richard and the caddies. Inkster playfully pumps her fist and dances a quick little dance—kind of a Texas two-step of pleasure.

After a lay-up shot that catches thick rough on the edge of the fairway, her wedge just clears the front bunker and rolls straight toward the flag.

"Get in!" yells the five-deep throng ringing the green. It almost does, barely missing the stick and rolling six feet past.

Moment of truth.

All of Inkster's work for the last two and a half years, the thousands of hours beating balls on the practice range and stroking putts on the practice green, designed to improve her already phenomenal game, to turn a mere mortal into something closer to a divine golfing machine, capable of surviving and even thriving under the excruciating pressure cooker of the final holes of a major championship, is represented in the form of a six-foot birdie putt which will tie her for the lead.

The hush of the crowd dissolves in groans as Inkster comes off the putt and pushes it to the right. The moment is lost.

She fights on. On the 156-yard 17th hole, lined by a chute of trees, with wind howling through the swaying branches, Inkster fires an iron to 25 feet. "All right, Juli, good shot," says Richard, rooting for her playing partner.

But Inkster's birdie putt, much like her bid for victory, comes up an agonizing three inches short of pay dirt.

Pierce, meanwhile, is tossing a big payday to the wind, bogeying 17 and pushing her drive on the ferocious 399-yard 18th hole, a dogleg left with an uphill second shot to a green surrounded by grandstands that is playing dead into the wind.

Whacking her driver into the turf four times as she stalks off the tee, Pierce furiously berates herself. "I didn't trust my swing the last few holes," she'll say later. From the thick rough she is forced to lay up in front of a stream not more than 100 yards in front of her. She misses the green with a long-iron third shot and eventually double-bogeys. The last two holes cost her over $10,000, the kind of heavy price a pro usually pays for a late-round leakage of confidence.

Inkster, meanwhile, needs a miraculous birdie to tie Julie Piers, who finishes at one over par after a superlative 70. Piers (formerly Larson before her marriage last November) is at her best in big events, in bad weather, and on tough courses. She finished third in the 1995 U.S. Open and placed twenty-second on the money list with $258,602. She's in the clubhouse and catbird seat, as a host of contenders at one over par and two over par battle the weather, their nerves, and the final holes.

"A Hundred and ninety-five?" Inkster asks Johnston, after a drive that just catches the fairway.

"A Hundred and ninety-five," says Johnston.

Into the teeth of the wind, unprotected by the trees. The spectators along the ropes behind Inkster are hunched over against the gale, as Richard, in casual water on the edge of the rough, waits for a rules official to show up. Richard catches a break—her point of relief is in the fairway. Inkster, also in casual water, pondering her options as she peers over the creek and up the long steady incline to the green and the flagstick, asks the rules officials:

"Real quick [question], can I drop from fairway to rough?"

Yes, she's told. Inkster knows she can't get a 5-wood back to the pin in this wind. But a 3-wood is too much club. So if she takes relief by moving back a bit, the 3-wood will be closer to the right weapon.

Struck smartly, but pulled just a tiny bit, the shot runs through the green into the rough near the grandstand. With a near-impossible chip down a bank, she hits a mediocre shot and two-putts for bogey. A sparkly, fizzly, ice-cold 7-Up day, a day of sky-high hopes, ends on a flat, anticlimactic note.

"Can I have a ball?" a fan yells out as Inkster trudges through the packed gallery around the green to the scorer's tent.

Inkster throws up her hands in a gesture of frustration and resignation and irritation.

"You can have everything I have."

Inkster played magnificently. It's a big step forward for her, proof positive the swing changes are paying off. She ties for fifth, earns $37,800, and boosts her Solheim Cup chances. Not a bad Mother's Day. (Inkster and Dickinson, who bogeyed the final hole, are the week's leading mommy winners.)

But champions don't settle for also-ran finishes. At this moment, Inkster is disgusted, ready to give away golf balls, gloves, shoes, clubs, maybe everything except Brian and the kids and the Louisville Slugger from Ken Griffey, Jr.

Three reporters wait for her as she leaves the scorer's tent. Down in the dumps, Inkster laments a double-bogey on 8, which forced her to play catch-up the rest of the day. Back in January Inkster resolved not to be so tough on herself, to be her own best friend. She's not having much success at the moment, but finally she does offer herself a little pat on the back.

"I played about as good as I could."

As it turns out, not even a miracle last-hole birdie by Inkster would have done the trick. As Inkster is finishing her round, Laura Davies breaks out of a logjam of players at one and two over par, rolling in a 15-foot birdie putt on the 16th hole to assume the lead at even par.

What a difference a year makes. In 1995 Davies, dueling down the stretch womano-a-womano with Kelly Robbins, lost the tournament on 16 with a lousy wedge and even worse three-putt for bogey. Robbins took advantage of the gift, birdied the hole, and prevailed by one shot.

Davies has won 41 events around the globe. But she's never been known as a great closer. When Davies and Donna Andrews fought it out on the final nine at the 1994 Dinah Shore, the Blonde British Bomber shakily missed several short birdie putts before butchering the last hole by failing to find the fairway with a play-it-safe-and-smart 4-iron off the tee.

But yesterday Davies told the media how she's had to elevate her game to compete with Webb and Sorenstam and Robbins and Pepper. And today, she offers tangible proof. Davies has been near or at the top of the leader board all day, after playing two holes (double-bogey, par) to complete her second round this morning. And, under the dreadful conditions and intense pressure, she's been as steady as any golfer could be.

The birdie at No. 16 breaks a string of 15 straight final-round pars, featuring crucial three- and four-foot par saves time and time again. Usually, confronting such a series of must putts is like walking into a succession of lion's dens. Sooner or later, you're lunch meat.

But Davies is a different breed of cat this year. Last year she was labeled a tank and a casino rat and ended her week in Wilmington by kicking away a major tournament. This year she is extolled in the pages of *The New York Times* by Larry Dorman, who writes:

> She is to women's golf what John Daly is to men's golf, what Michael Jordan is to the NBA, what Frank Thomas is to major league baseball. She is the player who can take it deep, the force, the franchise.

Her peers, by and large, adore and marvel at her, going gaga when she pulls out her Maruman driver and aims over the tall white oaks that guard the left side of the dogleg on the 399-yard 18th hole, an act requiring such bravado and strength—it's a 240-yard carry over the dogleg and creek and trees—that it seems a superhuman feat.

Davies often seems larger than life. As Rhonda Glenn puts it, "She plays like Babe Ruth on the course and talks like Queen Elizabeth off it." Royalty without airs or arrogance: Davies isn't the straightest hitter on the links, but she's a straight-shooter the rest of the time, direct, unpretentious, and possessing a dry, deadpan wit.

During the Standard Register Ping in Phoenix, Davies played basketball several times with Karrie Webb, a few other players and caddies, and some local kids in a full-court gym above the pro shop. A few writers asked for her assessment of her game. Davies, who prides herself as a fine athlete—she plays a mean game of tennis, soccer, and cricket—laid it on the line.

"Absolute crap."

"How's your shooting?" she was asked.

"Absolute crap."

Never afraid to throw the dice, the 33-year-old is a high-roller on the green-felt tables of Las Vegas, casino royalty at Bally's, a pedal-to-the-metal hellion on the autobahn, a swooshing blur in a BMW cranked up to 160 mph, and a take-no-prisoners golfer who, in the words of Judy Rankin, "tries to grind her opponents into the dust" before she picks them up, brushes them off, and win or lose, tells them, "Jolly good show, mate." Davies marches to the beat of her own drummer, and it's a raise-the-roof, rock-the-heavens, roll over Beethoven, teeth-rattling joyous assault.

"She whacks it and finds it, and whacks it again, and doesn't worry about it," says Julie Piers. "I take dead aim down the middle, and dead aim at the pin," says Davies, who could be talking about her life off as well as on the course. "I hate laying up. I hate leaving it short. It's just all-out attack."

Her attitude is much admired by Inkster. "She plays for herself. She doesn't let anyone dictate her life. That's great to see in a woman."

It's not a bad life for someone who worked as a bookmaker's assistant, grocery store clerk, and a gas station attendant before turning pro. But it's not always easy being Laura Davies. She knows that people talk about her size. "Laura's a heavy subject," cracked a writer in the media center a few days ago. She may seem larger-than-life, but she bleeds as easily as the rest of us. She tries not to eat on the golf course, lest someone snap a picture. In 1992, after seeing an ad for Ultra-Slim Fast starring Tommy Lasorda, she used the diet drink to reduce from around 230 pounds to 180 pounds. It was too much. Now she carries about 200 pounds on her five-foot-ten frame and looks marvelous.

A shy person, Davies surrounds herself with family members on the road—her cousin and caddie, Matt, her father, Dave, who lives in the States and attends a number of tournaments. Older brother Tony, who introduced her to the game, serves as her business manager and scheduler. She shares an elegant $700,000 house near London, complete with a soccer field, tennis court, pitch-and-putt golf course, indoor pool, and 18 TV sets with her mother and stepfather, Rita and Mike Allen. If her pals aren't around—Davies is buddies with Australian sisters Mardi and Karen Lunn, Karrie Webb, Brandie Burton, and a number of European players—she'll call room service rather than venture to dinner on her own in a hotel restaurant.

So when Ben Wright teed off on her, the words angered her many friends on Tour. "A lovely person," says Pierce, "with a great perspective on life. She's very feminine for a big woman in speech and manners. That gets overlooked because of her size."

* * *

Clinging to a one-shot lead as she comes to No. 18, Davies confronts a final hole that, even for her, is brutal today. Not even the Bambino himself could launch a drive over the corner.

So instead she crunches a 2-iron down the fairway but pulls, ever so slightly, a 3-iron, which the wind blows into a bunker short and to the left of the green.

A playoff seems certain.

Even after Davies's superb long bunker shot checks up eight feet above the pin, a playoff still seems likely. The hole on No. 18, resting on a slight crown, has had a lid over it for most of the contenders.

It's the ultimate test of a delicate stroke and iron nerves, the ultimate test of steadiness under pressure, a test that Davies, for all her victories, often has failed.

Not now. Rock solid over the ball, brimming with confidence—"it's a dead straight putt," she tells herself—Davies rolls the ball into the heart, a final sweet redemption and reversal of fortune. "This was the best round of golf I've ever played under pressure. To have no bogeys on that golf course, the way it was playing, to make all my three- and four-footers. It didn't take that much to have one get away from you."

Somehow the saga seems incomplete. We need a fitting wrap-up to the year of upheaval created by the Ben Wright controversy. After all, as a source at CBS revealed, CBS employees have gone through sensitivity-training sessions in the wake of the controversy.

Has it paid off? Let's eavesdrop on the joke Jim Nantz will tell to a roomful of writers and golf officials, including a number of LPGA staffers, at the Metropolitan Golf Writers Dinner in New York in a few weeks. After a chicken dinner, Nantz ambles to the microphone and says, "That dinner reminds me of Hillary Clinton: All thigh and no breast." A bit of laughter is followed by an embarrassed silence.

Oops. Maybe Nantz fell asleep in class. Maybe a pig ate his homework assignment.

Obviously, what is needed is a voice of sanity, a voice of level-headed common sense, a voice of tolerance, a voice of experience, a voice of wisdom.

When the Ben Wright story broke last year, Betsy Rawls seemed to have blamed the messenger. "It was a terrible story," she said. "It never should have been printed."

But when asked a few days ago about the gay label that so often is slapped on women athletes, and particularly the LPGA, Rawls, after a moment of silence, warmed to the subject.

"It's not based on anything that makes *sense*," offered Rawls. "Women athletes don't fit the traditional stereotype of women, the image of house-wives and mothers who stay home and raise a family. In my day, most of us never considered mixing a career and a family life. Bob Hagge [husband of Alice Bauer Hagge] traveled with the Tour [in the 1950s and 1960s] and people looked at him with great scorn.

"The two lifestyles were not mixed then. Now they are. Maybe some people haven't gotten used to that.

"I don't know why physically talented women are associated with les-bianism. In a few years, the subject won't even come up. Women athletes *and* lesbians will be more accepted."

CHAPTER 6

Southern Pines:
A Coronation in a Cathedral

Open Fever.

At six o'clock on Monday morning, May 27, Carl Laib walks Pine Needles, the Donald Ross–designed course that rolls through a forest of towering longleaf pine trees. (Longleaf pines are distinguished by their long needles and jumbo-size cones, some almost as big as footballs.)

The Caddie Machine is the only person on the course, pacing out yardages and studying the lay of the land as the shadows of night slowly are washed away by the sun rising through the pines. Quail, rabbits, possums, woodpeckers, and foxes frolic in the forest, planted a century ago by entrepreneur James Walker Tufts, who turned the Pinehurst area from a wasteland into the mecca of American golf.

But by nine o'clock, when Laib steps off the final yardages on the 418-yard 18th hole, which doglegs left and then tumbles down a long, steep slope to a green set in a natural amphitheater and ringed by grandstands, the course, to Laib's surprise, "is a madhouse."

At most LPGA tournament sites, Monday is as quiet as a schoolyard during summer vacation, as players slowly drift into town. Not here. Not this week. Golfers flood the putting green, located just a few feet from the back door of the clubhouse, a two-story rustic lodge.

Open Fever.

That's what the players call it. "You get so set in your ways [on Tour]," says Caroline Pierce, playing in her eighth U.S. Women's Open. "Everything is quite structured. The Open upsets your routine. Players are so excited they play eighteen on Monday. You never see that anywhere else. I try to treat it like another tournament, with the same practice habits."

The practice green is center stage at Pine Needles, where everything seems to flow together with the Zen-like economy and grace of a Japanese garden.

A few paces to the left of the putting green, to the west, is the tee box of the 481-yard 1st hole, decorated with white and yellow and purple petunias. Framed by majestic pines, the hole rises steeply uphill, then doglegs sharply to the right, with the fairway flowing above and parallel to the putting green and practice range. Take a few more paces to the left of the first tee and you're standing on the 18th green.

Just right of the putting green, to the east, is a large white canvas merchandise tent; business is already brisk as local residents of the Sandhills and visitors from around the country scoop up rafts of swank apparel and souvenirs—golf shirts, sweaters, jackets, ball markers, water glasses, limited-edition prints of Pine Needles, straw hats, towels, nylon flags embossed with the Pine Needles logo, a longleaf pinecone with the words "1996 U.S. Women's Open" circling around the needles of the cone.

A few yards to the right of the tent are small, portable stands, placed at the back of the crowded practice range, which flows to the east and is bordered by a row of chocolate-brown Alpine chalet-style guest quarters. Vacationers to the resort can almost literally fall out of bed and onto the practice range. That's where the famed instructor Peggy Kirk Bell, 74, usually holds court. Bell, one of the early pioneers of the LPGA Tour, and her late husband, Warren "Bullet" Bell, a professional basketball player with the Fort Worth Pistons, bought Pine Needles in 1953, after the property had served as an Air Force headquarters base in World War II and then been sold to the Roman Catholic diocese of Raleigh.

In those days the "hotel" was a barracks with 50 bunk beds. Now it's a full-scale resort with lighted tennis courts, swimming pool, game room, two dining rooms, and spacious lounge with a huge stone fireplace.

"The result has been a destination of, by, and for golfers," writes Lee Pace, author of *Sandhills Classics: The Story of Mid Pines and Pine Needles*. "Opulence takes a backseat to comfort."

From the clubhouse area, only the 1st hole and 18th fairway and green are visible. The rest of the course to the north is tucked over the hills and out of sight, creating a delicious sense of anticipation, leaving the treasures to be found in the distant forest to the imagination.

Aaron Zydonick, a 24-year-old resident of the Sandhills, is collecting a few treasures of his own, displaying the signature of Patty Sheehan.

"I collect from all the greats," he says. "She's like the Jack Nicklaus of women's golf. And Michelle McGann, she's like the Arnold Palmer."

The analogies may be questionable. But it's refreshing to see a display of enthusiasm from a Generation Xer about anything; a display of enthusiasm from a Generation Xer about women's golf is mind-boggling. There can only be one explanation: Open Fever. Fortunately, the strain that infects a fan is relatively mild.

It's different for the pros. When Patty Sheehan contracted the disease in 1990, a particularly virulent strain known as the Atlanta Nightmare, it crushed her heart and spirit, transforming a happy-go-lucky Irish imp into a gloomy sad sack.

Six weeks after the 1990 U.S. Open, after squandering a nine-stroke final-day lead and breaking into agonized sobs at greenside when ABC's Judy Rankin thrust a microphone in her face, Sheehan sat on a picnic bench near the clubhouse at the Ping–Cellular One Championship in Portland, and gamely answered questions about the debacle. Sheehan was somber, on the verge of tears at times, wounds still oozing and raw. It was the journalist's equivalent of surgery without anesthesia.

"No, I'll never forget it," said Sheehan. "Hopefully, I'll learn from it."

Sheehan brightened, however, at the response from fans who had witnessed her collapse. "I got hundreds of letters," she said, "people pouring out their guts to me."

Two letters stood out. One was from then Denver Bronco football coach Dan Reeves, who knew a thing or two or three or four about losing the Big Ones. Reeves wrote that he had never felt worse for an athlete, and offered Sheehan an honorary uniform. Sheehan, a football fan who always wanted to give the game a whirl, wrote back, asking, "What's my number and where's my locker?"

The other letter was from Mickey Wright, who, after winning the U.S. Open in 1958 and 1959, stood on the brink of a historic three-peat in 1960, taking a seemingly comfortable lead into the final round.

But not even Wright, the greatest woman golfer in history, was immune from Open Fever. She shot an 82 and finished fifth. "That stands out as my worst moment in golf," said Wright.

The next year Wright fought off the demons and won the U.S. Open again. "You can do it too," was her message for Sheehan, and the words salved the pain a bit.

"I decided the Open shouldn't become so important that it disrupted my inner harmony, as it had in the past," says Sheehan. By the time of the 1992 U.S. Open at Oakmont, she had made a certain peace with herself.

And, as she hoped, Sheehan learned some concrete, practical lessons from the Atlanta Nightmare that made her a better, stronger, tougher golfer.

Sheehan always insisted her collapse was more physical than mental. And there's no question she was physically beaten into the ground during a week of 90-degree-plus heat and savage midsummer southern humidity, as well as thunderstorms that continually disrupted play. On Friday, after an opening round 66, Sheehan arrived at the course at noon, warmed up three separate times, sat out three separate rain delays, teed off at 7:35 at night, and played three holes before darkness fell. On Saturday morning, saddled with a 7:15 A.M. tee-off time, Sheehan arrived in a predawn down-pour, finally teed off at 1:30, and completed a second round 68 at 6:00 at night.

When the USGA decided to play 36 holes on Sunday, the Atlanta Nightmare attacked her weakened system. "I knew 36 would be long and hard," said Sheehan. "I didn't sleep much or eat much for breakfast."

By late morning the wheels started to wobble, as Sheehan tried to nav-igate her way through a Fun House with swaying floors and rotating mirrors.

"My legs weren't there," says Sheehan. "I got a little dizzy and felt faint a couple times. Mentally I was fine, but physically I was really struggling. Sometimes the body doesn't listen to the brain." Sheehan shot 75-76. Afterward she was diagnosed with dehydration and hypoglycemia.

A sadder but wiser Sheehan was ready at Oakmont. Coming into the 1992 U.S. Open on a roll, with two wins in her last three starts, Sheehan stocked up on rest and fluids and kept her swing keys simple—"turn and tempo." Her mental approach was basic as well. "Just keep plugging away," she reminded herself in mantralike fashion.

And the golf gods rewarded her perseverance with, as her friends called it, "The Miracle," a fast-moving thunderstorm that suspended play with two holes to go. The delay gave Sheehan a chance to regroup after three-putting 16. After cussing a blue streak at herself, Sheehan mellowed out, psyched up, and, when the all-clear siren sounded to resume play, did what she had to do.

"I knew I needed to birdie 17 and 18 to tie. Juli was playing so solidly—I knew she wasn't going to make any mistakes." Sheehan's dramatic birdies forced a playoff. No one expected a woman to break par at Oakmont, but Inkster and Sheehan shot four under par 280 as they broke away from the pack. When Sheehan defeated her close friend the next day, Inkster was saddled with her own demon: the loss still pains her four years later.

Sheehan hits the practice range at Pine Needles early Monday afternoon, after tying for eighth behind winner Rosie Jones at the LPGA Corning Classic in New York, where the Tour stopped after the LPGA Champi-onship in Wilmington, on an ugly, rainy, hand warmer and long underwear day. Sheehan, Inkster, and a handful of other pros got a lift to the Moore County Airport last night on Corning's private jet. When they arrived, a batch of player courtesy cars sat near the tarmac, but the driver in charge wouldn't release a car to Sheehan or Inkster, claiming they were reserved for players on later flights. Tired and irritated, dumbfounded at the mind-less bureaucracy, Sheehan and Inkster argued with the man until he burst into tears. There may not be any crying in baseball, but at the U.S. Open—

the men's as well as the women's—tears always seem to flow, tears of joy, tears of sorrow, tears of confusion, stress, and strain.

The Caddie Machine takes Sheehan's Wilson sand wedge over to Dave Baker's equipment repair van, which travels with the Tour and contains hundreds of shafts and grips and a full-scale tool room to tinker with or repair clubs. The wedge has a few dings on the edge of the blade that Sheehan wants ground smooth.

"Grinding with Dave," says Sheehan, in a sassy mood. "One of the few men who ever asked me to grind with them."

Sheehan struggled with her fairway woods in Corning. She asks Callaway rep Todd Strible to check the swingweights on her 3- and 5-woods. Strible returns, clubs in hand, and tells Sheehan they're right on the money.

But they still feel heavy to her. It's a bit of a mystery. The difference between swingweights—a D-0 to a D-1, for example—is no more than the weight of a dollar bill or two. Strible doesn't believe players can detect such a subtle change. Others disagree—some pros demand clubs that are identical down to a fraction of a gram.

If anyone can sense the difference of a dollar bill or two in weight it probably would be Sheehan, a "feel" player with an artist's sensitivity. (Feel players, like Sheehan and Lopez, are holistic, concentrating on touch, balance, and rhythm, striving for a sense of grace and harmony. Mechanical players, such as Nick Faldo and Betsy King, break down their swing into the smallest component parts—left heel position at the top of the backswing, right elbow at impact, etc.—tinker with them obsessively, and reconstruct the pieces like an auto mechanic tearing down and rebuilding an engine.)

"Maybe it's the grips," says Laib. Sheehan's fairway woods recently were regripped; the new ones are a tad thicker. Strible is inclined to agree. "A small change in the thickness of the grip will make a huge difference in feel." He recommends new Golf Pride grips, specifically, a thinner grip that LPGA player Cindy Rarick just started using called Tour Velvet.

A touch of Tour Velvet does the trick. "Feels like a toothpick," says Laib, waving one of the newly regripped clubs. Sheehan begins smoking the ball, pounding out a succession of screamers, balls rising into the Carolina blue sky like airplanes lifting off a runway, banking softly to the left in Sheehan's trademark draw.

"It drives me crazy when I hit it great on Monday," Sheehan confides, mopping her face with a white towel as the warm, humid early-summer sunshine beats down.

After 90 minutes on the range, Team Sheehan—Patty, Laib, and manager Rebecca Gaston—hop on a golf cart and travel about 300 yards up the left side of the range, just below the pines lining the 1st fairway, to a practice area reserved for pitches and bunker shots. Standing in a bunker below the green, Sheehan softly carves shots out of the light tan sand, ball after ball rolling gently near the flagstick. Rebecca rakes the traps.

"Therapy," she grins, as a gallery of about ten people, with rapt expressions on their faces, watch Sheehan's labors.

The green is too slow to practice pitch shots, however, so it's back to the main putting green. Strible has given Sheehan a batch of new Callaway caps and visors for the week, and as she rides back on the cart, Sheehan tries them on. All at once. The caps rising from the top of her head make her look like a golfing conehead.

"I wear many hats," she quips.

One of them is a celebrity bonnet. Whenever Sheehan leaves the roped-off confines of the putting green or the practice range, she is besieged for autographs. On her way to the putting green, Sheehan spots two other celebrities sitting in a golf cart, Peggy Kirk Bell and Patty Berg, and goes over to give them a hug.

One of the LPGA's founders, Berg, 78, won 57 tournaments, including the inaugural U.S. Women's Open in Spokane in 1946, and toured the globe for Wilson Sporting Goods, giving exhibitions and promoting women's golf. Bell, winner of the Titleholders in 1949, was a star as well, the first pro, male or female, to pilot her own plane to tournaments, although she cut short her touring pro career after a few years to return to help build Pine Needles and raise a family.

The two legends begin arguing over, of all things, Sheehan's wardrobe. Knickers are Sheehan's trademark, but she wears shorts more often these days, especially in hot weather.

"I really like you in shorts," says Bell.

"Well, *I* like her in her knickers," growls Berg, in a deep, raspy voice that Sheehan loves to imitate.

Back and forth it goes, as a bemused Sheehan looks on. Finally Berg growls, "Aw, Patty'd look good in a gunnysack," and Sheehan returns to the putting green, signing a few more programs and caps along the way.

After two and a half hours of practice, Sheehan is satisfied. "A good day's work," she says. And a day that isn't over, even though her labors at the golf course are complete. When she's home in Reno, Sheehan jogs about three miles every morning. On the road, she takes her traveling poodles, Sherlock and Quincey, out for a one-and-a-half-mile spin.

"I try to run every day. If I force myself to run after a tiring day, I seem to have more energy."

Tonight she'll try to relax a bit. She and Gaston plan to have dinner with

Don Kettleborough, the artist Sheehan "painted" with in Florida, and the gallery owner who sold their creation. Afterward, Sheehan, fueled by a little wine, will try to create another masterpiece, rifling some paint-soaked golf balls into a canvas.

On Monday evening the Caddie Machine gingerly walks down a corridor at the Comfort Inn in Pinehurst, carrying a container of ice to apply to his knees, still aching after surgery last fall. He hurt the left knee last spring in Atlanta, the right compensating for that injury. Both were scoped; holes were drilled in the kneecaps to allow blood to flow more easily through the joints.

Formerly a production supervisor at Nabisco and Stroh's Brewing Company, Laib, tired of factory work and union hassles, quit to join the Tour in 1986.

"It's tough to break in," says Laib, who did his share of "parking-lot duty"—hanging around in hopes of hooking up with a player lacking a looper for the week. But after working for Nancy Rubin for eight months, Laib acquired a reputation as a dogged employee. The Caddie Machine was born.

"It's fine," says Laib, shrugging at the mention of his nickname. "Now players will say, 'Well, you're the machine.' I guess it means you don't do anything wrong." Laib's services were in sufficient demand that, in a golfing version of a man-bites-dog story, he dumped a superstar, Betsy King, to go to work for Sheehan in 1991. Laib, ultraserious about his work, but also an irreverent jokester, blended better with Sheehan, a witty, mellow soul, than with King, ultraserious both on and off the course.

In 1995 Laib was hired as a short-term assistant coach for the women's golf team at Stanford, in part to teach them course-management skills. He played nine holes with Tiger Woods one day and was duly impressed.

"A very nice kid," says Laib. "All he wants to do is play golf. A lot of class too. At the girls' tournaments he was in the gallery, cheering them on."

Laib was impressed with Woods's Cobra driver as well. "It has the stiffest damn shaft I've ever seen," says Laib. "It felt like a two by four." Although Laib is burly and strong and a fine golfer, he wasn't able to generate anywhere near the clubhead speed necessary to use such a weapon. "I couldn't get it around—everything went dead right."

Laib, 47, may have bad knees, but he also has four flags from the 72nd hole of the U.S. Open hanging on the walls of his condo in Phoenix after teaming with Betsy King to win in 1989 and 1990, and with Sheehan to win in 1992 and 1994.

The collection is not unlike a matador's trophy case containing the ears of bulls slain in front of cheering fans in blood-stained arenas. If the U.S. Open is the ultimate arena for a golfer, it is for caddies as well.

Open Fever. Laib packed a 40-pound bag six miles through the rain in Corning, New York, yesterday, got off the course last night, flew to Pinehurst, slept for a few hours, and arose to greet the daybreak for his six-mile trek up and down the undulating hills of Pine Needles, meticulously surveying the land. As the Caddie Machine shuffles off to his room, to ice down his aging, creaking joints he says, with a tired smile, "I'll be ready."

It's cool and cloudy on Tuesday morning as Sheehan, Inkster, Dottie Pepper, and Cathy Gerring tee off. Big crowds surround the tee box and the adjacent practice green.

A phone rings somewhere in the background. "Hey, if it's for me, tell them I'm not here!" yells Sheehan, and the gallery laughs.

After overnight thunderstorms, the fairways are soft and the rough high and matted. Although nearby Pinehurst No. 2, which will play host to the men's 1999 U.S. Open, gets most of the glory, often ranking among listings of the ten top courses in the world, Pine Needles, built in 1927, is in the same league. It was the favorite of Donald Ross, who designed both courses with the classical grace of a Renaissance master.

Yet Pine Needles is also a duffer's delight. Mature longleaf pines are barren of branches or foliage near their base. So it's tough to lose a ball in the forest. You may not be able to hit it over the infantry green branches of the pines or slash it off the slippery cinnamon-colored pine straw carpeting the ground beneath the trees. But unlike many resort courses, which swallow up $40 per dozen Titleists like Clinton downs doughnuts, you can at least find the damn thing.

The quartet is tracked by about 100 spectators—about 99 more than usual for a practice round—as they walk up the hill toward their drives: Sheehan, in black-and-white checkered shorts and a white shirt, Inkster, in an aqua shirt and white shorts, Pepper, in khaki shorts and a white shirt with flashy red, blue, and tan designs, and Gerring, in brown shorts and a tan shirt, gossip about the Skins Game played two days ago in Texas.

On the 14th hole, after a succession of carryovers, Laura Davies sank a 12-foot putt worth $300,000, a record for a single shot in any professional Skins Game. Her total take was $340,000. Pepper and Sorenstam each won $100,000. Beth Daniel was shut out.

After Sorenstam birdied the 1st hole, she was stripped of the Skin, worth $20,000, for using an artificial device—a compass. Under normal tournament play, Sorenstam would have been disqualified and sent packing. But it was deemed a bit harsh to bundle her on a plane and send her home from a made-for-TV event, especially since she was a prime attraction. "The camera loves her," says former commissioner Charlie Mechem.

The consensus is that Sorenstam, who took the blame for the incident, was covering up for her fiancé, David Esch, making a rare appearance as her caddie.

"The wind was howling," says Ralph Scarinzi, who was in Texas caddying for Pepper. "So why do you need a compass?"

Compasses can be useful, in some cases, to find true north, if players are on a course where greens tend to break in a common direction. Laser-beam distance finders, currently the latest high-tech rage, can be helpful too. The devices, which resemble binoculars and sell for up to $3,300, yield yardage measurements between the viewer and a selected target. Some caddies swear by them; others find them unreliable. The most futuristic tool on the market is computer printouts from satellite photos, which measure the difference in elevation from sprinkler heads to the middle of each green.

"That's making it more complicated than it really is," says Scarinzi, who, like most veteran caddies, does his work the old-fashioned way, walking off distances one step at a time, gauging the effects of wind and elevation by experience, common sense, and field tests, such as today's practice round.

Players experiment with different clubs, preferred angles into the greens, and, particularly at Pine Needles, various strategies around the greens. Most greens are crowned like an inverted bowl. It's a Donald Ross trademark. As *Sports Illustrated*'s John Garrity so neatly puts it, they melt off at the edges "like a Salvador Dalí watch." Shots that are not struck the precise direction or distance tend to dribble off the front or back or sides of greens into a variety of slopes and hollows. Wisely, the USGA, which usually mandates thick rough around the green, has shaved the fringes at Pine Needles, presenting players with several options: pitch, chip and run, or putt.

The caddies pace off distances on the greens, double-checking their earlier work, and compare notes. Laib measures release distances—how far the ball rolls on the putting surface after it lands. Two weeks ago, after the McDonald's LPGA Championship in Wilmington, Laib traveled to the Sandhills and spent two days rolling balls on the Pine Needles greens. No, not putting. Simply rolling balls from various locations to learn how putts will break. When he finished, he had a drawing of each green filled with curving arrows that look like Egyptian hieroglyphics. Few caddies go to such lengths—it is Laib's obsession to such detail that earned him the sobriquet "Caddie Machine." Originally, it was a derisive tag from coworkers, who thought he was showing them up; now it is an acknowledgment of respect as well, and even some of the TV commentators use it.

Laib's hieroglyphics may only come into play two or three times a round, since Sheehan usually reads her own putts. But that may be enough to make a critical difference, especially since the Pine Needles greens are so tough to decipher.

"It's always a good idea to have an answer for her," says Laib with a smile, although he's not really kidding, "instead of saying, 'I don't know.'"

Most of the holes at Pine Needles are separate, isolated, entities with wide ribbons of parrot-green fairways, a combination of yellow-green Bermuda and darker rye grass, lined on both sides by groves of soaring pines. Yet the holes flow into each other as naturally as the tributaries of a mighty river. If golf courses had theme songs, Pine Needles might be matched with music conveying something ethereal and timeless, perhaps "Watermark" by Enya. (The course at Mission Hills? A remarkably lovely version of "California Dreaming" by Dinah Shore, her ownself, which was played at the gala Nabisco Dinah Shore dinner in March. The LPGA International? "Welcome to the Jungle" by Guns 'N Roses.) Plenty of sunlight seeps through the branches of the pine trees; the effect is airy and majestic and serene. Each hole is a cathedral of nature and Sheehan, a budding golf architect—she devours books on the subject and helped route a course in Angels Camp, California—is duly worshipful.

"It's every designer's dream," she says. "The holes work with the land. Ross didn't have to move around a lot of dirt. There aren't many pieces of land like this left, so today's designers have to be more creative."

Even the fairways, a bit wider than usual at a U.S. Open site, present problems. Almost all are sloped or contoured, steering balls toward the rough, or resulting in slight to severe uphill or downhill or sidehill lies.

"It makes you think on every single shot," says Sheehan.

On the 4th hole, a lovely 355-yard dogleg left which requires a drive over a lake near the dogleg and an approach shot up a steep hill, Sheehan bangs her drive into the rough. She can barely see the top of the ball.

"Oh, oh. That is not pretty," says Sheehan, bending over the orb, nestled in the thick, wet grass.

"That's brutal," says Laib. "You're going to have to hit fairways this week."

In many respects it's a typical practice round—"chip, chip, chip, chip, chip, putt, putt, putt, putt, putt," as Sheehan puts it. Inkster, often the last to leave the green, has earned a nickname for her obsessive work habits—"Chipper." Her instructor, Mike McGetrick, joins the foursome midway through the front nine. Yesterday they labored on the practice green, moving the ball up farther in her stance, quickening her preputt routine, keeping her body steadier, and accelerating through the ball.

The atmosphere is both businesslike and jovial. The best players in the world talk to each other like other golfing buddies do. They talk about their families and sports (the ongoing NHL and NBA playoffs spark lively discussions), tell each other "Good shot," and abuse the hell out of each other.

"I'm going to play a Juli Inkster cut," announces Pepper after driving into the right rough on the 327-yard 8th hole and finding pine branches blocking her path to the green. She curves the ball smartly around the branches but comes up short.

"Nice club, Ralph," says Inkster, giving her former looper the needle. (Scarinzi caddied for Inkster until she dropped off the Tour early in 1994 to give birth to Cori. He intended to pick up Inkster's bag when she returned, but Pepper was looking for a caddie, and Juli told him he'd be crazy to pass up the opportunity.)

"Tough crowd," smiles Pepper, sticking up for her caddie and boyfriend. Pepper and Scarinzi began dating after her divorce last spring from Doug Mochrie, who was her teacher and caddie for most of their almost nine-year marriage. Her relationship with Scarinzi is an open secret inside, but not outside the ropes of the Tour. (It soon will become public knowledge when a writer from *Golf World* identifies Scarinzi as Pepper's "significant other.")

Lunchtime.

Sheehan chows down on carrots, raisins, and gingersnap cookies while swigging from a plastic container filled with Shaklee Performance Drink. Among his other duties, the Caddie Machine is in charge of nutrition and hydration—he mixes the Shaklee powder with water before every round.

Gerring and Inkster joke about a late-night phone call in 1993, just after Gerring learned she was pregnant with Jayme, her second son.

"The rabbit died," Gerring told Inkster.

"You don't *have* a rabbit," replied Inkster.

"You never heard that expression before?" Inkster is asked.

"No," she says, slightly embarrassed.

But Inkster quickly gets her revenge. Playing out of the heavy rough on the 350-yard 12th hole, Gerring grunts loudly as she slashes an iron through the tangled grass.

"Was that Monica?" Inkster calls out, a reference to tennis player Monica Seles, who grunts like a stevedore when she serves.

Gerring turns to Inkster. Slowly and deliberately she rubs her nose with her middle finger. And suddenly it seems like 1990 again, when Gerring won three tournaments and placed fourth on the money list with $487,326.

The solidly built five-foot-four Gerring, with the pixie blonde haircut and flashing blue eyes, played the game like a fullback bulling through the line of scrimmage. Instead of mascara, you pictured her with black grease paint under her eyes. Her friend John Killeen said, with admiration, "She's a feisty bitch on the course. That's what it takes."

It took all of her feistiness and an ocean of courage to survive and recover from the horrific accident four years ago that destroyed her career and almost ended her life. On April 25, 1992, at the Sara Lee Classic in Nashville, Gerring and her husband Jim were standing in a buffet line, about to have lunch, when a catering company employee poured alcohol into a warming dish that was still lit, igniting a blaze that engulfed Gerring in flames. "From the waist up, she was a complete ball of fire," said a witness.

As her husband and several horrified onlookers tried to blanket the flames, as the inferno melted the skin off her head and her hands, Gerring remembers thinking, "I'm going to die. I can't take this pain much longer. My brain is burning up. My hands are burning up."

Inkster visited her friend in the hospital 36 hours later. "Her head looked like a beach ball, her hair was singed, and she was in a lot of pain. She didn't know anybody, didn't know where she was."

The damage was deep and irrevocable. Six to eight layers of skin were burned off her hands. She endured endless skin grafts. "People can never imagine how badly I was burned, how painful it was."

No one, including Gerring, expected her to play golf again. But last December, three and a half years after the fire, Gerring teed it up with Jay Haas in a mixed team event, the JCPenney Classic. Last month, she competed in her first LPGA tournament in four years at the Sprint Titleholders Championship in Daytona Beach, firing 75-74 to miss the cut by five strokes, smiling with pleasure and satisfaction all the way, even though fire has left her, as a professional golfer, a shadow of her former self. Her drives are 25 yards shorter; she's a club shorter with her irons. Her touch is erratic, varying, literally, with the weather.

"I know I'll never be able to come back on a full-time basis, and I know I'll never have the shot-making ability I used to have. My hands don't have the stamina or strength to do that. I just miss the competition *so* much."

During her forced absence Gerring, 36, filled her time with charity affairs, working with athletes at her alma mater, Ohio State, and the day-to-day tasks of raising her boys, 7-year-old Zachary and 20-month-old

Jayme. But the daughter of club pro Bill Kratzert, sister of PGA player Bill Kratzert Jr., and wife of Muirfield Village head pro Jim Gerring couldn't resist the lure of the links. She hopes to become a semiregular on the LPGA Tour, picking and choosing her spots. (Money isn't a problem. Gerring settled a $25 million lawsuit against the catering company for an undisclosed but hefty sum.)

It won't be easy. Gerring's face shows little trace of the flames that almost consumed her, but her hands, as critical to a golfer as they are to a surgeon or concert pianist, tell another story. They're marked by red skin graft scars and grayish white patches where deep tissue was burned away.

When the temperature falls below 65 degrees her hands ache. When it's over 80 degrees they begin to swell to something resembling oven mittens, since the fire destroyed her pores, preventing perspiration from escaping. Either way, her touch is lost.

So Gerring journeyed from her home in Cincinnati to Charlotte, North Carolina, to qualify for the U.S. Open a few weeks ago, hoping for temperate weather. She got it and fired a 73, just good enough to squeak into the field.

On the 401-yard 14th hole Pepper buries her second shot a few inches from the front lip of a greenside bunker. At first she agrees with Scarinzi, who urges her to drop it in the middle of the bunker.

Then she reconsiders. "I gotta *try*," she says.

Is she nuts?

If Pepper takes a rip at the plugged golf ball, she stands a good chance of smashing the club into the overhanging lip on her follow-through. She could jam a hand, jam a wrist, perhaps even break a bone.

For what? A meaningless practice shot two days before the biggest tournament of the year?

But there's really no such thing as a meaningless shot to the full-throttle, take-no-prisoners, get-the-fuck-out-of-my-way, Hall-of-Fame-or-bust Dottie Pepper, tagged with the perfect nickname—"Hot"—when she was a junior golfer in upstate New York. Look up "feisty" in the dictionary and you just might find a picture of Pepper, with her thick blonde mane and big, bold, blue eyes, each ear pierced with three silver studs above a dangling gold earring.

Earlier in her career the Saratoga Springs native, a daughter of former major league baseball player Don Pepper, wore her blonde hair spiked on top and occasionally painted her nails black. A neo-punk princess with chips on both shoulders, and a naked ambition reminiscent of Tonya Harding, she blew onto the Tour in 1988 like a hurricane, yelling at her shots like a Bronx cabdriver.

Her colleagues reacted like she had spit in their soup. "We all yell at the ball," said one, "but Dottie's the only one who expects it to listen."

Paired in 1990 with an idol Pat Bradley (who, deliberately or not, turned intimidation into a fine art with her frozen mask of a game face, labeled by her competitors as "The Gaze"), Pepper played right through, walking to the second tee before Bradley and Colleen Walker, the third player in the group, had putted out on the first green. Bradley was furiously and publicly critical, and Pepper, lost in her own little white-hot world between the ropes, was privately abashed by her behavior.

Whether you love or loathe her, it's hard to take your eyes off Pepper. When charismatic players such as Lopez or Sheehan are in contention and charging, they generate electric waves of energy. When Pepper is in contention, she generates pure heat. Watching golf on TV often is enervating enough to induce a light coma, but Pepper's laserlike intensity burns right through the screen. It's hard to tell if she is more likely to explode, implode, or do both simultaneously.

She did a little of both during her early years on Tour, soaring to stardom in 1992, capturing the Nabisco Dinah Shore, the money title ($693,335), Player of the Year honors, and the Vare Trophy for lowest scoring average (70.80), while suffering from colitis and a hiatal hernia, as her ambition chewed at her innards like battery acid. Pepper carried around a prescription bottle of Zantac, the drug of choice for the fanatical careerist.

Slowly she began to mellow a bit. And to fit in a little bit, as she figured out "the lines of acceptability," as Pepper puts it, that govern the Tour.

Her game stayed red-hot. Pepper placed fourth on the money list in 1993, 1994, and 1995. When she captured the 1995 Stratton Mountain Classic in Vermont last August, her tenth career victory, she became the youngest and fastest LPGA player to top the $3 million mark in career earnings.

But her behavior was always suspect. At the Solheim Cup in 1994, she shouted "Yes!" and pumped a fist when opponents Laura Davis and Alison Nicholas missed a putt. In a year-end review, *Golfweek*, appalled by the display, wrote, "On behalf of a grateful nation, Dottie's dog Shank sank its teeth into her leg." (The wound required 15 stitches. Pepper fired her caddie for violating the confidentiality of the player-caddie relationship, akin to a doctor-patient relationship, and leaking the story to the media.)

The LPGA is the Hugging Tour: after the final putt is holed, the winner and runner-up customarily embrace. Something a bit different occurred when Pepper lost a five-hole playoff to English rookie Helen Dobson in 1993 at the State Farm Rail Classic. No hugs. No smiles. Pepper greeted the young victor with a stony-cold glare and a curt handshake before turning her back and stalking off. It was repugnant. I've rooted against her ever since.

So I've been tiptoeing gingerly around her all day. Even in a practice round, Pepper glowers and scowls and yells almost as intensely as in the heat of battle. And she's played poorly this year, by her standards, with just two top-ten finishes in ten starts. Tinkering with her swing and experimenting with a set of DCI cast irons from Titleist, her major endorser, haven't helped her mood.

Yet, to my great surprise, Pepper proves to be extremely likable: intelligent, thoroughly unpretentious, and vulnerable. She's got a nice, barbed, heavily sarcastic sense of humor, which she applies to herself as well as others. It's the type of sarcasm that often masks deep insecurities.

"She's sacrificed a lot, she's very hard on herself," said a friend earlier this year. "Being the best is what it's all about. Golf is so much of her life— once she's off the course, she has no confidence in herself."

Fans who can't stomach Pepper might be shocked to see her after she hits her tee shot on the 172-yard 16th hole. As Sheehan, Inkster, and Gerring walk to the green, Pepper finds a friend in the gallery, a tan and white Welsh Corgi, a sheep-herding dog, out for a walk with his master. Pepper crouches down and the dog puts his paws on her shoulders and nuzzles her face as Sheehan, Inkster, and Gerring look back and roll their eyes.

Although Shank is no longer with her—Doug claimed him in the divorce settlement—Pepper travels with another chow named Furman, named after Pepper's alma mater. Pepper dotes on the creature, bragging about his ability to push tapes into her car's cassette player. "Traveling with a dog makes it easier to leave golf at the golf course," says Pepper. "They're so excited to see you. They have to go for walks and be fed."

Maybe it's Furman, maybe it's the divorce, maybe it's Ralph, maybe it's maturity, maybe it's all of the above. Despite her mediocre play so far in 1996, Pepper seems to have called for a truce in the battle that rages inside herself, if not in the weekly wars against her competitors.

And if ongoing negotiations for an endorsement deal with Dr Pepper pan out, expect to see her starring in commercials next year. You already know the tag line:

"She's a Pepper."

Meanwhile Sheehan keeps hitting long irons to the par threes and par fours. "We're gonna wear a hole in this thing," she mutters, after hitting a 4-iron to the green on the 405-yard 15th hole.

"It'll be easy to warm up tomorrow," says Laib. "A half-bucket of four-irons and a half-bucket of drivers."

The sun finally burns through the clouds and the afternoon turns steamy. Sheehan needs a driver and 3-wood to reach the downhill 418-yard 18th hole. Sheehan hit eight 3- and 4-irons today; unless the fairways dry out, Pine Needles will be a brutal marathon for the shorter hitters.

After the round Sheehan signs autographs and practices until 4:15. Then she goes back to the rental house in Pinehurst, runs with the dogs, and has dinner on a lovely early summer evening, basking in the soothing warmth and charm of an area that is a throwback to yesteryear.

The Pinehurst area, also known as the Sandhills, is anchored by the towns of Pinehurst, Southern Pines, and Aberdeen. The towns form a rough triangle in the heart of Moore County. Call it the Golf Triangle, a counterpoint to the Research Triangle of Chapel Hill, Durham, and Raleigh, located an hour or so away.

Or call it the "Golf Capital of the World," as the Pinehurst Area Convention and Visitors Bureau describes it. The boosters aren't just whistling Dixie. A drive from Aberdeen to Pinehurst Village to Southern Pines, which takes about ten minutes, passes 17 golf courses: Pit Golf Links, the nine courses of the Pinehurst Resort, Midland Country Club, Club at Longleaf, Talamore, Pinehurst National, Pinehurst Country Club, Mid Pines, and Pine Needles. There are over forty courses in the Sandhills, with more on the drawing boards or under construction.

Long-term residents grouse about the population boom. Pinehurst alone has quadrupled in size since 1980 to about 7,000 residents, including many retirees lured by the near year-around golf, the tranquillity, and the relatively cheap living costs. (A flyer stuck under my car windshield wiper advertised a three-bedroom, two-bath, cathedral-ceilinged home in Pinehurst with a membership in Pinehurst Country Club for just $124,900.) Still, by urban standards, it's horse and buggy country, with thick forests and dairy and farm land just outside the triangle.

It's All Golf All the Time in the Sandhills. One Aberdeen car wash is named Par Three. Another is called the 19th Hole. Kids board yellow school buses for after-school activities with bags of clubs in their hands. The Sandhills Community College library is displaying a photo exhibit called "Growth and Grace: The Story of Women's Golf in America." The lounge at the Comfort Inn is named Putters. A sign on every TV reads, "Your TV's been fixed so it always shows golf," and it does—channel 34 beams in The Golf Channel round-the-clock.

Soda fountain magnet James Tufts, who founded Pinehurst in 1885, buying up 5,500 acres of harvested timberland in the Sandhills for about $1 an acre, dreamed big dreams. He envisioned a winter health resort that would lure visitors and businessmen from the North and South. He hired the firm of Frederick Law Olmsted, architect of New York's Central Park, to design the village of Pinehurst. In 1896 he opened the Holly Inn, which charged $3 a day and offered tennis, croquet, lawn bowling, bicycling, and hiking. When some guests from the North brought their golf clubs and began whacking balls around nearby dairy farms, Tufts saw green—fairways and dollar bills. In 1890 he hired Donald Ross, a young Scot who had apprenticed as a teenager at St. Andrews with Old Tom Morris before journeying to America.

Ross spent the next 48 years at Pinehurst, designing, among many others, Pinehurst No. 2, three other courses at Pinehurst Resort, Pine Needles, and Mid Pines. He watched golf slowly overtake the other leisure pursuits—equestrian farms and racetracks, gun and hunt clubs—that drew wealthy East Coast businessman and the southern aristocracy to the Sandhills. The golf boom, Ross said in his later years, was inevitable.

"Americans did not have much time for play—it was all work. In Scotland, every man, woman, and child had some interest outside his work. I knew that Americans would someday find time to play. And I knew the game would be golf."

Today a shop in Pinehurst Village sells a needlepoint pillow stitched with the motto, "Golf is not a matter of life and death. It is much more important than that." The Olmsted-designed village, a few quaint square blocks, mixes New England style red-brick buildings and Southern plantation style white clapboard structures. Some, such as the Holly Inn (which now charges $139 per night), are a century old. Shops, restaurants, and thriving, pulsating real estate offices fill the village. All of the surrounding lanes curl gently around the square. There are no straight roads around Pinehurst Village, and few straight putts on Donald Ross courses.

On a sultry early summer day a visitor to the village strolls along lanes sheltered by pine trees, holly trees, and dogwoods, which act like umbrellas to soothe the wicked yellow-white rays of the sun. Huge white magnolia blossoms, in full bloom, lend their sweet fragrance to the fresh scent of the pines. Flowerbeds sprout all over the village, a riot of red, yellow, white, pink, and violet annuals, begonias, impatiens, and petunias. Hopping through the flowerbeds and flitting through the trees, catbirds, mourning doves, red and brown cardinals, robins, sparrows, purple finches, and mockingbirds sing songs.

The beauty is breathtaking, the pace bucolic, the atmosphere primarily Old South overlaid with a touch of Yankee carpetbagger eye-for-the-main-chance hustle. "There's more tradition in the air and more magic on the ground here than at any other destination this side of St. Andrews," gushed *Golf* magazine.

In most respects, Pinehurst is a glorious partnership of man and nature, an exquisite natural setting that has been enhanced by the wisdom and brilliance and vision of Tufts, Ross, and Olmsted. Next month the village, the grandiloquent Pinehurst Hotel (built in 1901 and known as "the Queen of the South," the hotel now is the ritzy five-star centerpiece of Pinehurst Resort), Pinehurst No. 2 and No. 4, Midland Road (the first four-lane road in North Carolina), and Pinehurst Harness Track will be designated as historical landmarks by President Clinton, the first golf course community to be so honored. The area deserves the honor, but the cynical political analyst may wonder whether the First Golfer is currying favor in return for preferred tee times.

Pinehurst isn't perfect. Its aristocratic past, which lingers like the scent of the magnolia blossoms, has its drawbacks as well as its charms. One drawback is a brand of finely graduated snobbishness. Another is the often glacial service in the hotel dining rooms.

But when you can eat, drink, and breathe golf, food is secondary. One of the best places to feast is at the Tufts Archives in Pinehurst Village, which devotes a separate wing to two intertwined subjects: golf and the history of the Sandhills.

Among the hundreds of volumes of golf books is the fine new book by Tarheel writer Lee Pace, *Sandhills Classics: The Story of Mid Pines and Pine Needles.* The courses were built by the Tufts family in the Roaring Twenties to handle the overflow from their booming business at Pinehurst Resort. Good idea; bad timing. The stock market crash of 1929 forced the family to sell both properties. After it passed through the hands of the air force and the Roman Catholic church, newlyweds Warren and Peggy Kirk Bell paid $50,000 for a one-third share of Pine Needles in 1953. Two years later the Bells bought out their partners, former PGA star Julius Boros and his inlaws.

Peggy had turned pro in 1950, seduced by Spalding's contract of $10,000 a year and $50 for one-day exhibitions. The offer was much more attractive than her other option, a schoolteacher's job and annual salary of $3,500. Peggy barnstormed in her plane around the country giving clinics, often two a day, in between tournaments. "Peggy didn't care what the world thought of her," Hollis Stacy told Pace. "She went out and helped start this tour. She's a nonconformist. . . . Playing golf wasn't the typical fashion for women back then. I'm very thankful we had pioneers of that sort."

"When we were struggling to get the Women's Open going," said Bell, "Babe Zaharias suggested that each LPGA player put up some money and we announce that we were playing for a purse of $10,000. But Babe's idea was that none of us would really contribute money and neither would we win any money. We'd just announce it to attract the attention of the press. We've come a long way since then."

So has Pine Needles.

Warren and Peggy built the resort almost from scratch. It was a labor of love and 18-hour days. It was also a long haul to prosperity. "I remember when Bullet raised the greens fee from $2.50 to $3.00," Peggy told *Golfweek*. "We all thought we'd go out of business."

Eventually the Bells created a down-home masterpiece. (Bullet died of cancer in 1984.) Peggy acquired a reputation as one of the game's finest instructors—her Golfari Schools at the extensive practice and teaching facilities at Pine Needles draw women golfers of all skill levels from around the country. In 1993 Bell and her children bought Mid Pines across the street.

One thing, however, has remained constant: The operation still is a family enterprise. Son-in-law Kelly Miller is the general manager. Son-in-law and former PGA pro Pat McGowen is a teaching pro. Daughters Bonnie and Peggy Ann work in management. Son Kirk, a Pinehurst mortgage broker, used to give lessons at Pine Needles.

Today the resort is a bustling, thriving business, offering golf packages that are a relative steal. A three-day, two-night peak season rate of $492 includes everything from range balls to lodging, meals, and golf on both courses. "When you're at Pine Needles, you feel you're there to have a golf experience, not to see how much of your net worth you can leave behind," says former PGA player Joe Inman, a Carolina native who has known the Bell family for years.

Pine Needles has always labored in the shadows of the bigger, glitzier, world-famous Pinehurst Resort. But this week Peggy Kirk Bell will host a party for over 100,000 guests, an international press corps, and a world-wide TV audience, as the women professional golfers who follow in the footsteps of Bell and the other pioneers of the LPGA Tour battle it out for $1.2 million and the most prized silver trophy in the game.

The greatest woman athlete in the history of the Sandhills is also a star attraction at the Tufts Archives: Annie Oakley, who lived in Pinehurst from 1915 until her death in 1926.

Caricatured by Ethel Merman in the smash Broadway musical *Annie Get Your Gun*, Oakley seemed lost in the mists of history and legend.

However, a picture in a display case of a small, slender, pretty woman in a prim long dress, with a grave expression on her face and a rifle in her hand, stopped me cold.

Born into abject poverty in Ohio in 1860 as Phoebe Ann Moses, Annie picked up a rifle at the age of 8 and began hunting to put food on her family's table. Soon she was supplying quail and pheasant to hotel dining rooms in Cincinnati, killing the birds with head shots so as not to impair their value.

In 1875 she bested celebrated marksman Frank Butler in a trap-shooting contest. A year later they were married. Annie learned to read and write as well as to perform on stage. By the time Butler and Oakley signed up with Buffalo Bill Cody's famed road show in 1885, the five-foot-tall star, who weighed less than 100 pounds, had developed into a "consummate actress," with a personality "that made itself felt as soon as she entered the arena."

"Buffalo Bill and Annie were among the nation's first modern media darlings, but their rise to prominence was not entirely due to flattery," wrote Damaine Vonada in *Smithsonian*. Not even close. Oakley's style was far surpassed by her substance; she was one of the great athletes and clutch performers of her era. She shot dimes from men's fingers; she stood on the back of a galloping horse and shot glass balls out of the air. When she whipped noted marksman Miles Johnson, 30,000 people jammed the playing field.

Touring with Buffalo Bill for 17 years, Oakley earned $1,000 a week, a fortune in her day. The great Sioux leader Chief Sitting Bull adopted Annie as a surrogate daughter, dubbing her "Little Sure Shot." Oakley's European tour caused a sensation. She dazzled Baron de Rothschild, played a command performance for Queen Victoria, who called her a "very, very, clever little girl," and shot a lit cigarette from the mouth of Crown Prince Wilhelm in an exhibition for the German royal family. (After Wilhelm became kaiser and a key figure in the start of World War I, Oakley said, "If my aim had been poorer, I might have averted the Great War.")

Although her stage shows bordered on the risqué—Annie wore knee-length skirts and her long auburn hair down around her shoulders, provocative attire in the late nineteenth century—offstage Mrs. Frank Butler was a model of rectitude. She read the Bible, embroidered, worked with poor children, and dressed in high collars and long dresses. She was married to Butler for 50 years without a hint of impropriety. "To be considered a lady has always been my highest ambition," she told an interviewer.

"No wonder many in her audiences regarded Annie with a bemused mixture of fascination and awe," wrote Vonada. "Here was a wholesome little character presenting herself as the essence of femininity while brandishing a potent symbol of manhood, yet leading a married life as prim and circumspect as that of any middle-class housewife. She was provocative, appealing, and reassuring, all at once."

In 1915 Oakley began working in Pinehurst. She taught women to shoot and gave occasional exhibitions. One of her signature tricks was to shoot an apple off the head of her beloved Irish setter, who would calmly pose on a stool about 20 paces in front of her master's rifle. (Memo to Dottie Pepper and Furman: Don't try this trick at home.)

Oakley was not universally loved. In many respects, she faced the same sort of societal tut-tutting that women golfers faced when they took up *their* weapons.

"When I began shooting in public," said Oakley, "it was considered almost shameful for a woman to shoot. That was a man's business, you see. Sometimes when I was invited to shoot at trap-shooting clubs the wives and women friends of the members would be invited. They would look me over, often disdainfully, but I would not mind them at all. If they wished to be friendly, they could. If they did not, I did not care."

A consummate perfectionist, Oakley even orchestrated her own funeral, ordering the gown she was to be buried in shortened to precisely the proper length just before her death in 1926. In 1993 she was inducted into the National Women's Hall of Fame with 34 others, including Shirley Chisholm, Rosa Parks, Gloria Steinem, and a woman who would be the patron saint of the most radical of feminists based on her name alone, Cherokee Nation chief Wilma Mankiller.

Two years after the death of Oakley, who shattered stereotypes as easily as clay targets, the first national golf championship for women was played at Pine Needles.

On a sunny, warm Wednesday morning a crowd of about 200 happy fans gather to follow "The Match," a best-ball duel pitting Sheehan and Laura Davies against Jane Geddes and Liselotte Neumann.

The Match, a $50 Nassau with presses, closest to the pin, birdies, eagles, the whole schmeer, has become a day-before-the-U.S.-Open tradition.

Usually Geddes is paired with Amy Benz, which sounds like a mismatch. It is—Geddes and Benz regularly pummel Sheehan and Davies. Benz, a solid player but a nonwinner in her 14 years on Tour, usually steals the show and the dough, saving some of her career rounds for The Match.

Sheehan and Davies still wince at their defeat at Indianwood in 1990. "We were one down on seventeen," says Sheehan. "Laura was the only one on the green. She three-putts and Benz sinks a twenty-footer for par."

"Every year I just bring my money," she says. Sheehan has made over $5 million playing golf, yet her losses in The Match are burned into her memory bank: $210 in 1989; $485 in 1990 when Benz shot 65 in Atlanta. "It took me about six months to pay up," smiles Sheehan, who estimates her total losses from The Match to be in the thousands. Despite the dismal past performance record, Sheehan is pumped. "It's the only time all year I do this," says the Reno resident, who normally eschews gambling and the casinos. "That's why I get so excited."

Everyone congratulates Davies on her $340,000 haul from the Skins Game. Davies plans to buy herself a new toy with the windfall, a year-old fire-engine-red Ferrari 456 for $137,000.

It will give her a smoother ride than the plane trip back from Texas to North Carolina. Davies abhors small planes, so she took a Valium to soothe her nerves when she boarded. "I relaxed to the point where I was drinking like a fish," laughs Davies, who wound up neck deep in a barf bag.

But she seems fit as a Ferrari today, crushing a drive over the hill on the first hole.

"Man, she hits it like Daly!" exclaims a man hanging over the tee box.

Neumann rolls in a birdie putt on the rugged 414-yard 2nd hole as Geddes raises a fist and cries, "Way to go, partner!" "Here we go again," mutters Sheehan. It appears another bath may be forthcoming.

Especially when Neumann cans a 30-foot birdie putt on the 127-yard 3rd hole.

"I know how to pick 'em, don't I," crows Geddes. Sheehan, looking like she just bit into some moldy cheese, drops her putter and visor on the green and stares silently at Geddes.

"An amazing phenomenon," says Geddes, rubbing it in.

"You don't need to swing or anything," Davies sarcastically tells Geddes. "You might as well just carry her bag."

Geddes laughs. She's an intelligent, voluble, strongly built, five-foot five-inch blue-eyed blonde, whose first victory came in the U.S. Open in 1986. But a few years later she seemed burned-out, a scowling and grumpy figure on the course. In 1990 caddie John Killeen nominated her and Patty Rizzo (who fled the Tour in 1992 for a year on the Japanese Tour before marriage and semiretirement) as the Tour's biggest underachievers. "It's the biggest waste I've ever seen," he said.

"I was ready to retire," says Geddes. "I couldn't find any motivation. Finally, I told myself, 'You've got a little more pride than this.'"

Geddes realized her job was running, and in some ways ruining, her life. "The happiest people out here are able to separate their golf score from their life, instead of living the rest of the day according to what they shoot, which everyone does at some point."

These days Geddes, 35, radiates an upbeat energy. She earned $263,149 in 1993, $273,600 in 1994, $332,014 in 1995, and already has recorded three top-five finishes in 1996. Nicknamed "Spanky" for her power, the long-driving Geddes "tries to enjoy life on the road more," treating herself to nice hotels and eating at good restaurants.

Currently she's pursuing a degree in business administration via the Internet as she travels the Tour. "I wanted to do something to use my brain a bit," Geddes told *Golf Digest*, "and I always regretted not getting my degree." She figures it will take about five years to earn her sheepskin. Tuition shouldn't be a problem.

On the 195-yard 5th hole, the cup is tucked up front on a steep downslope near a ridge bifurcating the green. Neumann, chipping from the back fringe, watches her ball cross the ridge, accelerate past the pin, and roll off the green into the front fringe. Geddes, just off the left side of the green about 40 feet from the cup, strokes a putt a trifle too firmly and watches it race down the slope and off the green.

Neumann and Geddes, two of the best female golfers in the world, can't keep a chip or putt on a green somewhat dulled by recent rains. If the USGA locates the pin up front during the tournament, we could see double figures on this hole, players batting balls back and forth like kids at Putt-Putt.

Beth Daniel, standing on the tee on the opposite hillside, watches the carnage and then yells out, "Patty!"

"We halved the hole with bogeys!" Sheehan hollers back.

Sheehan is playing well, despite sacrificing chunks of real estate to her playing partners. "I *killed* that drive," she says ruefully on one hole, peering up the fairway at Neumann's drive, about 15 yards ahead of her, Geddes, about 30 yards ahead, and Davies, who is off somewhere in another zip code.

But she's having a grand old time. As Neumann prepares to drive on the 327-yard 8th hole, Sheehan loudly scrapes her cleats on a concrete pathway. Neumann backs away, laughing, although she remains mum.

But the laughter speaks volumes.

When Newmann defeated Sheehan to win the U.S. Open in 1988, the then 22-year-old rookie found herself with a trophy in her hands and the golf world at her feet. Companies, particularly in Japan, showered her with six-figure endorsement deals.

It simply overwhelmed her.

"Everything happened so fast," says Neumann. "I wasn't quite comfortable on Tour yet. I'd go to the range and hit balls between Patty Sheehan and Betsy King and say to myself, 'Wow!' I don't think I considered myself one of the best players in the world at the time."

Yet she was expected to perform with the elite. "I kept thinking, 'What can I do to get better?' I wanted to hit the ball higher and longer. I started working on the wrong things."

Life in a goldfish bowl of fan and media and sponsor obligations proved equally difficult. She describes her three years after the U.S. Open as "kind of a hard time." Given Neumann's stoical nature, it's safe to assume she was close to miserable. She fell to 51st on the money list in 1990.

But she kept working. Asked if she ever considered quitting, Neumann instantly replies, "Nope!" then smiles and adds, "I never give up."

During her lean years, the book on Neumann was simple: short hitter, inconsistent ball-striker, great putter. So she gradually rewrote it, building a reliable, compact swing and adding 20–30 yards in distance.

She also created a happier life outside the ropes. A resident of Boca Raton, Neumann has lots of interests outside golf—Miami Dolphins football, tennis, music, wine collecting, and decorating. She also may have the best fashion sense on Tour.

In 1994 she rejoined the elite, placing third on the money list with $505,701. This time it wasn't a fluke. Neumann won $305,157 in 1995. She kicked off the 1996 season with an amazing nine-stroke victory in the Chrysler-Plymouth Tournament of Champions in January and won again in Tuscon in March.

Last week Neumann turned 30. As Pia Nilsson notes, there's a maturity in her as a golfer and a person, a quiet confidence, a serenity, an understated elegance.

She's the Ingrid Bergman of golf.

As Sheehan walks down the fairway on the 8th hole she acts out a joke that Caroline Pierce told her last summer at the du Maurier Classic. It is, as Pierce notes, quite politically incorrect, one of those jokes that make you laugh out loud and then slap your forehead and groan. (The joke is about the wheelchair Olympics. The punch line is "Wheelchair hurdles." You can fill in the rest.)

The kick that Sheehan gets out of telling the joke is funnier than the joke itself. She's still grinning when she comes off an 8-iron and pushes it into a greenside bunker. "The only short iron I get to hit all day, and I miss it," she says, quickly getting back to business by birdieing the 374-yard 9th hole, which squares the match.

The gallery crowds around the shallow, narrow tee box on No. 10, a gorgeous 440-yard par five that plays from an elevated tee over a lake and up a steep hill before doglegging sharply to the left. A strategically placed fairway bunker prevents players from shaving too much off the dogleg.

Except for Davies. Ben Wright was wrong. Davies isn't a tank. She's much too coordinated and nimble an athlete. She also has a back as broad as Paul Bunyan and swings a club like she's trying to chop down a tree with an ax.

So when she pulls out a pencil about four inches long and tees up her ball on the eraserless tip, the fans start buzzing. It's one of Davies's patented crowd-pleasers, but it's more than just a stunt. The extra height of the pencil-tee reduces the spin on the ball and makes Laura Longest even longer.

"Maybe you should try it," someone says to Sheehan.

"The pencil's almost as tall as she is," says Geddes.

"Yeah," says Sheehan. "It would be like T-ball."

Davies seems to shake the earth with the force of the blow. The ball soars into orbit, a towering drive that clears the bunker at the top of the hill, a blast of about 250 yards in the air. Her colleagues have seen it before, but they, along with the fans, shake their heads in awe.

"Having fun?" a fan says to Davies after she pulls the pencil out of the turf.

"Not yet," she replies.

Not yet.

Not yet!!

Two days ago Davies won $340,000. Two weeks ago in Wilmington, she won the McDonald's LPGA Championship. Yet she's grinding her heart out in a practice round that may cost the multimillionaire, at most, a thousand bucks or so. Tip money. Teddy bear money. (Davies collects teddy bears as well as TV sets and sports cars.)

Those two little words—"Not yet"—illustrate the vast gulf that separates a Davies or Sheehan or Neumann or Pepper or Webb or Sorenstam from the rest of us. Sure, there's a huge talent gap. But, above all else, they possess a competitive drive light-years beyond most mortals. Maybe it's one of these hereditary things, like a predisposition toward baldness or nearsightedness. Maybe it's one of those mutant genes that scientists can mark and eventually stamp out. (Competitors on the LPGA Tour and in other sports have a healthy outlet for their killer instincts, but those who gravitate into other fields—law, politics, business, religion, the military— are the scariest people on the planet.)

Donna Caponi, winner of 24 LPGA tournaments and two U.S. Opens, now an analyst for The Golf Channel, comes out to check on the progress of The Match after Sheehan birdies No. 10.

"We're one up," says Davies. "For the first time in six years," she adds sardonically.

"I haven't done a thing all day, partner," Davies tells Sheehan on the 405-yard 15th hole, just before she rolls in a 15-foot sidehill slider for birdie. Sheehan skips in delight, then covers her mouth like a schoolgirl caught celebrating a perfect score on a math test.

"She's a lot peppier when she's winning," says Geddes.

"I'm a lot more fun," agrees Sheehan.

NBC technicians are testing cameras behind the 16th green as the players arrive at the tee, as Open Fever continues to build. Although they didn't plan it that way, The Match offers a great diversion for the quartet, a device that compels them to play with intensity while forgetting, temporarily, the real battle that begins tomorrow.

Davies laces an iron that tracks toward the flag on the 172-yard hole.

"Get all over it!" yells Sheehan. "Get in, honey!" It almost does.

"Partner," says Sheehan, hugging Davies after she sinks her short birdie putt. "We won."

Davies is happy but not totally content. "We're one and oh on the press," she says as the group tees off on the 17th. But Neumann, who opened the match with three straight birdies, saves a sweet one for last, snaking in a 30-footer on the 418-yard home hole to win the final presses and save herself and Geddes $300 each.

The players troop off to the merchandise tent, where the victors receive the spoils—chic $120 wind jackets with flags signifying past U.S. Open champions, including Sheehan, Davies, Neumann, and Geddes, on the back. The winners model their jackets in the midst of a gaggle of fans; the losers whip out their credit cards.

The Caddie Machine pockets $10 from Neumann's looper, Mark Scott. Laib is ready for the big show. His memo books are filled with notes and numbers and arrows: yardage figures, release distances, driving distances, breaks on the greens. During the tournament Laib adds to and updates the numbers. By the weekend, barring big changes in the weather, Laib and Sheehan will have a clear idea of precisely how far every club will fly, how far every ball will roll, and how much every putt will break.

"She's ready," says Laib. "She's hitting it good. All we've got to do is play smart. If you're over the majority of the greens, you're dead. You've got to leave the ball below the hole, or you'll be kicking yourself in the head all day."

"I played really well," says Sheehan, wrapped in her new jacket. She's tired, a bit glassy-eyed, but pleased with her preparation. "I'll go home and rest and get ready to go tomorrow."

Today was good clean fun; tomorrow is another story. "At the Open you have to play your absolute best," says Sheehan. "Do that, or the course will destroy you."

* * *

Unfortunately, the best-laid plans of mice and men and women and USGA officials and golfers . . .

Deb Richard, Wendy Ward, and Michiko Hattori kick off the fifty-first U.S. Women's Open at precisely 7:00 on Thursday morning.

It's bitter cold. Players and caddies and marshals shiver and shake as a frigid wind rustles the tops of the pines and the sun hides in the forest.

By 11:20, however, when Caroline Pierce, Marianne Morris, and Cindy Rarick tee off, the skies are blue, the sun is sparkling, and the program sellers are almost out of programs. It's still windy, though—stray pine needles, carried by the gusts, blow through the air.

When the trio reaches the 414-yard 2nd hole, it is confronted by the site of Sherri Steinhauer, Martha Nause, and Gail Graham, the 11:10 group, just sitting around talking.

"It's been slow since the second group went through at 7:10," says a marshal. The hole *looks* fairly benign—a straightaway drive over a hill with a second shot down a long, gradual slope to the green. But it's a typical Donald Ross classic, lulling and luring players into disaster. The fairway kicks right, and many players, trying to avoid the pines on the left, wind up in forest on the other side. And everyone seems fooled on their second shots, as balls come up well short or skip over the green, which proves unwilling to accept a long iron or fairway wood.

Pierce munches on an apple. She's never matched or bettered par in any of the 22 rounds of her seven previous U.S. Opens—a tie for fifty-first at Colonial in 1991 is her best finish. But she begins play with confidence after a busy two weeks when she moved from her apartment into a house she just bought in Scottsdale, caddied for Rick Aune in an annual caddie tournament in Corning ("Mostly we sit in carts and abuse them"), attended Melissa McNamara's thirtieth birthday party and a baby shower for Nancy Ramsbottom, expecting in August, and tried to catch up on her sleep.

The stretch from Nashville through the U.S. Open has been, says Pierce, "very tiring," and players are exhibiting the wear and tear. "Everyone at McDonald's was bitching. At Corning the range is very small, and there were arguments over space. That never happens earlier in the year. It's because the big tournaments are so close together [this year]."

Staying above the fray, Pierce tied for thirteenth at Corning. "I trusted my golf swing all the way around." Her putting was better, too. Pierce switched from a Tad Moore putter to an Odyssey, the current rage on the pro tours since Nick Faldo rode the Rossi II model to victory at the Masters. (Mike Eggling, husband of LPGA player Dale Eggling, reps for

Odyssey. He says 37 LPGA players are now using the putter. The company estimates that TV coverage of Faldo's victory with the distinctive blade and its black plasticlike Stronomic insert in the face, will translate into $5 million in sales.)

Although the new tool probably helped, it was a change in technique that really turned Pierce's putting around. "I'm relaxing my hands more," she explains. "When you get a death grip on the putter, you get to jabbing it."

Corning eased a few insecurities as well. Pierce hasn't played well on Sunday or with, in Pierce's mind, the physically superior Sheehan. So when they were paired together for the final round, and Sheehan froze her with a look when she entered the locker room that Pierce interpreted as "play well today or I'll kill you," she responded to the challenge with a solid 72.

Rarick, a slender, blonde 36-year-old, and something of a fashion plate, talks to a fan who compliments her on her hip two-tone black and tan Italian golf shoes. Her game hasn't been as snazzy lately. Rarick, who won four times in 1987–1991, hasn't tallied since, slipping back in the pack.

Morris, 30, on the verge of stardom after earning $191,050 last year in her fifth year on Tour, snacks on some crackers.

"Share, Marianne," says Gail Graham. Morris does. A criminal justice major at the University of South Carolina, Morris dreams of being a cop someday, and spends plenty of her off-hours watching *NYPD Blue* and reruns of *Cagney and Lacey*, *Adam 12*, and *The Rookie*. She knows, however, just how dangerous real police work can be: a college friend who worked as a DEA agent was blown out of the sky a few years ago on a plane returning from Colombia, probably the result of terrorism.

For now, maybe Morris can use her detective skills to ferret out the cause of the delay. Actually, the greenest rookie could crack this case. It's the stubborn traditionalists at Golf House, the headquarters of the USGA in Far Hills, New Jersey.

The pace of play at the U.S. Open has become an annual joke. In 1991 Lori Garbacz, waiting endlessly on the 17th tee at Colonial, phoned in an order for a pizza, had it delivered, and chowed down.

This year the USGA's target time for pace of play is 4:04. It could happen. And pigs could fly. Consider the recipe the USGA concocts: A field with 30 mini-tour or club pros and 15 amateurs, who qualified at ten sectional tournaments or received USGA exemptions, including all eight members of the U.S. Curtis Cup team.

Part of the tradition of the U.S. Open is that it is truly open. Any woman with a handicap of 4.4 or less can tee it up in the sectionals. And part of the charm of the U.S. Open is watching the amateurs, especially the youngsters (a 14-year-old qualified in 1995), often accompanied by excited parents, walk wide-eyed onto the practice range to hit balls next to a Betsy King or Beth Daniel or Nancy Lopez.

Just don't expect a threesome of, for example, Lori Atsedes (Futures Tour), Stephanie Keever (17-year-old Las Vegas high school student), or Lori Wilkes (mini-tour player and substitute teacher) to whip around a course like Pine Needles.

That is, however, just what the USGA expects. It also expects to send 150 players (a mob larger than the normal 144-player LPGA field) off the 1st tee, instead of starting players off both No. 1 and No. 10, without turning Pine Needles into something resembling rush hour in Manhattan.

If it weren't so indispensable, the USGA, founded in 1894, would be awfully exasperating. A nonprofit association of over 8,500 member clubs and 650,000 golf fans, the USGA has an annual budget around $50 million and a staff of close to 200. The growth of the USGA has mirrored the exploding popularity of the game: in the late 1980s, the USGA staff numbered only about 35.

The USGA stages 13 national championships. In conjunction with the Royal and Ancient Golf Club of St. Andrews, the USGA is responsible for the Rules of Golf, the Bible of the links. The USGA also subjects clubs and balls to exacting performance tests and standards, an increasingly vital role in an era where golf has become an enormous business and equipment companies seek to exploit the tiniest edge in the marketplace. If the USGA weren't standing at the gate, protecting the integrity of the game from the barbarians and their space age scientists, clubs would be designed to fire golf balls like rocket launchers and balls would be equipped with miniaturized motors and homing devices which locked onto flagsticks. If it weren't for the USGA, everyone would shoot 18, go numb with boredom, and take up Parcheesi. Some pros think standards have become too lax, and equipment improvements have altered the game, replacing skill with technology. Beth Daniel is one of the most outspoken. She's written USGA president Judy Bell (no relation to Peggy Kirk Bell) to urge the USGA to crack down.

Actually, the USGA, which for almost a century prided itself on its hidebound conservative, elitist, snotty, stubborn resistance to change, has undergone something of a revolution in recent years. When 43-year-old David Fay was hired as its executive director in 1989, the devotee of both classical music and Springsteen accelerated the merger of a traditional structure with a progressive concern about issues such as gender and racial equality. Since 1990 clubs hosting USGA national championships and sectional qualifiers are required to have open membership policies. "It just wasn't right," Fay told *Golf World.* "To judge someone on their race or their sexual preference or their religion is crazy."

Awash in cash—the USGA's television deal with NBC is worth $65 million over five years, merchandise sales have skyrocketed, golf fans who join the USGA contribute millions in dues, and the stock market boom has sent USGA investments through the roof—the USGA is funding an array of environmental programs (including a $3 million project to investigate the effects of pesticides on golf courses) and spent over $800,000 last year for youth and education programs focusing on junior, minority, and physically disadvantaged golfers.

Although the hierarchy of the USGA, which is controlled by a 16-member committee, is still dominated by wealthy men from private clubs, minorities and women now have a place at the table.

In fact, a woman sits at the head of the table. In January 1996 Judy Bell, 59, became the first female president in the history of the USGA, an ascension that had nothing to do with tokenism or affirmative action.

An outstanding amateur golfer, Bell held 9-hole (31) and 18-hole (67) U.S. Open scoring records that stood for 30 and 21 years. Passing up a potential pro career in favor of business, she and partner Barbara McIntire (a high-ranking USGA Committee member who almost won the U.S. Open as an amateur, losing in a playoff to Kathy Cornelius in 1956) opened a clothing shop at The Broadmoor that grew into a small empire consisting of four stores and two restaurants in the Colorado Springs area. After rising through the ranks over a 35-year period to become vice president, Bell orchestrated the hugely successful U.S. Open in her own backyard last year that lured a record 94,000 spectators to The Broadmoor.

The power that the USGA exerts over the golf world has never corrupted it, absolutely or even a smidge. Au contraire. The USGA is a model of rectitude in a rudderless world where the prevailing ethos is a combination of "Just Do It" (no matter who gets trampled under foot, or sneaker) and "Don't Look at Me, It Wasn't My Fault."

Instead, the USGA's power tends to manifest itself in displays of arbitrariness and eccentricity. Sometimes it seems as if there's a deranged old coot in a tattered blue blazer running around the attic of Golf House, who sneaks downstairs in the dead of night and sends out faxes and directives on official stationary.

Suzy Green, first alternate from sectional qualifying in Charlotte, was invited into the field a few days ago when Colleen Walker withdrew. She was thrilled but puzzled, with no idea why she got the nod over alternates who had posted lower scores in other regions. (In fact, Green was the first alternate from the fifth-ranked allotment site, and was, accordingly, the fifth alternate to join the field. But why was she given the same tee times Walker would have received, instead of the least preferential times?)

And how can one rationalize the USGA's 1996 special exemptions? JoAnne Carner, Hollis Stacy, and Pinehurst resident Donna Andrews are in. Amy Alcott is out. The decision was made by the USGA Women's Committee (one of over 30 such committees composed of over 1,500 volunteers, which sometimes make the organization as unwieldy as a truck with 30 tires of different sizes). It was harshly criticized by several golf publications for choosing Andrews, a big-gate attraction in her hometown, over Alcott.

The critics missed the boat. Andrews deserved an exemption from qualifying and a spot in the field. Her U.S. Open record, which includes a second and a third in six starts, is superb. She surely would have earned a spot in the field on the course (the top 40 LPGA money earners from last season are automatically exempt) if not for her back injury. But Alcott, winner of five majors and two USGA titles, including the U.S. Open in 1980, also deserved a place in the field. Her exclusion, as she nears the end of a marvelous career, is a slap in the face to a great champion.

And, what about the Rules of Golf? You can fix ball marks but not spike marks? Why? Because the USGA says it will slow down play to tamp down spike marks? Absurd. Pros who miss short putts on national TV spend, cumulatively, about a month of Sundays muttering and peering at spike marks, real or imaginary.

And how about the rule that allows caddies to line up players like toy figures in a computer golf game? And tell them if their putter blade is facing the target? It's the most disgraceful sight in the game. Players may as well just drop a club on the turf to line themselves up, the way they do on the range.

Some golfers eschew the assistance, even if it might put them at a competitive advantage to their peers. "If you can't line yourself up," says Sheehan, "maybe you shouldn't be out here." Beth Daniel agrees. Her letter to Judy Bell echoed Sheehan's belief that real woman can align themselves without a helping hand.

What does the USGA say? "It is a matter that is being reviewed by the Rules of Golf Committee." Expect a decision sometime in the next century, which, to be fair, is only a few years down the road.

This *round* may not conclude until the next century. After their long delay at No. 2, Pierce, Morris, and Rarick reach the 195-yard 5th hole and come to a screeching halt. Three groups are waiting near the tee box. One of the kids carrying a portable scoreboard is lying flat out on the grass, a baseball cap over his head, napping while still holding the board aloft.

Rarick cadges a banana Powerbar from Lonnie Hellwig, Sherri Steinhauer's caddy.

"I'll pay you for it," says Rarick. "How much?"

"A dollar fifty plus tip," says Steinhauer.

The course is playing ferociously long for Pierce and the other short hitters. Facing a fierce wind on the 355-yard 4th hole, she needed a fairway wood to reach the green, hooked it into the trees onto a bed of pine straw, and hit a marvelous wedge to scramble for par.

After about a 30-minute wait, the green finally clears. The hole is stunning. Both tee and green are on hillsides, with a mini-canyon in between. It's a beautiful hole, but it's playing dead into the wind.

Pierce pulls out a driver and hits it absolutely flush. The ball barely reaches the front edge of the green. (She'll take it—the hole will bedevil the field today, partly because an NBC mini-blimp with a camera attached is tethered down the hill to the right of the green, and a number of players, including Dottie Pepper, find themselves faced with shots near the blimp and its cables, necessitating long discussions with rules officials and even more delays. One player bounces a shot off the blimp and pars the hole, a "blimpie," which should be worth a month's supply of submarine sandwiches.)

On the 402-yard, 7th hole, Pierce wails on a driver and a 3-wood and winds up on the front fringe with a putt of about 100 feet over a big ridge. She misjudges the slope and leaves it 20 feet short. It's easy to see how quickly a U.S. Open course can frustrate and overwhelm a player.

Pierce battles her heart out to keep Pine Needles from destroying her. When the long par putt is halfway to the hole, she begins walking toward it, confidently motioning with her arm like a bowler rolling a strike. It's in all the way.

After a tooth and claw struggle that lasts almost five and a half hours, a struggle that requires 9 fairway-wood second shots on the 12 par fours and a driver and a 7-wood on two of the par threes, Pierce walks off the last green with a 16-par, 2-bogey 72.

"What's true par today?" Pierce is asked, after she signs her card and reporters from Europe, Australia, and America encircle her.

"At least 72," she says.

She's being modest. The field will average 75.66 today. In terms of sheer grit, this is a round for Pierce's scrapbook. In terms of sheer weirdness, a question she gets from the Australian writer is also one for her scrapbook.

"Which LPGA players smoke cigars?"

*   *   *

It may be hellaciously difficult for the players, but the U.S. Open at Pine Needles is heaven for golf fans. By the time Sorenstam, Webb, and the 19-year-old Texas University student Kelli Kuehne, 1995 U.S. Amateur champ, tee off at 2:00, the course is swarming with some 14,000 spectators, a first-round record. It feels like the final round of an ordinary event, with a buzz of excitement in the air. The air itself, temperature in the mid 70s, with the chill winds of the morning turned into a caressing breeze, is just about dead solid perfect. "If you had your hand on the thermostat," says a spectator, "I don't know which way you'd turn it."

With two groups stacked up on the 2nd tee, Sorenstam and Webb find a spot in the shade, plop down on their golf bags, idly pluck blades of grass from the turf, and kill time like chums on a coffee break.

Webb is smiling on the outside, but not on the inside. Last week she picked up a $10,000 appearance fee in Japan, but she lost a caddie and, much more importantly, a fiancé. After an argument in the Far East, Todd Haller returned to Australia. The relationship, Webb says privately, is over.

When the 2:10 pairing of Sheehan, Inkster, and Neumann walk off the 1st green and see three groups, including Sorenstam, Webb, and Kuehne, stacked up like planes over O'Hare, Inkster says, "We've played one hole and we've already got a twenty-five-minute wait. This must be the Open."

Yes, it's the Open. But why are Sorenstam, Webb, Sheehan, Inkster, and Neumann teeing off in the middle of the afternoon, times usually reserved for the lowest on the totem pole, trash-sweeping times? Why is Suzy Green, the last player to make the field, blessed with excellent 8:00 and 12:00 starting times?

One guess.

That's right, The Great God Television raises its long lens once again. ESPN is showing an afternoon telecast of the PGA's Memorial tournament from two to four, with two chunks of U.S. Open sandwiched around it from twelve to two and from five to seven. So the stars, including Mallon, Davies, Bradley, Robbins, Lopez, King, and Daniel are booked for the late show, with spiked-up greens, a finish in the twilight, and a pace of play that feels like moonwalking.

"Brutal," says Caroline Pierce of midafternoon starting times. "It's tiring more than anything else, the waiting around."

Sheehan spent the morning trying to quell Open Fever. She arrived at the course and warmed up with confidence.

But this is the U.S. Open. "At the Open you have to play your best. Do that or the course will destroy you." And on the 2nd hole, the best-laid plans of the meticulous, disciplined Sheehan go kablooey. She drives into the rough, lays up short, and guns a wedge at the flag, which is near the back of the green. It runs off the unyielding surface and Sheehan pitches up and two-putts for a double-bogey.

"I was going after the pin, which you can't do at the Open," Sheehan says later. "It was a stupid shot." After that Sheehan feels like she's swimming upstream all day. "When you're two-over after two [holes], you feel like you can't make any more mistakes. Making birdies is so difficult at the Open anyway—it puts you in a hole right off the bat."

At 7:15 there are still eight groups out on the course. It's All Golf All the Time in the Sandhills and at the U.S. Open, where play runs from sunrise to and beyond sunset. The sun kisses the tips of the pine branches. Deep shadows seep over the course. Spectators in the half-full grandstand put on coats and sweaters and begin to shiver as the temperature rapidly plummets.

Reporters camp out near the scorer's tent, actually a silver mobile home parked beside the grandstand. There are 314 media representatives at Pine Needles; 14 Japanese cameramen, photographers, radio broadcasters, and writers engulf Hiromi Kobayashi when she walks off No. 18 after shooting 77.

Sunset arrives at 8:24; play concludes at 8:38. Sorenstam finishes with a 70, one stroke behind co-leaders Kim Willimas and Beth Daniel. Webb shoots a no-birdie 74. "I hit the ball as good as I have all year, but I left every putt six feet short."

"What's the deal with Todd?" asks a writer from *Golf World*.

"I'd rather not discuss it," says Webb. The Australian press is not as willing to take no comment for an answer. They spend the rest of the week digging for dirt, and Webb's face becomes more and more morose, especially when she fails to decipher the exceedingly subtle greens.

Sheehan, Inkster, and Neumann all finish with disappointing 74s.

"Ridiculous," says Inkster about the late tee times.

"It was impossible to read the greens the last few holes with the shadows on them," says the Caddie Machine.

Davies, who also shoots 74, is livid. Slow play drives her batty anyway, and the combination of slow play and a lousy tee time is too much.

"The tee times were a joke. I don't know why name players and former champions have to [finish] in the dark. I couldn't see the back of the ball the last five holes. I don't care if it's TV. This is the bloody U.S. Open. I wouldn't mind a 2:30 starting time, if it were drawn out of a hat. But the [better] players weren't given a fair chance. The lesson here is don't win a U.S. Open or be a leading money winner and you won't get a bad tee time."

Playing in the next-to-last group, Nancy Lopez tees off at 3:00 and finishes at 8:30. Lopez's eyesight isn't what it used to be. Like Jack Nicklaus, she often has trouble picking up the flight of the ball or seeing where it lands. She also has night blindness.

She could have used a miner's cap on the last few holes—or would that have been considered an "artificial device" by the rules pooh-bahs of the USGA? Finishing bogey-bogey-bogey, Lopez staggers in with a 76, her chances of winning her first U.S. Open lost in the gloaming.

Lopez is so angry and disheartened, she swears she never wants to play in another U.S. Open. "I couldn't see the breaks at all on the last few holes. Everything looked flat. It scares you. I missed a one-foot putt on the last hole."

"The Open has always had the imprimatur of being the world's toughest golf tournament," David Fay told *Golf World*. "I would hate to see it become something less than that."

Fair enough.

Sometimes, however, the USGA seems to take perverse pleasure in watching the best players in the world suffer. Sometimes, it seems to be sending out a message that life is often unfair, unkind, and arbitrary. Sometimes, it seems to be reminding golfers, and the rest of us, that powerful, implacable forces, whether the work of man or nature, control us.

Those are good things to be reminded of, at least once a year. Still, my guess is that the gatekeeper of the sacred playing fields, the guardian of integrity, the arbitrator of the rules, probably wishes, in its newly sensitized heart, it could reach into its tailored blue blazer, pull out a fresh white handkerchief, and offer it to Nancy Lopez, who sits in a silver mobile home next to the 18th green and weeps as she signs her card, the darkness falling around her.

Move Day on Saturday is hot, sunny, and gorgeous, with a hint of a breeze. Almost as hot as Annika Sorenstam, who fired the tournament's low round yesterday, a three under par 67, to take a three-shot lead over Brandie Burton, Emilee Klein, and Jane Geddes. It may be lonely at the top, but Sorenstam seems comfortable there. For one thing, she loves Pine Needles. "It's just a beautiful place. Great golf holes—there's meaning to each one. You have to think a lot, there's a lot of strategy here."

All week she's been, as usual, a bit of a loner, putting on the seldom-used auxiliary practice green tucked above the clubhouse, and hitting balls on the opposite side of the range, accompanied by caddie Colin Cann, who, like the Caddie Machine, came to Pine Needles early to roll balls across the greens.

"She's so much calmer and so much more centered," said coach Pia

Nilsson a few days ago. "The Swedish and European media have noticed it. She doesn't get as off-balance. I don't worry about her too much. I'll be very surprised if she doesn't keep getting better the next few years."

A mind-boggling thought. Since Sorenstam switched from graphite to steel shafts before the McDonald's LPGA Championship, which corrected a slight fade, she's been hitting the ball as straight as an arrow. "She's at her peak," thought caddie Cann as the tournament began.

The course dried out and played much shorter for yesterday's second round—Davies, Val Skinner, Wendy Ward, and Meg Mallon all shot 68—but it was hardly a walk in the park. The field averaged 74.26, an improvement of a little over a stroke from the first round. The 36-hole cut that sliced the field to 63 players (low 60 plus ties) fell at a whopping eight over par. Hollis Stacy (+9), Donna Andrews (+9), JoAnne Carner (+11), Nancy Lopez (+12), Helen Alfredsson (+12), Cathy Gerring (+13), Dottie Pepper (+13), and Betsy King (+18) spent last night packing their bags.

In fact Pepper was stranded in the Pine Needles parking lot after her round yesterday, as furious as she's been in her entire career, after loaning her courtesy car to her mother. Sick of the game that so consumes her, she told caddie Scarinzi after the 11th hole he should temporarily find another bag—she was taking the next two months off. (The vow lasts less than 24 hours: today Pepper is beating balls on the opposite side of the range, out of sight of the fans.)

Sheehan and Inkster matched cards again yesterday; they stand at 145 after firing 71s. Exhausted after the first round, Sheehan simply gutted it out, missing nine greens but recovering time and time again with clutch chips and putts. "She couldn't get her legs through on her irons," said the Caddie Machine. Inkster squandered a potentially excellent round with bogeys at 17 and 18, again bedeviled with inconsistent putting.

With bogeys on 2, 3, 4, and 5, Pierce fell back in the pack, then played smoothly to shoot 75 and survive the cut.

It's crunch time for Sheehan and Inkster, who need superb rounds to move into contention.

Sheehan seems up to the challenge. Refreshed and focused, she strikes the ball flawlessly on the early holes, piercing the fairway with drives and flagging irons at the stick.

"Patty Sheehan has the best golf swing in the world," a dazzled fan says to his wife after another sizzling drive.

But the great swings and shots go for naught. Sheehan strokes lovely putts that hang on or curl over the edge of the cup on the first five holes. The small, purse-lipped frown on her face tells the story. No U.S. Open glory this year.

Inkster can't get anything going either, although she and playing partner Meg Mallon share a laugh on the 393-yard 6th tee when Juli reaches into Meg's bag and starts to pull out Meg's driver. It's an easy mistake to make—both endorse Wilson and carry red and white Wilson Staff bags, with matching red and white Wilson head covers.

(Neither plays Wilson woods, however. Inkster packs a Big Bertha driver and 3-wood and a Taylor-Made 5-wood. Mallon uses a Cobra driver, Taylor-Made 3-wood, and Callaway 7-wood. Earlier in the season Wilson ran ads for their Invex driver, which John Daly rode to victory at the 1995 British Open, containing photos of other Wilson reps, including Mallon, Inkster, Bernhard Langer, and Vijay Singh. The ads clearly gave the impression that all of the pictured golfers played the Invex; just the opposite was true. Mallon and Inkster can't hit it a lick; Mallon says none of the men, except Daly, use it either. Apparently all is fair in love and war and golf equipment marketing.)

The atmosphere around the course is electrifying. After yesterday's record Friday attendance of 22,000, a third straight mark is shattered as 30,000 fans flood Pine Needles today.

Sitting in back of the hillside green on the 195-yard 5th hole, ringed ten deep with fans, and watching contenders arrive at the tee box high on the opposite side of the mini-canyon is a joy. The scenery alone is worth the price of admission. A few puffy white clouds with a bit of ash gray mixed in gently drift through turquoise skies. The dark branches of the pines, with their beds of cinnamon pine straw, encircle the green. The putting surface itself, a light green with a tinge of yellow, is ringed by three cuts of fringe of gradually deeper grass and darker shades, culminating in the seaweed-colored rough.

Players tee off, walk down the hill, and stride up to the green as rivers of fans, a mobile Monet of pastel shirts and shorts, flow up and down the pathway alongside the fairway. The rivers keep widening and deepening as the final groups crest the hill, fans whooping as an all-business Laura Davies drills a 15-foot birdie putt, wincing in silent, sympathetic agony as her playing partner, Joan Pitcock, plays Ping-Pong across the treacherous green for a ghastly triple-bogey, groaning as Sorenstam, playing in the final group with Burton, misses a 10-foot par putt.

The tee across the canyon is deserted now. The rivers of fans flow into a mighty ocean behind the leaders, Sorenstam and Burton. The thunder of competition is up ahead; behind it a tiny bird hops across the now silent, peaceful, deserted green. And I have an overwhelming desire to jog to the car, pop open the trunk, haul out my clubs, and tee it up.

Open Fever.

The crowd flows around the tee boxes and the greens and down the length of both sides of the fairways as Sorenstam, in a soft salmon-colored shirt and pale yellow shorts, and Burton, in a white shirt with bold brown designs and brown shorts, battle through the back nine, threatening to break from the pack.

By the time they reach the 401-yard 14th hole, Sorenstam (-5) and Burton (-3) are the only two golfers under par.

After a booming drive, Sorenstam, with 161 yards to the hole, pulls out a 6-iron and laces it at the flag. She watches in amazement as the ball lands softly just in front of the stick, then keeps trickling and trickling past the pin, over the crown, and down a short, steep slope into the rough.

About ten photographers are dogging the duo, walking just inside the ropes, as photographers and writers are allowed to do. (NBC, however, just like TV broadcasters at other tournaments, is in the middle of the fairway with cameras, microphones, and cable, breathing down the necks of the players.) The photographers walk around the back of the green, looking for prime shooting positions.

Suddenly a sharp, loud "Oh!" bursts from the packed gallery behind the green, as a photographer steps on Sorenstam's ball. Marshals are supposed to stand guard in such situations, shooing away anyone who comes near. This marshal was dozing at his post.

The USGA's Barbara McIntire, acting as rules official for the final group, arrives to adjudicate. The marshal points to the spot where he thinks the ball was before it was stepped on. The fans along the ropes voice their disagreement.

"How does he know?" calls out a fan. "He wasn't watching anyway." Other voices murmur in agreement. The galleries at Pine Needles, golf fans from the Carolinas and across the country, are as classy as the course itself, knowledgeable, respectful, and enthusiastic. No screams of "You da woman!" from *this* crowd.

Sorenstam laughs. She points toward the green, jokingly urging McIntire to place her ball on the putting surface. Finally she's allowed to pick it up and place it on the original spot, and everyone, including the embarrassed photographer, is happy.

But Sorenstam isn't laughing after bungling her flop shot, leaving it in the fringe some 15 feet above the cup. She spins the wedge in her hand and starts to bury it in the turf before she collects herself, a huge display of temper from the normally cool one.

Her par putt rims out and rolls three feet away. Sorenstam hits short putts firmly—she advocates driving the ball into the back of the cup. But this putt is a hair off-target; it spins around the cup a full 360 degrees and sits there, still above ground, mocking her.

Burton, after a tremendous bunker shot, pars the hole and suddenly the two are tied at three under par.

After a good drive on the 405-yard 15th hole, Sorenstam pulls an iron into a greenside bunker. The sweet little machine, who has hit almost nothing but fairways and greens since the tournament began, is leaking oil, and the pressure is in the red zone. As she waits for Burton to play her second shot, Sorenstam walks up the fairway a bit and stands near the ropes on the right side. Only a few spectators are near her.

Just then a little girl, probably about 5 years old, long, dark hair flying, dashes from the pine trees toward the ropes, laughing and yelling, "Grandpa!"

Sorenstam turns toward the noise. She's just blown a two-shot advantage after leading the U.S. Open for two days. She's just hit one of her worst shots of the tournament. Her Swedish temper may heat up slowly, but it came close to boiling over a few minutes ago. Now this! A kid running around like it's some sort of amusement park!

What would Albert Belle do at a moment like this? Most likely grab a 2-iron and, next thing you know, the head of the little long-haired girl would be rolling across the fairway.

What would Dottie Pepper do at a moment like this? Probably stop the tot dead in her tracks with a glare powerful enough to traumatize her for years.

What does Sorenstam do?

She . . . smiles. One of those little Annika-smiles, unfeigned, cheerful, and encouraging. The little girl is corralled by her mother and carried away from the ropes. Sorenstam goes back to work.

Just a little smile. Just a quiet display of grace under the noose-tightening pressure of the U.S. Open. When Pia Nilsson hears the story later, she nods in satisfaction. "That shows she's right where she should be."

Sorenstam scrambles for par, sliding in a six-foot putt on the high side. She rims out an eight-foot birdie putt on the 172-yard 16th hole. She blasts a drive 50 yards past Burton on the beastly 424-yard 17th hole. ("Not bad if you like perfect," says a marshal) leaving her just a 7-iron to the green. Later Sorenstam, who would like to fly military jets some day, sounds like she felt *herself* soaring into space when she describes the drive. "I hit it real solid, and I think all the anger from 14 was done in me. And I just flew."

Sorenstam rolls in a 30-foot birdie putt on No. 17 and pumps a fist as the ball seeks shelter. Burton bogeys Nos. 16 and 17. The lead is three again.

The walk down the hill from the 18th fairway to the green is overwhelming. At the top of the hill, the players stand above the level of the grandstand, gazing down a chute lined with people packing every inch of the ropes on both sides of the fairway and ringed around the green. It seems as if every one of the 30,000 people at Pine Needles today is waiting to greet them. As they walk down the steep slope, the stands and the people seem to rise, and the applause and the whoops and the shouts mingle with the rays of the sun and float down like a benediction.

Soon Burton, who won the U.S. Girls' Junior title at Pine Needles in 1989 when she was 17, is in the interview room. This gallery is not as beneficent. After a brief light moment (Reporter—"What's Sunday going to be like?" Burton—"Hopefully 75 and sunny." [Laughter]) things get a mite testy:

Q: Brandie, is it frustrating playing against a player like Annika who doesn't make very many mistakes? And does her right-down-the-middle shot all the time, does that make you feel like sometimes you need to make things happen?

Burton: No, I wasn't playing against her today. I was playing against myself. And that's also a big key, because it's not match play, you've got to beat the golf course. I was so into my game, that doesn't even bother me.

Q: Jane Geddes said that Annika showed she wasn't an iron woman today, that she's capable of being caught and maybe passed. What was your perception of what you had to do to catch her today, and what's your perception now following the round? What, if anything, has changed in your mind about her being in the lead?

Burton: See, that's the way I think everybody is getting a little out of control about that. I'm not worried about Annika, I'm worried about the golf course. The golf course is tough enough, and to have two variables come into play—some players may think they need to catch that person. If you get wrapped up in that person, you're not going to put a hundred percent in your game. That just adds to another variable that I've worked on this year, just to beat the golf course and make as many birdies as you possibly can.

Q: Annika has missed three fairways in three days. A player that straight, does she actually equalize her distance disadvantage?

Burton: You guys want Annika up here right now? I'm not describing Annika's game, and I'm not talking about her game. I'm up here to talk about my game.

The media aren't altogether happy campers. Late finishes on the first two days played havoc with deadlines, especially for the European press. And, there's no such thing as a free lunch at the U.S. Open—the buffet in the media center costs $6.95.

Sorenstam sails serenely through her interview. Last year at The Broadmoor, another Donald Ross design, she snuck up on Meg Mallon in the final round when Mallon triple-bogeyed an early par three. This year Sorenstam carries the weight of leadership on her shoulders.

Leading any golf tournament is, for most players, traumatic, playing havoc with a normally aggressive approach to the game. A few players, such as Raymond Floyd, relish a lead, figuring it gives them an extra margin of error. But most react like first-time drivers on the LA freeways, continually glancing at the rearview mirror, terrified of what might be coming up behind them.

Carrying a lead into the final rounds of the U.S. Open is the toughest challenge in sports.

The best in the game, the bravest and strongest have buckled—Sam Snead, Arnold Palmer, Mickey Wright, Patty Sheehan. Talented players—Gil Morgan, who built a seven-stroke lead at Pebble Beach in 1992, Helen Alfredsson, who confidently opened up a seven-shot margin on the field at Indianwood in 1994—have watched in horror, almost transfixed, as the relentless pressure, tightening and tightening minute-by-minute, suddenly cracked them like a soft-boiled egg, spilling runny, yellow nerve endings all over the fairway. "You don't win the Open: It wins you," said Cary Middlecoff, alluding to the fact that many Opens fall into the victor's lap. Final-round heroics, such as Johnny Miller's 63 in 1973 or Patty Sheehan's birdie-birdie finish in 1992, are incredibly rare.

But the woman of steel has already bought her ticket to the biggest, scariest Fun House of them all, and looks forward to the journey. "I don't mind being chased," she tells the media. "I think it's a good experience, and I've got to be able to handle this too. You cannot always chase someone. I think it's important to be able to hold the lead, also. You learn a lot from that, and that's the way golf is. You've got to be able to adjust to every situation."

A short time later Sorenstam and Burton are grinding away on the practice range as the sun sinks behind them. A few reporters, photographers, and die-hard fans sit and watch. So do Pia Nilsson and fiancé David Esch behind Sorenstam, and Burton's mother and father, Roger and Barbara, behind her.

"Will she be the first repeat winner?" asks a young, bearded fan from Los Angeles, gesturing at Sorenstam.

"No," says Steve Elling from the Raleigh *News & Observer*, who marvels at the way Sorenstam picks the ball from the turf with her irons, barely taking a divot. "The sixth." (Mickey Wright, Donna Caponi, Susie Maxwell Berning, Hollis Stacy, and Betsy King previously won back-to-back U.S. Opens.)

"But she'll be the first *babe*," says the dude from California. Perhaps so. *Esquire*, which last year, in the wake of the Ben Wright controversy, named the LPGA, along with Melissa Etheridge, Julie Cypher, Rachell Williams, and Ingrid Casares, among the "Women We Love Who Will Almost Certainly Never Love Us Back," just anointed Sorenstam, along with Mia Hamm, Jackie Joyner-Kersee, Holly McPeak, and Mary Jo Fernandez, as one of its "Women Whose Locker Rooms We'd Like to Hang Around."

At any rate, with her sun-bleached blonde hair, gold engagement band, gold earrings, slender gold bracelet—and a three-stroke lead—Sorenstam certainly *looks* golden.

Sorenstam wakes up with a case of Open Fever. She has a stomachache, as butterflies loop-de-loop in her gut. But it doesn't last long. "She was fine when she got to the course," says Colin Cann.

She joins Burton, Geddes, Green, Bradley, Tschetter, and Davies on the range. Another Carolina blue sky bathes another record crowd of 34,000 with 80-degree temperatures. A lively breeze ruffles Sorenstam's yellow shirt and black shorts. Shades shielding her eyes, she begins hitting short irons in front of a throng of onlookers. Children sit cross-legged under the gallery rope in front of the portable stands. One little girl in a pink shirt holds a pink soccer ball. Another girl in a blue U.S. Open cap collects autographs from players, including Davies, who signs a few before heading to the putting green, calling out "Good Luck" as she passes Geddes and Burton.

"Annika with a two-shot lead is my worst nightmare," Davies once said. After three rounds she trails by six, as does Michele Redman, Nancy Harvey, Mayumi Hirase, and Kris Tschetter. Tammie Green and Pat Bradley are five behind, Geddes four back. Burton trails by three; after Burton's press conference last evening, it's clear that Sorenstam is also *her* worst nightmare.

A fan near the range is wearing a white T-shirt, perhaps designed by the USGA, with the message of the day. The front reads:

No Charity
No Sympathy
No Mulligans

And on the back, in bold red letters inside a golf ball:

No Mercy

As the contenders warm up, players who began the final round at or near the back of the pack are finishing on No. 18. Caroline Pierce sinks a nice ten-foot par putt for a fine 70, her best-ever round in a U.S. Open. It vaults her to her best-ever U.S. Open finish, a tie for thirty-fourth with Inkster.

"It's starting to play like an Open course," says Pierce. "You hit a good shot into the green, and then wait five minutes till it stops rolling to see if it's *really* a good shot."

Buried midpack after a third-round 72, Sheehan rallies for a 69 and a tie for fourteenth.

"It was a different Open week," says Sheehan. Usually she takes the week off before the U.S. Open to prepare. This year she played in Corning, and it hurt her. "Being home the week before you can concentrate on specific shots—chipping from high rough, putting Open-speed greens. It's real intense practice, as opposed to playing a tournament, which isn't practice at all. Carl [Laib] needs to get into his mind-set too, and get to the site to study the course and learn the ideal spots to hit the ball. It takes him a week to absorb that."

In the 1960s it was Arnie's army.

In the late 1970s and 1980s it was Nancy's navy.

In the 1990s, at a site once used for an air force base it can only be Annika's air force. And the fans are out in full force. From the back of the crowd around the 1st green, it's barely possible to see the top of Sorenstam's black Callaway cap.

The early holes follow a familiar pattern. Burton, dressed in a light purple shirt with cream trim and cream shorts, scrambles from the rough. Sorenstam hits nothing but fairways and greens.

Burton has been working with Senior Tour star Dave Stockton on her short game since January, and talking to him every night this week. Stockton is one of the finest putters in the game, a magician with the flat stick, and he seems to have passed his gift to Burton, who has sunk a career's worth of long putts this year. Maybe it's one of those Vulcan, or Stockton,

Mind Meld things. On the 127-yard 3rd hole, Burton snakes home a 25-footer for birdie; Sorenstam, repulsing the early challenge, trumps it with a 7-footer of her own.

About 20 photographers and 10 writers trail the golfers through the enormous crowds and onto the tee boxes, crouching down in back or along the sides. NBC's Roger Maltbie, looking like a rumpled walrus in blue khakis, a wrinkled sport shirt, tennis shoes and white cap, blows cigarette smoke out his nose on the tee of the 195-yard 5th hole. Maltbie, a skilled golf analyst, is paid a small fortune. But on-course reporting isn't glamorous work. A headset delivers a tinny feed of NBC's telecast in his ear; all day long he listens to promos for NBC's "Must See TV," which Must Drive Him Crazy.

For the golfers, hemmed in by writers, photographers, cameramen and microphones, and surrounded by dense packs of fans, it's almost like swinging in a phone booth, with a bunch of faces pressed up against the glass.

"God, I hope I don't kill anybody," murmurs Burton, as she yanks a long iron toward the crowd. She winds up in the pine straw and works hard to salvage bogey.

Sorenstam gets her first test of the day: a three-foot par putt on a spiked-up green. Although she rotates her head when swinging her woods and irons, Sorenstam anchors it when she putts, waiting to hear the sound of the ball plunking into the cup. She does, the crowd applauds, and Sorenstam offers a tense "thank you."

On the 393-yard 6th hole, Sorenstam hooks her drive into the second cut of rough. It's one of only five fairways she will miss in the entire tournament, and it brings an exasperated frown. After playing safely short of the green, Sorenstam pitches nicely to four feet.

No little Annika smiles now. She looks tense, perhaps a bit scared, as she fidgets over the par putt. But her stroke is bulletproof.

"She has the game and the temperament suited for this kind of pressure," Jane Geddes will say later. "She is so precise, so poised, way beyond her years. Catching her today was a thought some of us had. But that was all it was—a thought." Her opposition is treading water. Sorenstam holds a commanding five-stroke lead over Burton and Geddes.

Like all great players, Sorenstam is an inveterate scoreboard watcher. As Johnny Miller puts it, "In the heat of a major championship, it's a jungle out there, and when there's a noise, the small animals look for cover while the lions find out what caused it. They're not afraid of anything.

"Jack Nicklaus was that way. So was Arnold Palmer. . . . They were kings of the jungle."

When Sorenstam sees she is firmly in command, she seems to relax a little. With 220 yards to the pin on the 440-yard 10th hole, from a sidehill lie with the ball above her feet, Sorenstam scorches a magnificent 3-wood which rolls up 20 feet from the cup. When she slam-dunks the eagle putt, she raises both hands overhead, breaks into a high-beam smile that lights up the roaring gallery, and floats from the green to the next tee on waves of applause. Up ahead Kris Tschetter, in the process of shooting a 66 that will sweep her into second place, sees Sorenstam move to eight under par, and says to herself, "What golf course is *she* playing?"

"This isn't a golf tournament," says a fan watching Annika's air force, worshipping in her wake, "it's a coronation."

Even the cautious, conservative, play-it-as-it-lies, take-nothing-for granted USGA agrees. As Sorenstam cruises through No. 12 with a seven-shot lead, it does something astonishing, not to mention unprecedented. It issues a press release which reads:

"Annika Sorenstam's winning 72-hole total of 2__ [sic] is a new U.S. Women's Open scoring record. . . . [Sorenstam] is only the sixth woman to have won back-to-back U.S. Open titles."

As if to remind everyone she's human, Sorenstam bogeys Nos. 13 and 14. But she birdies No. 15, and then, on the 172-yard 16th hole, turns a coronation into an exhibition for the ages. Armed with a 6-iron, she pulls the trigger on a rifle shot that almost literally knocks the pin down—the ball takes one bounce and clangs off the flagstick. Sorenstam can't see it—she doesn't wear her contacts on breezy days—but the screams from the crowd around the green reverberate all the way back to the tee box.

And the mind flashes to the exploits of another great athlete, Annie Oakley, when she coolly blasted targets from the sky in front of 30,000 cheering fans. A prim, proper lady, a bit of a loner offstage, and a dazzling, steely-willed competitor of almost otherworldly skill and poise onstage. Years later 39,000 cheering fans shake the heavens with applause as Sorenstam walks down the 18th fairway and into the history books. Her final round 66 ties the record for lowest final round at the U.S. Open; her 72-hole total of 272 shatters the previous mark of 277 set by Liselotte Neumann in 1988, when Sorenstam sat up all night, glued to the tube, dreaming a teenager's dreams about following in her countrywoman's footsteps.

A faint sound of music drifts down from over the hill above the 18th green as the sun sinks toward the pines. A bagpiper in Scotch kilts appears at the top of the hill, slowly moving toward the green. USGA officials in blue blazers and white shirts stretch across the green. Judy Bell, shattering tradition once again, announces the site of the 2001 U.S. Women's Open:

Pine Needles. The crowd goes wild. Peggy Kirk Bell and her family almost fall off their chairs in surprise.

Actually, it's a no-brainer. Above almost all else, the USGA seeks crowds at the U.S. Women's Open, big enthusiastic crowds, grandstands overflowing with cheering fans, fans transmitting the wonder and thrill of the U.S. Open to the viewers at home, who might get the notion that the women's game ain't just beanbag. Pine Needles delivered the bodies and a whole lot more, a grace and charm that are so rare these days they almost seem quaint.

"It's been like a storybook," says Chip King, director of golf at Pine Needles and Mid Pines. "Just a magical week. The facility, the golf course, the weather, the two thousand volunteers, the fans. Mostly how everybody enjoyed it here. I really think it's because of the Bell family. They invited everyone into their home for a week."

Sorenstam, who dreads public speaking—she used to tank junior tournaments in Sweden to avoid the victory stand oratory—expresses her gratitude and tears up when she thanks her family. Her father, mother, and aunt traveled from Sweden to the Sandhills for the U.S. Open; since they rarely get to see her play, it's an extraspecial occasion.

Then Sorenstam parades the big silver trophy for a semicircle of about 50 photographers spread out across the green, shutters clicking like locusts, yelling like Hollywood paparazzi.

"Annika! Annika!"

"Annika! Over here!"

Later Sorenstam meets the press in the media center. "Now I can breathe again," she says. But the pressure on the head of a champion never completely lifts. A writer asks her about her chances of a three-peat in 1997.

"Let's take one thing at a time," she pleads. "I'm just going to enjoy these two for now."

Sorenstam will try to become the first woman to win three straight U.S. Opens at Pumpkin Ridge near Portland, Oregon, next July. The odds are against her. But it would be foolish to bet against her. At the U.S. Open, which demands the ultimate in precision and the ultimate in determination and preparation and will, Annika Sorenstam is the strongest player, male or female, in the world.

Her preparation this year offers ample proof. Pros routinely visualize golf shots. Sorenstam went well beyond that. Before she arrived at Pine Needles, she visualized everything a defending champion would need to cope with in order to defend her crown.

"I imagined myself being there, and really prepared for a lot of distractions. Everything was under control. There was time to practice and sign autographs. It could be a shock if you weren't prepared. But it turned out to be nothing, almost."

When she tees it up at Pumpkin Ridge, she'll have one great champion rooting for her. "I'm just so impressed with her composure, her maturity, her smarts," Mickey Wright told *Golf Journal*. "I hope she wins three in a row."

Several years ago, before fame arrived, Sorenstam played in a tournament in the Sandhills. Peggy Kirk Bell invited her to stay at Pine Needles. The older woman and the shy youngster became friends. But Bell couldn't pronounce Annika's name. She calls her "Heineken."

Cute, but it just doesn't fit. Since Sorenstam has joined the pantheon of the greatest athletes to perform in the Sandhills, she needs a nickname befitting her. The choice is obvious:

Call her Annie.

CHAPTER 7

$\mathcal{A}$tlantic City and Toledo: Independence Day

Juli Inkster is frustrated.

It's the last week of June and Inkster is sitting on a bench of the temporary bleachers at the back of the practice range at Greate Bay Resort and Country Club in Somers Point, New Jersey, site of the $750,000 ShopRite LPGA Classic. "I'm playing better. I know I'm *hitting* it better. But I've got to learn how to win again and know I *can* win again."

Inkster took two weeks off after the U.S. Open. She skipped the $600,000 Oldsmobile Classic in East Lansing, Michigan (won by Michelle McGann over Liselotte Neumann after a four-hole sudden-death playoff) and the $550,000 Edina Realty LPGA Classic just outside Minneapolis (won by Neumann in front of galleries packed with transplanted Scandinavians).

The tournament in Minneapolis is not one of Inkster's favorites. She hates the course—"wind and a lot of lay-up holes." But her memory may be influenced by her visit in 1990, the culmination of the worst travel experience of her career.

It was August and Hayley was still teething. Juli and her parents, Jack and Carole, who were serving as baby-sitters, endured a four-and-a-half-hour delay before flying from San Jose into JFK Airport for the JAL Big Apple Classic in New Rochelle. On a sweltering New York midsummer day they hopped into a cab. A malfunctioning heater was cranked up full blast. The cab driver promptly got lost. Inkster missed the cut.

On to Minneapolis via Pan Am, which turned into a little flight of horrors. Hayley pooped all over Juli's shirt. A beverage cart careened down the aisle and flattened a stewardess against the rear of the plane; Jack had to pry the cart away to free her. Finally the landing gear wouldn't engage. The pilot and copilot, armed with flashlights, ventured back into the passenger section and peered through the floor at the mechanism—not the most reassuring of sights for the terrified travelers—while the plane circled and circled and circled.

Eventually they landed. But midsummer in Minnesota was no picnic.

The course, says Jack, was under attack by swarms of mosquitoes that were "just a little bit smaller than airplanes."

Inkster's return to the fray last week at the $550,000 Rochester International in upstate New York was relatively uneventful. Actually, says Inkster, "last week was wasted."

After hitting it well early in the week, Inkster lost her rhythm as the rains descended, and she missed the cut. She now ranks twenty-seventh on the money list with $101,070.

A deluge washed out Thursday's first round. More thunderstorms led to a 6:44 rain delay on Saturday. "Never saw anything like it," says the Caddie Machine, who could have used hip boots to slog around the course. It's the sixth week in a row where rain has marred the proceedings. The LPGA now has a new nickname—the Thunder and Lightning Tour.

The range at Somers Point is quiet and peaceful on Monday afternoon, populated by a few golfers and a number of swooping, squawking white and gray seagulls. Somers Point is ringed by Great Egg Harbor Bay, to the south and east. The bay is separated from the Atlantic Ocean by narrow fringes of land. Ocean City, directly across the bay to the east, is a seaside resort town with a two-mile wooden boardwalk along the ocean. The population swells from around 20,000 to 110,000 in the summertime. Atlantic City is a 20-minute drive to the north.

A scent of sea salt is carried by the breeze on a mild, gray day. Inkster lugs her heavy golf bag onto the range. Caddie Greg Johnston is moving into the Ocean City house he's renting for the week with several other caddies. Nanny Tina England and daughter Cori are at the grocery store.

Juli and 6-year-old Hayley have just returned from the Ocean City boardwalk, a honky-tonk strip of shops, restaurants, movie theaters, miniature golf courses, a towering Ferris wheel and roller coaster, and every variety of junk food known to man, woman, or child, including salt-water taffy, caramel corn, licorice, corn dogs, and snow cones. In fact, Juli is wearing a few red streaks of cherry ice on her white sweater. The board-walk is a daily event—today's entertainment, for both Juli and Hayley, was riding the water slide.

Last night they celebrated, in a very low-key manner, Juli's thirty-fifth birthday, with a dinner that included ice cream and green beans. Hayley went to bed at 8:30, Juli at 9:30.

Hayley, dressed in a blue outfit decorated with blue and red flowers, her straight, cropped, ear-length blonde hair topped by a beaded headband, sits on Juli's red and white Wilson Staff golf bag as Juli goes to work.

"Mom, can you do that thing where you balance the balls?"

Inkster delicately stacks one golf ball on top of another, no easy feat in itself. Then she takes an iron and whacks the bottom ball, which goes sailing down the range. The top ball pops up about 30 feet in the air.

Hayley's eyes widen in delight. The idea is for Juli to catch the pop-up like an infielder. But this one would be a tough grab for Cal Ripken, and Inkster, who, after all, is now 35, declines to dive for it. "Didn't want to kill myself," she shrugs.

Like most precocious kids, Hayley has a few zillion questions on her mind.

"What's the other way to spell Juli?"

"What's that?" she says, pointing to a scoreboard.

"Can you get me a tee?"

It's a well-established routine for Inkster, who chats cheerfully with Hayley between shots. And Hayley finds plenty of activities to amuse herself. She eats some red candy—"Yum!" She peers into a Viewmaster. She hits a few balls, displaying an athletic lunge of a swing. She plays catch with a bystander, tossing a miniature white basketball back and forth. She serves as caddie—rolling new Titleists, one-by-one, to Juli, while sitting so close that the force generated by Inkster's powerful swing ruffles her hair.

"Aaagh! Aaagh!" says Juli.

"What's wrong?" Hayley asks.

"I'm not driving very well."

During her two-week break, Inkster went to Hayley's kindergarten graduation and picnic, a swim party, the Great America amusement park, and her parents. She didn't play or practice very much.

The Tour has been a grind this season, more so than usual. The biggest tournaments of the year are already over, and it's not even July. Instead of the glories of the U.S. Open or the Nabisco Dinah Shore, players face the mundane prospect of traveling to Ohio next week for two events, the Jamie Farr Kroger Classic in Toledo and the Youngstown-Warren Classic. In short, the dog days of summer have already arrived.

"The schedule is so front-loaded this year," says Inkster. "You had to peak really early." And to make matters more difficult, the next six weeks require players to crisscross North America, journeying from New Jersey to Ohio to Massachusetts to Missouri, to Alberta, Canada, and then back to Massachusetts. It's the most convoluted path the LPGA has ever trudged, and caddies as well as players are flying a lot more often than in past seasons.

But it's crunch time for Inkster. To make the Solheim Cup team, she needs to win a tournament and play well at the final major, the du Maurier Classic in Edmonton, which means she needs to start holing some putts.

"I'm putting better," says Inkster. "I'm just not making anything. Miss on the left edge, miss on the right edge, lip out. When I hit the ball good, I'm one or two under. When I hit it bad, I'm two or three over."

Before the season began, Inkster said, "I have a lot of confidence off the course. I think I'm a good person. On the course I need a little more confidence, a few more pats on the back. It's a tough thing to learn, to be my own best friend."

Six months later, Inkster is asked if she's making any progress. She shakes her head. "I'm not doing very good with that. I still get really mad. It's good that the kids are out. I'm *trying* to enjoy myself a little more."

Inkster beats balls a while longer.

"Two more, Hay," she says. "Then we'll go putt some."

"Can I putt too?" asks Hayley.

"You can."

Later this evening they'll return to the boardwalk, after taking care of some necessities of life on the road: finding a stroller for Cori and doing laundry, practically a daily occurrence with the kids. "We go through clothes like Kleenex," says Inkster.

"Mom, I'm a finger puppet," says Hayley, waving around a white tee.

Inkster hits two more, then two more, then two more.

"Moh-uhm!" says Hayley.

"Just two more."

Leslie Spalding is worried.

She hits the practice range on Monday too, after missing her fourth straight cut at Rochester last week. After wilting in the spotlight at the McDonald's LPGA Championship, Spalding missed the cut at the Corning Classic, watched the U.S. Open on TV, skipped the Oldsmobile Classic in East Lansing to spend a week in Montana, and missed the cut in Minneapolis. She's slipped all the way to 120th on the money list, right on the borderline of the top 125. Like the sands of an hourglass suddenly turned upside down, the optimism and confidence she carried with her from the Sprint Titleholders Championship have, bit by bit, ebbed away. "It's hard not to think about the future, about keeping my card. Wilmington set me back a little. I think I've seen the worst times. I've learned a lot—you keep trying harder, and harder, and that makes you score worse and worse. You just have to rip it and go for it."

Easier said than done. After the McDonald's LPGA Championship, Spalding traveled from Wilmington to Philadelphia and shot 80 in the sectional qualifying for the U.S. Open, missing out by four strokes. "It was at the end of the first long trip and I was really sick of golf," says Spalding. "I got too mad out there and made a stupid double [bogey] on number six. I didn't have fun."

She didn't have fun at the Corning Classic in upstate New York later that week. Spalding shot 74-74 to miss the cut by one stroke.

"Dumb mistakes," says Spalding. The crushing final-round miscues were a missed two-foot putt, a three-putt from 15 feet on No. 16, and the mistaken notion she needed to birdie the last two holes to make the cut.

"I'm focusing too much on scoring instead of playing." Not even a trip to the psychologist—sports psychologist Bob Rotella, one of the best-known golf shrinks—helped. Rotella has been a guru to many of the stars of the PGA and LPGA Tours. Spalding read his book, *Golf Is Not a Game of Perfect*. religiously during Q-School last year, as did fellow rookie Susan Veasey, and it was a valuable asset in helping them survive and secure their Tour cards. But Rotella had no magic words for Spalding after she shelled out $3,100 for a two-day session at Rotella's office in Charlottesville, Virginia.

On the first day Rotella accompanied Spalding for 18 holes. "He said I've definitely got the goods." But Spalding knew she could play before she wrote out the check.

"He seemed kind of distracted," says Spalding. Part of the time she watched videos of Rotella discussing the mental side of the game with Tom Kite, Jack Nicklaus, and Brad Faxon.

"It was good to listen to other players," says Spalding. "You don't come out here [on Tour] and ask other players [what they are thinking]." Nodding her head at Inkster, hitting balls nearby on the practice range, Spalding adds, "It would be neat to know what *she's* thinking."

Spalding did have fun during her week off. She served as a bridesmaid at a friend's wedding in Tampa, then flew to Montana where she visited relatives and friends, including her pals at a TV station in Billings where she worked as an intern during college summer breaks. "We played studio golf," says Spalding, with putting targets set up around the studio. "The loser has to buy drinks."

But the short vacation didn't help her game or ease her concerns. In Minnesota she shot 75-72 and again missed the cut by one stroke. It was a lonely week inside the ropes. Spalding and fellow rookies Susan Veasey and Jill McGill, who are sharing quarters this week at the Residence Inn located right across the street from Greate Bay, agree that the less successful players tend to be the least friendly. Paired with Nancy Taylor and Adele Peterson in Minnesota, the silence was deafening. Spalding brought a friend to caddie for her, "and *he* didn't even cheer for me."

"It was a huge mistake on my part," says Spalding. "I had to tell him everything. How to rake bunkers. Where to stand. When to get out of the way. How to clean clubs. You need a very positive person, but you need a good caddie too."

At one point Spalding needed to coax in a four-foot putt for a double-bogey. She did. Then she lost it.

"You better start talking to me and complimenting me!" she yelled at her friend/caddie. "'Cause no one else is and you're the one on my side!"

Her friend lost it too. "He got nervous and started muttering to himself," says Spalding, now able to laugh at the spectacle.

She wasn't laughing after shooting 78-78 in Rochester last week to miss the cut by eight strokes, one of her worst performances of the year. Three days ago, during the first round on Friday, she lipped out eight putts. On Saturday she played eight holes before the storms descended, endured the 6:44 rain delay, and slogged it out to the finish, even though she had no chance of making the cut. (Players are allowed to withdraw midround or midtournament at their own discretion, whether due to injury, illness, or plain old disgust with their performance.)

Spalding's slump, if it hadn't come at such a crucial time, would barely merit the label. Almost every golfer on tour, male or female, loses it at one time or another, sometimes for months, sometimes for years, sometimes forever. The causes range from injuries to illness to equipment changes to personal problems to a loss of motivation to you name it.

Sometimes the fall from grace is as sudden and shocking as stepping into an open elevator shaft.

A few weeks after his triumph at the Masters in 1980, still flying high and playing brilliantly, Ben Crenshaw came to the Memorial loaded with confidence. He left a broken husk, as he explained to Tom Boswell, author of *Strokes of Genius*:

"I can still remember the shot when it changed. I tried to hit a wood out of a trap. Hit it sideways, made eight on a par-four, and it was like somebody turned out the lights."

As Boswell notes:

"No man is at peace with the game of golf. Always there is the nightmare of a tiny injury that will change the magic stroke, or the subtle aging of the body, or the hundred things that can make the mysterious golf swing disintegrate. 'All the vital technical parts of the swing take place in back of you, or above your head,' [NBC's Roger] Maltbie says. 'It's terrifying to think of all the gremlins that can creep into your game. Our margin for error is infinitesimal.' "

Spalding is grinding away on the practice green; her practice sessions include 30 eight-foot putts and 50 ten-foot putts. But so far the long hours haven't yielded the desired results.

"I'm hitting the ball the same, but I haven't scored. I'm rolling the ball well, but I haven't made any putts."

About all Spalding can do is to maintain a positive attitude and keep working. So it's back to the practice range, back to the putting green, back to the affirmations newly revised:

1. "I trust my abilities."
2. "I am a great putter."
3. "I chip in every chip I have."
4. "I am the best."
5. "I belong out here."

Caroline Pierce is tired.

After opening with a fine 71 last Friday in Rochester, Pierce teed off late on Saturday.

How late? Try 8:05 at night, after the 6:44 rain delay. Pierce played three holes in the gloaming before total darkness descended. She may as well have pitched a tent on the 4th tee and awaited the sunrise and yesterday's marathon double-round finish. By late afternoon, near the end of her 33-hole day, Pierce was so groggy she committed one of the bonehead moves of the season. With the fairways almost underwater, players were allowed to mark, lift, clean, and place their ball. Only Pierce forgot the first step, picking up her ball before marking the location with a tee, and incurring a one-stroke penalty. Since she finished sixty-fourth after closing rounds of 76-77, the damage to her pocketbook was minimal.

Today was another predawn wake-up call. Pierce hitched a ride with caddie Rick Aune. They left Rochester at six o'clock this morning, arrived at Somers Point at one o'clock, and went straight to the practice range, determined to work through the swing problems that plagued Pierce in Rochester yesterday.

Despite just one top-ten finish in 1996, way back in January at the HealthSouth Inaugural, Pierce is having a decent year. She ranks forty-seventh on the money list with $71,576. She has a good shot at making the field for the Toray Cup in Japan in October (top 46 players get automatic invitations) and some chance of cracking the top 30 and making the field for the season-ending ITT Tour Championship in November. At the least, she wants to finish in the top 50, in order to receive a two-year exemption, an insurance policy against a poor season.

After the U.S. Open four weeks ago, Pierce tied for twenty-first in East

Lansing at the Oldsmobile Classic, where weather delays frazzled her nerves. The forecast for the third round on Saturday called for sunshine, but when Pierce opened the blinds in the morning, and confronted another gray, crying sky, she hollered to roommate Missie Berteotti.

"I can't stand it! I can't stand it! I'm going to quit!"

Instead she played solid golf, sank a bunch of par-saving putts on Sunday when she shot an even-par 72, and banked a $6,281 paycheck.

After the round she left for "the pro-am from hell," scheduled Monday morning in Peoria. Flying through several thunderstorms on Sunday night from East Lansing to Chicago, Pierce and the other passengers were bounced around for an hour as the plane circled O'Hare. Finally they touched down. Baggage arrived three and a half hours later. By then the last flight to Peoria had already departed. So Pierce, Jane Crafter, Wendy Ward, Denise Killeen, and Michelle Estill rented a 19-passenger van and drove for three hours through the darkness and the rain, arriving in Peoria at 3:30 in the morning. Tee time was 9:00. Pierce's paycheck for playing was $1,300.

Then she skipped Minnesota and took a week off. Pierce returned to her new house in Scottsdale, saw a bunch of movies (*Braveheart, Cold Comfort Farm, Persuasion* for the third time), and ran up massive phone bills talking to her twin sister, Jane, in England, who was coping with boyfriend problems.

It was back to action last week in Rochester. In addition to fatigue, Pierce is fighting the mental, as well as the physical, monotony of the Tour.

"Sometimes golf doesn't stimulate me enough," says Pierce, who prefers The History Channel to ESPN. "Intellectually, I get bored. It's hard to find people to hang around with." Pierce is very popular with her peers. She has plenty of friends on Tour. Still, she says, "I don't have an awful lot in common with a lot of people out here." She spends some time with Aune—both are extremely well read, with lots of common interests—but players and caddies generally try to avoid each other after the workday is over. "It's just too much," says Pierce. (The time they do spend together is enough, says Pierce, to falsely fuel the Tour's gossip mill with rumors that she and Aune are more than just good friends.)

Executive Committee business offers some variety. The committee currently is discussing whether to hire an agronomist. The PGA has a full-time agronomist, one reason their courses are in such uniformly good shape. The LPGA wants to upgrade playing conditions in general and particularly in places such as Atlanta and Corning, which were in pathetic shape this year. The committee is also trying to find a spot on the schedule for Enesco, which makes "precious-moments" figurines. The company has deposited money into an escrow account to secure dates for a new tournament in Chicago, but late spring to mid fall is booked solid. "We never used to have this issue," says Pierce, which is quite an understatement. Thirdly, the committee is figuring out the logistics of the Samsung World Championship of Women's Golf in South Korea in October. Samsung wants a 72-hole affair, but transporting players from the last regular-season full-field event in Pennsylvania to South Korea in time for four days of competition looms as a headache.

At the moment, Pierce has plenty of physical and mental challenges. A caddie who has just arrived at Greate Bay sees Pierce and Aune on the range and calls out, "No days off?"

"I hit it so poorly yesterday," says Pierce.

"How'd you play?"

"We're here," Aune answers succinctly. "With a camera."

Fellow pro Jenny Lidback has loaned Pierce her hand-held video camera, and Pierce and Aune are rifling through the instruction manual. They discover that removing the lens cap helps considerably.

Pierce is working on her takeaway, trying to get the club in the right position as she starts her backswing. "If I whip it inside, the swing gets too vertical. I start casting the club at the top, cutting across [the ball] and slicing it."

It's exceedingly technical. The correct takeaway position that Pierce is seeking looks virtually identical with the wrong one. Pierce and Aune peer through the lens and play back the tape, trying to pinpoint the problem. The focus seems a bit blurry. To the layperson, it appears that she's simply coming off a lot of shots, instead of driving through the ball with her characteristic swooping motion.

One thing is clear, however. Pierce is hitting it like crap, "skanking the ball," as she puts it, terrifying the seagulls with low line drives and sickly fades. If she makes the cut this week, it will be a miracle.

Her putting isn't so hot either.

Pierce has developed a little outside-in loop on her backswing, which gives her putts a tiny bit of hook spin. So she positions a wooden block that resembles a thick ruler to the right of the ball on the practice putting green. It's one of the most widely used training aids on Tour, a simple and effective method of grooving a putting stroke (by using blocks on both sides of the ball) or curing an inside-out or outside-in stroke.

No rest for the weary. Pierce spends four hours on the practice range and putting green.

Patty Sheehan is "bombed," or so she says, after a Wednesday pro-am round that turns into a raucous on-course wine-guzzling and cigar-smoking bacchanal. Playing in a group that includes casino high-rollers (the fivesome is marking its ball on the greens with a $1,000 chip) and cigar aficionados, Sheehan was inveigled into lighting up a stogie. "It's so totally out of character," she says. "I started acting like the guys."

After the U.S. Open, Sheehan flew home to Reno for two weeks. "When she doesn't want to play, she doesn't," says Inkster. "I think that's why she's done so well." And for so long. Sheehan isn't quite like PGA player Bruce Lietzke, who could put the clubs in the garage for six weeks and then tee it up and challenge the best in the game. But she's the closest equivalent on the LPGA Tour, as her desire to play wanes more and more with every passing season. Sheehan still loves to compete, but she doesn't love the lifestyle of the Tour or the travel.

"You have to protect yourself out here," Sheehan told *Seattle Post-Intelligencer* columnist Laura Vecsey. "We're very exposed. I've been hurt by a lot of stuff. I'm hurt when people say stuff about me. I'm hurt when people say bad stuff about the LPGA. I'm hurt when my friends get hurt."

In 1990, shortly after Sheehan had blown the U.S. Open in Atlanta, she was involved in a pretournament Shoot-Out in Seattle, which usually involves plenty of good-natured razzing. When she lined up a long putt on the 18th green in front of a grandstand of spectators, Judy Dickinson loudly called out, "C'mon, Patty, hit this putt like you did in the Open."

"It was just like somebody had stabbed me," says Sheehan. She walked back down the fairway by herself, in tears. The next day Dickinson said she hoped she hadn't hurt her feelings. Sheehan told her not to worry about it. Then she shot a tournament record 18 under par 270 to almost lap the field. But the sting of the remark still makes her wince six years later.

During her break after the U.S. Open, Sheehan dug around in her 1,000-square-foot garden, borrowing a neighbor's tractor to spread steer manure and planting a variety of vegetables. Prized seeds include Chinese cabbages and white radishes, a gift from Ayako Okamoto, whose parents are farmers.

Last week she returned to action in Rochester, a tournament she owns—Sheehan won there in 1989, 1990, 1992, and 1995. But the rain slowed her to a crawl; she finished thirtieth. After the ShopRite she plans another month-long vacation before the du Maurier Classic, then another break before she cranks it up in preparation for the Solheim Cup on September 20–22.

Today is a weird day, but it's probably fitting. The ShopRite LPGA Classic is a strange event. In some ways, the tournament mirrors the recent growth of the LPGA itself. Just a few years ago, when Jane Geddes won in 1991, the event offered the smallest purse of the year, an anemic $300,000, and the greens were a joke—"scarred, burned-out *Poa annua* slabs of asphalt," wrote Geoff Russell in *Golf World*. Top players stayed away in droves. The whole affair was as depressing as the slums that lap up around the edges of the monolithic casino towers in downtown Atlantic City.

But the tournament has undergone a renaissance. The course and the greens have been extensively renovated. The purse is up to $750,000, one of the most lucrative events remaining in the season. As a result, most of the top money-winners are here to try their luck. Many will plunk down a few coins at the casinos as well, which is also fitting—Gene Galti, 73, who bought Great Bay in an auction in 1972, was one of the original founders of the gambling industry in Atlantic City, part owner and operator of the Brighton Hotel and Casino, which opened in 1980. Atlantic City, currently undergoing a renaissance of its own, is a boomtown. Major casino operators, facing a backlash against legalized gambling in a number of other states, are pouring money into Nevada and New Jersey. Mirage Resorts, Hilton, Circus Circus, and MGM Grand, all powerhouses in Vegas, are seeking new pigeons in the East. The lead story in *The Press of Atlantic City* trumpets the announcement of a new $490 million joint casino venture by ITT and Planet Hollywood ("The city's sizzling gaming industry turned white hot . . ."). Casino moguls Steve Wynn and Donald Trump are wrangling over a proposal for a tunnel that will link expressways with new casinos to encourage more visitors; Governor Christine Todd Whitman is caught in the middle of the dispute.

Two of the principals—Whitman and Trump—are competing in the pro-am today. All morning black and white stretch limousines roll up to the clubhouse at Great Bay and disgorge casino industry executives and their high-rolling guests.

It's not a pretty sight.

In addition to a rather garish display of gold jewelry, loud attire, and chest hair, the casino crowd collectively swings at a golf ball with as much grace as Jersey Holsteins on ice skates. The assortment of shanks, skulls, dubs, and dribbles on the practice range is a study in ineptitude. If these guys gamble as badly as they golf, their losses probably finance much of the cost of the 3,152 new rooms The Donald is adding to Trump's Castle, Trump Plaza, and Trump Taj Mahal.

"The main thing you want to do is get it airborne off the first tee, right?" Trump says after pushing a drive to the right on the first hole. Wearing a white cap with yellow piping, hair long and shaggy, Trump looks like a shambling yachtsman. He may be a New Yorker, but Trump exhibits a kind of bovine aggressiveness that seems so common in "Joysie." Players enjoy the amenities at the ShopRite—the beaches, boardwalks, fishing, casinos—but roll their eyes at some of the human creatures they encounter, who mumble and bray like barnyard animals.

Trump receives tepid applause from ShopRite volunteers, dressed in pink flamingo-hued shirts, and a few curious fans. He's in good spirits; Trump just sold his interest in one of his hotels to a corporation he owns which will put a cool $150 million cash in his pocket. The art of the deal, indeed.

But his affability may not last long. A few years ago Meg Mallon played in the pro-am with Trump, who brought along some of his high-rolling casino customers. "He was really nice to me," says Mallon, "but he was brutal to those guys." Mallon recalls that Trump brought along a bodyguard who shadowed him inside the ropes.

The day had a happy ending, however. Mallon and Trump's team won. "He was beside himself," says Mallon. "He called up Marla [Maples] on the phone and we talked to her."

Only golf could unite Donald Trump and Christine Todd Whitman in a shared passion. Whitman is playing in the Atlantic City pro-am for the third straight year. Her partners include Val Skinner and LPGA commissioner Jim Ritts. If golf reveals character, as many people assert, Whitman is the coolest Republican on the planet. She's distinct from most politicians, who develop a waxy yellow buildup over the years, the result of too many soggy chicken dinners, too many broken promises, too many sleazy solicitations for campaign moola, too many compromised and abandoned principles, too much utter bullshit.

Fortunately, there's little bullshit to wade through on the links. When Whitman pulls an iron to the left on the 8th hole, no one tells her "Good shot," which seems to suit Whitman just fine. Asked which was more nerve-wracking—dancing with David Letterman on his show last night or teeing off this morning in the pro-am, Whitman smiles and says, "Oh, this."

"I don't stay up late, so I wasn't as cognizant as I should have been about how I could make a fool of myself [with Letterman]. But one thing you learn as governor—there's always someone around with a camera."

Whitman hits a decent ball, especially for someone who has played only three 9-hole rounds all year. The unorthodox politician has an unorthodox putting stroke, hunched over in a crouch, elbows almost resting on her knees. When she sinks a ten-foot putt to give her team a birdie on No. 9, she flashes an emphatic thumbs-up sign to go along with a big, beaming smile.

As Sheehan and her partners pass by Whitman's group, Sheehan, a stogie in her mouth, calls out, "Hey! Come follow us. It's a lot more fun."

Probably so. Sheehan's group orders three bottles of wine at the turn. The 1989 Berringer Reserve arrives two holes later and is inhaled during the last seven holes. After the pro-am round, Sheehan climbs the stairs to the media room, housed in the clubhouse, and sits down on an outdoor balcony to record a radio interview.

It's a rollicking conversation, full of good humor, destined to become the centerpiece of the show. Afterward Sheehan walks back into the clubhouse and quietly confesses, "I'm bombed."

"You sounded fine in there," she's told.

"Rilly?" says Sheehan, slurring the word just a bit. Indeed, Sheehan is a little tipsy, but the old pro, as usual, comes through with a winning performance.

Caroline Pierce spends three more hours on the practice range and putting green after her pro-am round on Tuesday. She spends five hours practicing on Wednesday and four more on Thursday. Other players are starting to take notice.

"You're still out here?" they say.

On Friday at 7:50 A.M., Pierce tees it up in the first round of the 54-hole event with 18-year-old phenom Cristie Kerr and Susie Redman. Redman, 30, travels the circuit with her husband and caddie, Bo, and their sons John, 6, Benjamin, 3, and Bo Jess, 18 months. Last year Redman tied for second at the Dinah Shore and won $133,008 in 13 tournaments before leaving the Tour in June when Bo Jess was diagnosed with neuroblastoma, a childhood form of cancer.

Redman credits LPGA day-care director Tony Verive and assistant Lisa DeLosh with possibly saving her son's life. Bo Jess had been sick for months, but doctors kept diagnosing his illness as something minor, such as bronchitis. But when Bo Jess was wheezing more than usual during a tournament in East Lansing, Verive took him to the emergency room. X-rays revealed a large tumor in his throat, which almost killed him in the next few days. Now Bo Jess is in remission and doing splendidly. And the family is back on Tour, traveling to as many tournaments as possible in a 1993 Ford Conversion van.

Crowds are scarce. There are more volunteers, dressed in their flamingo-hued shirts, than fans. Too bad. It's a pretty course and a fabulous day, sunny with temperatures in the 70s. A fountain in a small lake near the 13th fairway creates a soothing splash for a Canadian goose and her babies, who lie in the shade near the water.

Kerr is a baby too; but the youngster is already a professional, renouncing her amateur status after playing in the Curtis Cup matches against a team from Great Britain last week. (The Brits upset the favored Americans.) She's playing in the ShopRite via a sponsor's exemption. In October she'll try to win her Tour card for the 1997 season at Q-School.

Like Michelle McGann, Kerr is skipping college to try to go directly to the big-leagues as a teenager.

She's got the talent. Last year in a junior tournament at Du Pont Country Club in Wilmington, site of the McDonald's LPGA Championship, Kerr shot 64. The tees were up a bit, but a 64 is major league golf in practically any ballpark.

She's got the attitude. Or maybe *an* attitude is closer to the truth. Kerr raised eyebrows among the pros when she competed in the HealthSouth Inaugural in January, treating her elders with disdain. She told a bunch of astonished players in the locker room that competing against the pros wasn't any different than playing in a junior event.

Kerr raised more eyebrows at the Nabisco Dinah Shore in April. Her expression, during the holes I saw her play in the first round, was a cross between a scowl and a pout. Rumors that she cursed out her caddie and father, Mike Kerr, were rampant.

Both father and daughter admit that things sometimes get a bit tempestuous. But they are also each other's biggest fan. Mike plans to quit his job next year as a fourth-grade teacher to work full-time for Cristie as her caddie/agent/scheduler. He's been portrayed as a pushy stage parent, but it seems clear that Cristie is pulling at least as hard as Mike is pushing.

"Yeah, Mike can be a little strong at times," mother Linda told *Golf World*. "But you can't push Cristie into anything. She likes it. She wants it. She'll do it."

Young phenoms are always great copy. Kerr, winner of 11 amateur and junior events in 1995, has been profiled in *USA Today, Golf World*, and, yesterday, *The Press of Atlantic City*.

It's clear she reads her clippings, including the critical comments from the pros. Kerr came into the interview room two days ago determined to win friends. With a smile she introduced herself individually to several reporters.

But Kerr, like a lot of bright but immature youngsters, assumes that anyone over the age of 25 is an idiot. Her haughtiness kept spilling out from under the edges of her pleasant public relations game face.

"Her world is so small," says an LPGA official. Indeed, it's hard not to feel some sympathy for Kerr, who is the human equivalent of a partially completed metal sculpture with sharp, jagged edges. Her outside interests are limited to shopping and fishing. She admits to having very few friends in high school. Asked about her abilities in other sports, Kerr, five-foot-five

LAURA DAVIES (*Credit:* © Kim)

LISELOTTE NEUMANN (*Credit:* © Kim)

DOTTIE PEPPER (*Credit: © Kim*)

MICHELLE MCGANN (*Credit: © Kim*)

CAROLINE PIERCE (*Credit: © Kim*)

KARRIE WEBB (*Credit: © Kim*)

THE TORAY QUEENS CUP CADDIES (*Credit: © Kim*)

JANE GEDDES (*Credit: © Kim*)

KELLY ROBBINS (*Credit: © Kim*)

LESLIE SPALDING (*Credit: Photo by David P. Hall*)

JUDY RANKIN (CENTER) WITH SOLHEIM CUP PLAYERS AND CADDIES (*Credit: © Kim*)

JULI INKSTER (*Credit: © Kim*)

ANNIKA SORENSTAM (*Credit: © Kim*)

THE U.S. SOLHEIM CUP TEAM (*Credit: © Kim*)

PATTY SHEEHAN *(Credit: Photo by Marc Glassman)*

HIROMI KOBAYASHI *(Credit: © Kim)*

and stocky, mentioned an aptitude for tennis, bowling, gymnastics, and ballet, then added, "if you can believe that."

She probably never ran track. Kerr is slow as molasses. By the 14th hole an LPGA official is timing the group. Kerr comes within six seconds of incurring a two-stroke penalty for slow play.

Pierce and Redman have been giggling or shaking their heads all day over her behavior. Kerr is an extremely long hitter, but on the 5th hole Pierce caught her drive solidly and belted it out there with the kid.

"You hit it a long way for a little girl," Kerr told her. "I'm sorry—a little woman."

"I'm older than you think," said Pierce, too amused at the remark to be angry.

Like daughter, like father, except Mike Kerr's antics prove less amusing. "He moves around a lot," says Pierce. "You can give her some leeway because she's young, but he's got no excuse."

Kerr struggles to keep the ball in the fairway en route to a 73. Mary Bryan, who is scouting the course in preparation for the regional television broadcast on Saturday and Sunday, notes that Kerr needs work on her swing as well as her manners.

"She has a little bit of a tilt," says Bryan. "Instead of a real good turn, she's a rocker and blocker. She does it with great consistency, it's worked to this point, but maybe not when she gets older."

Meanwhile Pierce is hitting fairways and greens and stroking putts with authority. Cruising along at three under par through 15 holes, she finishes with a startling flourish, rolling in 15- to 20-foot birdie putts on Nos. 16, 17, and 18 to complete a dazzling six under par 65, the lowest round of her career.

Four days ago Pierce was scaring the seagulls on the practice range with her wayward efforts. Today she shoots 65 and makes it look easy. It takes a course record 64 by Amy Benz to knock her out of the first-round lead. It's an awfully satisfying round for Pierce, a testament to the old-fashioned work ethic.

Earlier this week Pierce received her green card. It took two years. During that time she was only allowed in the U.S. on a six-month work visa, so she had to return to England at least twice a year. Now she has the freedom to stay as long as she wants. According to her green card (which actually is pink) Pierce is considered to be "an alien of extraordinary ability."

Not that anyone else particularly notices. Pierce is dissed and dismissed all day, and not just by Cristie Kerr. The starter on the first tee and the tournament public relations director mispronounced her name (Carolyn instead of Caroline). A reporter for *The Press of Atlantic City*, writing a story about Pierce for tomorrow morning's paper, focuses on the fact that Pierce hasn't won after playing in 212 LPGA tournaments during her nine-year career.

Benz, who, like Pierce, is extremely popular with her colleagues, doesn't fare any better. She hasn't won in 319 starts dating back to her debut on Tour in 1983. Later in the afternoon, a pudgy reporter who probably can't break 64 for *nine* holes will ask Jane Geddes, who fired 68 today, what she thinks when she sees players like Benz and Pierce atop the leader board with scores of 64 and 65.

"Do you say to yourself, 'Wow, that's a pretty good round for *them?*'" Geddes, remarkably diplomatic, notes that both golfers are fully capable of shooting the lights out.

Pierce is still tired. But her fatigue is mixed with satisfaction for a job well done.

Juli Inkster is still frustrated. She walks toward the clubhouse after shooting a one over par 72. Her mouth is turned down in a frown; her face is furrowed with deep lines of fatigue and displeasure.

Leslie Spalding is still worried. On the 380-yard 13th hole, her fourth of the day, Spalding hooks a drive "in the exact wrong place" and, seven blows later, records a quadruple-bogey eight en route to a 75. One lousy shot and her hopes of making the cut are as dim as a 40-watt light bulb.

Patty Sheehan isn't still bombed, although she may be soon.

"I'm going to go back [to my hotel] and take about five PMS pills," she grumbles after a 69. Sheehan leafs through the latest copy of *Sports Illustrated*. She comes to a story about PGA players who own their own airplanes. "That's the difference between the PGA and the LPGA," says Sheehan. "They have their own air force." Sheehan will try her darndest the next two days—she always does—but mentally she's already back in Reno digging around in her garden, getting her hands dirty and clearing her mind of the travails of the Tour.

Professional golfers are like horseplayers. The changing mood at a golf tournament during the course of a day resembles the mood at the racetrack.

At the beginning of each day, hope springs eternal. The morning is filled with promise. Excitement mingles with a nervous buzz. Cheerful chatter fills the air.

"Good luck," players tell each other.

"Have a good day."

In their mind, everyone is a winner before the deal goes down.

As the losing tickets—or the bogeys and double-bogeys—pile up throughout the day, hope slowly evaporates and is replaced by fatigue, teeth-grinding apprehension, futility, and despair. The words that George Plimpton wrote in *The Bogey Man* in 1967 are just as true today:

"The exercise of the game itself in top competition was an ugly combination of tension and frustration, broken only occasionally by a pleasant surprise, but more often by disaster."

Like the racetrack, at its core the Tour is as cold as the Arctic and as impersonal as the IRS. And the all-consuming worlds of the track and Tour are linked in another way: golf and gambling are two of the most narcissistic of activities.

In fact, golf may be worse. Be honest, golfers. Is there anything more enjoyable than reliving your round, shot by shot, hole by hole, for your playing partners or spouse or even the grocery store clerk? And, conversely, is there anything more excruciating than *listening* to another golfer replay a round, shot by shot and hole by hole?

Researchers are studying a promising new form of treatment for juvenile offenders. Miscreants are locked in a tiny room and forced to listen to a parade of paunchy, florid, middle-aged men in Dockers drone on and on about their 97 at DuckSoup Muni or their 132 at Poisoned Oak (hey, it was from the tips!), a round that took seven hours to play and almost as long to recount. Preliminary findings indicate that even the most hardened offenders crack after several hours of such torture, and vow, with utmost sincerity, to sin no more.

"Given the suffocating internality of tournament golf," wrote Michael Bamberger in *To the Linksland*, "it is surprising to me that the professional game does not routinely produce examples of mentally unstable behavior."

Professional golf is the "toughest way in sports to make a living," says John Brophy, a former NHL coach who sometimes caddies for his wife, LPGA player Nancy White-Brophy.

Brophy has achieved fame—or infamy—in hockey circles for his intensity as a coach and player. Among other accomplishments, Brophy is remembered for biting the ear of an opponent in a fight and throwing a shoe that smashed a four-stitch gash in the mouth of a slumbering teammate.

But Brophy insists the frustration level in hockey, or any other sport, pales in comparison to golf. "The way I'm wired, I couldn't play. [It's] like losing fourteen games in a row in overtime."

Golf at the highest level takes its toll, sometimes in dramatic ways.

Laura Baugh, 41, the Tour's Great Blonde Hope in the 1970s, recently emerged from the Betty Ford Center after being treated for alcoholism. Baugh, mother of six kids, the five youngest ranging in age from 14 months to 8 years, still has the figure of a teenager. Her beauty earned her a small fortune in endorsement deals after she became the youngest player to win the U.S. Women's Amateur as a 16-year-old in 1971 before turning pro in 1973. As Tim Rosaforte wrote in *SI*: "There was always a Norma Jean Baker quality about Laura Baugh, the blonde starlet who was supposed to take women's golf to Madison Avenue."

She did. Her ads for Ultra-Brite, with the tag line, "Laura Baugh, how's your love life?" were a sensation. So were her risque calendars in Japan. But her golf career wasn't as successful. Baugh has never won on the LPGA Tour. A short hitter, she could have added yards to her drives by bulking up her slender frame. But, as she told *SI*, "I don't want to be just heavy. It's a bit of an ego trip for me, and it's one of the dilemmas I have." Some pros believed she was bulimic or anorexic.

Working as a commentator for ESPN last June, she was booted from the tower by producer Larry Cirillo, who later said she was incoherent. Players gossiped that they smelled liquor on her breath.

Muffin Spencer-Devlin, who has battled manic-depression for over 20 years, suffered a manic episode in 1990 that ended when she raised a ruckus at a banquet before a tournament in England, was removed from the field, and hustled into a clinic.

Since coming out at the 1996 Dinah Shore, she has dropped off the Tour to work with a psychologist, in an attempt to better control the ups and downs of her illness. (She's also on the "Gay A-List," has attended a number of celebrity events, and plans to be at the Democratic Convention.)

(Both Spencer-Devlin and Baugh will resurface in Youngstown in two weeks. Spencer-Devlin will shoot 78-71, miss the cut by two strokes, and end her season. Baugh, with her hair cropped punk-style in back, and wearing blue nail polish, will shoot 82-74. Although she refuses to talk to the media, Baugh is observed talking a mile a minute to her agent, IMG's Jay Burton, who noted that only 10 percent of alcoholics are able to avoid a relapse. Baugh will play six more events in 1996, and grant an interview to *Golfweek*, discussing two occurrences when she almost died in March and May, the result of alcohol abuse. She will deny that she has an eating disorder.)

Professional golfers are high-stakes gamblers of the first magnitude. Every round they bet the table limit on themselves. The next day their score is posted for all the world to see in the agate type of the sports section. Today Caroline Pierce is a seven-birdie 65, a winner, a star. Tomorrow Pierce will be a no-birdie 75, a failure, a screwup. On the telecast of the ShopRite, analyst Mary Bryan will tell the viewing audience that Pierce appears nervous as she misses several short birdie chances and tumbles out of contention, a loser for the two hundred and thirteenth consecutive time.

"It takes a unique person not to be affected by bad play," says Pierce. Pierce handles the ups and downs of the Tour better than most, but she's wrong and she knows it. A golfer would have to be superhuman not to be affected by bad play.

The underlying Arctic chilliness of the Tour, coupled with the obsessive nature of the game, and the brutal demands of traveling and practicing and playing at the highest level make it a lonely life for many players.

In 1988 Pat Bradley's game suddenly disintegrated when the superstar developed hyperthyroidism, also known as Graves' disease, a sometimes fatal illness that can be inherited or triggered by severe stress. Bradley's self-image revolved around her career. When Graves' disease sawed off the lofty limb Bradley perched on as one of the world's finest golfers, she fell to earth and broke apart. After topping the money list with $492,021 in 1986, she won only $140,132 in 1987, as the disease attacked, and then just $14,965 in the throes of the illness in 1987. For several months she staggered from one tournament to the next, missing cut after cut.

"After a while, I thought I must be having a nervous breakdown," Bradley told *People* magazine. "I assumed I was the talk of the locker room, although I never really heard anyone discussing me. No one came up and asked what was wrong, but I don't hold that against anybody. We all have our own problems to deal with on the Tour. I just hid in the privacy of my own room."

Bradley finally saw a doctor and learned the problem was physical rather than mental. Medication brought almost instant relief—Bradley won $423,714 in 1989, regaining her position near the top of the pecking order.

The ordeal changed her. Once described by Geoff Russell of *Golf World* as "so tenacious a competitor she'd play her mother for her last nickel and probably beat her 10 and 8," she remained a ferocious opponent. But her icy on-course demeanor, which held fans and her fellow pros at bay, began to soften. Eventually Bradley, who earned Hall of Fame honors in 1991, became something of a crowd favorite. Last month at the U.S. Open, when Bradley birdied the 72nd hole to claim a tie for third, a sterling achievement for a 45-year-old, she received a thunderous ovation from the huge gallery.

Outside the ropes Bradley is a different person as well. Rookie Wendy Ward was startled—and grateful—when Bradley sat down next to her at a banquet and said, "Okay, Wen, tell me how your season is going."

How many Tour players are happy with their lives?

Fifty to 60 percent, estimates Pierce. In a separate interview Lauri

Merten, winner of the U.S. Open in 1993, came up with the exact same numbers.

Rosie Jones thinks 50 percent is close to the mark. Jones laughingly says the Tour breeds "social chaos." But she's dead serious when she describes its schizoid nature.

"You have competitive, competitive, very competitive women out here. You can't get too close. But there's also a deep compassion, respect, and loyalty, which I think is really unique to women."

Jones is very well-liked by her peers. Yet she describes herself as something of a loner.

"The Tour is real cliquey. I don't belong to any of them. It doesn't bother me. I'm really good being by myself. A lot of people aren't. I have friends out here, but not close, close friends.

"The hardest thing is to keep everything balanced," adds Jones. "Professional life, personal life, family, business obligations—and maintain all that while you're on the road dealing with equipment, transportation, and clothing. And the physical, emotional, and psychological parts of a person have to stay intact, too. All of that walks out on the tee box with us."

Just staying healthy is a major accomplishment. Keith Kennedy, a HealthSouth employee who manages the LPGA's fitness van, a mobile exercise and therapy center which travels from site to site, commonly sees about 50 players a day during the dog days of summer. Most are treated for back, neck, or shoulder problems.

How many professional golfers have back problems?

"If they play long enough, one hundred percent," says Kennedy, who spent nine years as a physical therapist with Tennessee Tech University and one year with the Birmingham Bullets of the Continental Basketball League before being assigned to the LPGA Tour in 1992.

The fitness van houses two StairMasters, Nautilus machines, free weights, three stationary bikes, and a trampoline. All of the equipment gets a workout. So do the training tables. "Sometimes it takes a little spit and bailing wire to get them out there," says Kennedy.

Last season Dottie Pepper spent as much as two hours in the fitness center before teeing off, loosening up a sore rotator cuff and a sprained back. Stretching, Kennedy's manipulations, and bottles of Advil got her through the season. Barely.

Now she's a self-described "stretching maniac. I've actually hurt myself stretching," laughs Pepper, who spends 45 minutes per day on her routine and has been relatively pain-free in 1996.

Jones, like Pepper, stretches religiously. "From 1987 to 1990 I was in a lot of pain. I used to walk off the course and into a bag of ice. I hardly even went out to eat." Now Jones stretches 20–30 minutes in the morning and 30–60 minutes in the afternoons or evening. "I used to have lots of bad days and a few good ones. Now it's lots of great days and a few bad ones."

"If they miss one day of stretching, they're really hurting," says Kennedy of players with chronic back problems. "Many are continually working on the course to keep flexible. We're educating a lot more. So far we haven't had the sudden traumatic stuff [this season], where a player can't complete a round."

Under the stress and strain of a golf career, relationships, as well as bodies, take a beating.

A number of LPGA players have divorced in the last few years, including Pepper, Cindy Rarick, Kris Tschetter, Tammie Green, and Tina Tombs (formerly Purtzer), who reclaimed her maiden name after splitting with her former husband in 1993. (Tombs went through a bitter but ultimately successful custody battle for her daughters, Sarah, who is 8, and Heidi, who is 6. Her on-the-road lifestyle was an issue in the custody fight.)

Lauri Merten divorced Paul Peterson in 1988 after six years of marriage. "When you're young, you're hungry for success," says Merten. "You think golf is everything." In 1994 Merten married Louis Capano, a wealthy real estate developer from Wilmington, Delaware. "It's very difficult to find a true relationship," says Merten. "And when you do it's very hard to maintain it. You have to make it the most important thing."

"You have to do it as a team," says Inkster, who has been married for 15 years. "You can't really have an ego—the woman *or* the man."

"It's tough," says Kris Tschetter, divorced in 1992, and engaged to be married later this year to fiancé/instructor/caddie Kirk Lucas. "I think it takes a real special guy. Someone who is willing to support you but someone who also has his own thing going—so he has enough self-esteem that it doesn't bruise his ego if you are making more money than he is or are in the spotlight."

When unmarried players are asked, "What kind of guys do you meet out here?" most of the answers are not encouraging.

"Caddies," says Leslie Spalding, dateless for most of the season.

"Married ones," says Pierce, who now assumes, usually correctly, that a nice guy she meets during a pro-am round is hitched.

"Salesmen, very flashy, very fun," says 31-year-old Maggie Will, a three-time winner on Tour. Will is a slender blonde who didn't lack for suiters. But in 1994, unhappy with both her game and her personal life, she almost quit the Tour to become a stockbroker. She had met, she said, too many "Mr. Wrongs" during her first six years on the road. "People think we get up, play some golf and go out at night. They think we're wild partyers. I had dinner with Lauri Merten for her birthday and had a couple glasses of wine and thought, 'Wow, I never do this.'"

"It can be a very lonely existence out here," says Will. "Maybe it is for every career woman. It's a very charmed life—we're very lucky and we're spoiled rotten—but it's a very difficult life."

The loneliness of the Tour sometimes causes smart women to make hasty, sometimes foolish choices. In 1979, Nancy Lopez, a 22-year-old superstar lauded by the fans but shunned by many of her peers, met and married sportscaster Tim Melton after announcing her engagement to 50 million viewers on the *Today* show.

In her autobiography, written shortly before her marriage, a head-over-heels Lopez wrote of the "chemistry" between her and Melton, and contemplated giving up her career, and even her Catholic religion for her Mormon husband-to-be. The union lasted about three years.

By the time Lopez married Ray Knight, she was strong and secure enough to blend a traditionally based marriage with a high-flying career, and strong and secure enough to hire and then fire her husband after Knight caddied for her at several tournaments. ("I still let Ray carry my clubs," she joked, "from the garage to the trunk of the car.")

And compassionate enough to leave a note in Dottie Pepper's locker at the Pinewild Classic in North Carolina last April when Pepper announced she was divorcing Doug Mochrie. Dottie met Doug when she was just 13. They married when Pepper was a 19-year-old student at Furman University. Doug, a club professional, became Dottie's instructor and caddie.

Looking back on it, Pepper says she was "much too young" for marriage.

"It takes a special commitment in terms of both parties involved on and off the course that was definitely lacking," says Pepper. "It's different when the woman is the center of attention and making most of the income. Both people have to be very, very sure of themselves and the relationship, and that was lacking as well."

The note from Lopez, her childhood hero, led to "heart-to-heart discussions," says Pepper. "Nancy went through the same thing I did. If I have a problem in the future, I wouldn't hesitate to talk to her. Her opinion would be honest, heartfelt, and well-thought-out."

Even when a player finds someone she likes, the demands of the Tour and life on the road make relationships difficult, if not impossible. Last year Tracy Kerdyk, 30, broke off a serious relationship that seemed to be leading toward marriage and kids. Stretched too thin to devote herself to the relationship and her career, she opted for the latter. When she subsequently won the JAL Big Apple Classic in New York, her first victory in seven years on Tour, she concluded her decision had been the correct one.

Pierce's "on-and-off" two-year relationship with Bruce Stephen, who owns a small public relations firm in Pittsburgh, recently came to an end. They're still close friends—Pierce spent time with him and his three daughters recently—but the romance is over. The kids were a factor—Pierce isn't prepared to be a mom in a ready-made family. So was Pittsburgh, a city that holds little charm for Pierce, especially in the off-season when it's tough to beat balls in the snow. But time might be the greatest obstacle—at this point in the season, Pierce spends much of her limited amount of free time sleeping, replenishing her energy and escaping from the pressures inside the ropes.

She's one of the lucky ones. Many pros can't escape the game even in their sleep. Golf saturates their unconscious and seeps into their dreams.

"Weird dreams," says Pepper, who has two nightmares that recur occasionally during the year and more often when she is preparing for a new season. In one dream, Pepper is in an office. Her ball is stuck in the corner of a file cabinet and she can't hit it out. In the other dream, Pepper is on the tee, driver in hand, and a tree is right behind her, preventing her from swinging.

Lopez suffers from an almost identical nightmare. "I've always said that if I've got a swing, I'm all right." In her dream, Lopez is on the tee, ready to hit, but a tree blocks her backswing. She picks up her tee, moves to another location, gets ready to swing—and the tree has moved behind her again. So has a rules official, stopwatch in hand, ready to nail her for slow play.

Sue Thomas, 30, an eight-year pro from Texas, struggling to escape from the fringe after several dismal seasons, has been visited by two high-anxiety dreams in the past, although none has haunted her recently. In one dream, she's late for her tee time, running as fast as she can to make it, but never arriving soon enough. In the other dream, she finds her ball lodged in tree roots or up in tree branches. Thomas swings and swings and swings at it, missing and missing and missing.

The strangest golf dream Rosie Jones experienced occurred shortly before a tournament in Rochester in 1991. She was on the final green with a 30-foot putt for victory. The Rochester event is a community-wide celebration with huge crowds; fans were everywhere. Jones stood over the putt, raised her head to take one more look at the hole—and the hole was gone. The fans were gone. Everyone was gone.

"Wait a minute!" yelled Jones. "You're not even giving me a chance here!"

Ironically Jones won the 1991 Rochester Classic. "Now I interpret the dream to mean that I wasn't getting a fair shake. Sometimes golf and life don't *give* you a fair shake."

* * *

On a cool, windy Sunday, punctuated by savage thunderstorms that create several rain delays lasting a total of over five hours, Dottie Pepper shoots 69 for a course record 202 and tallies her second victory in two weeks. Amy Benz, who held a four-shot lead entering the final round, falls apart after the first rain delay, which lasts over three hours. She shoots 76 and barely hangs on for second place.

Play concludes at 8:22 at night. Cars near the course have had the headlights on for the past hour. Benz is near tears in the interview room. Tomorrow's paper will describe her as a loser of 320 consecutive events.

The "traveling circus," as Maggie Will aptly describes it, rolls on to Ohio for next week's $550,000 Jamie Farr Kroger Classic near Toledo.

Toledo.

Uggh. A downtown core marked by decay, broken glass in the streets, and rusted-out Oldsmobiles and Chevys. Mile after mile of strip malls.

The first week of July. Pass the bug spray.

The $550,000 Jamie Farr Kroger Classic on July 5–7. Jamie Farr? The dude who played Klinger on M*A*S*H a millennium ago? Aren't we scraping the bottom of the celebrity barrel? (The pro-am, however, is interesting. Everyone cross-dresses. Players wear pin-striped business suits. Caddies dress in Klinger-style print dresses and feather boas and tote handbags.)

Strange faces on the practice range. Laura Davies, Annika Sorenstam, and Liselotte Neumann are in Europe. Patty Sheehan is rooting around in her vegetable garden in Reno.

Instead of 20, 30, or 40 players dueling for the last two spots in the field in the Monday qualifier, just 11 tee it up at Highland Meadows Country Club, located in the Toledo suburb of Sylvania. Connie Chillemi, who has played in just four events in 1996, and Anna Acker-Macosko, who has played in three, fire 69 to qualify. They join conditional players who are far down the priority list, such as Myra Blackwelder, Tish Certo, Mary Bea Porter-King, and Laura Witvoet. The latter quartet has combined to compete in only eight tournaments in 1996, but so many players are taking a break this week that the field has opened up to numerous fringe dwellers.

If Highland Meadows wasn't such a classy layout—"a great course where you have to hit every club," says Pierce—and the tournament so well run, perhaps no one would show up. Many players and caddies, mired in the tedium and bone-deep fatigue of the dog days of summer, seem more interested in the Fourth of July fireworks in downtown Toledo or the opening of the movie Independence Day than in the tournament.

But the Tour is a hard hook even for those who are running on empty. Just ask Terry McNamara, who caddies for Rosie Jones.

"Sometimes I think about quitting," says McNamara, who has caddied on the LPGA Tour since 1983, after a brief shot as a player on the men's mini-tour circuit. "But after a couple of weeks I'm ready to go again."

McNamara has worked for Jones for nine of his thirteen years on Tour. It's one of the most stable player-caddie teams.

"I get along well with my boss, and I think she's a hell of a person also," says McNamara. "It's not brain surgery, but you've got to do your business and take care of what your player needs—and they need different things."

"The pace [of the Tour] is amazing," says McNamara. "You don't realize you're moving so fast until you stop. It's like driving down a freeway at a hundred miles an hour and then slowing down to thirty-five in a city zone. It's a jolt. It could make other things seem boring.

"Everything [on the Tour] is right now. When your boss asks you to make a decision, you have five seconds to make it and forty-five seconds to wonder how it's going to turn out."

"It's like a pitcher and catcher in baseball," says former looper Chuck Heath. "It's the next closest thing to being a professional athlete yourself. You're an integral part of an athlete's career."

Lonnie Hellwig, who caddies for Sherri Steinhauer, says, "There's an intimacy that takes place." He isn't referring to sex, although player-caddie relationships can develop, on rare occasion, to marriage (John Killeen married Denise Baldwin, now Killeen, last fall). Hellwig, who once worked in a hospital, says the Tour creates the same kind of bond between players and caddies that coworkers experience in the intensive care unit.

"So-called normal people can't relate to us," says equipment repairman Dave Baker. Baker used to be a jazz drummer; the rhythms of the LPGA Tour now are a part of him. "I can't relate to my family anymore when I go home. I have a hard time in the off-season. I miss it."

Baker used to work for the PGA Tour. He says, "There's no comparison. It's like a big family out here. The PGA Tour is a bunch of isolated pockets of individual groups."

"The Tour is very exciting," says Caroline Pierce, who shudders to think of her twin sister's nursing job, where every day and every paycheck are roughly the same. "It gets in your blood."

"Extremely addictive," says former player Cathy Mant, who played the Tour from 1976 to 1986 with limited success. Still, she says, "The public made you feel like a star, made you feel like something special. If I had to do it all over again, I'd do it in a New York minute."

LPGA employees often describe the Tour as a drug. The drug is pure adrenaline. Just ask Dottie Pepper, who is almost giddy from a megadose after two straight victories in Rochester and Atlantic City. Dottie Pepper once again feels like a star.

"I haven't slept much this week," says Pepper, as she sits on a picnic table in the sunshine by the Highland Meadows clubhouse on Wednesday, July 3. "I've been too excited."

Her dismal play at the U.S. Open was a turning point for Pepper. She junked her clubs, a set of Titleist DCI cast irons, in favor of a duplicate set of 1972 forged Titleist blades that she played until this spring. She junked her instructor, returning to Ted Ossoff, her previous coach. They watched videotape of Pepper in action, and the conclusion was simple: Let Dottie be Dottie. "I went back to a little more upright swing and a little more left-side dominant," Pepper told reporters. "I went back to things I trusted and not what the new-fangled gurus say is right and what the golf swing is supposed to look like. It didn't work for me."

Above all, it meant beating balls until her hands bled. Pepper displays her palms, which have red calluses the size of 50-cent pieces. It's a small price to pay for two trips to the winner's circle, which ensure Pepper a spot on the Solheim Cup team, her foremost goal for the season.

"I thought I'd be staying home until two weeks ago," says Pepper, the star, albeit a controversial one, of the winning U.S. team in 1994. "I didn't want to be a captain's pick."

(Ten of the 12 members of the U.S. team are chosen by a point system based on top-ten finishes over a two-year period. The other two teammates will be selected by captain Judy Rankin after the Star Bank LPGA Classic in Dayton on August 23–25.)

Life couldn't be better for Pepper, inside or outside the ropes. Although she threatened to junk her boyfriend and caddie, Ralph Scarinzi—"He was quaking in his boots," Pepper jovially told the press—along with her clubs and her instructor, it was a joke.

"We're just best buddies," Pepper says of the almost year-old relationship with Scarinzi. The couple shares common interests—movies, jet skiing, politics, and, of course, golf. Scarinzi plays to a four handicap. He receives two shots a side when he and Dottie tee it up. "I can't get him to snow ski, though," says Pepper, whose family owned a ski shop and started her on the slopes at the age of 3. (Asked what she'd be if she weren't a golfer, Pepper says, "An airline pilot or a ski bum.")

"He knows how to laugh, and that's definitely something new for me," says Pepper, who has loosened up a lot after untying the knot. "I want to live a little before I make another full-time commitment, and know that it's right. There's no rush."

Although it's hard to believe, Scarinzi is more likely to take golf home with him than is Pepper when their workday on the links is over. "I'll say, 'No, talk about something else,' " says Pepper, who used to eat, sleep, and dream the game 24 hours a day.

The game makes Sue Thomas feel like someone special. Two years ago it made her feel like a bag of garbage tossed into a landfill.

Thomas relishes the toughest of challenges. As a youngster she practiced classical piano for over five years. Her teacher envisioned a professional career for her star pupil. But at the age of 13, when push came to shove, and Thomas was forced to choose between three or four hours a day pounding the keyboards or beating balls on the practice range, she opted for golf.

"[My teacher] was *so* disappointed when I quit," says Thomas on a sun-splashed Fourth of July at Highland Meadows. "She thought sports had no place, especially a girl playing sports."

The training for golf and for piano is not as dissimilar as one might think. "You break it down into pieces," says Thomas. "Left hand and right hand. Golf is kind of like that too. And it made me understand you have to work hard at something to be good."

By high school Thomas was dreaming of the Tour. A scholar-athlete at the University of Georgia, Thomas earned All-American honors while graduating with a degree in economics in 1989. Thomas expected to play the mini-tours to hone her game but surprised herself by acing Q-School.

"I didn't belong out here at all," she says. "I was totally lost." Thomas earned just $2,629 in her rookie season, lost her card, returned to Q-School, and, once again, sailed through it. In her sophomore year she registered two top-ten finishes and placed fifty-ninth on the money list with $38,285.

Thomas saw stardom on the horizon. "Who wouldn't?" she says with a smile.

But it was a mirage. Her game hit a plateau and then nose-dived. Her record over the next few seasons was a stark recitation of futility and failure.

1991:	$30,127	1994:	$ 2,676
1992:	$20,220	1995:	$ 9,175
1993:	$6,680		

Thomas hit bottom in the fall of 1994. At Portland she bombed out in a Monday qualifier. Later she walked into the media center, lines so deeply etched into her dark scowling face it looked as if she were wearing a mask.

In Seattle the following week, Thomas received a phone call. Her grandmother, in a coma for six weeks, had passed away. Grieving and deeply depressed, Thomas flew home. She wound up sitting next to B. D. Mooring, a chiropractor in his seventies from Idabel, Oklahoma.

At least that's who he told Thomas he was. For all she knows, she suddenly found herself in the middle of a true-life episode of *Touched by an Angel*. When Thomas floated off the plane in Texas, her attitude and her life had been transformed.

"He talked to me for three hours. He gave me a new way of looking at life. He said, 'Try to make the most of every single day. Enjoy yourself. You don't have to go through life feeling like a failure.'

"Golf was everything to me. It's not the focus of my life now. I try not to be so hard on myself—my goodness, we're not perfect."

Although Thomas is religious, "I don't go around beating my Bible." Since her encounter with Mooring, she has worked on both her spiritual growth and her golf swing. She reads primarily books about kinesiology (Thomas, like so many players, has a bad back) and New Age philosophy, such as *Mutant Message Down Under* and *Celestine Prophecy*.

She treats people differently now. "I smile more, especially at kids, and make eye contact with the people in the gallery. I never did that before. We're no different than anybody else, just because we make a living playing golf."

The results of her personal transformation didn't show up immediately on the scorecard. Some relatives openly questioned why she persisted with the sport.

"That's a tough thing to hear. I'm making progress, but it's difficult to explain to people. It's hard for them to understand that your scores don't necessarily reflect your progress."

In 1993 Thomas began working with a new teacher. He revamped her swing plane. "It took two years to get to a point where I was somewhat comfortable enough with my swing to trust it out here under pressure."

After another successful trip to Q-School in the fall of 1994, Thomas was exempt for the 1995 season. But she needed a $10,000 loan from her parents and $22,000 in wages from Monday pro-ams to make it through the year.

So it was back to Q-School for the sixth time last fall, but she only placed high enough to secure conditional status. So far she has played in seven tournaments this season. She expects to get into the field in about eight more events.

Instead of raising expense money by playing in the Monday pro-ams, Thomas is teeing it up in the Monday qualifiers and shelling out $100 for the privilege of competing for one of the last two spots in the 144-player field. So far she's succeeded in Hawaii, Sacramento, and Atlanta, and fallen short in Tucson, Phoenix, Lansing, and Atlantic City, despite shooting 72s in the latter two qualifiers.

"Mistakes are more costly," says Thomas of the Monday qualifiers. "A bad hole can really get you." Players who fall short at Monday qualifiers spend the next six days—an eternity—ruing the cost and aggravation of journeying all the way to Arizona or Michigan or New Jersey to play one fruitless round.

Yet Thomas, in her attempt to climb Mt. Everest without ropes or boots, is inching her way up the steep, icy slope. She's earned $18,263 so far in 1996. Her chances of securing her card by finishing in the top 125, and ensuring a spot in about 25 events in 1997, are promising. (Conditional players who finish between 90 and 125 on the money list are higher on the pecking order than players who earn their conditional status at Q-School.)

Two weeks ago in Rochester, after rounds of 72 and 69, Thomas had a golden opportunity to vault into the top 90 and perhaps even win her first title. But she shot 76 in the final round and earned $6,277 after tying for seventeenth.

Discouraging?

Not for the new, improved Thomas.

"I wasn't disappointed," she says with a smile. "I haven't been in that position—in the third-to-last group [on a Sunday] for the last five or six years. It was fatiguing—I played 32 holes that day. I shot four over [par] on the front, and was proud of myself for hanging in there. It was a good experience."

After her flight with the angel—or the chiropractor—most of Thomas's experiences seem to be good ones. "It's funny how things work out," she says. "There's no such thing as coincidence. You know the old saying, 'When a student is ready, a teacher will appear?' You just have to be open to the possibilities."

Huge crowds revel in the drama at Highland Meadows where Joan Pitcock, a nonwinner in her nine years on Tour, fires 68-66 to open up a three-stroke lead going into the final round.

And on Sunday, a hot and muggy day with thunderstorms in the forecast for later in the afternoon, the Tour once again seems a place of limitless possibilities, especially around the 18th green, ringed by big grandstands and even larger crowds. Families flood the course. Tournament organizers have announced a whopping increase in the purse next year from $550,000 to $750,000, as well as the expansion of the event from 54 to 72 holes.

As the players approach the final green of the par-five finishing hole, an announcer calls out the name of each contestant. Every golfer receives a nice ovation as she briefly occupies center stage. It's one of the small, sweet, often overlooked perks of the profession—not many of us receive a round of applause at the end of the workweek.

"Leslie Spalding!" calls the announcer. "From Billings, Montana!"

After holing their final putts, players turn in their scorecards just behind the green and exit the area through a waist-high green mesh fence.

About two dozen of the smallest, cutest kids of the season, fairly evenly divided between boys and girls, hang out by the fence and wait for autographs. One 5-year-old girl carries a Minnie Mouse autograph book. The kids gaze wide-eyed as their new sports heroes sign their shirts, caps, and programs.

Spalding emerges from the scorer's tent with a big smile on her face, and picks up a Sharpie pen as the kids swarm around her. It's the exclamation point to a terrifically satisfying week. Spalding was five over par after the first 13 holes of the tournament. The ax of another missed cut already was starting to descend. But she played the next 41 holes in five under par and finishes tied for thirty-fourth. Her $3,675 paycheck boosts Spalding to 118 on the money list with $18,664.

"The slumps over," Spalding says cheerfully, as she continues to sign her name.

What a difference a week makes. Last Sunday in Atlantic City, after missing the cut, Spalding sat around the Residence Inn, "watched TV and ate junk food and got fat. It didn't make me feel any better."

This week she stayed in private housing with a wonderful family, the McVickers, swam and played tennis with a cousin visiting from Montana, sank a few putts—"It's all confidence"—and regained her best form. "I was trying to be too technical and think too much. I'm more of a feel player."

Tonight she'll celebrate at a local pub. Celebrate a bit too much, in fact. "I didn't know you're not supposed to chug wheat beers," she'll say tomorrow, nursing a hangover.

But right now, for Leslie Spalding, professional golfer, life is sweet.

"Dana Dormann! From Orlando, Florida!" calls the announcer.

Four months ago at the Nabisco Dinah Shore, husband John Dormann, who caddies for Meg Mallon, sounded as if he was at the end of his rope. Son William, at the time 12 months old, had been sick, and Dana was in the process of shooting 79-76. Unlike some who travel the Tour with a nanny or baby-sitting parents, John and Dana are shouldering the parental burdens all alone.

"Playing is the last thing on her mind," John said at the Dinah Shore. "You try to have some kind of normal life but it's just impossible. I don't know how long we can keep this up."

What a difference four months make. Dormann shoots a superlative 66 to finish tied for tenth, her best showing of the season.

"I think I've finally made it back," she says. "It was a tough time after the baby was born. I lost about ten pounds and I wasn't that big before," says the slender athlete. "It took about a year to put the weight back on."

The joys of motherhood relegated golf to the back burner for a while. To an extent, they still do. "I want to be the best mother I can be. I cut down on my practice time. It's a lot more desirable to spend a half-hour with William than to hit bunker shots."

Last year Dormann didn't practice at all after her rounds. She earned $28,582 in 17 tournaments. Now she opts for quality time on the practice range as well as with John and William. "I don't socialize on the range as much. I figure out what I need to work on before I go to the range and work on that."

Before she became pregnant, Dormann, 28, was knocking on the door of stardom. She won tournaments in her second and third year on Tour, earning $270,413 in 1992 and $234,415 in 1993. She may never attain such exalted status again. But she's well on her way to combining a successful career with a happy family life.

"Cathy Gerring! From Dublin, Ohio!"

Playing in just her third tournament of the year, Gerring is all smiles after making the cut and shooting 73-71-74 to finish tied for sixty-fourth. It's the first time she has made a cut on the LPGA Tour since 1992.

"I think it's coming," she says as she greets friends after the round. "I didn't hit the ball well but scored the best yesterday. It's encouraging, because good players score well when they're *not* hitting it good. *Anyone* can score when they hit it good."

Gerring will skip the next three events to avoid likely steamy weather and swollen hands in Youngstown, St. Louis, and Massachusetts. Her next appearance will be at the du Maurier Classic in Edmonton in early August. She can hardly wait.

* * *

"Kris Monaghan! From Spokane, Washington!"

In an astonishing turnaround, Monaghan recovers from an opening-round 75 to tie for sixth. Monaghan was six over par for the tournament after 26 holes midway through her second round yesterday, before scorching the front nine (she began play on No. 10) in 29. Today she skied all the way to 30 on the front nine, which means Monaghan played 18 consecutive holes in 59.

"A career highlight," says Monaghan.

Especially after last season. Monaghan won the Kyocera Inamori Classic and $208,987 in 1993, slipped to $51,847 in 1994, then played just one event in 1995, the Tournament of Champions in January, before she left the Tour.

She left to help care for her brother Todd Carey, dying of AIDS. Carey was diagnosed HIV-positive in 1986. His career as a nuclear engineer in the U.S. Navy ended, and he spent a lot of time in the VA Hospital in Albuquerque. He was angry and bitter.

When Monaghan returned from Albuquerque for Christmas in 1994, she found Carey bedridden. Monaghan took "a normal job" as a sales manager at a country club and helped Todd's twin sister Teri care for him. He died five months later.

"It threw me for a tizzy," says Monaghan. She didn't play competitive golf for a year. Last winter she moved back to her hometown of Spokane and spent a few months skiing. She teed it up in an LPGA tournament for the first time in 14 months in Tucson in March.

Monaghan, 35, is happy she left the Tour to spend time with her brother. Now she's glad she's back.

Working for someone else isn't her cup of tea. "We're able to be our own boss and set our own hours."

She returns with a broader perspective. "Watching somebody close to me die made me appreciate life more and appreciate my talents more. I'm more calm and patient."

The bad rounds no longer sting as much. And the good rounds? The spectacular 29s and 30s?

"Those rounds are for Todd. He's at peace now, watching me play golf."

"Maggie Will! From Whiteville, North Carolina!"

Will finishes tied for eighteenth, only her second top-20 finish of the season. But it's evidence she's on the right track after slumping badly last year and early in 1996.

Outside the ropes, everything is rosy. Will sports a big diamond engagement ring; in November she will marry Tom Halpin, who owns a jet engine repair business in Sarasota, Florida.

They met in the summer of 1994, a few months after Will had broken up with another "Mr. Wrong." At first she was skeptical. Halpin was a golf nut who had played the pro-am before, a tournament in Vermont with Will's friend and fellow pro Katie Peterson-Parker.

"Oh, I know your type," Will told him. "You just want to date a professional golfer."

Slowly, he won her over. "He understands the value of things," says Will. "He's honest; he treats people extremely well. He proved to me there are good guys in the world."

But there were problems. "I was playing the worst of my life. Everybody blamed Tom. They'd say things like 'He's distracting you,' or 'Here's another guy who is going to wreck your game.'

"These were friends who liked me for what I did, not who I was. I was playing bad before I met him."

Will took her golf difficulties to sports psychologists Bob Rotella and Deborah Graham: the former adjusted her attitude; the latter helped her become better organized on the golf course. Gradually Will saw a glimmer of improvement. Best of all, she began to enjoy the game again, partly due to Halpin's enthusiasm—he reveres the history of golf and plays to an eight handicap.

The romance weathered its own crisis. Last summer, after dating for a year, the 41-year-old Halpin told Will he was a confirmed bachelor. She broke up with him.

"It was the hardest thing I ever had to do. I knew I was losing a great person. The next eight weeks were awful."

Finally Halpin called. Shortly thereafter he proposed. "Being happy together," says Will with a grin, "beats being happy alone."

"Joan Pitcock! From Fresno, California!"

It's been a wild ride for the 28-year-old, whose goal at the beginning of the week was extremely modest—to make the cut. Pitcock, who resembles a young Sally Field, came to Toledo after poor performances in Rochester, where she tied for fifty-ninth, and Atlantic City, where she tied for fifty-sixth. She met with her instructor before the ShopRite, who pointed out that her alignment and ball position were out of whack. "I felt silly," says Pitcock, who has developed, writes *Toledo Blade* reporter Dave Hackenberg, "a reputation for her friendliness and honesty."

Pitcock is a fine player. She finished thirtieth on the money list last year with $ 204,407. She was third in Corning this year and contended at the U.S. Open before a disheartening final-round 78, but she hasn't won in nine years on Tour after dropping out of Fresno State University to turn pro in 1988. And she hasn't *felt* like a winner in a long, long time.

In 1994, when she placed forty-seventh on the money list with $114,735, Pitcock contemplated hanging up the sticks and finding another profession. "I thought I could do other things and make the same money and stay in the same city." In addition to the frustrations of the Tour, Pitcock missed her family. Her father suffered a heart attack in 1985 when Pitcock was a senior in high school. He underwent triple bypass surgery in 1993. Pitcock calls her parents every day. She returns to Fresno to visit every month. "I miss them more now than when I came out on Tour."

What was she planning to do instead?

"I had no idea," says Pitcock. "I'm qualified to do absolutely nothing."

So she stuck with it and played well in 1995. But not well enough to alleviate her frustration. "I have a little money saved," Pitcock would tell herself. "I can walk away if I want to."

She felt like doing so earlier in the week, after what Pitcock describes as a "dark moment" of self-doubt and dissatisfaction.

"It was frustration with my game and the weather. A lot of *how* you play depends on *when* you play," says Pitcock, who drew the worst of "the flip" in a number of tournaments this season. "You *try* to let it bounce off you."

Pitcock played Friday morning under favorable weather conditions and shot 68. She followed with a marvelous 66 yesterday. Last night she flipped on CNN and watched the sports ticker on the bottom of the screen flash her name every few minutes. And as her name continued to flash on the screen, Pitcock acknowledged her obsession with winning, stronger than ever after 225 trips to the starting gate on the LPGA Tour.

"The more I went on [in my career], the more I realized I didn't want to be someone who never won. All the pressure I put on myself was to win." She prepared herself for the heat of Sunday afternoon. "It was my tournament to win or lose. I hadn't been in that position before."

Pitcock's nerves this morning were strung as tautly as piano wire. Bogeying the 1st hole didn't help. "Holy cow," she said to herself. "I hope I don't do that again."

Pitcock's game plan is intelligent and conservative. She shoots for the fat part of the green and grinds on her approach putts. "I knew that's where the nerves would come in, on the short putts, so I tried to avoid the three- and four-footers." She avoids looking at the leader board as well. "I never, ever felt good out there," Pitcock says later. "It was a short rope and I was at the end of it."

* * *

As thunder rumbles in the distance, Pitcock, clinging to a one-shot lead over Marianne Morris, reaches the par-5 18th tee. Three solid shots later Pitcock, 12 feet from the pin, watches Morris barely miss a 14-foot birdie attempt.

With her putter "shaking as far from side to side as going back," Pitcock cozies the approach putt to two inches of the cup.

"It's a gimme!" yells a fan from the packed grandstands just behind Pitcock.

"I'll take it!" Pitcock calls back.

She taps it in and raises her arms in victory as the massive gallery stands and roars its approval.

Pitcock assumed that if she won, she would "break down and cry and be pitiful out there." But a beaming smile lights up her weary, fatigue-creased face. Several of her colleagues race onto the green and drench her with champagne, a tradition for first-time winners.

"You get a lot of neat stuff when you win," Pitcock happily tells the media. The windfall includes the use of a customized van for a year (particularly useful since Pitcock's car was stolen in Wilmington and vandalized last week in Atlantic City), a Rolex ("the official timepiece of the LPGA," presented to every first-time winner), and a check for $86,250.

Later Pitcock poses for pictures by the club swimming pool with tournament sponsors and organizers. The sweet smell of champagne is on her breath as well as her navy shirt and tan shorts. Tonight she'll watch CNN again, as her name is flashed around the world, and her triumph will begin to sink in.

It hasn't yet. Pitcock, despite her happiness, is concerned that winning will create higher expectations from herself and from others.

"You're always under pressure and there's always the need to make another putt. You try as hard as you can; that's all you can do. Try to have your own expectations and satisfy these if you can."

Tomorrow she'll fly home to Fresno, and surrounded by her family, she'll discover that winning truly is joyous. A big cake awaits her—Pitcock's twenty-ninth birthday is next Friday. The whole week will seem "like one long birthday party." Her friends will congratulate her. "People really don't think you can win until you do. They don't know if you can play against Lopez 'cause you're the gal who lives next door." Her family will celebrate. Her mother will tell her, "I'm glad you finally won, because you needed to do it for yourself." Pitcock will find some peace of mind, and bask in a new-found sense of accomplishment.

* * *

The traveling circus rolls on. Players point their rental cars east and drive toward Youngstown. The Tour can be harsh and brutal. But it is also an open road winding through a landscape of opportunity that few people—and particularly few women—are fortunate enough to experience. Up ahead lies a new town. Up ahead is another chance. Up ahead is the possibility of failing miserably. Or succeeding spectacularly, erasing years of pain, frustration, and hardship in a few magical days. Up ahead lies freedom. For a professional golfer, every day is Independence Day.

CHAPTER 8

*E*dmonton: Smoke and Mirrors

"Good luck and bonne chance," reads a scoreboard by the 18th green at the Edmonton Country Club as players complete their practice rounds for the final major of the season, the du Maurier Classic on August 1–4.

It's been a long July for LPGA players, after a month that took them from Joan Pitcock's triumph in Toledo to the Youngstown-Warren LPGA Classic (where Michelle McGann defended her title in front of adoring crowds), to the Friendly's Classic in Agawam, Massachusetts (a town just outside Springfield where Dottie Pepper won her third tournament in five weeks), to the Michelob Light Heartland Classic in St. Louis, where, to her astonishment, Vicki Fergon shot one of the great rounds of the year, a nine under par 63 on a tight, tough course en route to her first victory since 1984.

(While it might have been Fergon's career round, it's not her best-ever score. She shot 62 in the 1984 San Jose Classic, joining Mickey Wright, Laura Davies, and Hollis Stacy in the LPGA record book for lowest 18-hole total.)

"I've been getting so mad at myself," Fergon said after the 63. "I've been really miserable on the golf course. . . . So I just tried to forget it. I just tried to change my attitude around."

No one knows what to expect this week. The du Maurier hopscotches around Canada year-by-year. But this is the first time since its inception in 1973 that the tournament has ventured to the windswept prairies of Alberta.

It's virgin territory for most players, too. Nancy Lopez thought she might be able to visit husband Ray Knight this week, managing the Cincinnati Reds in Montreal, until she pulled out a map and realized she was three-quarters of a continent away.

A few players fail to cross the border, including Dottie Pepper and Patty Sheehan. The hottest golfer in the world, Pepper played through a measles-like virus to win the Friendly's Classic, but paid the price. For the second straight week she's bedridden at her home in Glassy Mountain, South Carolina. Sheehan, on the other hand, is feeling fine. She's been having too much fun at home to feel properly prepared to play, even if the du Maurier is a major.

It's not the first time a star has given the du Maurier the cold shoulder. Lopez often skips the tournament. In 1991 Beth Daniel withdrew prior to the event after her 8-month-old dog died. (When Daniel was mocked in some golf publications for her decision, Amy Alcott, in an unfortunate attempt to defend her, said, "I went through a depression for two years. I'd rank the loss of my dog with the death of my mother and father.")

Hard to imagine Daniel or any other star skipping the U.S. Open because of the death of a pet. But as majors go, the du Maurier has been a minor. Until this year television coverage has been abysmal, usually tape-delayed on the weekend and shown in the U.S. on Prime network. In 1994, during a 45-minute rain delay in the final round at Ottawa, the network cut away to show a replay of the 1993 event and continued to do so, even after live action had resumed. Martha Nause, completing her dramatic comeback from Ramsay Hunt syndrome, won the first major of her 17-year career. Viewers never saw it.

(This year ESPN, which is televising the du Maurier, and the LPGA insisted on bringing in additional cameras and placing control of the telecast in the hands of veteran U.S. producer Larry Cirillo, bruising a few egos at Canadian network CTV, which has held the reins in the past.)

Course conditions have been bush league too. Greens at the 1995 du Maurier at Beaconsfield Golf Club in Montreal were described as "brown rugs" by *The Edmonton Sun* columnist Dick Chubey. One player told *Golf World*, "It's hard to putt on dirt."

No such problems at the superbly conditioned Edmonton Country Club, the first golf club in the city, which is celebrating its hundredth birthday. Over the years it has shared its grounds with a toboggan club, an isolation hospital during a smallpox epidemic, and an oil field, where members drilled for crude in the 1940s when the city became a boomtown. Edmonton C.C. was one of the few courses in the world where a *really* fat wedge could pay off big-time.

Since the original members leased land from the Hudson's Bay Company in 1896 to build a five-hole layout, Edmonton C.C. has acquired a storied history. The Prince of Wales (later King Edward VIII) played the course in 1919. Walter Hagen, fresh off a victory at the British Open, played an exhibition in 1925. A half-century later, in 1974, Debbie Massey defeated Amy Alcott in the Canadian Women's Amateur Championship.

"It's a great little golf course," Pat Bradley told *The Edmonton Journal*, in an article entitled "Country Club Gussied Up for the Girls." While it's no Pine Needles, the course has a stylish, classical feel to it, with soaring aspens, Colorado spruce, and pine trees framing the fairways and small greens.

In short, it's a fine course in a charming city of 850,000. Edmonton is the fifth largest city in Canada, but it doesn't seem a bit congested, not even in July and August when visitors swarm "Canada's Festival City" for a host of events: the Edmonton International Street Performers Festival, a riot of clowns and entertainers; Klondike Days, a salute to the pioneer era; Edmonton Heritage Festival, a celebration of the wide-ranging ethnic diversity of the city; the Edmonton Folk Music Festival, highlighted this year by the return of Alberta native k. d. lang; and Fringe Theater Event, a dazzling array of original plays scattered around numerous stages in Old Strathcona, a gentrified, bohemian district beehived with shops, coffee-houses, restaurants, and theaters.

The festivals are almost as famous as the West Edmonton Mall, biggest mall in the world. It's located just minutes from the hotels where many players are staying. They're dropping enough loonies (the Canadian dollar coin with a picture of a loon on it) and toonies (the new Canadian two-dollar coin) to earn West Edmonton designation as "the official mall of the LPGA."

It truly is a monstrosity, with over 800 stores and services, a casino, 19 movie screens, 110 restaurants and fast-food vendors, a five-acre water park, an NFL-sized ice-skating rink, various rides at Galaxyland, and a miniature golf course.

"The roller coaster is unbelievable," says Leslie Spalding, who already has been to the mall twice.

Spalding is sitting in the comfortable clubhouse at Edmonton C.C. on Thursday, August 1, after firing a first-round 76.

"Course record?" asks Dina Ammaccapane as she walks toward the locker room.

"Yeah," Spalding says sarcastically. "You, too?"

"Yeah," says Ammaccapane, who also played poorly and shot 74. "The other way."

Spalding's game has been on a roller coaster of its own since her fine performance in Toledo. She shot 73-74 and missed the cut by two strokes in Youngstown and 74-77 in Agawam to again miss the cut by two strokes after finishing bogey-bogey. On 17 she hit a decent drive into a horrible lie and missed a four-foot par putt. On 18 she hit a drive through the fairway onto a severe slope, dooming her to another weekend of unemployment.

"It was real frustrating," says Spalding, who has slipped to 126th on the money list. "I've been hitting the ball real well."

So she skipped last week's tournament in St. Louis and returned to

Tampa to work on her putting. Coach Paul Enright suggested opening up her stance, keeping her hands from getting ahead at impact, and adopting more of a pendulum stroke.

Outside the ropes life has been more enjoyable. Although her endorsement deal with Pervonia skin care products never materialized, Spalding did sign with Bobby Jones apparel. No money, but lots of nifty new threads. She also scored a free Dirt Devil after playing in a pro-am with some guys who work for the vacuum cleaner company. In Youngstown, Spalding played tennis and visited with the McVicker family (who housed her in Toledo), after they drove cross-state to root for her. In Massachusetts she stayed with a woman who works for the tournament sponsor, Friendly's, and toured its ice cream plant. (Free samples!) Last week in Tampa she swam, played tennis, visited with friends, and flew to Cleveland one day for an outing sponsored by Anderson Consulting, joining 17 other LPGA players and a number of Senior PGA Tour players.

"It was a nice golf course and dinner," says Spalding, who pocketed $1,000 plus travel and hotel expenses for the day. She wasn't as impressed, however, with the attitude of the hosts, who are sponsoring the $3.6 million World Match Play Tournament for men. They told her that any significant involvement with the LPGA was "down the road."

The hosts this week earn rave reviews from Spalding and the other players; du Maurier provides lavish treatment. When Spalding heads upstairs to the clubhouse Hospitality Room for lunch, she'll be greeted by tables decorated with ice sculptures and laden with a pasta bar, salad and fruit bar, assorted hot entrees, and a desert bar. In the morning she chows down at a waffle bar. Du Maurier doesn't neglect the care and feeding of the media either, providing meals and gifts, including a black vinyl briefcase and a pen.

Du Maurier, an arm of Imperial Tobacco Limited, can afford it. Imperial, which controls over 60 percent of the Canadian cigarette market, is in turn a subsidiary of Imasco Limited, whose companies produced over $8 billion in sales and over $500 million in profits in 1994.

Imperial's major cigarette brands include du Maurier, Player's, which sponsors motor sports, and Matinée, a brand primarily pitched to women through fashion magazines and tennis tournament sponsorships. The du Maurier is the only LPGA event of the year in North America that allows smoking in the media center. Open containers of du Maurier cigarettes are strewn across the tables where the du Maurier publicity representatives work. They don't actually tell the media, "Thank you for smoking," but the message is clear. (A small percentage of LPGA playeres smoke, but it is rare to see a golfer puffing on a cigarette inside the ropes.)

*   *   *

Caroline Pierce won't be standing in line at Galaxyland to ride the roller coaster after her opening-round 71.

Heights scare her. Bridges freak her out. At Wykagyl Country Club in New York, site of the JAL Big Apple Classic, Pierce is the only player in the field who won't cross a bridge on the 3rd hole that leads from a point near the tee box over a gully to the fairway. Instead she walks down the hill and under the bridge. So when some of the caddies heard about the bridge on the 9th hole at Edmonton, they rushed up to Rick Aune three weeks ago in Youngstown and proclaimed,

"Caroline won't be able to play Canada!"

They had a point. The bridge on the 175-yard par three is unavoidable. It's a spectacular hole. A golfer sees leaves fluttering in the breeze at ground level about 20 yards in front of the tee; they continue for about another 80 yards toward the green. At first glance they appear to be some sort of low-lying plants or shrubs.

They are, in fact, the very tip tops of a forest of aspen trees sheltered in a ravine that plunges down about 80 feet. The only route from tee to green (or, for that matter, from the clubhouse to the 1st tee or driving range, which both are near the 9th tee) is over an open, swaying suspension bridge. It conjures up visions of Galloping Gertie, the suspension bridge over Puget Sound near Tacoma, Washington, famously captured in a film that showed it swaying violently in a storm before buckling and breaking apart.

The bridge at Edmonton seems sturdy enough, anchored by thick silver steel cables. And it offers a spectacular walk over the ravine, eye-level with the treetops, floating with the birds in the uppermost branches, which are lit by golden sunshine. Far below is the floor of the deep green forest, with its cool, dark shadows and rocky terrain.

But the bridge is barely wide enough for two people walking side-by-side over its wooden planks, and it bounces with every footstep. For safety reasons only about 25 people can be on it at once.

"It'll be all right if I don't look down," says a woman to her friend, walking gingerly over the forest.

"It gives me the heebie-jeebies," says Pierce, who does what she has to do and crisscrosses the span several times a day. But not without some serious jitters.

The final round and final few holes of tournaments also are starting to spook Pierce. She's struggled on Sunday ever since her collapse at Nashville.

"I'm trying not to make it a big issue. It could *become* a big issue."

After a tie for thirty-fourth in Toledo, Pierce skipped Youngstown and took care of a few immigration matters, getting a medical exam and visiting the INS office in Pittsburgh. Officials took a picture of her right ear, used like a fingerprint for identification purposes. She tied for thirty-seventh in Awagam; after a double-bogey on the 17th hole Sunday she birdied the difficult final hole, to stem the last-round blues a bit.

Pierce, like Spalding, is working on her putting, which has been erratic. Mostly she's focusing on her rhythm, trying to accelerate the blade through the ball at impact.

Later today she'll call her twin sister, Jane, in England to wish her a happy thirty-third birthday. Tomorrow Jane will call her to return the greeting. (They were born several minutes apart around midnight on the first—and second—of August.) A friend from Houston is visiting Pierce this week, and they will celebrate at one of the restaurants in Old Strathcona.

Juli Inkster vegged out at home for two weeks after a tie for twenty-sixth in Toledo.

"What'd I do? Not much," she says, vainly trying to remember any highlights. "We ate dinner outside every night."

Toledo was a step forward for her. Husband Brian made a rare appearance as her caddie. "It helped me," says Inkster. "I relaxed and had a little more fun." Although she missed a ton of makable putts, she hit the ball superbly. "I'm doing everything better," she says. "Thinking better, chipping better."

Proof came in St. Louis last week when Inkster finished fourth, her best showing of the year. "It was not my type of course. It's real narrow and you can't hit driver on a lot of holes. But I played steady—made a triple in the first round but didn't get down about it and came back to finish even par. On Sunday I hit it OB on the second hole and came back to be one under. The bottom line is that I putted good—good putts for pars and good putts for birdies."

Caddie Greg Johnston recently started lining Inkster up on the greens; she thinks it has helped considerably. "It frees [my mind] up. I just have to think about the speed."

She's absolutely striping the ball on the range, swinging with seemingly effortless power and precision. "That was so good it should count as two," says Johnston, as a Titleist rockets into the pristine blue Alberta sky.

"Two more," says Inkster, who proceeds to hit about a dozen.

"Is that better?" she finally asks Johnston.

"Much."

"I like the way you think."

Inkster heads from the range toward the suspension bridge, passing

Laura Davies, who is on the 9th tee with her pro-am group. The globe-trotting Davies has been in Europe for the last seven weeks since the U.S. Open. She flew in yesterday on Tuesday from the Irish Open in Dublin, where she tied for third.

"Hey, mate," calls out Inkster. "Welcome back."

Davies smiles and waves.

A fan says to Inkster, "Got it straightened out, Juli?"

It appears that she does.

So does Nancy Lopez, who tees off on the 10th hole at 12:40 on Thursday with Brandie Burton and Kelly Robbins. A big gallery follows the trio on a beautiful summer day. A few puffs of white clouds mark deep blue skies. The temperature is a breezy 80 degrees. Sellers ran out of admission tickets this morning as 7,000 fans flowed through the gates, a fine opening-round crowd. Edmonton has hosted some big events in recent years, including the World Figure Skating Championships, but the du Maurier is the first major golf tournament and interest is keen.

An army of volunteers in du Maurier colors, red (golf shirts) and black (pants), patrol the course. The marshals, like the fans, are appreciative, unjaded, and a bit naive. Expected to be impassive, they applaud every shot that gets airborne. A newspaper article with tips for spectators advises them not to walk through traps or across the greens. A spectator on the 15th picks up Burton's ball and then puts it back down.

Lopez has finished twelfth, seventh, and seventy-first in her three appearances since the U.S. Open. Her chances of making the Solheim Cup team are heavily dependent on her performance this week.

Playing superbly and buoyed by an early eagle on the 470-yard 15th hole, Lopez stands at four under par as the trio reaches the 360-yard 7th hole, which rivals the ravine-spanning 9th hole for beauty and difficulty.

The right side of the tree-lined fairway hugs the banks of the North Saskatchewan River. Push a drive—or a second shot—to the right and say farewell to your ball as it plunges hundreds of feet down the bluff toward the flowing brown water.

Ingeniously designed, the hole offers golfers a classic risk-reward option. The fairway splits left and right with a patch of thick rough in between. The safe shot is an iron to the left portion of the fairway (a driver will reach a grove of trees beyond the fairway), leaving a blind shot with a long iron from beneath a hill to a narrow, sloping green with a bunker to the left and the riverbank to the right. The risky tee shot is along a narrow strip of fairway bordering the riverbank; it leaves a golfer with a clear view of the green and a medium or short iron. Most of the field plays safely to the left; their attitude, says Pierce, is "Give me a par and I'll leave."

All three golfers hit shots safely to the left. The hill in front of them is so steep that even Lopez's caddie, the tall Tom Thorpe, has to jump like a basketball player to spot the top of the flagstick in order to give Lopez a reference point to aim at.

Lopez pulls her second shot into the greenside bunker and hits a tremendous trap shot to three feet. While she waits for Burton and Robbins to finish, Lopez, wearing pink shorts and a white jersey with thin, faint pink horizontal stripes, practices her putting stroke over and over. Then she rolls in her par putt and the golfers and about 200 spectators walk along a dirt path overlooking the river.

"Beautiful, isn't it?" says Thorpe, who resides in Portland, Oregon. "Just like the Columbia Gorge."

Burton and Robbins aren't as sanguine. After finishing second at Agawam two weeks ago, Burton is four over par. Robbins, after missing only her second cut of the year last week in St. Louis, is seven over par, falling apart after a good front nine. The kid carrying the group's portable scoreboard doesn't have a 7 in his bag of numbers, so there is a blank spot next to her name, lending the impression she is some sort of tagalong.

Robbins fights back, ripping two massive woods onto the front of the green at the 517-yard 8th hole and two-putting for birdie. Yet she looks as if she's in a fog; studying her approach putt, she walks right on top of Burton's line. When she apologizes, Burton laughs and says, "Don't worry about it."

After a wedge that brakes to a screeching stop, Lopez rams in a four-foot birdie putt. On the 175-yard 9th hole she flags an iron over the ravine and forest at the stick, but the ball trickles into the back fringe. She smashes a horrible lag putt eight feet past the hole. Her comebacker slithers in and out of the cup.

Lopez slaps her thigh. Pros hate to finish a round by three-whacking (the latest lingo for three-putting) the last hole. But the crowd applauds long and loud for her, as she finishes with a 68. It ties her for second behind Karrie Webb, who hits 17 greens en route to a phenomenal 65.

"That's the best first round in a while," Thorpe says as he removes his sweaty uniform, a red jumpsuit. He notes that Lopez, despite three-whacking the last hole, only needed 30 putts today. More practice time and the use of a laser device which indicates if the head moves during the putting stroke have helped. So has a switch from a mallet putter, which Lopez has used almost her entire career, to an Odyssey Rossi II, which continues to be the hottest weapon of choice on the LPGA Tour.

Lopez greets a large contingent of reporters and camera crews in the media center for the second straight day. After watching her yesterday, for-mer CTV anchor Daphne Kuehn told *The Edmonton Journal,* "I don't care how many interviews you watch in your life, it's always special to see some-thing done as well as Nancy just did it."

It's dinnertime. Lopez is dying to get the hell out of the interview room, let the therapist soothe a stiff neck and back, and work out in the fitness van. (Lopez has now lost 37 pounds in 1996, and aims to drop 10 more.) She's still shaking off lingering traces of jet-lag. "Your muscles feel different when adjusting for time changes." When she flew into Edmonton on Mon-day she couldn't sleep, and wound up staring like a zombie at the TV screen at three o'clock in the morning.

But Lopez is as gracious and patient as a saint with the reporters, who hang on her every word.

"When I play a pretty good first round the tempo is much the same the next few days, and I feel good about that. The last couple of months I've built a lot of confidence in myself. . . . I don't feel uncomfortable close to the lead; I did early in the year."

Cincinnati Reds baseball was a topic of discussion yesterday, with owner Marge Schott recently getting the boot by major league owners. Late last night Lopez talked to her husband, who said, "Oh, by the way, I got thrown out last night."

"What inning?" Nancy asked.

"About the seventh."

It's not the first time Knight, whose competitiveness matches that of his spouse, has gotten the heave-ho. Both Knight and Lopez are appalled by the lackadaisical attitude of many of today's professionals.

"Ray gave one hundred percent as a player," says Lopez. "He played with a torn Achilles [tendon], bad rotator cuff, chips in his elbow. Sometimes managers have to beg players to play. It bothers Ray a lot, especially when you see how much more money they make."

As an amateur, Lopez took her cues from veterans such as Judy Rankin, Donna Caponi, and JoAnne "Big Momma" Carner. "I loved Carner more than anybody. She never had a defeatist attitude. She never got upset at a bad shot. I'd say to myself, 'I want to be just like that if I ever get on Tour.' "

Lopez earnestly discusses the issue of sports stars as role models.

"Pro athletes, a lot of them, feel like they're owed something. Lots of players in all sports forget that you have to give back or appreciate. So they win a tournament and think they're untouchable. Well, I've won forty-seven tournaments. How am *I* supposed to feel?" she says, breaking into a laugh.

Motherhood has deepened Lopez's sense of responsibility to the fans, especially the younger ones. "Kids are watching you all the time. You don't want to disappoint them."

She doesn't want to let her own children down either. Retiring to become a full-time mom has become an attractive notion. She candidly admits she might already have done so except for her contractual agreements with Sara Lee and Tommy Armour clubs, which run for a couple of more years. "I'm only thirty-nine but it does seem like I've been playing golf forever."

Her dilemma is simple. On the one hand, Lopez is "trying to see if I really can win, trying to see if I have the mental attitude. You have to be able to outthink everybody else."

On the other hand, Lopez wants her kids "to be as normal as they can." Last week she thought about taking them to the Olympics in Atlanta, at least until the pipe bomb explosion in Centennial Park that killed one spectator and injured scores of other fans. (Rosie Jones and Tracy Kerdyk attended the Games last week. Kerdyk, staying near the park, heard the blast.)

Lopez segues into a subject seldom discussed at a golf tournament, terrorism. The LPGA media rep beside Lopez stops taking notes, puts down her pen, and starts looking uneasy.

"It's getting worse," says Lopez, last week's explosion of TWA Flight 800, possibly caused by a bomb or missile, fresh in her mind. "I hate getting on a plane. There's no safe place anymore. You never know on a golf course. We're out in the open. Anybody could shoot us. It's scary."

Her fears are not just theoretical. In 1985, the final round of a tournament in South Carolina was temporarily suspended when a guard spotted a man in a car with, the guard claimed, a gun on his lap. When the car was searched, a pairing sheet was found with three names circled, Beth Daniel, Betsy King, and Hollis Stacy. A few years later a fan in Lopez's gallery made a remark that she found threatening. "I was a basket case after that."

More recently Laura Davies has been obsessively pursued by a retired surgeon named Henry Lee, a Korean-born Canadian who became infatuated with Davies when he attended the du Maurier a few years ago.

As Davies details in her new autobiography, Lee followed her at various tournament sites and sent her a stream of marriage proposals as well as a copy of his divorce papers. Davies shrugged it off until Lee wrote her a note in 1995 stating, "If I can't have you, no one else will." At that point LPGA commissioner Charlie Mechem notified the FBI, which prevented Lee from attending the Safeco Classic in Seattle; this March the FBI dragged him, screaming, from the course at the Ping/Welch's Championship in Tucson. Although it's not mentioned in the book, Davies says the FBI finger-printed Lee in Tucson, which seems to have scared him off. Since then Davies has received only an occasional note from him.

"I don't go out at night too often," says Lopez, who has had men follow her back to her hotel. "I hate to live my life afraid. I don't let my kids stay out alone too long. I can't sit down when the kids are alone outside."

Nancy Lopez knows she and her family can't escape from the real world. Sometimes, however, the LPGA seems to try. Particularly when it journeys to Canada.

More than any other organization in sports, the LPGA and its players walk the walk and talk the talk in terms of giving back to society. Players host charity events that aid everything from juvenile diabetes (Michelle McGann), to breast cancer (Val Skinner), to rape crisis and domestic violence (Val Skinner again), to the handicapped (Lopez), to youth organizations (Sheehan), to multiple sclerosis (Amy Alcott), to abused and neglected children (Shirley Furlong). These events are not just grin 'n' shake photo ops; they demand months of planning and personal involvement.

Betsy King travels to Romania to help bring back orphans of war and organizes teams of players and caddies to build houses with Habitat for Humanity. Patty Sheehan was recognized by *Sports Illustrated* in 1987 as one of eight "Sportsmen of the Year" for her six-figure financial support of Tigh Sheehan, a home for abused and neglected teenage girls. Patty Jordan works with an organization promoting sexual abstinence for teenagers. Kay Cockerill was honored by *Golf Digest* and *Sports Illustrated For Kids* for her work with the LPGA's Urban Youth Golf Program. Hollis Stacy works with the Scleroderma Research Foundation. Kim Shipman volunteers at the Women's Community Bakery in Washington, D.C. Rosie Jones solicited about $2,500 from 40 players and caddies at the ShopRite in June to help keep the Animal Orphanage in Voorhees, New Jersey, open after watching a local news station report the shelter was on the verge of closure. LPGA players donate every dime of the money they win in Wednesday pro-ams back to the organization to help support the LPGA's catastrophic illness fund.

Caddies, who struggle to make ends meet, raise money every year for tournament charities at a site that treats them well. Last year they donated over $5,000 in Portland.

Two innovative kids' programs are at the heart of the LPGA. One is the LPGA Urban Youth Golf Program, started in Los Angeles in 1989, which brings golf to minority and underprivileged children and teenagers in the inner cities of Los Angeles, Detroit, Portland, and Wilmington, with expansion plans to add more cities to the list.

"Of all the major organizations in golf, the LPGA is the most progressive," writes *Golf Week* columnist James Achenbach. "Its Urban Youth Golf Programs are sensational."

Just as impressive is the LPGA Girls Golf Club, which encourages girls 7–17 to learn the game, compete, and form friendships in a nonthreatening environment. Begun in Phoenix in 1989 by LPGA teaching pro Sandy LaBauve, it was expanded to 27 cities in 1995 with plans to reach over 100 cities worldwide by 1998.

From 1981 to 1995 LPGA tournaments raised $78 million for charity. In 1992 it named the Susan G. Komen Breast Cancer Foundation as its official national charity. The LPGA Player Guide states:

> As a woman's organization with strong family priorities, the LPGA unfortunately has been affected first-hand by breast cancer and knows only too well the devastating results of the disease on the patient, family and friends. On November 20, 1993, the LPGA lost a very good friend. Heather Farr, who joined the LPGA in 1985, fought a 4½-year battle with breast cancer, after being diagnosed in 1989 at the age of 24. Her spirit will live forever in the heart of LPGA. The Susan G. Komen Breast Cancer Foundation has made remarkable strides to raise funds for advanced research into the disease and to provide further education for early detection and prevention. The LPGA provides the Komen Foundation with another avenue through which to focus its goals and spread its message.

The LPGA's popular tournament director, Suzanne Jackson, has waged a five-year struggle against breast cancer. A thin and smiling Jackson, who has endured two bone marrow transplants, is in Edmonton this week. It's her first appearance at a tournament site in 1996.

Several weeks ago, on July 9, Kathy Ahern, who won the LPGA Championship in 1972 and played the Tour until 1991, when she was diagnosed with breast cancer, died at the age of 47.

"I'm exactly Kathy's age," breast cancer survivor Shelley Hamlin said a few days ago as sunshine streamed down on the practice range. "We were diagnosed the same week. I was just lucky. I had better doctors, more checkups."

Last week Hamlin, Lopez, and about 50 other players attended a memorial service in St. Louis for Ahern. Hamlin was touched at the turnout. "It was an emotional week for all of us."

Hamlin is a friendly woman with a nice sense of humor—she performed a standup routine for players at the Sprint Titleholders in Daytona Beach in May. She's smart, too, a graduate from Stanford University with a degree in political science. Her victory at the Phar-Mor at Inverrary in 1992, just seven months after a modified radical mastectomy, was one of the most remarkable sports stories of the year. (Actually, it was a miracle Hamlin still was on the Tour. Ten weeks after surgery, she had to return to Q-School. She kept her card. The experience, she says, was "horrific.")

"She's an inspiration," says Callaway's Jan Thompson, who hired Hamlin to speak and teach at golf clinics when Thompson was at Mazda and used LPGA players to help the company sell more cars to women. Hamlin, saddled with medical bills, was in debt until she picked up the winner's check of $70,000 at the Phar-Mor.

"Sometimes the golf gods smile," Thompson says.

Hamlin won again at the ShopRite Classic in 1993. But she struggled with her game last year, banking just $20,504. This year has been worse, at least until last week when she tied for tenth in Agawam.

"This year hasn't been much fun at all," she says. "I haven't had a sense of where my backswing is. It's like Silly Putty; it changes from day-to-day." Hamlin laughs. "I've worked really hard to be this bad."

Although she describes last week as "delightful—it recharged me a bit"—Hamlin is contemplating a career change.

"It seems like everyone coming onto the Tour is tall and blonde and hits it three hundred yards. It puts pressure on older players to keep improving their game. I've been having a little talk with myself. If I don't get better soon, I won't do this again next year." Instead Hamlin will become a teacher of the sport.

How does the future educator and breast cancer survivor feel about a cigarette company sponsoring an LPGA event?

"Du Maurier has been unbelievably great to us. They sponsor our fitness van. I think there is a place for a cigarette company. Smoking is probably not that bad for you as long as you don't smoke very much or for very long."

Smoking probably is not that bad for you as long as you don't smoke very much or for very long?

Shelley Hamlin is smart and well read. So are most LPGA staffers and players. Perhaps they know that *Lancet*, regarded as the world's most respected medical journal, predicts millions of worldwide smoking-related deaths by the end of the century. Perhaps they know that over 400,000 Americans die every year from smoking-related illnesses. Perhaps they know that in the mid-1990s, for the first time in history, there were more women smokers than men. Perhaps they know that lung cancer tops breast cancer as the leading cancer killer among women. Perhaps they know that studies suggest women smokers may be more susceptible to lung cancer than men. Perhaps they know that cigarette smoking has been linked to blindness, colon and rectal cancer, and, yes, even breast cancer, although research concerning breast cancer has yielded mixed results. Perhaps they know that smokers start young. The average age is 13. Of those who refrain from smoking until the age of 20, only 10 percent take up the habit as adults. Perhaps they know that 3,000 kids start smoking every day, and that one in three eventually will die of a smoking-related disease. Perhaps they know that, according to the *Journal of the American Medical Association* (JAMA), cigarette usage among teenage girls went through the roof when tobacco companies began targeting brands such as Virginia Slims (longtime—now former—sponsor of the women's tennis tour) and Eve to women in the 1960s. Perhaps they know that in 1993 the Surgeon General's office reported that the fastest growing segment of smokers in the U.S. consists of females under the age of 23. Perhaps they know that the Centers for Disease Control in Atlanta found that children exposed to smoke in their homes miss 7,000,000 more school days than other kids as a result of colds, flu, bronchitis, and pneumonia.

Perhaps they know that studies cited in JAMA found that Joe Camel is recognized as a symbol of smoking by 91 percent of 6-year-olds, which means Joe Camel is about as famous among children as Mickey Mouse.

Perhaps they even know that a 1988 marketing plan from Imperial Tobacco, parent company of du Maurier, stated, "If the last 10 years have taught us anything, it is that *the industry is dominated by the companies who respond most effectively to the needs of younger smokers.*" (Emphasis as in the original). And that a 1980 media plan outlined target groups for each of its brands; some were targeted to males and females in the 12- to 17-year-old age group.

Tobacco companies claim that their promotions are designed to induce brand switching. Period. Those assertions were undercut by internal documents produced as evidence during the industry's challenge to the Tobacco Products Control Act in Canada in 1995. The documents constitute, as it were, the smoking gun, as summarized by Rick Pollay and Cynthia Collard in an article in the *Ottawa Citizen* in December 1995.

"Tobacco promotion is not, as the industry claims, merely to encourage brand switching. Its twin goals are to keep smokers from quitting and to get adolescents to use cigarettes as a symbol of adulthood. . . .

"How do we know the real intent and strategies of the tobacco advertisers? Because they told us. . . .

"These previously secret files reveal tobacco manufacturers agonizing over ways to discourage current smokers from quitting and to encourage adolescents to smoke. They chronicle the industry's efforts to analyze the adolescent psyche and to persuade it to smoke."

What do younger smokers need? Other than to stop smoking? They need—or want—to know that their brand of choice is hip, cool, and happening.

Direct cigarette advertising is illegal in Canada. But tobacco companies are allowed to sponsor cultural activities and sports events; currently du Maurier sponsors sports, art and music groups, and festivals to the tune of $35–40 million a year nationwide.

It's a subtle but effective form of advertising. The du Maurier black and red logo is ubiquitous at the du Maurier Classic and other sponsored events. Posters promoting the tournament are all over Edmonton, wrapped around many street-lamp poles. The subliminal message associates du Maurier with clean, healthy, youthful, fun activities.

The strategy, says Cynthia Callard, director of Physicians for a Smoke-Free Canada, is to link the company logo, on TV in particular, with athletes. "A nice, healthy tennis star is a nice picture to have beside their name. It's consistent with direct advertising in other countries."

Sponsoring such events also generates tremendous goodwill for cigarette companies. In addition to the du Maurier Classic, the company sponsors five tournaments for Canadian women professionals leading up to the Classic, plus clinics and support for women teaching pros. The series offers $100,000 in total prize money; du Maurier grants automatic exemptions into the Classic to the top five finishers in the series. Such sponsorships foster the notion, says Callard, that cigarette companies "aren't really evil, they're nice."

Recipients of such sponsorship become as addicted to tobacco money as smokers do to nicotine. When proposals surfaced in the Canadian Parliament this year to require cigarettes to be sold in plain packaging (to help deglamorize smoking for youngsters) and prohibit or restrict event sponsorship, arts organizations across Canada wailed that it would sound the death knell for many symphonies, dance companies, and arts and music festivals.

How does the LPGA explain its acceptance of cigarette sponsorship?

It rarely, if ever, has to. At the two du Maurier tournaments I've attended in Edmonton and Vancouver (1991), the issue barely caused a ripple, although antismoking activists picketed outside the gates of the Vancouver Golf Club. The Physicians for a Smoke-Free Canada attempted to buy ad space in the tournament program in 1995 at the tournament in Ottawa. The proposed ad read: "Last year cigarettes killed twice as many women as breast cancer." Du Maurier refused to sell them space, which generated a flurry of stories in Canadian newspapers, but little attention from the media at the tournament itself.

When I asked then-commissioner Charlie Mechem about the propriety of the du Maurier sponsorship in 1995, he was startled by the question.

"Really, the issue has simply just never been raised. By anyone. We've never been criticized for it, and we have never, ever, so far as I'm aware, given serious thought to doing anything other than what we're doing. I look upon it as a company of integrity, a company that has been extremely supportive of young women, particularly in Canada, in developing their skills. They sponsor our fitness van. They've been a great company for us."

Players, including Inkster and Pierce, tend to parrot the party line— "Smoking is a personal choice"—in almost Stepfordian fashion. Commissioner Jim Ritts defends cigarette sponsorship on several grounds.

"Du Maurier supported the Tour in a very big way when others didn't. To me, a strong argument is that as long as the product is legal, we shouldn't play judge or jury. There's no attempt [at the tournament] to market tobacco to young people. There's not a level of discomfort among the players. They've been good partners. I think you should dance with the ones that bring you."

The rationale makes a certain amount of sense. For 46 years the LPGA has been on its knees, tin cup in hand, begging for corporate support. As Val Skinner, who tepidly defends the du Maurier sponsorship ("They're sponsoring fitness, even though it seems like kind of a contradiction"), notes, "We haven't been in a position to say no to *any* sponsor until now."

So when the LPGA secures a loyal backer, it seems eternally grateful. If necessary, players will hang around town for a week to tee it up on a course wriggling with water moccasins, as it did in Beaumont in 1967. Or say, as good and loyal LPGA player Shelley Hamlin says, "Smoking probably is not that bad for you as long as you don't smoke very much or for very long."

Du Maurier has been a pillar of support for the LPGA since 1973. It doesn't make players walk over snake-infested fairways; instead it lavishes $1 million purses, fitness vans, and waffle bars on them. That's why the LPGA designated it a major in 1979 (when the tournament was called the Peter Jackson Classic), even though the fields, the quality of the courses, and the lousy TV coverage often were less than first-rate.

(The poor media coverage, in some ways, has been a blessing for the LPGA. One LPGA official believes that scrutiny of the cigarette company sponsorship would have been more intense if the tournament was covered as extensively as the other three majors. Lots of people don't know du Maurier is a cigarette company. And most people probably assumed Peter Jackson was a person rather than a brand of smokes.)

The LPGA's eagerness to please is one of its greatest assets. LPGA officials believe, correctly, that their product sells itself to anyone who actually comes into contact with it. As *Golf World*'s Bill Fields puts it, "The handshake theory is thriving on the LPGA Tour. The golfers and their commissioner believe, like politicians, if they can touch one more palm, they'll get one more vote." As Dottie Pepper puts it, "If we can get people through the gate the first time, they'll be back."

Proof of the validity of the theory abounds. The LPGA is embraced in enclaves across America, in Nashville and Corning and Youngstown and Rochester and Portland. The image of the Tour, in those communities, is vastly different, and better, than its image among the general public.

Ask Ray Burgoo, CEO of Giant Eagle, a chain of 136 grocery stores in Ohio, Pennsylvania, and West Virginia. Last month at the Youngstown-Warren Classic, Burgoo announced that Giant Eagle would become the sponsor of the tournament beginning in 1997. For Burgoo, who has seen the LPGA's appeal in the community, the sponsorship is a natural. Most Giant Eagle customers are women; golf is a fast-growing women's sport. "It meshes nicely from a marketing perspective."

The gay stereotypes about the LPGA and the Ben Wright controversy are irrelevant to Burgoo. "We never even thought about it," he says, adding that Giant Eagle "has worked hard to create diversity" in its own workforce. In Youngstown, the LPGA represents exciting competition and great athletes who help raise money for children's charities (hit hard by the economic problems in the region), put on clinics for the physically handicapped, and interact with the fans. The LPGA's image in Youngstown, says Burgoo, "is a plus."

So the goal of the LPGA is to build bridges to the larger world. But in that context, its eagerness to please, a tremendous asset in attracting and keeping sponsors, turns into a liability. The LPGA's embrace of a cigarette company illustrates a larger, more fundamental get-along, go-along, don't-rock-the-boat philosophy that creates the impression that the organization has no core values. "We backpeddle too much," Juli Inkster said early in the year, discussing the Tour's response to the Ben Wright controversy. "We need to believe in ourselves instead of taking the pansy way out."

Example: The LPGA's eagerness to support a 1992 proposal to hold a golf competition at Augusta National G.C. during the 1996 Olympics, even though Augusta has no women members. The LPGA was left with egg on its face when local civil rights leaders helped torpedo the proposal, claiming the home of the Masters was racist and sexist and thus an unsuitable venue for an Olympic event.

Example: The LPGA did not adopt a nondiscrimination policy until 1991, long after the PGA and Senior Tour.

Example: The timidity of the LPGA in addressing the lesbian issue, which lasted until Ben Wright unwittingly did the LPGA a favor by helping bring it out of the closet.

Example: Allowing the producers of NBC's *Mad About You* to perpetrate the gay stereotype about the LPGA without a peep of protest.

Example: Allowing TV golf commentators to call LPGA players "girls" without a peep of protest. Ritts says, "I don't know how to deal with that issue," noting, correctly, that LPGA players and LPGA players-turned-commentators refer to each other as "girls" and "gals" on and off the air. "Is it okay for Donna [Caponi] but not Johnny [Miller]?" And Ritts, rightly, is more concerned about commentators' lack of familiarity with LPGA players and their talent, which leads "to filling the void with inanities."

Yet language matters, as Ritts, formerly an advertising whiz, should understand. It's another instance when the LPGA's deference to TV networks or sponsors, and its silence in the face of major insults, or even minor disrespect, invites disdain from the public at large and despair from millions of women golfers looking to the LPGA for leadership in their fight for equal treatment on the links.

Why does the general public still connect the LPGA with lesbianism? Why are so many of the references to the LPGA in the nongolf media, on *Mad About You* or the *Tracey Ullman Show* (which featured an episode about a gay woman golfer coming out of the closet), or in *Esquire* (which lumped the LPGA into a group of gay celebrities), about sexual orientation?

Is it sexism? Homophobia? Long-standing stereotypes about female athletes?

Sure, to a large extent.

But it's also because the LPGA hasn't given the public a different image to take the place of the stereotypes. This is not a criticism of the image makers—LPGA publicity people sell the LPGA as an organization of world-class, approachable, socially concerned, family-oriented athletes with skill and fervor, despite puny budgets. (The LPGA is funded partly from tournament sponsors; 6.5 percent of the total purse money, about $1.7 million, goes into the organization's coffers for staff and programs. Licensing fees, merchandise sales, and TV rights money raise the total 1996 operating budget to about $7 million. The PGA, which is receiving a reported $65 million in 1996 just for TV rights to telecast its tournaments, runs superslick "Anything Is Possible" ads and sponsors weekly magazine shows for the PGA and Senior Tour on ESPN. The LPGA lacks the money to do the same.)

It is a matter of policy. When the LPGA takes cigarette money, it undercuts its concern with health issues and children. When it fights breast cancer with one hand and supports a company whose product causes lung cancer on the other, it sends out messages that blur its identity and induce cognitive dissonance headaches. When it turns the other cheek and allows TV networks to demean its players, it emboldens others to do so. How big was the audience for the *Mad About You* episode? 23.8 million. How does the LPGA counteract the impression left in the minds of these viewers? Good question.

Ritts and the LPGA are not oblivious to these issues. The *Mad About You* episode touched off an internal debate within the organization: Should the LPGA lead, follow, or get out of the way? Evidence indicates the choice may be much starker: Lead or be trampled. The LPGA needs to decide what kind of message it intends to send out to the kids in its junior golf programs and its fans watching LPGA events on TV, 45 percent of whom are women. All too often the LPGA—composed of talented, dynamic, intelligent women of the 1990s—comes across as an organization of timid, acquiescent, subservient women of the 1950s. (The name of the organization doesn't help. "Ladies" conjures up images of, at best, quilting bees and sewing circles and, at worst, old Jerry Lewis movies—"Hey la-dy!" The LPGA is toying with a name change: from the LPGA to the WPGA, perhaps to coincide with the turn of the century.)

In his first year in office, Ritts has proven himself an able cheerleader. That's a compliment—the rah-rah rallying of players, sponsors, and media is an important element of his job. He also has handled the gay issue with a cool nonchalance and an underlying message of tolerance, stating "There are elements of society that have a problem with diversity, including sexual preference. But that narrow mind-set doesn't dovetail with our fan base or corporate base."

The bigger question is whether Ritts can, and will, lead. And if so, in what direction? And will the players, hunkered down between the ropes, where they see the trees bordering the fairways of the narrow, conservative golf world, but often overlook the larger forests beyond, follow? Many LPGA players argued it was "too soon" for a female commissioner when Charlie Mechem announced his retirement in 1995. They were worried about the reaction of potential sponsors. Perhaps they should have been listening to their fans. As Barbara King wrote in a letter to *Golf World,*

I'm sure there are women who can just as effectively "schmooze" the corporate world while boosting the status and image of the LPGA, but more importantly, inspire women golfers and fans at the same time. Choosing another "good old boy" as commissioner will disenfranchise and discourage many women who would like to look at the LPGA for enlightened leadership.

For an entity that sees itself as the leading women's sports organization in the world, enlightened leadership, at a minimum, should include a clear maternity leave policy. The LPGA grants maternity leave under its policy for sickness and injury exemptions, but it's been an issue of considerable debate among players. "Girls who don't have kids say, 'That was your choice,' says Inkster. Or they say women will get pregnant to get an exemption. That's ridiculous!"

And it should preclude almost hiring a commissioner who socializes at a club that wouldn't let Nancy Lopez or Patty Sheehan walk through the front or back door. Former Centel Corporation CEO Jack Frazee was one of three finalists to replace Charlie Mechem. He adamantly refused to resign from the all-male Old Elm Golf Club in Chicago. A vocal group of LPGA players backed him to the hilt anyway, and were bitterly disappointed when Frazee lost out to Jim Ritts.

Pierce and Inkster and other players and officials are correct. Smoking is a personal choice. Accepting cigarette company sponsorship also is a choice.

In the past the LPGA understandably chose survival over all else. But the LPGA no longer is starving. It is healthy and strong enough to stand up and look sponsors and TV executives in the eye and itself in the mirror.

The LPGA's loyalty toward du Maurier is misplaced. It's a business deal. Du Maurier doesn't sponsor the LPGA because it has bad lungs but a good heart. It sponsors the LPGA to help it push its product.

If the LPGA quietly and graciously told du Maurier it was terminating its relationship when the present contract expires, it would be taking care of business as well. It would be telling Shelley Hamlin she didn't have to defend the indefensible. It would be telling all of the kids in the Urban Youth Golf Program and the Girls Golf Club that the LPGA was willing to walk the walk and talk the talk on health issues affecting children. It would be telling the world that the things it holds closest to its heart are not for sale.

Unfortunately, the Tour is heading in the opposite direction, finalizing plans to add the Australian Ladies Masters to the 1997 schedule as an official LPGA event. The sponsor? Alpine, a cigarette brand owned by Philip Morris. (Philip Morris also manufactures Marlboro, the overwhelming smoke of choice among American teenagers.) Perhaps the LPGA believes no one will notice: the tournament is being played Down Under and Alpine sounds like a mountain meadow.

Too good to be true.

The weather, that is. Hail, thunder, wind, and rain descend on Edmonton C.C. late in the afternoon on Friday, suspending play for 83 minutes. It's the eighth time in the last ten weeks that inclement weather has marred the proceedings on the Thunder and Lightning Tour. But it's not much of a surprise to the locals. Despite the past few days of hot, sunny weather, Edmonton has been, in the words of *Edmonton Journal* writer John Stock, "The 1996 rain capital of the universe."

Karrie Webb follows her opening round 65 with a crisp 68 to take a four-stroke lead over Meg Mallon and a six-stroke lead over Lopez, Dana Dormann, and Pat Hurst, before she and Mallon head for the mall and the rides at Galaxyland.

With the fearlessness of youth, Webb tells the media, "They've got bungee-jumping there, but I don't know if I'll do that, not during the tournament. I did skydive once last year. I really enjoyed it and I'll do it again when I get back to Australia."

Leslie Spalding is ready to bungee-jump without a rope. She shoots 72 and misses the cut by one stroke.

"I knew I had to ace number nine to make it," says Spalding, who began play on the back side. She tried, drilling a 3-iron to 12 feet and sinking the birdie putt. Now she again faces a weekend without work. Not even the world's biggest mall and the best free grub of the season can disguise the fact that she barely missed a paycheck, perhaps a substantial one, in the last $1 million, double-coupon tournament of the year.

It's a good-news, bad-news day for Pierce and Inkster. Pierce celebrates her birthday with a 75 for a total of 146 and survives the cut after hitting the ball poorly but sinking some nice putts. Inkster, hitting it nicely but missing putts, is buried midpack after rounds of 73 and 72.

Friday's storm is a drop in the bucket compared with the deluge that hits Edmonton on Saturday.

"I guess I didn't pray in bilingual enough," jokes tournament director Jocelyne Bourassa, who became the first and only Canadian to win the du Maurier, then called La Canadienne, in its inaugural presentation in 1973 in Montreal.

Kathy Postlewait remembers it well. "The crowds were a little more boisterous when Jocelyne was leading and winning. They were pro-

Jocelyne and damn the rest of the field. They were still hockey fans at the time."

A boisterous crowd of golf fans arrives early on Saturday. Edmonton, like many midsized cities in the U.S., has embraced the LPGA.

"At every opportunity," writes John Stock, "players and tour officials praise the community's ability to put out a welcome mat. Equally often, volunteers, members of the media, and paying customers go into rhapsodies about the class, cooperation, and commitment demonstrated by the players."

But most of the fans sprint for the exits when an early-morning drizzle turns into a torrential rainstorm. Play is suspended at 10:54, as the sand traps become wading pools.

Players and caddies stream off the course and back to the clubhouse, a chocolate-brown two-story wood structure with a narrow circular driveway at the entrance. After splashing through several inches of water covering the driveway, players seek shelter in the Hospitality Room or the locker room, known as "The Black Hole."

"It sucks you in there and you can't get out," says Lauri Merten. "No one can grab you. It's so cool." (The media is barred from the locker room on the LPGA Tour, as are fans, sponsors, equipment reps, caddies, agents, etc. It's the only place at tournament sites, other than Porta-Johns, where players are off-stage.)

Caddies huddle under the clubhouse eaves on a cement walkway that links the clubhouse and pro shop. They wipe off their face and hair with white towels. They empty clubs from the bag and wipe them dry. They encase yardage books in plastic. They discuss the caddie baseball pool. They eat sandwiches and drink coffee. Rick Aune reads a book. They stand around—there's no place to sit. Mostly they do what caddies do: They wait.

The players have it better. Some return to their hotel. Some watch the Olympics, where the Canadian 4 x 100 relay team shocked the favored U.S. squad and erased some of the wailing and moaning by Canadian fans over their paltry medal total. Liselotte Neumann watches TV, eats, listens to music, and visits the on-site chiropractor, who cracks her neck a few times. Meg Mallon talks to Suzanne Jackson, visits the chiropractor for a chronic shoulder problem, and is interviewed by CTV. Karrie Webb returns to the house she is sharing with a few other golfers and watches TV and plays cards.

Judy Rankin, in town to work as a TV commentator and to evaluate players for the Solheim Cup, says the main challenge during rain delays is "not to eat too much." That isn't easy, given the lure of the du Maurier pasta, salad, fruit, and dessert bars.

It's still drizzling at 3:30 as a patch of blue sky on the horizon spreads toward the river. Players in black or blue rain suits flood the putting green. There's little chatter. It's like the last-minute cramming before an examination, as golfers try to evaluate how much the rains have dulled the greens.

Play resumes at 4:00. There's plenty of time to finish—this is the land of 17-hour days, even if summer suddenly feels like fall. Only a small percentage of the 15,000 fans that arrived this morning have stuck it out. About 30 of them gather around the green at the 360-yard 7th hole, watching the leaders in the last few groups. Traps are half-filled with water. Beads of rainwater cling to the needles of the spruce trees behind the green. Chill winds invade from the prairie.

The scene is surreal. The kids who carry the portable scoreboards have been sent home. Fans are almost nonexistent. It's the third round of a major and the atmosphere is as devoid of excitement as a practice round.

It feels like a dream to Karrie Webb. Two over par for the day when play was halted, Webb promptly double-bogeys her first hole after it resumes. "It was another kick in the gut," she'll say later. Suddenly a gaggle of golfers are back in contention.

About 50 people are following the final group. Webb, seeming invincible on Thursday and Friday, looks small and forlorn now. Something finally scared her. Taking a four-shot lead to bed last night, Webb suffered through a nightmare. She dreamed she was playing in the third round. Playing miserably, struggling to subdue the phantoms of her subconscious, the doubts and fears that afflict even the bravest and most confident human being.

Now she's mired in a true-life replay. Webb leaves a 35-foot putt 5 feet short on No. 7, a horrendous lag, then misses again. She sighs deeply, tosses her putter down, and strips off a red and black plaid rain suit. Playing partner Meg Mallon takes the lead with Pat Hurst at eight under par after a sensational iron to four feet, then knocks the pin down with a wedge on the 517-yard 8th hole for a tap-in birdie.

Everyone is shivering. Black clouds stream across the sky. Webb, digging deep, rolls in a ten-foot birdie putt, then stands grimly, eyes vacant, as caddie Evan Minster whispers encouragement in her ear.

Webb hopes that the birdie will get her on track. But she's still fighting her swing and her tempo, which is too quick, a sign of anxiety, a legacy of bad dreams. On the 175-yard 9th hole she blocks an iron badly to the right.

"ARRGH!!" she screams, as the ball plunges toward heavy rough. "JESUS!! CHRIST!!"

"Did she swear?" a woman behind the ropes asks her husband.

He nods. "See, honey, I'm not the only one who does that on the golf course."

Walking to the left of the tee box, Webb crouches down and puts her hands over her head. She has rarely been so angry and upset. "I didn't think I was going to get my swing back. I just felt myself getting deeper and deeper in the hole."

Webb stares toward the ravine. She bogeys No. 9 to turn in 40. She tells herself to calm down, tells herself she has played brilliantly on the back nine all week, tells herself there are birdies out there, tells herself that it was just a bad dream.

By the time the final group finishes at 8:00 about 500 devoted fans fill the grandstands at the 18th green. Devoted and half-frozen fans. It's utterly raw now, but Webb, fueled by anger and determination, is down to her shirtsleeves. After a booming drive, she hits the 465-yard par five in two shots. She rolls in a four-foot birdie putt and pumps a fist after playing the back nine in three under par. She and Pat Hurst trail Meg Mallon, who is in at 206 after rounds of 72-65-69. Lopez is at 208, Rosie Jones at 209, and a trio of foreign stars are at 210 (Sorenstam, Neumann) and 211 (Davies).

The top Canadian in the field, at 214, is Chris Greatrex, hardly a household word. Well, maybe in Canada. The Canadian contestants, who are eating meals together and wearing caps with Canadian flags, are besieged by the media. Greatrex played on the LPGA Tour in 1995 after earning exempt status at Q-School. Actually, as Greatrex describes it, "I only played part-time, just Thursdays and Fridays." She's barely exaggerating. Greatrex teed it up in 24 tournaments and earned exactly $939 to finish 199th on the money list.

She's back on the LPGA Tour this year—as a caddie for fellow Canadian and best friend Nancy Harvey.

"It's the greatest thing I could have done. I'm learning everything I needed to learn: course management; patience; seeing how your attitude can affect your game. You see it all in black-and-white behind the bag."

After toying with the notion of playing the mini-tours in 1996, Greatrex decided she could learn more by observing the stars. Her decision was derided by some of her former playing partners.

"What are you doing caddying?" they said. "You're lowering yourself. You're not playing or practicing enough."

But, says Greatrex, "Some of the best players thought it was a great idea."

A humbling one, though. Greatrex was so deep in the fringe as a player that she was the equivalent of a lost ball, yet she held a higher social status than the most successful caddie.

"The first couple of tournaments I felt like a real outsider. What a let-down. I was a second-class citizen—couldn't go to the locker room or in the clubhouse for food. It made me all the more hungry to get back."

But Greatrex discovered that caddying has its own vicarious pleasures. When Nancy Harvey began the final round at the U.S. Open in sixth place, "It was the biggest thrill of my life. I could hardly sleep the night before."

Her performance this week is enough to render her sleepless in Edmonton. "Did I expect this? Not in a million years. I'm hitting the ball worse [every day] and my scoring has gotten better."

Credit the course management skills she's learned as a looper and a student of the game: (1) Figuring out the preferred area to hit her drive. "I used to just bust it down the middle." (2) Playing to her strengths and hitting shots she knows she can hit. (3) Getting the ball on the putting surface quickly when chipping, instead of lobbing shots and trying "the ridiculous or the miraculous." (4) Playing for bogey when necessary.

She'll be back at Q-School in two months for a comprehensive final exam.

Karrie Webb runs into Meg Mallon near the interview room.

"I wanted to birdie the last hole so I could play with you [tomorrow]," says Webb, who will get her wish. In addition to being friends, Webb likes playing with Mallon because she has the tempo of a metronome, a smoothness that sometimes rubs off on a playing partner.

Mallon's smooth moves have rubbed off on the entire golf world. In some respects, Mallon is a younger Lopez, with a gracious warmth and a sunshine smile that rarely flickers.

Her first love was basketball. Her father owned a Massachusetts car dealership and hired some of the Boston Celtics for promotional work.

While there are enough former basketball players in the LPGA to field a league, not just a team, Mallon is the only one to draw NBA stars such as Bob Cousy and K. C. Jones to her christening. The youngest of six children, Mallon remembers Jones and Cousy shooting hoops in the driveway with her older brothers.

"The Celtics were like family," says Mallon. Jones, a class act in every respect, became her role model. "He stressed what it takes to be a professional. I knew I'd have to be patient and work hard. I also knew I'd have setbacks and I'd have to go through them. Even now, when K.C. watches me play, he never watches my shots. All he watches is my face to see how I'm handling stuff."

Joining the Tour in 1987 on a self-described "Five-Year Plan," Mallon gave herself five years to succeed or find another profession. She spent the first year in Chris Greatrex territory, earning $1,572, averaging 76.91 strokes per round, and languishing in the deepest fringe. Slowly and steadily she improved, earning $24,002, $42,574, and $129,381 the next three years, observing and absorbing everything around her.

"I listened to interviews, watched people practice, stuck around when I missed the cut and watched them on weekends, sat in the locker room and listened to stories. They were the best teachers in the world."

She watched Sheehan blow a nine-shot lead at the U.S. Open in 1990. "You could see she was getting exhausted physically. But she never got upset."

She watched Pat Bradley, engulfed in the throes of Graves' disease, shoot 74. "Best 74 I've ever seen. She couldn't get the ball above knee high, but she never lost her poise."

By her fifth year Mallon had poise o' plenty to go with her always solid ball-striking and her painstakingly manufactured, silky-smooth putting stroke. In the space of three weeks she won the LPGA Championship with a 15-foot birdie putt on the last hole and the U.S. Open in stifling 100-degree heat at Colonial in Texas.

Suddenly the woman with the megawatt smile was a megastar, a gallery favorite and a locker room favorite as well. "Everyone likes Meg," says Caroline Pierce, who is somewhat intimidated by her talent. "She's so consistent." That she is—Mallon has ranked in the top 15 the last six years and earned over $2.6 million. She has placed in the top 20 in 11 consecutive majors.

She's also more complex than the ever-present smile might suggest, an extremely intelligent, perceptive, and forthright woman who sets high standards for herself and others. At the HealthSouth Inaugural in January, Mallon finished the tournament and turned to the crowd. Smiling on the outside but furious on the inside, she announced, "Ladies and gentleman, I three-putted seven times this week." Then she hurled her putter like a discus into a lake. In Toledo in July, taking the second-round lead, she tossed and turned all night when she realized she might have committed a rules violation. (Mallon let a moving putt hang on the lip of the cup for more than ten seconds before it tumbled in. She should have given herself a penalty stroke but was unaware of the rule.) The next morning she turned herself in and was disqualified for signing an incorrect scorecard.

Her honesty contains a critical edge. "It's unfortunate we have to play so early [tomorrow]," Mallon tells the media. "I would like to get a good night's sleep." The last tee time for Sunday's final round is 9:11, a schedule dictated, as always, by the demands of television. So Mallon will have to forego her front-row seats for Ottawa-born Alanis Morissette's concert in favor of some shut-eye.

But not before she praises her playing partner. "I like to watch Karrie. She hits it so good." Asked about Webb's outburst on No. 9, Mallon says, "It's nice to see she's got a little temper, a little red behind the ears. But she uses it to help her. For twenty-one, she's very composed."

Not as composed as usual, though.

"Today has been the longest day of my life," says Webb, who hopes the golf demons that infiltrated her dreams will let her sleep in peace tonight.

Wicked arctic winds and frigid sunshine greet the contestants on Sunday morning as they venture forth into battle.

It's the most important round Nancy Lopez has played in a long time. For all her storied success, she owns only three major titles, and all were LPGA Championships. (She also won the 1981 Dinah Shore two years before it officially was designated as a major.) She hasn't won a tournament since 1993. And, says Lopez, "It's do or die for me to make the Solheim Cup."

Lopez birdies No. 1 then promptly bogeys No. 2 and No. 3, after missing a two-foot putt.

"I'm not going to do that anymore," she lectures herself.

As the winds gust up to 30 miles per hour, another force of nature, Laura Davies, makes her presence felt. "When I woke up this morning and saw how windy it was," says Davies, who conquered similar conditions to win the McDonald's LPGA Championship in Wilmington, "I thought if I shot a sixty-nine maybe something good would happen."

She gets busy early today, holing out from a bunker on the 3rd hole. Then she confronts the 7th, which almost destroyed her yesterday—Davies shanked a 4-iron tee shot about 90 yards. It almost tumbled down the cliff bank into the North Saskatchewan. She was fortunate to make bogey. The memory has her "shaking like a leaf" on the tee. But Davies crushes a 6-iron down the right side of the fairway, follows with a wedge on the 360-yard hole, rolls in the putt, and walks off the green with a birdie and a truckload of momentum. She turns in an amazing 32, the only contender to play the front nine in even-par or better.

Everyone else is struggling. Mallon, the great wind player with the silky-smooth putting stroke, three-whacks it on two early holes then leaves a long approach putt on the 9th hole six feet short. She angrily swings her putter like a baseball bat as she marches up to mark her ball.

"I'm Irish," Mallon said earlier in the year. "I can get furious. The blood rushes to my head. I'm half-embarrassed and half-mad."

She misses her par putt. She stalks off the green glowering, the megawatt smile switched off by a trio of three-whacks.

"God!!" she yells, slamming the ball into the hand of caddie John Dormann.

Up ahead the Davies Express rolls on. After a bogey at No. 11, she chips in for birdie at No. 12 and birdies No. 13 to take the lead at nine under par.

"And don't think," Judy Rankin is telling the television audience, "when the players reach the next scoreboard, it doesn't make a difference to see Laura Davies at the top."

The green at the 371-yard 12th hole is adjacent to the clubhouse. It is ringed by so many spectators that it is impossible to see who is on the putting surface.

Suddenly a huge roar erupts.

A Nancy Lopez birdie roar. Nancy's navy has a new Canadian division. She's playing with Liselotte Neumann and Rosie Jones. Although Jones and Neumann are struggling, they share a light moment—a laugh and a high-five in the middle of the fairway—after both bounce approach shots out of a greenside bunker packed with wet sand on the 341-yard 13th hole.

Lopez's birdie moves her to eight under par, just one stroke from the lead. But Lopez is oblivious to Davies, who birdies the 470-yard 15th hole to get to ten under par.

It's not because Lopez is avoiding the leader boards. Like all great champions, Lopez wants to know exactly where she stands. The problem is that Lopez literally does not see Davies's name at the top of the board. To her eyes, it blurs right into the du Maurier name above it. So Lopez believes she's tied for the lead with Pat Hurst.

Lopez crushes a drive on the 15th hole. She's left with a 3-wood to a slightly elevated, narrow green, and she hits it dead solid perfect, the ball rolling onto the green 60 feet short of the flagstick.

"I hit it exactly the way I planned," she'll say later. "It's been a long time since I responded to that kind of pressure."

The massive gallery whoops and hollers as Lopez, in a blood-red sweater, white turtleneck, and navy slacks, walks onto the green, smiles, and says, "Thank you."

She strikes a perfect lag putt, the ball trickling to a stop six inches from the cup, and the crowd groans and applauds simultaneously. Tap-in birdie. Nine under par. Lopez thinks she's in the lead.

Rain begins to pelt down. Caddies coordinate umbrellas, towels, rain gear, a virtuoso juggling act to keep clubs and golfers dry. The 371-yard 16th hole flows to the farthest point from the clubhouse. Almost all the fans have gone ahead to watch the final groups play Nos. 17 and 18. A small knot of spectators under umbrellas and rain slickers around the green watch as Lopez flags an iron through the raindrops to ten feet of the stick.

Lopez gets a great read from Neumann's longer putt, which is almost on the identical line. This is *the* putt, although Lopez doesn't realize it, since Davies is almost certain to birdie No.18 to finish at 11 under par. Unless she sinks it, Lopez will need to birdie Nos. 17 and 18 to tie.

"C'mon, Nancy," whispers a woman at greenside.

The putt is dead in the jaws—and three inches short.

"Hit it!" Lopez says. She stares at the heavens for a long moment. Then she walks through the small crowd, eyes on the horizon, as regal as in her glory days, when a journalist, marveling at her aristocratic bearing and common touch, dubbed her the "Spanish Queen."

"Go get 'em, Nancy!" a man calls out.

"Thank you," she says, eyes still fixed in the distance. She thinks she's still leading.

After a big drive on the 356-yard 17th hole, Lopez pulls a short iron onto the left fringe. Switching from a sand wedge to a pitching wedge, she hits a terrible chip, running it 12 feet past the cup. Her bid, for all practical purposes, is almost over.

Except in Lopez's mind. She believes she needs the putt to maintain her lead over Hurst and Webb, who has birdied 15 to move to eight under par.

These are the putts she used to make in her sleep. These are the putts that won her 47 tournaments. These are the putts that measure the heart and guts and determination and pride of an athlete. These are the putts that Lopez has been missing.

She rolls it home. Lopez pumps both fists overhead. The crowd roars, happy for her, even if they think she's playing for second place. Playing for pride rather than a championship, although maybe they are, in some ways, one and the same. "That was a prove-it-to-yourself putt," Lopez says later.

Lopez splits the fairway on 465-yard 18th hole to the cries of "That's it! and "Go get 'em, Nancy!" from fans around the tee box, praying for a last-hole eagle.

Davies paces nervously near the 18th green after hitting the green in two with a conservative 2-iron and 6-iron. (Yesterday she reached the green with a Tiger Woodsian drive and 9-iron.) Her two-putt birdie is good for a mind-boggling 66. But she's not counting her loonies and toonies yet. In 1988 Sally Little canned a 30-foot putt on the final hole to defeat her by one stroke. The memory is fresh in her mind.

With 220 yards to the green from a slightly depressed lie, Lopez busts a superb shot ("I just missed catching it perfect") that checks up about ten yards short of the green.

Then she looks at the board. And sees, for the first time, DAVIES at the top.

"Damn!" a stunned Lopez says to herself. "How'd she get up there?" In Lopez's mind, Davies must have finished ace-ace-ace to rise from nowhere to the top.

Knowing, finally, what everyone else in the gallery and the TV audience knows—that she needs a chip-in eagle to tie, Lopez gives it a go. But the chip runs well past the cup. After missing the comebacker, Lopez settles for a tie for second with Webb, who closes with a birdie.

It's been a good news/bad news week. The good news for Chris Greatrex, who finishes with a 72 to tie for twelfth and earn $14,808, is that she proved she could rub shoulders with the stars inside the ropes as a player as well as a caddie. The bad news? She'll have to pass that comprehensive final exam at Q-School in October to earn a promotion from looper to golfer in 1997.

The good news for Caroline Pierce is that she crosses the bridge and closes with a final-round 70, after birdieing 7 and 9, two of her last three holes. It's the second-best round of the day. Major relief for those last-round final-hole blues. The bad news is that she skanked the ball most of the week. Her great round today elevates her from the bottom of the heap to a tie for forty-ninth.

The good news for Juli Inkster is that she continues to play well, tying for twelfth. The bad news is that she finished twelfth, since only top-ten finishers earn Solheim Cup points. Inkster's three-whack on the final hole, after hitting the green in two, cost her a tie for tenth place. "It just about killed me," she says.

The good news for Karrie Webb is that she shook off her nightmare and battled to the wire. On 15 she told her caddie that she could tie Davies with birdies on the last four holes. She almost did it, with two birdies and two near misses. The bad news is that Webb lost a friend. She's crying when she enters the interview room; some reporters initially assume it's because she finished second. In fact, she's in tears after watching Davies on TV dedicating her victory to Colin Lunn, father of Mardi and Karen Lunn, who died last week from a massive heart attack at the age of 56.

The good news for Davies is that she shot 66 on a day when no one else in the field could break 70, captured her second major of the season, and cemented her status as the number-one ranked woman golfer in the world. She also gets to fly across the Atlantic to next week's Scottish Open in style. Earlier she told her brother Tony, who caddied for her this week, "If I win this bloody thing, I'm going to fly first-class." She draws a big laugh in the interview room when she adds, "I don't know if I'll move Tony up, though."

The bad news is that she lost a dear friend. "I spent a week with Colin in Germany two weeks ago and he was right as rain. He was like a second father to me."

"When I told [Mardi and Karen] I was coming to Australia for the funeral, they told me to do something better and win the du Maurier for their dad. They said the same thing to Karrie and Brandie [Burton] because we are all pretty close. He was a wonderful bloke and it's a sad time for all of us."

The good news for Nancy Lopez is that her immense competitive pride, battered and beaten over the past few seasons, has been restored.

"I was making the putts like I used to. It was a good day to look at myself as an LPGA player. I told myself, 'Nancy, this is a test for you,' and I felt like I was fighting under pressure the way I used to.

"I never really felt nervous. I was real focused. I haven't felt that way in a long time. I felt I was going to hit the next shot well. I feel like I won within myself."

The bad news for Lopez? She probably needs glasses.

The good news for du Maurier is that the antismoking activists were silent in 1996, reserving their fire for upcoming battles in Parliament. The good news for the LPGA is that it drew rave reviews in a new territory, the prairies of Alberta. Already Edmonton is clamoring for a return engagement in a few years.

It's just too bad about all those cigarette butts littering the lovely green fairways, eh?

CHAPTER 9

Chepstow, Wales: All the World's a Stage

The U.S. and European Solheim Cup teams arrive at the St. Pierre Hotel on Monday, September 16, under warm, sunny skies. A harpist plucks traditional Welsh hymns at the archway entrance of the castlelike, twin-turreted fourteenth-century Norman mansion. Built with ancient sand and tan colored stones from Roman ruins, the medieval structure once provided safekeeping for the Crown Jewels. The original estate was given to St. Pierre de Caen by William the Conqueror. Now it's an elegant 400-acre Marriott Resort, containing 11 acres of gardens and lakes, as well as 36 holes of golf.

Located in the Wye Valley in the southeast corner of Wales, a two-hour drive from London, St. Pierre is a few miles from the heart of Chepstow, an ancient walled port town of 10,000 where Chepstow Castle, built in 1067 after the battle of Hastings, stands guard on a cliff over a loop of the river Wye. The castle changed hands many times over the next six centuries. It was the site of war, rebellion, intrigue, and turmoil.

Just outside the castle-like hotel entrance at St. Pierre lies a small fifteenth-century French-designed circular courtyard. A carriageway turned driveway, about 50 yards in circumference, rings an immaculately trimmed lawn. Shrubs and flowerbeds frame the courtyard, a picture-perfect site for a wedding reception or a formal Solheim Cup photo session. (St. Pierre spent £1.5 million to renovate the golf course and hotel for the Solheim Cup, plus £50,000 to spruce up the landscape with flowers and plants.)

A two-story stone building stretches along one side of the courtyard. It once stabled horses downstairs and stored fruit from surrounding orchards upstairs. Now it houses tourists in plush guest quarters.

Just off the other side of the courtyard is a tiny eleventh-century church, about 30 yards long and 10 yards wide, built of white, beige, and tan stone, featuring beautiful stained glass archways and topped by a bell-tower. It remains a house of worship almost a millennium after its creation, serving as the parish church of Monmouth St. Pierre.

The church is framed on one side by a tiny auxiliary putting green and on the other side by a small graveyard. (Talk about a full-service resort!) About 60 stone and marble headstones memorialize people who died between 1805 and 1993. Guests tramp right between the headstones and over the grassy graves to reach the resort entrance.

Helen Alfredsson imagines a new headstone. As she walks through the graveyard on Monday afternoon, she spots LPGA commissioner Jim Ritts.

"Here's where all your players will be," she jokes.

At least Ritts took it as a joke.

In six short years, the Solheim Cup has developed its own remarkable history, an intense, albeit less lethal, arena of war, rebellion, turmoil, and intrigue, pitting an American team against a squad from Europe. The biennial matches began in 1990 in Orlando, Florida, to the sound of one-hand clapping. "It's embarrassing to say," Lauri Merten told *Golf* magazine, "but I didn't pay any attention to it." The U.S. cruised to an 11½ to 4½ victory.

The losers gained more than the winners. "Going into Orlando, our players had never played against the Americans," said Mickey Walker, captain of the European team since 1990. "We lost that match, but we also lost our sense of awe."

In 1992 the Europeans shocked the Americans, 11 to 6½, at Dalmahoy in Edinburgh, Scotland. In *Golf World* Geoff Russell wrote, "All forecasts called for frigid weather last week in Scotland but no one expected hell to freeze over." Laura Davies led the charge and the British press whipped up players and fans over a perceived insult from Beth Daniel: "You could put anyone of us on the European side and make it better. But the only Europeans that could help us are Laura Davies and Liselotte Neumann." Then little-known Europeans such as Helen Alfredsson, Catrin Nilsmark, and Alison Nicholas outplayed Yank superstars Bradley, King, Burton, Sheehan, and Pepper.

"Laura was simply willing the Solheim Cup victory," Walker told writer Liz Kahn. "No one could have imagined we would have won by such a huge margin, but Laura has an incredible influence and power over the players; it's as though she is God. She doesn't realize it, and they don't either."

Then-LPGA commissioner Charlie Mechem called the upset "a watershed event in the history of women's golf." It heralded an international boom; more players from Europe and the rest of the world ventured forth to try their luck on the LPGA Tour, and college coaches in the U.S. accelerated their search for fresh talent from around the globe. (The LPGA Tour has become golf's true world tour; 56 foreign players from 13 countries ranging from Japan to Peru are competing in 1996, including almost all of the best female golfers on the planet.)

By 1994 the Solheim Cup was the premiere event in women's golf, alternating with the Ryder Cup on NBC. Although both teams vowed the competition would be intense but friendly, just below the surface emotions ran high when play began at The Greenbrier in West Virginia.

It wasn't long before emotions rose above the surface. By the time Dottie Pepper and Brandie Burton bested Laura Davies and Alison Nicholas in a Saturday afternoon four-ball (best-ball) match, the tea party was over and the European media was in a snit fit, accusing Pepper of trampling the sacred traditions of the game: shouting "Yes!" and punching the air with a fist when Davies missed a putt; refusing, with Burton, to concede two putts in the 12- to 18-inch range; ignoring Davies's outstretched hand when the Brit tried to congratulate her after a U.S. win in another match.

Tied 5-5 after the first two days of team matches, Pepper, whose dyed red hair matched the flames shooting from her bulging eyes, tore up and spat out Catrin Nilsmark in the second singles pairing on Sunday morning. She threw seven birdies, including two near-aces, at the Swede in a 6 and 5 annihilation, scorching the earth with an intensity that seemed radioactive.

"She was enough to scare anyone," says Joan Pitcock, who paid her own way to The Greenbrier to watch the matches. Pitcock and Pepper aren't particularly friendly, but Pitcock made a point of shaking her hand afterward in admiration of her phenomenal performance.

At the du Maurier last month, Nilsmark said she had never seen anyone play better. Nilsmark struggled in 1995 and early in 1996, focusing, in coach Pia Nilsson's opinion, too much on mechanics. "She got a little lost there." But Nilsson also was concerned that the thrashing from Pepper could have left a psychological scar. "We talked about a possible subconscious effect," says Nilsson. "It could easily happen to someone and get you stuck."

The U.S. routed the Europeans 8-2 in the singles matches en route to a 13-7 victory that brought the Solheim Cup back to America. In the aftermath, sisterhood took a backseat.

"After getting our noses rubbed in the memory of Dalmahoy for two years," said Sheehan, "this feels great."

Pepper was singularly unapologetic. "I know what it takes to play well. I don't get in anybody's way. I have to be happy with myself before anyone else."

Davies, who gets along famously with almost everyone, called Pepper "the rudest golfer I ever met." And she issued an early warning for 1996.

"We'll be ready. The Americans better be too."

The barrage of give-and-take, generally good-humored, hasn't let up since. "You find yourself going out to dinner and if it's with other players, invariably the conversation comes round to the Solheim—who's on the team, who's not," Davies told the *Sunday Telegraph*. "If I'm dining with the Americans, there's generally a bit of banter." Earlier this spring in Arizona, Davies, referring to the fortysomething or near-fortysomething status of

Americans such as Sheehan (39), Bradley (45), and King (41), said, "We're getting stronger. They're getting older."

At the du Maurier Classic six weeks ago, U.S. captain Judy Rankin was feeling every one of her 51 years. She had been running full throttle since assuming the post in February after 1994 captain JoAnne Carner stepped down to care for her ailing husband.

It wasn't just the myriad duties of a captain, ranging from selecting team wardrobes to scouting the course to media interviews to concerns about the strength and endurance of her "older" team in Wales (she investigated the value of vitamin shots to build up the immune system of her players before the journey) that left Rankin running on empty.

She had been on the road for a solid month, broadcasting ABC tournaments in Detroit and Britain and scouting U.S. players at the Jamie Farr Kroger Classic in Toledo. After inspecting the course at St. Pierre, she embarked on a 24-hour "see-the-world route" from London to Cincinnati to Salt Lake City to Edmonton. Sitting in a hotel restaurant after the conclusion of her broadcast duties at the du Maurier, drinking decaf and eating greasy egg rolls, Rankin could barely hold her head up.

A small woman with black-rimmed glasses, Rankin has a serious mien, a direct, friendly manner, and low-key presence. It's easy to picture her as the president of a highly successful bank, perhaps one of those glass towers fueled by the oil business in her home of Midland, Texas.

She is, in fact, a pioneer. Not only is she one of the first women to combine a family and career on the LPGA Tour—she and husband Yippy, who is in the insurance business, traveled the Tour with son Tuey—she did so with stunning success. Rankin, who turned pro at 17, and married at 22, won 26 tournaments, despite, as one writer described it, "a hooker's grip of startling severity," and a very upright swing that may have exacerbated the back problems that eventually forced her retirement in 1983. Despite her calm demeanor, Rankin was a player consumed with emotion. "I was an intense player, who performed best when I gave it my all," she told Liz Kahn. Rankin says she's a lot like Sheehan—a keyed-up golfer who prospered by learning to control her nerves. Sheehan remembers Rankin as an excellent thinker on the course.

Rankin was the first woman to break the $100,000 barrier for earnings in a season—she shattered the grass ceiling in 1976 by winning six tournaments and placing in the top ten in 25 of 26 events (a record that will never be broken) and tallying $150,734. When she retired, she became the first woman to make a living covering golf on television.

Her unobtrusive approach has worn well. "It is her ability to let the action speak for itself that attracted ABC Sports to her [in 1984] and since has established her as one of the best announcers in the business," wrote Pete McDaniel earlier this year in *Golf World*.

Rankin's biggest burden in Edmonton was the upcoming decision over her two wild-card selections for the 12-member team. Her picks were due in three weeks, after the conclusion of the Star Bank Classic in Dayton, August 23–25.

Although she had known that the Solheim Cup was a goal—*the* goal—for many players, the intensity, the desire, the near-desperation to make the squad had amazed her.

"It's astounding how much they want to be part of the team," said Rankin. "I've never been this close to it. Now I'm so close to it my eyes are crossing. Right now there are four or five players I would like to pick. Invariably somebody is going to be saddened and hurt. There's pressure being the person who has to do that."

Three weeks later in Dayton, Rankin still was agonizing. A few players had eliminated themselves from contention—Kris Tschetter with poor recent play and Juli Inkster, whose fine recent play was too little and too late. But complicating matters were the two previous tournaments, the Ping/Welch's Championship outside Boston, and the Weetabix British Open in England, both won by rising star Emilee Klein. Suddenly, if erroneously, Klein, 22, was being hailed as a player with the talent of the Tour's other great youngster, Karrie Webb. Rankin's choices boiled down to Klein, Lopez, Burton, King, and Daniel, with King and Daniel dueling for the last automatic spot.

Despite Rankin's stated preference for a player with a hot hand, and a concern about the age and stamina of her veteran team, the kid was the first to be eliminated.

Inexperience was a factor. "It's a fearful thing being on the first tee in a hostile environment," said Rankin, "and a fearful thing being down in a match. Men call it being in a foxhole."

But a lack of support from the rest of her teammates ultimately doomed Klein's chances. Enthusiasm ran high for everyone except her. "No one on the team seemed to know her very well," said Rankin. "No one had connected with her yet."

Klein had turned pro after winning the 1994 NCAA Championship while a sophomore at Arizona State. She won $179,803 as a rookie last year using a 50-inch driver almost as tall as the five-foot-four, blue-eyed blonde. Other than a fondness for shopping—Klein joked that her shoe collection was beginning to rival that of Imelda Marcos—she seemed obsessed with her career to the exclusion of almost everything and everyone else. During the pro-am at the Toledo tournament in July, Klein and her caddie/boyfriend, Kenny Harmes, were observed furiously working on her stroke at the back of the 18th green while her amateur partners were still putting out at the front. Standard etiquette is to root your amateur partners, the people subsidizing the Tour, into the cup before doing your own thing.

In their spare time Klein and Harmes play golf, aiming to tee it up at every one of America's top-rated 100 courses. In many ways Klein and Harmes constitute a *duprass*, Kurt Vonnegut's characterization of a unit of two people totally sufficient unto themselves. Or perhaps it's a foursome, since Klein calls her parents, Bob and Randee, a well-to-do couple who live in southern California, after every round.

On the final green at Dayton, Beth Daniel lined up a three-foot putt which would vault her over King for the tenth and final automatic spot.

King was a real concern. She had begun the year in second spot in the Solheim Cup point standings before tumbling precipitously down the ladder.

"It doesn't say much for how her year has gone," said Rankin. "It hasn't left her in an upbeat mood. She talks too much about packing it in and retiring. Her slide has been a surprise."

Daniel missed the putt. King was in. Daniel was eleventh, Klein twelfth, Burton thirteenth, and the resurgent Lopez, fifth in Dayton after a two-week break following her runner-up effort in Edmonton, was fifteenth.

What's a captain to do?

Earlier in the season, Rankin said, "Nancy would be a great addition to the team. In Wales, her kind of outward composure would be a plus. But she's got to give me ammunition."

Rankin wasn't about to make the same mistake that Lanny Wadkins made in 1995, when he selected his friend Curtis Strange for the Ryder Cup team, which proved to be a disaster for Wadkins, Strange, and the American team when Strange tossed away a critical match against Nick Faldo.

"Mechanics were holding Curtis back," said Rankin. "No matter how big your heart is, you have to be able to hit the shot."

Lopez had given Rankin ammunition. But not quite enough to dislodge Daniel or Burton. Rankin thought Daniel's presence on the team was essential. "She's one of a handful of the best players in the world. She needs to be there." In addition, Daniel would have been a lock for an automatic spot if she hadn't missed part of the early 1996 season after popping a rib head out of place in her upper back. Burton was a relatively easy choice too, with a fine record in the 1996 majors and previous Solheim Cups.

Breaking the news to Lopez wasn't easy at all. "We both shed a couple of tears," said Rankin. "I knew how much she wanted it and I was in a position to make it happen. I knew I was going to have to gut up and do things that weren't pleasant. That wasn't pleasant."

Both emerged from the locker room in Dayton with red eyes. A rumor spread that they had argued. "It could not have been further from the truth," said Rankin. "Nancy said, 'Well, you've picked two great players.'"

(Klein didn't take the news as well. "Neither Brandie nor Beth has won in the past year. I've talked to Judy, but there's still a lot of unanswered questions in my mind. . . . I don't think Judy realizes how tough I am at twenty-two.")

Rankin withheld one bit of information from Lopez, which would have made her disappointment even more painful. She didn't tell Lopez that if Daniel had made that three-foot putt on the final hole at Dayton, Lopez and not King would be at St. Pierre as a member of the Solheim Cup team.

The Europeans were agonizing too. Three of Mickey Walker's five wild-card selections were automatic—the Swedes Neumann, Alfredsson, and Nilsmark, the latter two having broken out of slumps. (The Europeans get five wild-cards to two for the U.S. because their stars play mostly on the LPGA Tour, which often precludes them from earning enough Solheim Cup points on the European Tour to make the team automatically.)

But the last two spots were a puzzle: Carin Hj Koch, a 25-year-old Swede, forty-eighth on the LPGA money list; Dale Reid, a 37-year-old Scot who whipped Patty Sheehan and Dottie Pepper in singles in the 1990 and 1992 matches; or Kathryn Marshall, 29, a Scot who won on the LPGA Tour in 1995, then struggled until finishing second and sixth in Europe just prior to the selection date?

Marshall's hot hand clinched a spot for her. But the choice between Reid and Koch, says European vice captain Pia Nilsson, "was very, very tough. You could look at it in so many ways. We spent a lot of time talking about it." Walker made the call, selecting the veteran over the youngster just an hour before the deadline.

"I'm very disappointed," Koch said last week at the Safeco Classic in Seattle. "It's supposed to be a two-year [selection] process. Kathryn played good the last three weeks and Dale has the experience, but hasn't played well. It would be nice being part of the gang, but life goes on."

The selection of Reid fueled another rumor—that Laura Davies had pressured Walker to choose Reid.

An amused Davies denied it. "Not at all. I'm very disappointed for Carin, very surprised she's not in the top twelve. Mickey never asked our opinion. Normally, she goes *against* what you say and leaves you in complete confusion. She's a great captain."

She is also, like Rankin, a pioneer. Walker, curly-haired, tall, and slender, with an elegant manner, was one of the first Europeans to play the LPGA Tour, and later became one of the first female head professionals at a club in England.

As the harpist continues to serenade the arrivals at St. Pierre, Davies cruises into the courtyard behind the wheel of her fire-engine-red Ferrari 456.

Applause rings out. A handful of photographers leap to take pictures.

Yesterday Davies fired a final-round 67 to defeat a resurgent Alfredsson, currently on top of the European money list, by four strokes at the Wilkinson Sword English Open. It's the seventh victory of the year for Davies, and the forty-seventh of her career.

It was also her eighth tournament in eight weeks, as Davies continues her quest to match Sorenstam's 1995 feat in winning both the LPGA and European money titles.

No wonder she told the media at last week's launch for her new autobiography (written with Lewine Mair of the *Daily Telegraph*) that she hadn't read it. She shrugged off the book's major revelation—that Davies has lost almost $800,000 in 12 years of gambling. Although she didn't go as far as Charles Barkley, who claimed he was misquoted in his own autobiography, Davies asserted she had merely thrown out a figure "that could be hideously above or hideously below. I have no idea."

The revelation touched off a tabloid tempest. When the *Mirror* printed Davies's picture on the front page, one of her mates assumed she had died. It's the first "touch of aggro" for Davies, as she neatly describes the gleeful assault practiced by the tabloids, behavior reminiscent of the gang of thugs in *A Clockwork Orange*.

"It's annoying that I have won two major championships this year and not managed a mention in any golf magazine or anywhere," Davies told the *Daily Mail*. "If Colin Montgomerie or Nick Faldo had won two majors this year, they would have been royalty by now.

"Yet all of a sudden, a flippant remark in a book becomes front-page news. I find that a bit irritating."

Still, Davies wouldn't mind seeing the media stir up a bit of patriotic fervor. Nothing bordering on the old ultraviolence, of course ("Obviously, courtesy to them, there is no place in golf for cheering a bad shot, but English galleries are not like that."), but some soccer-style frenzy would be nice, the type of atmosphere she and her teammates encountered in 1994.

"That bloody 'U.S.A., U.S.A.' still haunts me from The Greenbrier," Davies told *The Independent*. "You could hear it echoing, getting louder and louder . . . I'm definitely calling for a partisan crowd."

For Davies, *nothing* surpasses the importance of the Solheim Cup, not U.S. Opens or money titles. "There isn't a player, hopefully none of the Europeans anyway, who wouldn't die for the win."

Tuesday, Sept. 17

"Gran, 85, Battered to Pulp in Her Sleep" *(Daily Record)*
"Dear Kids, I've Left You for a Bishop" *(Daily Mirror)*
"Accident-Prone American's Hole-in-One" *(Tee Times)*

On Tuesday afternoon Brandie Burton steps off the tee box on No. 7. Her right foot disappears into a deep hole covered with four inches of grass. She goes down like a shot. A nearby cameraman hears a loud popping noise.

"My ankle just snapped," Burton says, shaking and turning white. Rankin thinks it may be broken. Burton, whose threshold for pain is otherworldly, insists on continuing her practice round.

Calmer heads prevail. Trainer Keith Kennedy elevates and ices Burton's ankle and wraps it tightly to prevent swelling from reaching the joint. After 30 minutes Burton tries to swing. She can't even walk. She rides the rest of the way in a cart as the news quickly passes to her teammates.

"The next most ashen person was Dottie," says Rankin. Pepper and Burton, the foremost U.S. duo, are scheduled to team up Friday morning in foursome (alternate-shot) play at the kickoff of the Solheim Cup. "Not only do they play well together," says Rankin, "they enjoy doing it."

They're chomping at the bit, too. Pepper, fully recovered from the virus that knocked her out of the du Maurier, won her fourth tournament of the summer two weeks ago in Portland. And Burton, says Rankin, "is so prepared, utterly fine-tuned and ready. The kid is playing great."

Was playing great.

Burton insists she'll be okay. She tells her teammates she once sprained an ankle so badly while sliding in a softball game that she was on crutches, but recovered quickly. This sprain, she says, isn't as bad. But her confident exterior masks an agitated interior. Privately, Burton doubts that she'll be able to play. Rankin, who took Betsy King to the dentist earlier today with a chipped tooth ("There's a certain amount of nursing involved in being captain"), has until noon on Thursday to replace a golfer who is sick or injured. (In past years an alternate traveled with each team.)

She decides to sleep on it. Or toss and turn on it. Rankin admits she hasn't been sleeping much.

Pairings and matchups keep spinning through her head. When she was named captain, Rankin sought advice from her predecessors, Kathy Whitworth and JoAnne Carner, as well as from veteran Solheim Cup combatants. Whitworth recommended pairing like personalities. Carner advocated including one exceptional putter in each duo. Daniel and King, who teamed up in 1990 and 1992, told Rankin they benefited from hitting their irons roughly the same distance, helping them collaborate on club selection.

Little things sometimes become paramount. Little things such as golf balls. Mallon and Geddes play Precept, a two-piece ball that is harder and hotter than the three-piece balls (such as Titleist) used by most of the team. So Mallon and Geddes become foursome teammates.

Matchups are a combination of homework and guesswork. Captains submit their teams prior to each session in the order their teams will tee off: Friday morning foursomes (alternate-shot) and afternoon four-ball (best-ball), Saturday morning foursomes and afternoon four-ball, and Sunday singles. It's like a bridge game as Rankin and Walker try to figure out how the cards of the opposition will be deployed. Rankin has been studying Walker's patterns from past Solheim Cups for months.

By Tuesday night, after practice, a two-hour photo shoot in the courtyard, and media reception, the mood in the American camp, as well as the condition of Burton's ankle, is getting, says Rankin, "pretty ugly."

"The players are very unsettled about this. Every player on this team loves Brandie. But it becomes a bigger issue." Realistically, Rankin must decide by late tomorrow afternoon whether to replace her. She's prepared to call Nancy Lopez.

Players begin drifting from the reception back to their rooms, located in cottages by the 17th tee overlooking the lake. Sheehan and Jones say good-night to Rankin, a bit concerned about their leader. Pepper asks if she's eaten, then takes her dinner order like a waitress at a truck stop.

"Soup?"

"Salad?"

"What kind of dressing?"

Wednesday, Sept. 18

"Vinnie Throws Wobbly—Soccer Hardman Vinnie
    Jones and His Crazy Gang Yesterday
    Labelled [Broadcaster] Gary Lineker
    a 'Jellyfish, a Wimp, and a Coward' " (*Daily Star*)
"Wobbly Golfer Swings" (*Tee Times*)

Burton walks gingerly to breakfast Wednesday morning. The swelling around her ankle has eased. Rankin decides to dance with the ones that she's brought.

Ice, anti-inflammatories, an electrical stimulator, and the removal of the top three spikes from her right shoe are sufficient to render her mobile. The injury is worse than anyone will admit—a severe sprain which has strained three ligaments—but Keith Kennedy tells Rankin that Burton can play without suffering any further damage. Riding in a cart, Burton makes it through 12 practice holes. Then she tells the media she's ready to go.

"Are you accident-prone?" asks a British reporter.

"Obviously," Burton says with a smile.

Beth Daniel, whose comments were used to fire up the Europeans in 1992, explains to the media that the Solheim Cup is not a grudge match like the Ryder Cup, with its edge of jingoistic antagonism. (Some U.S. players wore Desert Storm caps in 1993, a grotesque linkage of the Gulf War with a golf tournament.)

"A lot of people on their team are friends with all of us, and it's very difficult for us in that respect. They're trying to drum up the Ryder Cup atmosphere of hate, hate, hate, but it's not like that for us. This week they're keeping us separated, but I know if this were a regular tournament I'd be having dinner one night with Liselotte Neumann."

Daniel is partly responsible for ending Alfredsson's early-season funk. Compensating for pain in the right side of her derrière, Alfredsson was tilting her weight to her left. Daniel noticed and told Alfredsson, who balanced her weight more evenly, and began to strike the ball well again. (Alfredsson soon will undergo surgery to remedy what she describes literally as "a pain in the butt," which is the result of tripping over a bicycle 11 years ago and dislodging a small bone.)

Still, the Solheim Cup is not just another tournament. Rankin has been concerned about the British media whipping up a furor over Pepper's behavior at The Greenbrier and throwing her ace off her game. She's talked to Pepper about it, telling her "the last thing we want to do is to shoot ourselves in the foot." Months ago Rankin cooked up her own line for the media.

"I intend to say to the press: 'Now and then Dottie gets overly enthusiastic.' And 'Dottie's hair was red two years ago, so now that she's a blonde again, she'll be cool, calm, and collected.'"

Thursday, Sept. 19

"Jilted Husband Kills Wife's Pets" (*Daily Mirror*)
"Solheim No Place for Dottie Behavior" (*The Guardian*)

Almost every story about the U.S. team this week has focused on Pepper. Only Davies has received more ink.

The drumbeat of coverage reaches a crescendo this morning in David Davies's scathing piece in *The Guardian*.

Two years ago, in the heat of battle for the Solheim Cup at The Greenbrier, West Virginia, an incident occurred that was, in itself, disgraceful, that brought discredit to its perpetrator and that came close to diminishing the competition itself.

So when Pepper walks into the interview room on Thursday afternoon, slapping hands with Rankin, who is finishing up her session with the press, the atmosphere is charged.

Wearing a red, white, and blue sweatshirt and a blue Solheim Cup cap, Pepper sits down, prepared for a British Inquisition.

But the first question—how has her week been so far?—is a softball.

"I've been so busy I'd like to get a good night's sleep," says Pepper, referring to the nonstop schedule of practice, social events, photo shoots, and media requests that have left players with little time to take a deep breath.

The rest of the questions are cotton balls. Pepper is asked about first-match opponent Alfredsson. "Helen's probably the only one who talks more on the golf course than I do." She's asked about her success with Burton. Pepper says they're both bold and aggressive. "We're not short on our putts."

Pepper escapes without a scratch. Perhaps, when confronted with the cool, calm, and collected golfer, the reporters are too surprised to react.

It's all so civilized. Later in the afternoon, it will be announced in the media center that "a spot of tea is being served."

The opening ceremonies are quite magnificent. On the edge of the 16th fairway the teams sit in one long row at the base of a towering scoreboard that seems to stretch several stories high and a city block long. The scoreboard is topped with flags representing the nationalities of all of the golfers—United States, England, Wales, Scotland, Sweden, France.

Armed with an array of cameras, caddies, family members, and friends of the players snap and shoot pictures, part of a crowd of about 1,500 spectators on a blustery, chilly afternoon. Bucky McGann says his daughter and the other golfers are raring to go. "The last few days have been like the extra week before the Super Bowl."

American fans wear their hearts on their sleeves, hats, lapels, and jackets. Rebecca Gaston sports a stars and stripes tie, a tiny U.S. flag in her pocket, a flag lapel pin, and a navy sweater with a big flag in the center.

Jim Ritts quotes Shakespeare: "I am wealthy in my friends." He reads a message from President Clinton. Terry Coates, the leader of the European Tour, draws knowing smiles with another quote. "The well-adjusted person can play golf as if it were [just] a game."

An oom-pah band plays. A Welsh men's choir sings. Six jets from the

Royal Air Force's Red Arrow Team, reportedly piloted by a group of golf nuts, scream in low over the scoreboard, white, red, and blue smoke streaming in their wake in an abstract flag design, then returning to kiss the sky with the European colors of green and yellow.

The long two-year wait is over. The Europeans are licking their chops. They have much in their favor: the probability of bad weather, partisan crowds, a gimpy Burton, a slump-ridden King, the indomitable Davies.

A change in format—two sets of team matches on Friday and Saturday instead of one set—cuts both ways. It plays to the main strength of the Americans, who have superior depth. But it also plays to the strength of the Europeans, a younger squad.

Endurance has been a key concern for Rankin. "It's an even bigger issue if we run into bad weather." At the Dinah Shore, Patty Sheehan, who turns 40 next month, was already half-jokingly reminding her captain that she wasn't as young as she used to be.

"You know, I'm only an eighteen-hole [a day] player. Pretty soon it will be nine."

Bookies have installed the Europeans as a 13-8 underdog. (You can bet on the Solheim Cup at the William Hill bookmaker shop in the village of Chepstow; punters can also wager on which player will accumulate the most individual points for each team.)

Rumor has it that Davies had placed a huge bet on the Europeans. At that price, it's hard to blame her. The matches loom as a toss-up.

And tomorrow morning's foursome pairings are a pip.

1. Robbins & McGann vs. Sorenstam & Nilsmark
2. Sheehan & Jones vs. Davies & Nicholas
3. Daniel & Skinner vs. de Lorenzi & Reid
4. Pepper & Burton vs. Alfredsson & Neumann

Based on previous Solheim Cups, Rankin correctly guessed that Davies and Nicholas, undefeated in foursome play, would be Walker's first or second duo on the course. She wanted to tackle them with a pair that includes a U.S. player she views as a team leader. Robbins, though a relatively youthful 27, fits the bill. ("Other players respect her ability. She is kind of a calming influence; it's her nature.) So does Sheehan, who was 4-0 in Curtis Cup matches at St. Pierre in 1980. ("She's a well-rounded player who has learned to cope with her nervous system. All players respect that, probably more than a player who doesn't seem to *have* a nervous system.")

Rankin gives the U.S. squad the matchups and watches their reaction. She tells Sheehan and Jones, who teamed for two wins in 1990 under much less pressure-packed circumstances, "I'm pleased that you didn't flinch."

Friday, Sept. 20

> "Give Up Sex, Charles: He Must Be Celibate
>   If He Wants to Be King, Says Churchman" *(Daily Express)*
> "Tiny Americans Topple Titans" *(Tee Times)*

The fourth Solheim Cup commences on a misty, gray, cold morning. The BBC broadcasts live from the scene during its morning news show. Three hundred fifty media badges have been issued, compared with 50 for the first contest in 1990. (The Ryder Cup attracts some 700 journalists.) Sky TV is beaming live coverage throughout Europe. Other networks carry the action around the world, across Asia to Australia to the U.S.

It's a pleasure to listen to the Sky announcers, who eschew the gabbiness that mars many U.S. golf telecasts A ball that checks up on a green is described as taking "a fox trot to the right as it lands."

Sheehan, Jones, Davies, and Nicholas arrive on the 1st tee, pose for pictures, and wish each other good luck. Davies's looper, Matt Adams, gallantly kisses Sheehan's hand.

Laib, the Caddie Machine, paces. Four weeks ago in Dayton his knee locked up after the 10th hole of the final round. Rebecca Gaston toted the bag the rest of the way as Sheehan finished thirty-first.

"No more hills," said Laib's doctor, diagnosing an inflamed tendon that could snap. Although his knee threatened to give out again two weeks ago in Portland, he didn't tell his boss he was on his last legs. He knew the Solheim Cup was right around the corner. "No way I won't be there."

He's here. In fact, Laib came over a few days early to walk the course and prepare a yardage book for the other caddies. "I knew there wouldn't be time on Monday, and the Europeans already had one." Laib discovered a decent, if not particularly distinguished, layout, a parkland as opposed to a links course.

"Better than I thought it would be," says Pepper. "Very American. Well-defined fairways, not 747 material." The definition is courtesy of a majestic collection of trees—sweet chestnut, horse chestnut, lime, maple, beech, elm, English oak, ash—planted, in the case of one massive chestnut tree, as many as 400 years ago.

Sheehan and Jones take a one-up lead on the 374-yard 5th hole when the Davies/Nicholas duo bogeys. The early holes climb steep hills and the views from the top are majestic. The twin Severn Bridges, which link England and Wales, soar above the glittering silver-blue river a few miles to the east. Dairy farms, orchards, and row houses on the outskirts of St. Pierre spill for miles down the valley to the north and the west.

Bundled up in parkas and woolen caps, the crowd following the match quickly multiplies. Over 10,000 fans will flock to St. Pierre today, four times as many as attended the entire Solheim Cup in 1990.

Concessionaires sell "Yum Yums." At least that's what is painted in large letters on the top of their stands. The menu—burgers, bacon rolls with cheese, bacon rolls with mushrooms, white coffee (coffee with milk substitute)—doesn't quite live up to the hype.

Big scoreboards scattered around the course post U.S. advantages in red figures and European advantages in blue figures. Fans, players, and caddies can tell at a glance how the matches are faring without even reading the numbers.

Those who have competed in previous Solheim Cup matches claim the atmosphere is different than at any other tournament. They're correct. For one thing, a herd of people are inside the ropes. Trish Johnson, who is not playing this morning, and some of the European caddies are following Davies and Nicholas and chatting them up during delays. So are some family members and close friends of Sheehan and Jones. So are the media; several dozen journalists wander much farther inside the ropes than is allowed at an LPGA event. It lends a certain intimacy, warmth, and intensity to the contest.

As does the team aspect. Last year Joan Pitcock played for the LPGA against the Japanese Tour in the Nichirei matches in Japan. "It was so nice to have people on your team, instead of constantly being pitted against each other like we are every other week."

Val Skinner, to her surprise, found herself rooting for Sheehan at the Safeco Classic in Seattle last week. Outside the ropes, Skinner is a true humanitarian. She will soon be selected as one of five "Most Caring Athletes" by *USA Weekend* magazine, in recognition of her efforts to raise money to fight breast cancer. But she isn't the LPGA's most popular playing partner. She doesn't take crap from anyone; she's not above directing an occasional remark at an opponent's lack of distance off the tee. So her cheerleading was a little out of character.

"I was getting a feel for the team spirit," Skinner told a Seattle paper. "Normally, you're trying to rip somebody's head off their neck, and now you're pulling for them."

Rankin describes the informal team breakfast every morning as "sort of like the Walton family." Players wander in, eat, joke, get the latest weather report and Brandie Burton injury report, and check out Rankin's "thought for the day." Despite her serious demeanor, Rankin believes it's vital for the team "to hang onto a little bit of an ability to laugh at ourselves."

This morning team members traipsed in to find a picture of a duck, drawn by Rebecca Gaston, and a message that read:

"Always behave like a duck. Stay calm and unruffled on the surface and paddle like hell underneath."

So players and caddies, passing teammates who are behind in their matches, offer a few "Quack, quacks" of support. Spectators within earshot must think the Americans have gone bonkers.

The bond is just as strong on the European side. Players have been recounting war stories from past Solheim Cups, shooting pool, listening to music, and, as Pia Nilsson puts it, "teasing each other in a nice way."

Nilsson, a student of the history of sports, notes that the original meaning of competition means "to strive together." That noble cause seems to be alive and kicking in Wales. As John Hopkins writes in *The Times:*

"This is as pure as professional sport can be. It is rare these days to see people who are paid to play sport give such commitment to an event for which they receive no direct financial recompense."

Weeks after the conclusion of the Solheim Cup, a reporter will ask Davies about the rumor she bet big on Europe. Davies, who wagers on everything that moves, and some things that don't—she and brother Tony used to play Trivial Pursuit for £5 per game, otherwise why bother—is appalled at the notion.

"Never. There's absolutely no point. It's much more important than money. The thought of betting is stupid."

It's just as well she didn't. Davies is struggling, missing putts and sending Nicholas into the rough and trees to chase down her errant drives. On the rugged 425-yard 7th hole, which plays from the hills down toward a stream and then up a gradual incline to the green, Davies thins an iron, a terrible shot that ends up 30 yards short of the green in the left rough. Sheehan, after a good drive by Jones, belts a classic, soaring 3-wood that rolls up 12 feet from the cup.

After a decent pitch by Nicholas, Davies faces a 12-foot par putt for redemption. She pushes it well to the right and the U.S. is two-up.

The crowd swells by the second. More and more caddies and players drift into the fairways, as a monumental upset looms.

The Europeans fight back. After Davies hits a rocket into the rough on the 540-yard 10th hole, Nicholas bangs it down the fairway from near the base of a vast chestnut tree, with its mushroom cloud of green and autumn yellow leaves. Nicholas stumbles into a deep hole on the edge of the rough and almost goes down. She gingerly flexes her ankle.

"We need to get this fixed," she tells a marshal. St. Pierre may not be exceptionally difficult, but it's definitely treacherous.

Davies fires a brilliant iron into a stiff left-to-right crosswind that comes to rest six feet from the flag. Sheehan almost matches her.

"Come on, Laur-rah!" implores the gallery along the ropes and sitting in the grandstand behind the green as the most popular female athlete in Britain strides onto the green.

Jones misses a ten-foot birdie putt. A huge roar erupts from the crowd when Nicholas's putt curls in. "It's exciting, isn't it!" says a middle-aged woman fan in a red windbreaker at greenside. As the five-foot Nicholas exits the green, Trish Johnson reaches out and ruffles her hair.

Nicholas, 34, once was called "Little Al," part of the "Little and Large" pairing with Davies. Even apart from her diminutive size, it was easy to overlook her. If one were to ask to pick a professional athlete out of a lineup, Nicholas, who enjoys scuba diving, skiing, and bird watching, likely would be the last pick. With her straight brown hair simply cut around her oval face, Nicholas could be mistaken for a librarian, or perhaps a maid, serving tea and scones to the master and mistress.

Until recently Nicholas was primarily known as Laura Davies's little buddy, a feisty sidekick who kept the ball in the fairway and putted like a demon. (Davies says Nicholas is the best lag putter, male or female, in the world.) On her own, Nicholas was respected but hardly feared. When she whipped Sheehan in their 1994 Solheim Cup singles match, it was regarded as a huge upset.

But Nicholas, who splits her time between the U.S. and European Tours, won twice on the LPGA Tour in 1995, the result of swing changes (primarily a flatter arc) and a rigorous exercise program of stretching, sit-ups, and thrice-weekly cardiovascular workouts, which transformed a couch potato ("I had to be conditioned before I could even begin to be conditioned") into an energetic 128-pound transatlantic road warrior. Nicholas captured her twelfth European victory at the Irish Open in July, and has retained her splendid form since then.

She'll never be the model for an instructional video. Like many smaller players, she yanks the club outside on her backswing. But her record speaks volumes, and she has marched out from the considerable shadow cast by Davies into the sunshine. Now the British media call her "Big Al."

"She's such a sweetheart," says Sheehan. "She's a jewel." The scrappy Nicholas once had words with Betsy King at a previous Solheim Cup. Now they're fast friends—she and several other LPGA players accompanied the king to Romania in 1994 to provide assistance for orphans of war.

In some ways the 36-year-old Jones, a savior of animal shelter puppies and kittens in Atlantic City, is an ideal counterpart. The rail-thin redhead has won over $2.8 million and seven tournaments in her 15-year career. Despite struggling with swing changes this season, she won in Corning in May and ranks sixteenth on the money list.

A fine softball player in her youth, Jones plays golf with a scrappiness that conjures up images of torn uniforms and skinned knees. "She's my favorite," says Inkster. "Spunky, a big heart. A genuine good person who calls a spade a spade."

Ask Davies. In their singles match at the Solheim Cup in 1990, Davies hit a 2-iron off the 1st tee, prompting Jones to sassily ask if a screw was missing from her driver. An irked Davies won 3 and 2.

Maybe she's missing a screw on her driver today. Davies continues to send Nicholas into the rough and trees to rescue her wayward tee shots.

Alternate-shot golf is unique. "It puts a lot of stress on your game," says Rankin. It is, as one of the British writers puts it, "vaguely socialistic." Maybe that's why the Europeans generally excel in it. American players often find partnership to be a burden rather than a comfort. "We're too worried about making a mistake," says Sheehan.

Drama ebbs and flows with every shot. As the players reach the 14th hole, Jones's caddie, Terry McNamara, realizes he's having trouble breathing. "It's like being in the lead the last day at the U.S. Open," he'll say later.

"It's worse," says the Caddie Machine.

Players describe Solheim Cup pressure in different ways. McGann, who soaked up the atmosphere as the U.S. alternate in 1994, says, "It's not like you're standing over a putt at the U.S. Open. It's ten times worse. You're playing for your country."

"It's a different kind of pressure, a fun pressure," says Inkster. "You don't want to screw up in front of your peers. Everyone is so into themselves [on Tour]. It's nice to be able to rally around teammates." (Inkster's attitude is one reason why many of the U.S. players hoped she would make the squad. All week players have been telling Rankin they wish Juli were here to compete, share the experience, and razz the opposition. "Europeans can talk a lot of trash," says Inkster, a hint of approval in her voice.)

"Everything is heightened a bit," says Pepper. "I don't know if it's the pressure as much as the anticipation."

"It would be the worst week of your life if you were playing badly," says Kathryn Marshall.

The tension multiplies as the players walk toward the green at the 340-yard 15th hole, which doglegs left and then funnels down a narrow channel with spectators lining hillsides on both sides of the fairway. It's a claustrophobic yet thrilling march through a gauntlet of fans to the peninsula green at the edge of the lake, where swans and ducks float on its serene surface.

The fans press down along the ropes as the golfers walk by. Unlike the bombastic, militaristic harshness of the "U.S.A., U.S.A." chants that haunted the Europeans in West Virginia in 1994, the home continent fans offer a more imploring, encouraging voice of support. "Come on, Eur-rope," delivered in a rhythmic sing-song, becomes almost mantralike.

Sheehan and Jones have been as solid as the centuries-old stone buildings at St. Pierre, reeling off 13 straight pars. When Jones grazes the cup with a birdie chip from the fringe, McNamara, heart in his throat, pulls his cap over his eyes. Davies laughs in relief and compliments Jones. But she's not laughing after her five-foot par putt spins out. "Every time a putt goes over the lip, it is like someone had stabbed you," Davies told *The Independent*. As she walks off the green, face drawn, eyes on the horizon, Davies feels as if she's been impaled. The U.S. team is two-up.

The 210-yard 16th hole is stunning. Players stand on a small circular tee box in front of a small grandstand full of fans hovering over their shoulders. The corner of the lake is just in front of the tee. Past the lake on the left, up near the green, is a stone building from the 1600s, covered with ivy and used as a storage shed. The fairway is framed on the right by the towering scoreboard topped by flags, site of the opening ceremonies. The fairway itself flows gradually up a slope to the well-bunkered green. Grandstands, more flags and the turrets and chimneys of the old medieval mansion house and the bell tower of the church rise into the sky behind the green.

It's a beautiful beast. On Wednesday Daniel, Skinner, Geddes, and Mallon each hit two balls from the tee and never sniffed the green. Uphill and into strong headwinds or crosswinds, the hole is playing more like 230 yards, and is being attacked by most players with drivers.

Sheehan hooks hers badly.

"Gah!" she barks, disgusted.

The ball is buried in a thick tangle of ivy covering the stone wall and growing into the rock of the shed.

"Anyone allergic to bee stings, they ought to just exit," says Sheehan, stumbling near a wasp's nest as she searches through the foliage. Eventually the team double-bogeys. One-up.

Meanwhile the scoreboard turns red. Robbins and McGann, after going out in a fat 40, are scorching the back nine, birdieing four holes to come back from three-down against Sorenstam and Nilsmark and square the match. Daniel and Skinner, who trailed early, have forged a lead on de Lorenzi and Reid.

"Laur-rah, Laur-rah," implore the fans, pleading for a late comeback.

Sheehan strikes a beautiful iron on the 362-yard 17th hole, but the ball rolls to the back of the putting surface. A Brit in a tweed coat, watching her walk to the green, remarks, "She looks a bit grandmotherly doesn't she, with that gray hair. She must be about fifty."

When Jones runs their lag putt four feet past the cup—"Ho! Ho!" she hollers—Sheehan feels about 60. Davies and Nicholas are in with par. The 444-yard 18th, a reachable par five, favors the Europeans. The match, which seemed almost in hand, suddenly hangs in the balance.

For all of the success in her storied career, Sheehan's Solheim Cup record is dismal. She lost singles matches in 1990, 1992, and 1994. Apart from her wins with Jones in 1990, her doubles record is 1-2-1. In what may be her last Solheim Cup, she burns for redemption.

The crowd is barely breathing. The best clutch putter in the world strikes the ball straight and true, but it starts to die as it nears the cup. Sheehan's putter blade rises to eye level, as she attempts, with her best body American, to coax the ball a final few inches. The gallery, with its best body European, silently implores it to stop. The contest of wills ends as the ball trickles over the edge and tumbles to the bottom.

Davies, squandering her advantage, pushes another drive on the 18th. Nicholas, with no chance to get home, leaves her partner a 50-yard pitch from the rough. Davies bungles the shot, leaving it 20 feet from the cup. Heartsick, she stands for a long moment with her head down, swishing the wedge back and forth through the grass, near a scoreboard that is solid red.

No miracles from Big Al. When she misses a last chance to salvage a halve, Jones thrusts her arms skyward. Sheehan hugs Rankin. The Caddie Machine tells her, "That's two little bulldogs, captain."

"Who'd ever have thought the two little peewees would beat the big Laura," Sheehan says slyly in the interview room. "They didn't play their best. We didn't play our best. We were fortunate to make a good putt on seventeen."

Informed that Davies and Nicholas had been undefeated, Sheehan says, with an undercurrent of sarcasm, "Well, Howdy Dowdy, I did not know that," not bothering to mention that she and Jones also were—and still are—unbeaten as a duo.

Asked if their defeat of the seemingly invincible Davies had a psychological effect on the rest of her teammates, Sheehan says, "I think our match may have given them strength, seeing we were up fairly early on against Laura, as she is an enormous figure to be up against, not only because of the way she plays the game, but because of the enormous crowds that are behind her."

The morning ends with the U.S. leading 3½ to ½, a rout of stunning proportions. Robbins and McGann tie Sorenstam and Nilsmark. Daniel and Skinner outlast de Lorenzi and Reid despite a back nine 40. Pepper and the limping Burton, keyed by a rare birdie on No. 16, overcome a brilliant 33 on the front side by Neumann and Alfredsson.

The mood in the team dining rooms during the brief break is a study in opposites. The Europeans pick at their food in funereal silence. Finally Kathryn Marshall has an inspiration. She pops a disc by the group Snap into a CD player and the sounds of "We've Got the Power" vibrate the walls.

"I put it on at full volume because the first half of the lunch was as if somebody had died. They were all looking so solemn and serious and I just wanted to remind them that this is supposed to be fun."

The Americans, for their part, were celebrating. But they sober up in a hurry when Davies, paired in four-ball (best-ball) with Trish Johnson, explodes from the gate with three straight birdies.

"She's pissed," says Sheehan, a spectator this afternoon, as the board turns blue.

So is Judy Rankin. At herself. "I allowed them to be so pleased, and I was so pleased. It should have been thirty seconds for congratulations, then lace your shoes on tighter and keep going."

By the time the Americans lace up their Foot-Joys, the Europeans are beating them and St. Pierre to a pulp. On the 309-yard 8th hole, a narrow alley where most players hit irons off the tee, Davies launches a moon shot that kicks off a slight mound left of the green, rolls onto the putting surface, and burns the edge of the cup.

Everyone is agog.

"Did you see Laura's [shot]!" an excited Trish Johnson calls out to a group of European caddies and players near the green.

"It missed by this much," a caddie tells her, holding his fingers an inch apart.

A midafternoon sun peeks through and lightens the gray skies. Europe marches on. Their four teams throw front nines of 30, 31, 31, and 31 at the shell-shocked Yanks. Davies birdies seven out of 13 holes, Johnson adds two more, and they rout Robbins and Bradley 6 and 5.

All of the other matches go to the wire. Players and caddies drift over to the 18th hole and huddle in clumps behind the green. Camera crews zoom in on players and coaches for reaction shots. Rankin, drawn and somber, walks away to stand by herself. Joanne Morley, a Solheim Cup rookie (or "new cap," as they are called in Britain), didn't even play today, yet she's exhausted from the drama of spectating, deep circles around her eyes.

Sorenstam and Marshall shoot 65 and eke out a one-up victory over Skinner and Geddes in a tremendous match. Alfredsson and Nicholas shoot 67 to tie with Mallon and Daniel, who sinks a clutch 12-foot putt on the final green.

Only Pepper and King can post a victory, which preserves a 5-3 American lead. And it takes a 64 to do so against Neumann and Nilsmark. The pivotal holes are the 15th, where Pepper, after a 15-foot Nilsmark birdie putt sends the crowd into ecstasy, silences them with a 12-footer right on top of it, her fourth birdie in five holes, and the 18th, where King hits the green in two with a 5-wood from 212 yards and matches Neumann's closing birdie.

Players and caddies troop into the interview room, drained but exhilarated by what they have done and seen. Walker praises Pepper. "To follow Catrin's birdie on fifteen and hole it, two birdies, that was the mark of a great player and I admire her for it."

Pepper praises King, who came into the matches with her confidence so shaken that Rankin sat her down for a pep talk. "My heart couldn't have been beating any harder when Betsy hit that shot into eighteen. It was on the flag all the way."

King praises Pepper. "Dottie is the toughest competitor you can face, and to have her on my side is great. She may not necessarily have the most skill or hit it like Laura, but I have never seen her waste a shot on Tour, and I cannot say that about any other player."

Rankin praises Davies. "I'm not sure she couldn't have won [playing] alone." Then she praises everyone. "People who don't see women's golf in person don't realize how good they can play." The tally for the afternoon is irrefutable evidence: 50 birdies and 3 bogeys.

Saturday, Sept. 22.

> "Solheim Cup: Tuned-in Marshall Floors Yanks" (*Daily Star*)
> "Cheating Fergie Slept with Three Men at Once" (*The Mirror*)
> "Kathy's Power Play Fires Euro Fightback" (*Daily Record*)

Roars of joy reverberate around St. Pierre all day, as the Europeans take up where they left off. Each European birdie is worth a half-dozen hurrahs, the first from greenside, followed by a number of echoing cheers from around the course when the news is posted on scoreboards at different locations.

British and European flags, carried by many of the spectators, wave under chilly, windy, sunny skies. Davies drains a five-foot birdie putt on the 1st hole, and she and Trish Johnson never trail in their 4 and 3 victory against "the tiny American pair," as Sheehan and Jones are described in the *International Herald Tribune* this morning.

The Caddie Machine walks off the 15th green shaking his head. "They didn't miss one shot. They were so on."

Sheehan musters a small smile. "That wasn't very pretty."

In a mirror-image reversal of yesterday morning, Europe goes to lunch after pasting the U.S. 3½ to ½. Europe now leads the match 6½ to 5½. Their only casualty is captain Mickey Walker, stung on the left eyelid by a wasp. Walker makes her rounds wearing a white bandage wrapped around her eye and head, looking like a car-crash victim.

Not even Pepper and Burton can stem the tide and overcome a brilliant alternate-shot 69 by Sorenstam and Nilsmark, although they scare the bejesus out of the Europeans by getting up and down to halve No. 16, birdieing No. 17, and hitting the green in two on No. 18, leaving Pepper a 40-foot eagle putt to tie the match.

It is a putt that virtually defines Pepper, her awesome talent, her huge heart, her fourth-and-goal, give-me-the-ball guts, the refuse-to-lose mentality that might as well be stenciled on her forehead, the vast ambition that leads her right to the line of acceptability and, in the past, occasionally across it. It is a 40-foot, do-or-die eagle putt that slams into the back of the cup, pops up in the air but refuses to fall, as the crowd gasps, a mixture of astonishment, relief, and admiration.

Nerves fray and civility wanes in the afternoon. Rankin, desperately trying to hold the ship together, is balancing the needs of the moment with the demands of tomorrow's singles matches. Pepper, after leaving her guts strewn around the fairways of St. Pierre, is resting on the bench. So is Burton, and she's not happy about it, upset that she can't limp 36 holes today. Jones, a spectator as well, is not happy either, since she's only played in the alternate-shot matches. Bradley is idle for the third time in four sessions—her only appearance was with Robbins yesterday when they were flattened by the Laura Davies/Trish Johnson locomotive, and some of her teammates are extremely upset.

"I could detect a not real confident Pat Bradley," says Rankin, whose main concern was to find the right afternoon partner for Betsy King. "Betsy and Pat didn't have enough confidence and cheerleading ability to bolster each other."

Once that would have been a ludicrous notion; the two Hall of Famers, first and second on the all-time career earnings list with over $5 million each, have been stone-cold killers throughout their careers. Once the mere sight of the two of them together would have paralyzed the opposition. Not here. Not now.

So Rankin asked Kelly Robbins if she could play her fourth straight match.

"Put me in," said Robbins, and Bradley went back to her seat on the bench.

"She's one of the better players I've known in my life," says Rankin. "But I had to be tough in my thinking and remember, 'This is not the Y.' Pat never gave me twelve seconds of woe. She was great."

The Mallon and McGann versus Sorenstam and Johnson match is not so harmonious. Two controversies arise on the 14th hole with the U.S. holding a three-up lead.

Mallon is away on the green. She wants McGann to putt first, a common occurrence in best-ball play. But to do so, McGann will have to stand on Sorenstam's line. Sorenstam protests. Things get testy. A European rules official is called to adjudicate, and correctly rules in the U.S. favor.

However, what he fails to tell Mallon and McGann, and what they learn after they have trod on Sorenstam's line and putted out, is that the 1995 *Decisions on the Rules of Golf,* which interpret the rules, state: "It would be a sporting gesture to relinquish the right to putt first in these circumstances."

Sorenstam and Johnson are furious. They exact their revenge with birdies on the final four holes to halve the match with a must-make ten-foot putt by Sorenstam on No. 16, a tremendous wood and ten-foot putt by Johnson on the beastly No. 16, a fifteen-foot birdie putt on No. 17 by Johnson, and two magnificent shots by Sorenstam by No. 18, followed by her eagle attempt that dies on the lip.

(Two months after the Solheim Cup, Sorenstam is still ticked off. Asked if it was poor sportsmanship by the Americans, Sorenstam, usually so soft-spoken, snaps out an emphatic, "Yes! I would never do that.")

Friction increases when Rankin complains, after being notified by U.S. players and caddies following the match, that Martin Hall, Lisa Hackney's coach and boyfriend, was walking down the fairway with Johnson. Coaching inside the ropes is forbidden. Although Rankin is friendly with Hall and doubts he or Johnson would behave unethically, she feels compelled to stand up for her players. Hall, a well-known instructor, denies offering advice, explaining that Johnson simply had asked how Hackney had played. The explanation suffices, although Hall is advised to stay outside the ropes. Rankin and Walker exchange sharp words.

Robbins and King, whose birdies on No. 15 and No. 17 key a 2 and 1 decision over new cap Joanne Morley and de Lorenzi, are the only Americans to post a victory all day. The U.S. performance is summed up by a weary Sheehan, who crushes a driver into the wind on No. 16, the long par three, only to watch the ball land just short of the green in the fringe.

Sheehan raises her arms in resignation, smiles, and says to the gallery in the grandstand just behind her, "That's about all I can do." A few minutes later Sheehan and Geddes fall 3 and 1 to Neumann and Nilsmark.

A haggard Neumann is interviewed at greenside by several camera crews, asking questions in both English and Swedish. After four matches in two days, after a seemingly endless succession of white-knuckle putts (her clutch five-foot birdie putt this morning vanquished Pepper and Burton and produced "perhaps the loudest cheers this biennial event has ever heard," according to *Daily Express* reporter James Mossup), Neumann is wasted.

She praises the crowds. "Their cheering is keeping us alive, because we're getting pretty tired at the end of the day."

Europe leads 9-7. The team's confidence is sky-high. Marshall admits to a reporter she was disappointed at sitting out the afternoon session. Then she adds, "When we pick up the trophy tomorrow, it won't matter."

Rankin huddles with husband Yippy and LPGA general counsel Ty Votaw. They conclude that the third through sixth matches likely will determine whether the U.S. can turn it around. Rankin guesses Walker will stack her stars at the top, looking to strike quickly, put blue on the board, fire up the crowd, and land the knockout punch. She predicts Davies will play in the third to sixth position.

Her task is to match Europe's initial firepower while reserving a few aces for the final matches. (Two U.S. players ask Rankin not to place them in the anchor position, overwhelmed at the notion of standing on the final green with a putt to win or lose the Solheim Cup.)

The lineups for Sunday are due one hour after the completion of the afternoon session. In the media center Rankin watches as they are matched on a computer screen.

1. Bradley vs. Sorenstam
2. Skinner vs. Marshall
3. McGann vs. Davies
4. Daniel vs. Neumann
5. Burton vs. Hackney
6. Pepper vs. Johnson
7. Robbins vs. Nicholas
8. King vs. de Lorenzi
9. Jones vs. Morley
10. Geddes vs. Reid
11. Sheehan vs. Nilsmark
12. Mallon vs. Alfredsson

She feels like she's drawn a 12-card royal flush. "I didn't see one match on the board that was a gimme for the Europeans."

Ever since she was named captain eight months ago, Rankin has had one overriding thought in her mind: "to do everything in my power to win the first singles match." Back at the du Maurier, she toyed with the notion of sending Pepper into battle in the leadoff spot. "She's such an irritant to the Europeans. It could set a lovely tone for me."

But present circumstances obviate past theories. Months ago Rankin also said, "The most important thing is team unity." After benching Bradley twice today, she needs to unruffle the feathers of her players who saw it as a slap in the face.

So she leads with a shaky Bradley against a superconfident Sorenstam, playing almost as well as she did at the U.S. Open.

"It's a position of responsibility," says Rankin. "It's the right place to put her."

Rankin's message to her team on Saturday night is simple: Don't try to be more than you are, don't think you have to pull off miracles. "No one has to do anything they are not capable of, or have not done before." She suggests they think about, or dream about, some of those good times, some of the 187 victories this team has compiled.

Tomorrow Dottie Pepper will tell the media that "we definitely wanted to clear the air," implying some dissension and bickering in the ranks. But Rankin and other players say the mood wasn't confrontational at all.

"I thought everyone would get hyped up and out of control," says Jane Geddes. "But it was really mellow, really comforting. Dottie said a couple things. Judy said a couple things. Everybody was real calm."

The final message of the night comes from Rosie Jones. As she's leaving for her room, she turns, points her finger at her teammates, and says, "I'll tell you one thing. If I can beat you-all's asses every now and then, I can beat these people."

Sunday, Sept. 22

> "Find Me a Man, Orders Diana" (*Sunday Mirror*)
> "Mickey's Girls Sting Yanks" (*News of the World*)
> "Swinging to Laura's Theme" (*The Observer*)

The lesson for the Sunday sunrise service at the church at St. Pierre is from First Corinthians 9. One passage could suitably serve as a professional golfer's motto: "Know ye not that they which run in a race run all, but one receiveth the prize? So run that ye may obtain."

Music is provided a short time later by a chorus in the grandstand behind the 1st tee, basking under cool sunshine and mild breezes on a glorious morning. Flag-waving fans pack the right side of the fairway ten-deep.

After two days of practice, the chorus, led by former European Tour member Jane Connachan, is in peak form. Mickey Walker, wearing sunglasses over an eye patch, is greeted with voices humming theme music from *The Sting.* Sorenstam is serenaded with songs from the Swedish pop group Abba and a chant of "Number Two, Number Two, Number Two," in honor of her world ranking.

The choir sings "Flower of Scotland," the national anthem, for sparkplug Kathryn Marshall, matched up with Val Skinner.

It's been a magical week for new cap Skinner, who won the 1995 Sprint Championship and $430,248 last season but has never experienced anything as exciting as the Solheim Cup. When she arrived at St. Pierre, opened the door to her room, and saw the collection of sleek U.S. uniforms arrayed on hangers, it was "like waking up on Christmas morning when I was ten years old." When she and partner Beth Daniel joined Davies and partner Lisa Hackney on the 1st tee yesterday for their afternoon four-ball match, she was astounded at the outpouring of support for Davies. "Seeing a woman with that kind of popularity in golf is incredible to me."

But today Skinner is so deep into her "little pit bull" mode of concentration that the chorus doesn't even register as background music.

The other players get a kick out of the show. Alison Nicholas makes an entrance wearing a crimson wig and a tartan bonnet. Nilsmark is greeted with a hand-clapping, foot-stomping, grandstand-rattling chant—"If you're Europe and you know it and you really want to show it, clap your hands." A few lone voices try to counter with "Three Cheers for the Red, White, and Blue," for Sheehan.

"I'd like to bottle this atmosphere," says Jim Ritts, joking that the fans at Muirfield Village should be given lyric sheets when they walk through the gate at the 1998 Solheim Cup.

A reporter asks 1st tee announcer George Griffith if he's ever seen anything like it at another sporting event.

"It is most unusual. You couldn't pay for this kind of entertainment. It was literally born out of the atmosphere."

The chorus greets Alfredsson with "What's it all about, Alfie?" then it segues into the European clapping and stomping chant as a beaming Alfredsson, dressed in black slacks, yellow turtleneck, and blue and black plaid vest, dances to the beat.

When they stop, an American woman in the stands calls to Mallon, "They're brutal up here, Meg, but we're doing the best we can." Mallon, in tan slacks, a white turtleneck, and navy sweater with a tan stripe on the sleeves highlighted with white stars, replies, "Just hang in there. We are."

Mallon also has a final question for the chorus.

"What are you going to do when we leave?"

*   *   *

Suffer in silence.

By the time Mallon and Alfredsson hit their tee shots, the board is almost solid red. Skinner, Daniel, McGann, and Burton move ahead in the critical early matches. Europeans Morley and Nilsmark double-bogey the straightaway 540-yard 1st hole.

Most of the 15,000 spectators at St. Pierre seem to be in the enormous gallery tracking Davies and McGann. McGann's play is as solid as a 400-year-old oak tree. She turns in 33 and is two-up in a match that Rankin says "was one they had penciled in [as a victory] before they teed off."

Not in McGann's mind. Three weeks ago at the State Farm Rail Classic in Springfield, Illinois, she picked up her third win of the summer, defeating Davies and Barb Whitehead in a playoff. (When McGann lined up a ten-foot birdie putt on the third hole of sudden death, Davies told her, "Knock it in, mate." McGann did. Later she said, "That just shows what kind of sportsman Laura is.") Coming into the Solheim Cup, McGann, Pepper, and Davies were the hottest players in the world. When Rankin gave the team the singles pairings yesterday, McGann never flinched. In fact, she was excited.

Although McGann is only 26, her sterling play this summer has been a long time coming. When she was born, her parents, Bucky and Bernadette, sent out a birth announcement with a drawing of a baby climbing out of a golf bag. It read, "Announcing our future pro!" McGann joined the Tour in 1989, fresh out of Rosarian Academy, an all-girls prep school in West Palm Beach.

The five-foot-eleven youngster was a cross between a Clydesdale and a showgirl from the classiest revue in Vegas, combining a workhorse strength and power with brassy makeup, bright lipstick, gold jewelry, and a collection of gaudy, wide-brimmed hats that earned her a nickname—"The Hat Lady"—and a lucrative deal with Sonni Hats, which distributes her line to golf shops across the country. (McGann totes at least 12 hats with her on the road, packing them in empty drum kit containers.) McGann's 1993 club contract with Lynx, worth a reported $100,000 a year, was, at the time, second only to Jan Stephenson's deal with Dunlop.

Early in her career, McGann was known as a gracious competitor and a fine role model and spokesperson for the American Diabetes Association. (McGann was diagnosed with diabetes at 13. She injects herself with insulin twice a day.) She earned almost $1 million from 1989 to 1994.

Yet she remained a nonwinner. *The Wall Street Journal*'s Frederick C. Klein wrote an article in 1994 titled, "Lots of Hats but No Wins."

"The phenomenon of fame before significant accomplishment," wrote Klein, "is hardly unique in American sports, but seldom has it been better exemplified than by Michelle McGann."

Last year she finally clubbed the monkey off her back. McGann won in Nashville and Youngstown, ranking seventh on the money list with $449,296.

But by then a number of people were outfitting her in a black hat.

"Very into Michelle," sniffed one Tour veteran. "Very West Palm Beachy. College would have been good for her." Some of the backbiting from her colleagues was simple jealousy, which Laura Baugh and Jan Stephenson also experienced when they cashed in on their appearance. "Michelle rubs a lot of people the wrong way," says Inkster, "but she's always been nice to me."

Still, McGann's conduct gave the snipers an easy target. She seemed to be in the process of acquiring a new label—petulant golf diva. She whined that people kept asking "stupid questions" about her hats and outfits, even though her self-created image helped make her rich and famous. At the 1995 Friendly's Classic in Massachusetts, she blew her bonnet after missing the cut, bitching that the course was "no fun" and declaring "it might take a lot to get me back here."

Sylvia Bertolaccini, the tournament director and a former LPGA player, fired back: "There are superstars and there are money winners. Nancy Lopez is a superstar. I'm sure she saw some things along the way in her career that she didn't like, but she knew how to tell people in the right way."

Last year at Youngstown, McGann followed Lopez into the interview room. A TV reporter had asked Lopez to hold a microphone during her interview. When the same request was made of McGann, she said she was too tired. An LPGA official termed the scene "embarrassing."

What a difference a year makes. McGann has grown up this season, inside and outside the ropes. And her game has matured considerably.

"She's smarter off the tee," says caddie Donna Earley. "She knows when to lay up and hit a 5-wood." McGann acknowledges she often was overly aggressive, explaining, "My whole game, ever since I started, was based on great strength with my driver." She's also found a driver that suits her, after experimenting with various weapons, including Cobra and Taylor-Made. McGann latched onto a Great Big Bertha at the Oldsmobile Classic in June, site of the first of her three summertime triumphs, and hasn't let go since.

Improved short-game skills have added a new dimension to her game. McGann spends hours on the practice green and in the bunkers, where she "keeps hitting balls until I have them in a little pile around the cup." Her sand play has improved so much she sometimes aims for a bunker on a par five.

McGann says she simply didn't know the proper technique for some shots, such as a high lob from around the green. Now she does.

She also has learned how to treat the public. Part of the improvement is cosmetic. A sportscaster boyfriend, appalled at some tapes of her interviews, helped improve her speaking skills.

But the changes are more than just skin deep. McGann has a different outlook, courtesy of some schooling from Nancy Lopez at an outing earlier this season.

Marveling at Lopez's cheerful acquiescence to every fan request, McGann told her, "Gee, you're so good about it."

"These people have gotten us where we are," replied Lopez. "We wanted to be in this situation or we would have a desk job or something. We have to accept the role. It's not that hard to take a minute, because it means so much to them."

McGann is candid about the downside of fame.

"You have to be on all the time. You have to be *on* time. You can't just say, 'Whoa! Back up for a minute!' It's easier when you're playing well to be very gracious."

But Lopez's words hit home. "She is the legend," McGann says simply, and among her legacies are a handing down of a code of behavior to the younger generation.

McGann is close to vanquishing the British legend. The crowd, so giddy at the beginning of the day, now is so quiet you can hear a chestnut drop after Davies pushes a drive that bangs off a tree on the 412-yard 14th hole.

Forget the Yum Yums. These people need a Prozac vendor. After a terrible chip, which draws a low-pitched "ooww" from the gallery, Davies bogeys. McGann, who says, "I felt totally at ease once I got out there," nervelessly rolls in a four-foot par putt. She's three-up. She walks through the crowd with some of the old Lopez hauteur. Or perhaps hat-teur; McGann sports a glittery navy boater studded with silver sequins and "USA" in large silver letters on the front, a confident gunslinger marching through a hostile town.

"Come on, Laur-rah!" a few forlorn voices call out. Davies is pale and glum. She looks almost haunted. She pushes a drive into heavy rough on the 360-yard 15th.

"Haven't got much, have we?" she says to caddie Matt Adams. Her only play is a low punch down the slope toward the lake. She sends it onto the fairway, well short of the green. Bucky McGann, riding in a cart because of a recent broken hip, roars by like General Patton, handing out glossy photos of his daughter to the bemusement of fans and reporters.

But Davies won't quit. McGann dumps an easy 8-iron into the lake-front rocks to the right of the green. Davies grasps at the lifeline, hitting a sensational wedge to four feet and sinking it to ignite the fans. But only for a moment. The cheers turn to groans when Davies pushes a 2-iron wildly to the right on the 16th.

McGann has owned this hole all week, hitting it close in practice.

Almost all the other players whale away at it with drivers, but it's a smooth 3-wood for McGann.

Two hundred twenty-four yards to the flagstick. McGann can visualize the shot perfectly. "I knew it was all over the minute the ball came off the clubface." Soaring toward the green and the grandstand and the medieval stone walls and turrets, the ball gently falls to earth and rolls to a stop five feet from the cup.

Shot of the week. Shot of the year.

McGann's game face dissolves in joy.

"Yes!" she shouts, pumping a fist, turning to exchange a loud, smacking high-five with caddie Earley. A few minutes later Davies concedes the putt, the hole, and the match. For the stunned fans, who give McGann a brief smatter of applause, it's like watching Muhammad Ali topple to the canvas.

A beaming McGann is showered with congratulations from Bradley, Skinner, their caddies, and her family.

"All right!" she says. "We gotta get the rest of the crew in now."

It's not over yet. The U.S. leads in six matches, some by wide margins. But five others are close.

The second part of the devastating one-two punch comes a few minutes later on the 16th hole. Burton, clinging to a one-up lead over tenacious new cap Lisa Hackney, pushes a driver way to the right of the green. The ball vanishes into thick, matted grass. Hackney, after a magnificent tee shot, is 20 feet from the stick, almost certain to square the match.

Especially when Burton checks her lie. She figures she has two chances of scraping the ball out of the grass, over a yawning bunker, and onto the putting surface—"a hope and a prayer."

Burton opens up a sand wedge. Later she'll say she whacked at it as hard as she could. But her swing looks smooth and purposeful. The ball floats over the bunker, onto the green, and rolls right into the cup.

Forget the Prozac. These fans need electric shock treatment. Hackney, in the sporting gesture of the week, greets Burton with a high-five and a smiling "Bad time to do *that*."

The end is near. Kelly Robbins assures the U.S. of a tie, and retention of the Solheim Cup, when she halves with Alison Nicholas.

A pumped-up Sheehan, who couldn't reach the green yesterday, smokes a driver to 25 feet on the 16th and gives her teammates a curt nod when she reaches the green. Her beautifully struck birdie putt curls around the lip, but she closes out Catrin Nilsmark 2 and 1 with a par on the 17th. Her point officially assures the U.S. of victory.

"Yeah!" an exultant Sheehan yells as she exits the green. "Sing it!" She hugs Jim Ritts, his wife Linda, players, caddies, her mother, reporters, everyone and everything but the oak trees. The jigsaw puzzle of Sheehan's brilliant career is completed as the last small piece, a Solheim Cup singles victory, snaps into place. She has run out of worlds to conquer.

The teams gather around the 18th green. Sorenstam, quietly magnificent all week, is the only European to win a singles match. "I feel fine," she says. "I could go out again." Neumann, who, according to her friend and opponent Daniel, "was just dragging around the golf course," salvages a tie. Marshall, the diminutive spark plug who backed up her bold words with impressive deeds, loses 2 and 1 to Skinner despite being two under par in the best-played match of the day. Walker is in agony; a hive of wasps could not have stung so deeply. "I honestly felt we would comfortably win the Cup back." (Walker will soon announce her retirement as Solheim Cup captain; Pia Nilsson will lead the Europeans in 1998.) A crestfallen Davies, stabbed repeatedly by a balky putter, says, "At no point did I think we'd lose today."

The U.S. caddies, a scruffy and tired bunch—they went unshaven and dubbed themselves "The Dirty Dozen"—pose for pictures clutching cigars. One points to the scoreboard, drenched in red, grins, and says, "Sunday, bloody Sunday."

Kelly Robbins, the U.S. ironwoman who played all five matches and halved with Nicholas, gives McGann an emphatic high-ten, telling her, "Great playing! Way to take her on!" Mallon, who whipped Alfredsson 4 and 2, spots Geddes: "Janey, I got a bunker lesson from you! I was jammin' today!" King, who almost watched the Solheim Cup on TV at home in Limekiln, Pennsylvania, finishes with a 3-0 record after dispatching de Lorenzi 5 and 4. Burton, who inspired her teammates with a blend of guts, talent, and a glorious stroke of good fortune, is beaming.

So is Pepper., a come-from-behind 3 and 2 winner over Trish Johnson. The daughter of a major league baseball player pulls off an unassisted double-play: she triumphs on the course with sensational golf while silencing her critics by comporting herself with the poise of a Foreign Service career diplomat trapped behind enemy lines.

Weeks after the Solheim Cup, Davies, who called Pepper "the rudest golfer I ever met" after their 1994 dustup at The Greenbrier, offers a mellow assessment of her old foe.

"I like Dottie. When she's on the golf course, she's ferocious; I respect her competitive fire. She's a bit shy. I'm a bit shy also. So I wouldn't go up and initiate a conversation, but I like her."

Rankin, who orchestrated the matchups and mood so skillfully and smoothly she barely left fingerprints, can finally take a deep breath. Soon she will be reappointed as captain for the 1998 Solheim Cup.

The Waterford crystal Solheim Cup trophy is presented to the Americans at the closing ceremonies. Walker says, "The entertainment on the 1st tee this morning was absolutely memorable." Rankin applauds the galleries, "so partial and so gracious." She says, "It was torturous fun this week. I spent the week with twelve players and twelve friends."

Later that night the Europeans drop by to visit. Amidst the exhaustion, the exhilaration, and the disappointment, general merriment ensues. Drinks are served. Golf balls are blasted across the lake. Rankin, in her only clumsy moment of the week, makes "a feeble effort" to learn the macarena.

The evening ends when a golf cart driven by Joanne Morley crashes and hurls Beth Daniel into an iron fence, splitting open her head.

Sunday, bloody Sunday.

Monday, Sept. 23

"Camilla Sneaks Off to Balmoral" (Daily Mirror)
"Abject Europe Humiliated in Singles Battle" (The Independent)

Well before dawn the U.S. players gather in the lobby for bus rides to the airport and flights back to America. They walk through the castlelike entrance into the black night, tiptoeing through the graveyard. They take with them the crown jewel of women's golf, a bond with their teammates that is a rare treasure in a sport so relentlessly competitive and individualistic, and memories that will last a lifetime.

CHAPTER 10

New York and Pennsylvania: The Winnowing Process

Midway through the second round of the $725,000 JAL Big Apple Classic at the venerable Wykagyl Country Club in New Rochelle, New York, Caroline Pierce vaults to the top of the leader board.

Yesterday Pierce shot 72 on a wicked early October day that resembled the final-round conditions at the McDonald's LPGA Championship in Wilmington, with temperatures in the 40s and 50s and strong, cold winds. Only Dottie Pepper and Vicki Goetze matched par of 71. No less than 32 golfers shot snowmen—80 or above—on a day that seemed nippy enough to produce them.

The scores were abnormal. But everything is abnormal this year. Usually the tournament is played in midsummer. Usually it's a 72-hole event with weekend television coverage on NBC.

But NBC, a.k.a. The Great God Television, was booked up with the Olympics. It "suggested" the JAL Big Apple Classic might want to temporarily move to the first week of October in 1996. It "suggested" the tournament be reduced to 54 holes and end on Saturday, since NBC's Sunday schedule in October was filled up with NFL football and baseball playoff games.

JAL (Japan Airlines) and the LPGA bowed, kissed the master's ring, and bundled up in overcoats.

Even in the summer, Wykagyl is no walk in the park. Built in 1905 and subsequently remodeled by both Donald Ross and A. W. Tillinghast, the course is carved out of vast, towering, dense forests of dark-green-leafed oak and maple. On land where Native American tribes and Dutch and Huguenot pioneers once roamed, narrow ribbons of green fairway flow up and down hilly terrain marked with rock outcroppings.

Flames of orange and patches of rust, tan, brown, yellow, and red lick the trees. Pumpkins decorate the grounds and tee boxes. Pigskins and political platitudes mark the season.

Players rank Wykagyl among the top layouts on Tour. (Blasé locals, surrounded by some of the finest golf territory in the world, place it behind famed Winged Foot and Baltusrol, and lesser-known Quaker Ridge, site of the 1997 Walker Cup.) It is usually in immaculate condition. This week, even with fairways softened by recent rains, the sloping greens have retained their customary greased-lightning quickness.

Pierce loves Wykagyl. She tied for second last year, the best finish of her career, four strokes behind Tracy Kerdyk. She describes Wykagyl as "a wonderful golf course, very tricky, very difficult."

Few expected her to challenge this week. After wrestling with her swing at the du Maurier two months ago, she continued to struggle. In front of 30 family members and friends at the Weetabix British Open, on a short, narrow course that suited her game, she missed the cut. She skipped Dayton (but forgot to officially withdraw, so she was fined $100 and wrote letters of apology to the pro-am partners she stood up), missed the cut at the State Farm Rail Classic in Springfield, Illinois, hit the ball better but putted poorly to miss her third consecutive cut at the Safeway Classic in Portland, and started strong but suffered the final-round blues again at the Safeco Classic in Seattle, closing with a dispiriting 78 to tie for thirtieth.

"I couldn't even get it on the clubface. I felt a little bit beaten up at the end of it, exhausted."

To add insult to injury, one of her pro-am partners in Seattle told caddie Rick Aune, within earshot of Pierce, "She's got a little loop in her swing, doesn't she."

Aune was horrified. Pierce wasn't exactly brimming with confidence and he thought the comment might throw her for an even bigger loop.

There are times when Pierce seems to be a small bundle of insecurities. She doesn't like people staring at her. She's intimidated by some of her competitors. She was a basket case of nerves in Nashville, eventually able to admit to herself she didn't think she belonged in the final group. She gets the heebie-jeebies when confronted with heights or bridges. On the surface, she doesn't seem particularly well suited to a game that tests your confidence with each and every swing.

But like the graphite shafts of her Top-Flite irons, Pierce has a backbone of deceptive strength. She's more candid about her frailties than most people. And she survived and prospered after an experience that would have haunted most of us for the rest of our days. Almost three years later, she finally can discuss it, as she did in Seattle a few weeks ago, without her throat becoming dry and constricted.

In November 1993, Pierce was restlessly half-asleep in her ground-floor apartment in a gated community near The Woodlands in Houston at 2:30 in the morning.

Suddenly there was this huge *bang, like an explosion. I sat up and the next thing I knew these three guys, who had kicked in the door, are in my apartment shouting, "Police!"*

"You have the wrong apartment," I said.

The next thing I knew, they were on the bed. They pulled my comforter off and they threw me on the floor, and then they put the comforter over me and put a gun to my head.

They were asking me all sorts of questions like "Where's your money?" "What's your ATM number?" "Where's your jewelry?" They also got my car keys. They had smashed the window of my Honda, but couldn't get it started. So they looked on my State Farm insurance card for my apartment number, then broke in, in hopes of getting the keys as well as quick money.

At least two of them had guns. They were in there for about twenty minutes. I was in a crouching position with my head down most of the time. But I remember staring at one kid at one point. He was pointing a gun at my head and the gun was shaking.

I remember thinking I was never going to see my mom again. I thought I was going to die, I really did. Because I had seen them.

I guess I was lucky. There was a girl about three months before who had been raped by one of the guys during another robbery. I found out from the detectives afterward that the leaders of the gang were upset with the guy who raped the girl, because he was wasting time; they were there for money.

Finally they ran out the back door. One of them went to get my car, keys in hand. But my neighbor confronted him, so they decided just to run.

[LPGA player] Tara Fleming was the first person I called. She was an old roommate and lived just up the street with her parents. She and her mother came right down. Tara was wonderful.

I had to play in a tournament that week. I was extremely calm, spooky calm. Two or three months later I was playing in Tucson. On the 9th hole I hit two balls in the water and broke into tears. I made the turn and got on with it, but I spent the next three or four days crying a lot. You think you're fine and dandy with it, but you're not.

Pierce wound up testifying against one of her juvenile assailants, caught in a subsequent robbery. "They took us in a room and I was sitting opposite this kid. They said, 'Will you tell us what happened,' and it's almost like you're a victim all over again. I can't imagine these girls who get raped and then have to testify."

For a while, Pierce found it hard to sleep. She still feels uneasy whenever she visits Houston.

Pierce shrugged off the comment from the pro-am partner in Seattle. A few holes later, after she hit a particularly good drive, caddie Aune said loudly, "Pretty good shot for someone with a loop in their swing." The pro-am partner got the message; he said little the rest of the round.

After a week off at home in Scottsdale—Pierce got so pumped up watching the Solheim Cup on TV she plans to play enough tournaments in Europe in 1997 and 1998 to be eligible for the European team—she returned to action last week at the Fieldcrest Cannon Classic in Charlotte. Recovering from a heavy cold, Pierce tied for thirty-fifth, 13 shots behind Trish Johnson, who shot a final-round 64. (Johnson picked up a check for $75,000, and said, "I would still swap this for a victory [in the Solheim Cup] last week," which would have been worth, in monetary terms, zero.)

But Pierce found a rainbow glimmer of hope during a final-round 70. Armed with a new 9-wood and her old Tad Moore putter, Pierce hit the ball extremely well and left lots of good putts hanging on the lip of the slow greens.

So two days ago at Wykagyl, when another pro-am partner told her, "You got a funny loop in your swing, don't you?" Pierce just laughed.

"I've got that Jim Furyk swing going again, Rick," she said to Aune.

The only thing that bothered her yesterday, other than frigid weather, was the 164-yard 16th hole, requiring a tee shot over a swale to a macabre green set in a hillside. The green is an oval, cantilevered from left to right and back to front. Members come out to snicker at the sight of the best women golfers in the world three- and four-whacking. Or, in this case, nudging, as barely tapped putts careen down the slope like peas rolling across a tilted dinner plate. Pierce, after a wonderful iron to eight feet left of the pin, watched a carefully struck birdie effort curl just to the right of the cup and trickle ten feet down the slope. Easy bogey.

"It's a joke," she fumed after the round. "That hole should be blown up and redone."

By the time she reaches the back nine of the second round, Pierce is the only player in the field who is under par. Only about 40 people are following Pierce, Karrie Webb, and Hiromi Kobayashi. About half are Japanese—Kobayashi, sponsored by JAL, has been tracked by Japanese media and JAL functionaries all week. (When she won here in 1993, a victory broadcast in Japan, Kobayashi was touted as the next great Japanese star, the heir apparent to Ayako Okamoto.)

Prior to 1995, the JAL Big Apple Classic drew more volunteers than spectators. At least it seemed that way. In a city boasting the likes of the

Yankees and Knicks, the JAL Big Apple was lost in the frenetic shuffle. Last year, an aggressive marketing campaign lured 64,000 fans to Wykagyl. But now, as Yogi Berra would say, "It's déjà vu all over again," as the lousy fall weather and the obsession with the Yankees keeps spectators away in droves.

Leaves are falling and autumn colors deepening by the minute on another raw, windy, fall day. The cut, which falls at 153, is the highest of the year. Betsy King, who won here in 1990 and 1992, shoots 75-80. Helen Alfredsson shoots 75-80, Leslie Spalding shoots 80-84. Wykagyl assistant pro Cathy Ronan, who knows the subtleties of the layout the way a symphony musician understands the nuances of his favorite composer, shoots 86-94, a snowman and, what, a hangman?

But the small knot of fans is dazzled by Webb, who is crushing drives some 50 yards past Pierce and Kobayashi.

"Smoke!" says a younger fan in a baseball jacket.

"Holy shit!" exclaims a bearded dude in shades.

"This girl is, in my opinion, the best golfer in the world, pound for pound," says an opinionated middle-aged New Yorker, a stogie jammed between his teeth and a pink cap reading "Cornell Volleyball" on his head. "She has a better swing than Mickey Wright."

But Pierce is attracting some attention too. When she spanks a good drive on the 379-yard 14th hole, the dude in the shades says, "Can you imagine that? That little thing?"

Webb, as aggressive as always, is struggling on and around Wykagyl's speedy, tricky greens, hampered by a lack of local knowledge. Pierce, on the other hand, is finding the low side of the pin on her approach shots. After birdieing five holes on the front nine, she adds another on No. 14 after a glorious 7-wood to 12 feet.

After a three-putt bogey on No. 15, Pierce bounces right back. Her 6-iron on No. 16, the hole she suggested blowing up yesterday, rolls up four feet from the cup, leaving her a sidehill, uphill slider. It's almost an ideal position, yet on this green, the hardest, the most arbitrary and capricious, the most unfair that the pros confront all year, she's still in three-putt territory. But she coaxes in the birdie attempt, drawing an "ooh!" from the gallery.

On the 396-yard 17th hole, Pierce yanks her second shot into the trap, leaving a long bunker shot. Pierce leads the LPGA in sand saves with over 55 percent. Her shot, hit low, barely clears the top of the bunker, yet trickles up next to the pin. A great shot. A near disaster.

The type of break that a golfer needs to move to the top.

As the sun sinks below the treetops, Pierce pars the 18th hole to complete a seven-birdie, three-bogey 67, a masterpiece on a day when Michelle McGann, who also shoots 67, is the only other golfer in the field to break 70. Pierce leads by three over McGann and Pepper, who are at even par 142.

Pierce is interviewed at greenside by a few radio and TV reporters, the lights of the cameras illuminating the twilight. Then she meets the rest of the press in the interview room.

"I'm not a particularly long hitter," she tells the scribes, "but I hit the ball really straight." Asked if she's been in the lead going into the final round before, Pierce mentions Nashville, adding with a smile, "Don't ask me what I did there."

"What did you do there?"

"What did I do?" says Pierce, trying to remember. "Seventy-six. [Actually it was 77.] But I'm playing better now than I was then. I'm hitting the ball much better."

A reporter from *Newsday* asks Pierce if she ever considered quitting the Tour, given her early lack of success. Pierce replies that she thought about it a few times.

The reporter asks why she stuck with it for so long. Pierce explains there is always hope. "You can have a bad week and win the next."

The reporter asks if her career is a study in perseverance. He asks whether Pierce considers herself "a ten-year overnight sensation?"

By now Pierce is irritated, although she doesn't show it.

"I don't know how to answer that question. What do you think?"

"We'll find out tomorrow," he says.

When she leaves the interview room, Pierce walks over to two reporters she knows.

"Wasn't that guy a jerk?" says Pierce.

A female reporter who witnessed the exchange certainly thinks so. Later, she will say, "I think he showed a lot of disrespect. He was so busy with his own arrogance, he was completely missing the big picture. Basically, he was belittling her."

"Fortunately, her diplomacy was impeccable. Greg Norman never would have taken it. PGA players would have eaten him for lunch."

The dissing and dismissing of Caroline Pierce is nothing new to the LPGA or its players. Outside of the World Wrestling Federation, probably no organization in sports has been beaten up as often or as consistently as the LPGA.

In 1989 Frank Chirkinian, the most powerful golf producer in the business, ripped the LPGA for the physical unattractiveness of its star players. When the LPGA foolishly demeaned itself in 1990 by displaying some of its athletes in swimsuits in its own public relations vehicle, *Fairway*, it was attacked for selling cheesecake. "After Nancy Lopez, the two words most commonly associated with the LPGA have become, 'Who cares?'" wrote Jaime Diaz in *Sports Illustrated.*

When the LPGA highlights the lifestyle of players with kids, instead of praise for emphasizing wholesome family values, it often has been slammed for, its critics allege, promoting heterosexuality in order to disguise its "lesbian problem."

When LPGA golfers shoot the lights out, critics complain the courses are too short and easy. When scores are high, they say the women can't play.

Most major corporations, such as IBM, employ image consultants. Yet the LPGA has been mocked for hiring a beauty and fashion consultant, Beverly Willey, even though its players are on stage all day long. Willey's work ranges from cutting hair (some players with thick ponytails, such as Kelly Robbins, get smacked in the face on their follow-through if their hair is not trimmed to the correct length), to cancer prevention sunscreen recommendations, to personal shopping, to nutritional advice, to tips for speeding up a player's morning grooming routine, to fashion suggestions for television (blacks and "brights," such as pink and lime green look good, white makes people look heavier).

Even reporters generally sympathetic to the LPGA regularly weigh in with advice and criticism. After the Ben Wright controversy, Geoff Russell, who covered the LPGA superbly for five years for *Golf World*, urged gay players to come out of the closet, citing the example of Martina Navratilova. In fact, Navratilova was outed by Judy Nelson's "galimony" suit. And book writers blithely suggest the LPGA turn its back on a sponsor who puts up a $1 million purse (not to mention dessert and waffle bars) because it is in the cigarette business.

Maybe it's a men versus women thing: the overwhelmingly male media corps judges, while the women of the LPGA try to please. And the more they try to please, the harsher the judgment.

Sociologist Todd Crosset, author of a book about the LPGA, *Outsiders in the Clubhouse* (1995), was "struck by the propensity of reporters to lecture players about golf, make suggestions, and offer guidance on managing the LPGA."

As the comment indicates, individual players often fare no better at the hands of the media than does the LPGA as an organization. Late in 1989 Betsy King, who had won the McDonald's and the U.S. Open and sewn up Player of the Year honors, was asked by local reporters, "What kind of year are you having?"

Two years later when King went to Colonial in Fort Worth in search of her third straight U.S. Open title, she was almost tarred and feathered after rejecting a suggestion that the LPGA, which hadn't played in Texas for almost a decade, needed a regular event in the state to truly be considered a big league tour.

King responded, "There's a good ole boy mentality that's tough to go up against. We don't need to come to Texas to be successful."

The response from the media, wrote *Golf World*'s Terry Galvin, was to treat King "like a horse thief," roasting her in the local sports sections. King returned to the interview room Friday after a second-round 78, her chances for an historic three-peat as dead as Colonial's greens, fried to a crisp by midsummer temperatures approaching 100 degrees. She was assaulted again for having the temerity to criticize the deplorable putting surfaces. Finally King said, "When we [LPGA players] complain about conditions, we're just bitches. But when the men do it, people think, 'Well, it really must have been hard.'" Then she broke into tears.

Galvin wrote, "LPGA players face this media problem every week: a hockey writer, a basketball writer or even, in some cases, a bowling writer is assigned to cover their event. Many do not know golf. Many do not know Betsy King from Beth Daniel. Yet, for the most part, these players have great patience with some of the most absurd questions. And, they are honest to a fault."

But it's not only the local media that get it wrong. Early in her career Sheehan, a hard-charging competitor, was erroneously tagged with the same type of off-the-links aggressiveness by a *Sports Illustrated* writer who noted the bumper sticker on the car Sheehan was driving: WOMEN WHO SEEK EQUALITY WITH MEN LACK AMBITION.

The anecdote followed her for years. Only one problem—it wasn't Sheehan's car. "No, I don't describe myself as a feminist," said Sheehan in 1985, explaining the misunderstanding. "I just try to be a good person and be nice to people."

When Annika Sorenstam won her second-straight U.S. Open at Pine Needles in June, *SI*'s Michael Bamberger wrote a glowing piece comparing her accomplishemnt with that of Ben Hogan. Yet *SI* ran a story on Tom Watson's victory in the Memorial in its regular issue and banished Sorenstam to its "Golf Plus" insert and a much smaller circulation. Sure, Watson's first win in nine years was a nice story, but it hardly was on a par with back-to-back U.S. Open triumphs.

It may be impossible for an LPGA player to make the regular edition through her exploits inside the ropes. *SI* has run two stories about the LPGA in 1996 in the regular edition: the article about Muffin Spencer-

Devlin coming out, a Scorecard item detailing Laura Baugh's bout with alcoholism.

Even coverage about the LPGA in *SI*'s "Golf Plus" insert is hit or miss. Last year it annointed Michelle McGann and Laura Davies as the two best players on the Tour, after McGann's first two victories. Elevating McGann, after a brief hot streak, over Neumann, Pepper, Robbins, Mallon, and Daniel, was just plain ignorant.

The New York Times, although not so dumb, is just as dismissive. It played Watson's win on the front page of the sports section and buried Sorenstam. This year it didn't bother to send its ace golf writer, Larry Dorman, to either the U.S. Women's Open or the Solheim Cup.

Even the great Dan Jenkins, author of *Dead Solid Perfect,* turns into a puddin' head when he condescends to mention the ladies. In a rare reference to women in *Fairways & Greens* (1994), he votes for Babe Zaharias over Mickey Wright as the best woman golfer in history. ("Babe Zaharias couldn't carry Patty Berg's golf bag," said Mickey Wright.) In a 1994 preview piece in *Golf Digest,* Jenkins writes:

"Only a macho pig would say this and then duck before the feminists throw firebombs at him: The woman to watch in '94 is Helen Alfredsson, whether she is winning or not."

(Alfredsson, for her part, has eschewed the role of sex symbol. In Judy Rankin's book, *A Woman's Guide to Better Golf,* Alfredsson says, "I think we need to get the message out to women that it's okay to be an athlete. You can do other things, too, but it's a tough balancing act out here. It's hard trying to be pretty, trying to be feminine, trying to be skinny, trying to have your hair done nice, having long nails and then hitting the ball 300 yards. I mean, put that equation together. It does not work.")

After being kicked around for decades, it's not surprising that LPGA players welcome the media with smiles on their faces but a measure of fear and loathing in their hearts.

Liz Kahn, who spent years working on *The LPGA: The Unauthorized Version,* wrote that she was, for a long time, considered by the players as "unacceptable, because I represented the media, to [sic] whom they were very wary."

I found the same wariness from a number of players, caddies, and rules officials, particularly early in the season. Like the hippies who were figuratively either on the bus or off the bus in Tom Wolfe's *Electric Kool-Aid Acid Test,* people are either inside the ropes or outside the ropes on the LPGA Tour, and journalists are almost always outside.

Amy Alcott's manager had a cow when I tried to arrange an interview in

Los Angeles. Betsy King greeted me like a foot soldier for the Antichrist when I introduced myself in Tucson (but later went out of her way to provide interview time). Donna Andrews was so dismissive I felt like one of Leona Helmsley's servants. Stony-faced rules officials looked like they were dying to slap me with a minimum $200 "conduct-unbecoming" fine, but, to their amazement, couldn't find journalism listed as a sin along with cursing and club throwing. One star player advised other golfers not to talk to me.

The sins of sloth and ignorance comingle in the LPGA media center. Probably the biggest complaint by LPGA players is the sheer laziness of the golf media. Professional golfers work harder than almost any other group of people in the world. Then they observe reporters or broadcasters—making a not-so-small fortune—who can't even bother to open an *LPGA Player Guide* or show up on the range, much less the golf course.

"TV announcers need to do their homework," says Juli Inkster. "It's embarrassing." Several scholarly studies have found that women athletes are most often described on network TV and radio in ways that trivialize them or portray them as abnormal.

(Even when the announcers aren't denigrating them, the production quality of most LPGA telecasts helps consign the Tour and its players to Nielsen-ratings oblivion. If the LPGA didn't know bad TV, it wouldn't know TV at all. Except for the U.S. Open [NBC], Nabisco Dinah Shore [ABC], McDonald's LPGA Championship [CBS], and The Golf Channel's fine, but seldom seen coverage, most LPGA events are broadcast on the cheap, with fewer cameras and lesser announcers. Some telecasts seem to consist almost exclusively of long-lens shots of golfers with faces hidden under visors marching across drab, washed-out looking greenery while commentators try to compensate with foghorn blasts of hype and hot air. People who have only seen women's golf on the tube often are stunned when they go to a tournament and find themselves in the middle of a vibrant, colorful, dramatic world pulsating with energy and excitement.)

Mix some New Nastiness—the tabloid mentality that has saturated journalism and seeped into the media tent—in with the sloth and ignorance and the brew turns noxious. Both *Golf World* and *Golfweek* now run gossip columns. Golf writers stalk Tiger Woods's slender frame like jaguars on the scent of an impala. At least four books on Woods already are on the shelves or in production. In the preface to his new book *Tiger: The Making of a Champion,* Tim Rosaforte recounts how he "got in the face" of an uncooperative Woods to tell him that Woods needs the media (and Rosaforte) as much as the media needs Woods. Reports circulate that Woods has begun to shut out reporters and fans, closing himself off from the frenzy around him. Expect a critical backlash to follow.

As Bill Fields, a reporter for *Golf World*, wrote, "Second-guessing can be done with a smile or a sneer." The latter has become much more prevalent than the former, as the same kind of gratuitous nastiness that has turned political reporting into a swamp of cynicism begins to color golf writing as well.

Add a little narcissism—reporters more interested in their own golf games than in those of the pros they are covering—and the mix takes on a peculiar flavor. Case in point: Jeff Rude from *Golfweek*, who played golf with Laura Davies and wrote about trying to outdrive her. The title of the article: "Marlboro Man Gets Smoked by Davies."

Rude is an excellent writer and his piece was funny and suitably self-deprecating, especially when Davies borrowed a left-handed club and out-drove him as a southpaw. But as a letter to the editor from Bonnie Westfall of Leesburg, Virginia, asked, what was the point? "Men don't need to 'check their machismo at the pro-shop counter' if they play with a woman who hits the ball a long way. How about just saying, 'Nice shot' and getting on with the round?"

With a rare opportunity to spend a day with one of the most interesting people in golf, Rude chose to write primarily about himself.

Stir in a large dollop of often intertwined sexism and homophobia, and the mix turns poisonous. Reporters have been labeling women athletes as freaks for decades. In the 1930s Paul Gallico wrote that Babe Zaharias's amazing feats were a "compensation . . . she would not or could not compete with women at their own best game—man-snatching." In 1960 William Furlong wrote an article in *The New York Times Magazine* that was headlined, "Do Men Make Passes at Athletic Lasses?" Furlong concluded that, except for a few sports such as swimming, women jocks "surrendered" their sex. In 1995, Ben Wright railed about golfers playing a "butch game."

Perhaps the most perverse example came in 1995, shortly after the Ben Wright controversy, when *Sports Illustrated* offered a well-known LPGA player $10,000 to reveal her homosexuality. The offer was conveyed by an *SI* writer.

"The money could have helped," says the player, who, at the time, was struggling with her game. "But I said no. I'd rather scrub floors than be exploited like that."

Jim Ritts is almost amused at the media's obsession with homosexuality.

"The lesbian issue for some writers is like a flame to a moth," says Ritts. "A moth doesn't know why it goes to the flame; they don't know why they're asking the question."

As sociologist Todd Crosset discovered, the LPGA media center is a fascinating arena to study human behavior. He was amazed at the gossip about the private lives of the players, concluding that it was partly a way for reporters to establish status among their peers. (Golf writers swap gossip about PGA players, too, and no one is immune, not even Arnold Palmer.)

But Crosset thought the fascination with players' private lives also reflected "a desire to discredit the Tour and at the same time to sell stories about it." As one player told Crosset:

"I think that [the LPGA's image] is created by a lot of jealousy and envy. . . . I think men have a little problem with seeing women that make a couple of hundred thousand more than they do a year." Especially men stuck on the LPGA beat, which is considered to be, in golf media circles, the minor leagues.

Men have a bigger problem with women who are richer and hit a golf ball farther than they do. In some ways, LPGA players are quite intimidating. They are, generally speaking, bright, poised, articulate, and attractive. Most pro golfers are adults; many are wives and mothers.

They are not fantasy figures like ice skaters, nubile, scantily clad wisps selling grace and beauty in a sanitized, sexy sheen. (Nancy Kerrigan's pedestal was yanked away as soon as she revealed herself to be competitive and catty—i.e., human.) Or anorexic gymnasts, who prance and preen like toy poodles at the Westminster Dog Show.

Unlike female athletes in other sports, most of whom are kids and can be treated as such, pro golfers are formidable individuals.

Sports sociologist Don Sabo believes the put-downs of the LPGA Tour are a reaction to such unease. In 1989 he told SI:

"The L word is very much alive on the LPGA Tour, just as it is wherever single women are successful. By calling a woman a lesbian, men can discount a woman's achievement and keep her institutionally subordinate. There are some societies in the world that forbid two women to be alone for fear they will band together and try to break down male dominance, and there are traces of that same fear in America."

And there is real fear that male privileges in golf, most clearly expressed by discriminatory tee time and membership policies, are as outmoded as hickory shafts and gutta-percha balls. Hence the fierce opposition to change. As Marcia Chambers put it in The Unplayable Lie: The Untold Story of Women and Discrimination in American Golf, "If the Berlin Wall and communism could collapse in less than a year, might there be hope for an end to men's-only weekend tee times at America's private golf and country clubs? Probably not."

If LPGA players are treated seriously, it hastens the day that equality will be realized. When equality is realized, the game will be lost. (I know, I know, there's nothing worse than being stuck behind a foursome of women who can't play a lick. Except perhaps being stuck behind a foursome of men who can't play a lick and are too oblivious to their inadequacies to let anyone play through.) By putting the LPGA in its place, by raising the master's hand in warning, it helps preserve the status quo.

Crosset believes the media has a strong interest in preserving the status quo as well. "Sports writers and reporters have a personal stake in maintaining sport as a 'manly' institution and may have difficulty reconciling the existence of superb women athletes with their beliefs."

Seems plausible. And even if you don't buy the theory, it's a fact that very few women have achieved positions of power as golf writers, editors, or broadcasters.

As Charlie Mechem puts it, "What if tomorrow, ninty-five percent of the press room and ninety-five percent of the broadcast media at LPGA tournaments were women? I guarantee you, the reporting would be different."

For now, while every mother's son is chasing, or wishing he were chasing, the tale of the Tiger, great stories are strewn like diamonds on the fairways of the LPGA Tour, just waiting to be scooped up.

Caroline Pierce finds about ten notes on her locker from players wishing her good luck when she arrives at Wygakyl on Saturday. She's already dealt with her first dilemma—what to wear.

Last year Pierce sported an English straw hat for the final round. NBC's Bob Trumpy didn't like it. He told the nationwide audience she needed a new chapeau. NBC's Marlene Floyd leaped to her defense.

Top-Flite, naturally enough, wants its logo prominently displayed on TV. Pierce doesn't have a lot of Top-Flite-embossed clothes that are suitable for cold weather, so she improvises with an off-white short-sleeve jersey with Top-Flite on the sleeve over a white turtleneck, and a Top-Flite khaki baseball cap. When she enters the fitness van to stretch, Dottie Pepper does a double-take. They are wearing virtually identical pants, brown slacks with a subtle herringbone design.

Clothes are the least of her problems. Today Pierce has to handle: (1) the ups and downs of Wykagyl, the toughest course of the season; (2) playing partners Pepper and McGann, heroines of the Solheim Cup and winners of seven tournaments since June; (3) a crowd of about 19,000, a good percentage following the final threesome, staring at the underdog, expecting her to fold; (4) her own demons—nerves, her collapse at Nashville, the slights and slams and insults from pro-am partners to reporters, who view her as a loser.

Mary Bryan, who spoke to Pierce in the locker room, thinks she's ready for the test.

"She's focused enough that Michelle and Dottie won't bother her. The maturity in her game is a perfect example of how some players grow in a building block kind of way. Compared to last year her putting is better, her bad shots are better, and she's not as intimidated. The whole key is whether she can conquer the golf course."

Caddie Rick Aune thinks she's ready too.

"It's the best frame of mind I've seen her stay in for an entire week. You want to get mad, the course is so tough, but you just can't."

The butterflies are racing, although not as badly as in Nashville, as Pierce warms up on the range. She answers a few questions from NBC's Donna Caponi, gathering information for the afternoon telecast. To calm the jitters, Pierce mentally "plays" the first few holes on the range, as well as other shots she has felt uncomfortable with on specific holes. McGann, near the other end of the range, is wearing a broad-brimmed white hat with white sequins and black-and-white zebra stripes and a black bow, black slacks and sweater vest and a white turtleneck. She's the center of attention. She offers a toothpaste-ad smile for the photographers and fans as she launches mortar shots with her Great Big Bertha. "That was far!" says a wide-eyed boy. "That was so far I couldn't even *see* where it went."

It's a cool, sunny morning with a few high white clouds floating across a deep blue sky. The fierce winds have moderated, but it's chilly enough for Pierce to wear black handwarmers as she waits on the 1st tee, looking almost stricken as the adrenaline rushes and the tension builds. Pepper, in a heavy camel hair sweater, yawns nervously several times, antsy to be underway.

The packed crowd offers a few whoops for McGann and a big cheer for New York native Pepper, pride of Saratoga Springs.

Pierce enjoys playing with McGann. They were paired in the final round at the JAL Big Apple last year. Both shot 69 to finish in a four-way tie for second.

"She's very easy to play with," says Pierce. "Very complimentary and considerate." And, like Pierce, a fast player.

Although Pierce gets along fine with Pepper, she's not as happy about being paired with her. "We'll see," she said last evening, concerned about Pepper's intensity, tunnel vision, and methodical pace.

Soon she's really worried. After she "whiffs" an 8-iron into a bunker on the downhill 140-yard 2nd hole and explodes nicely to five feet from the pin, she watches Pepper ram in a 30-foot birdie putt.

"Here we go," Pierce thinks grimly. "She's gonna get fired up now." She already is—Pepper's eyes are blazing as she strides up to fish the ball from the cup.

Pierce hits a tentative putt. It rims out. Shades of Nashville. Her three-shot lead already has shrunk to a slender stroke.

"It's a long, hard golf course," Pierce consoles herself as she walks off the green. "There are going to be bogeys."

The players tee off on the 482-yard 3rd hole. Pepper and McGann and the caddies walk across a narrow wooden bridge, about 50 feet high and 100 yards long, that transports them over a steep drop-off. Pierce, however, trots down the hill and up the other side. The bridge seems innocuous, but Pierce says, "It's so narrow. It makes me dizzy looking down it."

But there are much bigger bridges that Pierce must cross today to achieve what she has worked for and dreamed of during the past nine years.

Pierce has bounced back from bogeys all week. After watching Pepper relentlessly stalk and thoroughly study a birdie putt for what seems like at least two minutes before missing, Pierce lines up a 12-foot birdie chance of her own. She strikes it smoothly, but as the ball approaches the cup, she fears she's misread it. When it holds the line and tumbles over the edge, a feeling of relief sweeps through her. ("Mentally, that was really big.")

Everything grinds to a halt on the tee at the 197-yard 4th hole, playing into a tough crosswind.

"Fancy meeting you here," Ralph Scarinzi says to Missie McGeorge and her caddie Teresa Durand as they wait for the green to clear. Another trio, Jane Geddes, Margaret Platt, and Gail Graham, who began play on No. 10, are waiting in the wings.

Pepper, the stretching maniac, limbers up a bit then sits on her Titleist bag. McGann talks fashion with some friends in the crowd. Geddes chats with tennis star Gigi Fernandez, a spectator today.

Trying to stay loose, Pierce makes the rounds, talking briefly with everyone—players, caddies, even reporters. She mentions Japan, where she'll be playing in two weeks. It's not her favorite place. "Take some laxatives with you," she advises me. "The rice will get you." The interview room is not her favorite place either. She's still mulling over her exchange last evening with the *Newsday* reporter.

"He was rude, wasn't he? Did I handle it okay?"

Eventually the green clears. Pierce smacks a solid 3-wood just short of the fringe. McGann and Pepper both hook shots behind a huge, double-trunk tree to the left of the green. Both are stymied; they have to chip out away from the putting surface. McGann misses a five-foot putt and double-bogeys. Pepper sinks a tough downhill four-footer and bogeys. Pierce, after a fine chip, knocks a three-foot par putt into the heart.

"Yes!" a few voices call out from the vast gallery.

The margin is three again. "Well, maybe I can do this," she tells herself, surprised at the poor tee shots by McGann and Pepper. Although she's not striking the ball as crisply today, her chipping is sharp. "If I can get the ball around the green," she thinks, "I'll be fine."

She puts on a short-game clinic the next few holes. Twenty yards short of the green on the 399-yard 5th hole, Pierce pitches up a slope to a blind green and the ball winds up inches from the cup, as "Good shot!" rings out from McGann and Pepper. Left of the green on the 357-yard 6th hole, Pierce delicately chips from wiry grass to a swift putting surface.

"Release!" she commands, as the ball trickles to tap-in distance.

The contrast with Nashville is stunning. Pierce's composure is as magnificent as her array of skill and touch.

Pepper appreciates the clinic. Unlike many people, she didn't expect Pierce to fold today. Last year they were paired in the final group at Tucson. Pepper won. But Pepper says that Pierce, who finished eighth, "hung right in there."

Meanwhile McGann is missing every makable putt. And Pepper has hit the wall as the exertion of the last two weeks at the Solheim Cup and in Charlotte, where she finished third after taking a lead into the final round, catches up with her. On the 196-yard 7th hole, after Pierce rifles a terrific 3-wood 20 feet from the stick, Pepper skanks a shot, a scrape so ugly it lands 30 yards short of the green. She double-bogeys. Suddenly Pierce is five in front of Laurie Brower and six up on McGann and Pepper.

Pierce continues to dazzle around the greens. When she dumps an 8-iron into the front trap on the 365-yard 8th hole and sees the lie, her heart sinks.

"Oh shit," she thinks. "Bad rake job." The ball is nestled into a ridge of sand. Pierce may be the leading bunker player on Tour, but she's not even sure she can escape from the beach, much less get it close. After a long, worried examination of the situation, she decides to cut it out with an exaggerated outside-in swing.

The ball floats out softly and checks to a halt next to the pin.

She digs out another shot on the 346-yard 9th hole, this one from a fairway divot onto the green. "Really good shot there," says Pepper, noticing the lie. Then Pierce, holding a six-shot lead, walks up a hill toward a huge crowd in back of the putting surface.

"Only Greg Norman could blow this kind of lead," says a reporter in the media center, just before Pierce pulls a three-foot putt and three-whacks for bogey.

Five-shot lead. Nine holes to play. An eternity.

Pierce exits the green and is swallowed up in the massive gallery.

"Excuse me, excuse me," she keeps saying. Pierce has forgotten about the three-putt. She's focusing on the rugged 401-yard 10th hole, which she double-bogeyed Thursday, as well as the next few holes of the back nine, which have brutalized the field.

"You can't get through them without a couple of bogeys," says Rick Aune. "Those holes are so hard. You know they're coming."

NBC is on the air. The introduction focuses exclusively on Pepper and McGann. Pierce's name is never mentioned. Johnny Miller isn't in the booth this week. Too bad. Without Miller, NBC is, at best, mediocre. But when the candid, brilliant, shoot-from-the lip announcer is on the air, he elevates NBC to the top of the chart.

The journey up and down the hills of the back nine begins. After the first two rounds, Pierce was surprised to be the only golfer under par. She didn't think the course was *that* difficult. Today, a fraction off her game, she knows what everyone else in the field knows—that Wykagyl is playing like a U.S. Open course. (The field will average 76.54, highest of the year.)

Her lead slowly erodes. Pierce survives the 10th with a superb fairway wood and a four-foot slider for par. But her relief is short-lived. The 365-yard 11th hole is a killer for short hitters. A deep fairway bunker was added in 1995, and it narrows the landing area for most players to about 15 yards. "You've got to be kidding," Pierce said when she saw the new trap.

It doesn't bother McGann; she simply bombs a drive over the bunkers. But both Pepper and Pierce find the sand and have to pitch out well short of the green. Suddenly feeling shaky, Pierce flies a wedge to the back of the green, leaving a long, treacherous downhill putt. She almost four-whacks, eventually coaxing in a downhill four-footer for double-bogey.

She bounces back, parring 12 and flagging a gorgeous 8-iron to four feet on the 139-yard 13th hole, drawing a "Whooh!" from the gallery on a hillside overlooking the green.

For the first time all day Pierce looks at the leader board, and it calms her. She's surprised to find no one is making a run at her. She's four up on McGann, who has steadied despite her putting woes.

Pierce backs off her putt when someone moving in the crowd breaks her concentration. "She's not comfortable with her line," NBC reporter Donna Caponi murmurs into her microphone at greenside. Actually, she's so focused on the line she forgets to hit the putt, and it creeps right to the lip of the cup and curls away. Pierce, amazed, laughs. But she knows peril lies ahead.

The 377-yard 14th hole is playing dead into the wind. After a good drive that sinks into a poor lie, Pierce tries to cut a 3-wood 175 yards to an elevated green. It squirts into the front right-hand bunker.

There are no gallery ropes on the 14th hole and the 15th fairway, so the crowds temporarily are left behind. Except for the damned Met Life blimp droning overhead, it's deathly quiet as the players walk to the green, with only a handful of NBC personnel and reporters and photographers accompanying them.

Pierce finds the solitude peaceful and soothing. She hits another great bunker shot, but it skids five feet past the pin. McGann, with a chance to apply noose-tightening pressure, leaves her 15-foot birdie try on the low side. Pierce hits the par putt just as she intends, but misreads it and watches the ball spin off the edge of the hole. Pierce has missed short putts on Nos. 9, 13, and 14. She's four over par for the day. Her lead is down to three.

Four holes to play, including two par fives, which McGann can reach in two. When Pierce won cross-country races in high school, "it was more determination than talent. I didn't like people in front of me." To hang on in this endurance test, she'll need large measures of both determination and talent.

McGann hits the uphill 432-yard 15th hole in two. The gallery, which has been waiting for the golfers at the green, is silent and tense as Pierce lines up a 20-foot birdie putt. Most of the crowd is rooting for the underdog now, but they can sense it slipping away. Pierce misses. McGann two-putts for birdie. Two-stroke lead over McGann and Tina Barrett, who has roared out of the pack with a final round 67.

Barrett began the day ten strokes behind Pierce. She left a good-luck note on the locker of her good friend. Now she's told to stick around for a possible playoff. She's interviewed in the NBC booth, watching the action with mixed feelings as Pierce teeters on the brink.

McGann hits a short iron to the front fringe of the tilted plate of the 16th green, playing 150 yards today, a good position beneath the flagstick, cut into the right front portion of the green.

Pierce, last to play, is almost unbearably nervous. She hates this hole. She knows it can destroy her. "Make a good solid swing," she tells herself. Under the heaviest pressure of her career, she does just that, crunching a 5-iron "as good as I could hit it."

The ball soars toward the center of the green. It lands and kicks toward the flag. Kicks hard. When it trickles past the pin, the crowd's cheering abruptly stops, as if someone had flicked off a light switch. Pierce faces a 12-foot sidehill, downhill putt. The fans know she's screwed.

In the locker room, players watching TV and rooting for Pierce yell, "Sit! Sit! Sit!" Then, "Aw, shit!" They know she's screwed too. The diabolical 16th green, which Pierce suggested blowing up, has devoured more victims today. Meg Mallon, standing on the tee earlier, watched a player tap a downhill putt that took off like it was on a greased baking sheet and rolled off the green. Mallon then hit an iron 15 feet above the hole, and did the same thing. Her subsequent four-putt was almost routine.

Only the NBC announcers don't seem to grasp the situation. After virtually ignoring Pierce most of the telecast, they're raving about her tee shot.

Pierce walks up to the green and marks her ball with a wry smile on her face. Under immense pressure, she hit a near-perfect shot, and she's screwed. "Boy, here we go," she says to herself. Later she will peg the chances of making the putt at 100–1. It's a fair estimate.

It's been a long day in the Fun House for Pierce. She's tiptoed across a succession of higher and narrower bridges. Now she's poised on a wire between two skyscrapers.

There's almost no chance of keeping the ball on the green. A 12-foot birdie putt is likely to become a 25-foot par putt or chip from the fringe. Maybe, if she catches a corner of the cup, the ball will stay on the green, but it won't be anywhere close. Maybe it's just not her lucky day.

McGann chips up 18 inches short of the cup. She's almost certain to head to No. 17 one shot behind (or even, if Pierce four-putts) with tons of momentum.

Pierce gets on with it. She picks a spot about six feet to the right of the cup. She'll try to putt up the slope to the spot, then let the ball descend, ever faster, toward its fate. Fans in a dense pack ring the back and sides of the green. Those closest to her can almost touch her as she lines up the putt.

Except for the thumping of their hearts, they stand as still as statues.

Pierce visualizes the putt rolling into the cup. She turns her body completely away from the hole, aiming for a spot in the universe, trusting her ability, trusting her nerve, trusting the faith that compelled her to join the Tour and pit herself against the best in the world, again and again and again, never quitting.

She strikes the putt as perfectly as is humanly possible. It rolls precisely over the spot Pierce has targeted, and begins to speed down the slope.

When the ball is four feet from the hole, Pierce yells, "Get in!" An instant later it disappears.

Pierce punches the air almost as violently as Tiger Woods. The explosive roar of the crowd envelops and deafens her. A singular thought, unbidden but incandescent, strikes her like a lightning bolt.

"I WON!!!!!!"

A stunned McGann misses her tap-in. As Pierce walks to the 17th tee, she marvels at her fist-pumping display. "Boy, that's not like me." She asks caddie Aune, "Was that obnoxious?"

Pierce bombs in a 30-foot birdie putt on the 396-yard 17th hole. "Big time," says an admiring fan at greenside. Pierce, who was just trying to two-putt, gives Aune an amused shrug and gets a pat on the back from McGann's looper, Donna Earley.

After popping two woods down the middle on the 481-yard 18th hole, Pierce approaches the green. Fall leaves are scattered over the fairway; a brilliant sun shines down. A few fans shout, "Caroline! Caroline!"

The golf has been brilliant, but Pierce could use some work on her victory stroll. After walking the wire and exiting the Fun House, Pierce finds herself a little dizzy. ("I was trying not to trip or fall on my ass.") She's a little embarrassed, too. ("I didn't know whether to wave my hat like the queen, or what.") But she's also filled with joy. "This is pretty cool," she tells Aune, giving the cheering crowd a sheepish little wave.

Up in the NBC booth, the commentators, who gave viewers little information about Pierce until her putt on No. 16, are gushing over her performance, especially when she delights the spectators with a final birdie by rolling home a 15-foot putt.

Pepper is the first to congratulate—and hug!—Pierce. She's showered with champagne by some of her pals. LPGA vice president Cindy Davis hugs her and quietly says, "See, nice people win, too."

Exhausted and relieved, Aune clutches the flag from the final hole. "It's fun when it's over. I never had a putt mean more to me than the one on sixteen."

It's the eighth victory for the 47-year-old Aune as an LPGA caddie. He calls it "the most rewarding. It was the hardest to get here. Nine years, 105 pounds, no one thought she could do it. *She* probably didn't think she could do it. She kept at it and kept at it and kept at it."

After interviews and the trophy presentation and an on-stage appearance to sing the chorus of "Under the Boardwalk" with The Drifters, who are entertaining at a posttournament party near the 18th green, Pierce gets into her rental car, closes the door, rolls up the window, and screams, "Yippie!!!" Then she starts laughing at herself.

Caroline goes into the city to celebrate with friends at dinner and the theater.

Later that night she dreams she is back on the 16th green, watching the most important putt of her career roll into the center of the cup as the roar of the crowd sweeps over her. When she awakes, her dream and reality are one and the same.

* * *

No mention of the JAL Big Apple on local news channels 2, 4, or 7 on Saturday night. On Sunday morning, *The New York Times* story ("Pierce Is Unlikely Winner in Big Apple") is on page 13 of the sports section.

The *New York Post* runs a tiny, four-paragraph blurb in its "Sports Shorts" section. It devotes almost a full page to an article by staffer Mark McLaughlin (complete with two pictures of the writer), detailing the 11-handicapper's performance in the JAL Big Apple pro-am a few days earlier. McLaughlin brags that he hit as many good shots as LPGA pro Allison Finney and claims she was impressed.

Pierce spends Sunday reliving her triumph. Almost literally. She plays in a posttournament pro-am at Wykagyl, with tees and pins unchanged from the final round.

The fruits of victory run deliciously through her mind: a check for $108,750; a silver trophy; a $2,500 certificate for a new Rolex; a three-year exemption; a spot in the field at the ITT Tour Championship in November, which is restricted to the top 30 money winners—Pierce now ranks twenty-third with $211,461; inclusion in the Chrysler-Plymouth Tournament of Champions in January (restricted to winners in 1995 and 1996); a $10,000 bonus from Top-Flite; a $5,000 bonus from Callaway; a big bottle of Korbel champagne; four pairs of preppy shoes from Pappagallo, which sponsored a booth at the tournament; "A" tee times ("I *love* 'A' tee times") for the next two years as Pierce takes her place among the Tour's elite.

Kutztown, Pennsylvania, located between Allentown and Reading, is two hours from Manhattan by car. In other respects it seems as distant from the Big Apple as the moon. Instead of the dizzying steel and glass towers of Manhattan, you see eight-foot-tall, tan-sheathed cornstalks waving in the breeze. Instead of yellow cabs, horns blaring, careening through snarled streets, you see black Amish buggies clip-clopping along the sides of the road. Tiny towns dot the area—Virginville, Fogelsville, Krumsville.

It is, in short, Betsy King country, a land of substance, values, and piety. King, one of the most remarkable people in sports, is roughly four parts ferocious competitor, four parts saint, one part shy schoolgirl, and one part scold. A resident of nearby Limekiln, King has spent the last five years working to get the inaugural edition of the $600,000 CoreStates Betsy King Classic off the launching pad.

Such hard work is nothing new for King. Although she's now in the Hall of Fame, it took her seven years to notch her first victory. After wandering in the wilderness, she found both Jesus and instructor Ed Oldfield in 1980. The former gave her faith and purpose; the latter gave her a reliable golf swing, one she honed the old-fashioned way. King worked like a dog, beating balls from sunrise to sunset. Rangy and strong, King was a basketball player as well as a golfer at Furman University before blowing out a knee. In many ways, she's the Larry Bird of golf, an excellent athlete who spent thousands of solitary hours practicing to become one of the all-time greats. "I enjoy practice more than playing," King said a few years ago. "It's more productive." From 1984 to 1995 King won 30 tournaments and five majors, a record unsurpassed, argued Geoff Russell in *Golf World,* by any player in the world, including Faldo or Norman.

A taciturn competitor, King clenches and grits her teeth as she starts her backswing, and peers intently at the ball as it soars toward the heavens. When King ran along the gallery rope slapping hands with the fans on the final hole of the 1992 LPGA Championship, which she won by 11 shots, it was as out of character as watching Clint Eastwood break into a song-and-dance routine.

She brings even more commitment, if that is possible, to religion. During an interview in 1991, she said that most people who go to church "just go through the motions. Then they walk out the door and that's it. You have to think about the Lord every day."

King walks the walk and talks the talk. She has, in fact, talked in tongues at church services. When she plays golf, hymns often run through her head.

John Dolaghan, director of the Fellowship of Christian Athletes (FCA), said, "I've never known anyone, let alone a professional athlete, who lives their faith more than Betsy."

King has been building houses for the poor with Habitat for Humanity for years. In 1987 she sacrificed a shot at year-end awards, skipping a late-season tournament to honor an HFH commitment. Next week King and about two dozen players and caddies will spend three days building a duplex in Reading for two families. (Even when she's serving the Lord, King remains a competitor. "We make up games," she told SI in 1991, "like who can hammer the most nails.") In 1993 and 1994 she and several other LPGA players visited Romania to provide aid for orphans of war. King shepherded a boy named Daniel, now 7, to his new adopted family in Seattle.

The 41-year-old King has a shy, soft-spoken manner. She doesn't preach; she prefers conversations to monologues. But the depth and intensity of her convictions invariably lead her to positions with a harsh edge. In 1991 King voiced admiration for the militant antiabortion protest group Operation Rescue, and expressed an interest in joining them.

"What about Christian tolerance," King was asked, a reference to the anger and hatred evidenced by many Operation Rescue demonstrators.

"Jesus wasn't tolerant," King replied. "He said, 'Hey, I'm the only way to God.' Tolerance is not what Christianity is based on."

But King, who has been harangued at tournaments by both pro-choice and antiabortion partisans, has softened a bit. She never marched with Operation Rescue. Although she opposes "the gay lifestyle," she "can see both sides of the issue" concerning gays in the military. She doesn't have an easy answer to a question concerning the line between sincere conviction and fanaticism. But she does offer a saying that religious activists sometimes use: "You're so heavenly-minded, you're no earthly-good."

That's a problem King will never have, whether she decides to rededicate herself to her golf game (King has earned just $136,459 and ranks forty-third on the money list, after placing in the top ten for 12 straight years and winning $481,149 last season), coach basketball, design golf courses, or work for a religious organization.

This week she's wrestling with the myriad duties of conducting a golf tournament—meeting with sponsors and staff, signing hundreds of autographs, granting interviews, ordering gravel delivered to cover muddy roads, providing a massage therapist for the players' locker room, checking out concession stands, and so on and so on. Trying, in short, to make the CoreStates Betsy King Classic, one of the few tournaments named in honor of a player, as successful as she has been, inside and outside the ropes.

Leslie Spalding is praying for a miracle. She ranks 136th on the money list, with $20,061. In the past two months, she has made only one cut.

She needs to win about $10,000 to move into the top 125 and ensure her card for 1997. The CoreStates Betsy King, the final full-field regular event of 1996, is her second-to-last shot. If she fails in Kutztown, her future will be decided in two weeks at Q-School in Daytona Beach.

The worst part is that she knows she can play in the big leagues. It's the little things that have killed her since the du Maurier in August.

During the final round of Ping/Welch's Championship near Boston she three-whacked Nos. 15 and 17, the latter from eight feet, and missed the cut by one. "I was very, very upset. I got off the green and started crying." A break during the Weetabix British Open soothed her spirits. Spalding went fly-fishing with her dad. Birdies have been scarce, but the fish were plentiful, even if Spalding was just learning to cast a line. "I hooked my dad in the ear and by the eye. I caught ten fish and one man."

Then came disaster in Dayton. Spalding scorched the back nine in three under par during the second round to survive the cut by one stroke.

"I was all excited," says Spalding. At least until second-year pro Pam Kometani told Spalding she may have taken an incorrect drop during the first round. Spalding had hit into the water, taken two club lengths from the hazard, and dropped another ball. It rolled a few inches outside the two-club-length area, so Spalding picked it up, redropped, and continued on.

Big mistake. A dropped ball that rolls outside the two-club-length area (unless it rolls an *extra* two club lengths away) is still in play.

"I had no idea," says Spalding. She turned herself in, was disqualified for signing an incorrect scorecard (picking up her ball was a one-stroke penalty), and learned a hard lesson—"Just call for a rules official to make sure."

At the State Farm Rail Classic in Springfield, played on a golf course with fairways conducive to 747 landings ("no jail at the Rail" is how players describe it), Spalding missed the cut by two. She survived by one stroke in Portland, shooting 71-75-72 to tie for fifty-third and bank $1,397. During the week Spalding and Jill McGill took the time to help Japanese rookie Mayumi Hirase with her English. Thanks to the tutoring, Hirase was able to greet her caddie on the range with a new phrase—"You peese of sheet"—to the amusement of all within earshot.

No such yuks in Seattle, however, where Spalding fired 71-76 to miss the cut by one stroke. It was closer to agony; Spalding finished her second round early and hung around all afternoon hoping the ax wouldn't fall.

The frustration started to take its toll. Spalding was beating almost half the field almost every week and earning next to nothing.

"Early in the year I was really relaxed. My attitude was to attack. I've gotten so enamored of making the cut that it makes it hard to function."

In Charlotte the wheels came off. Spalding shot 75-76 on a relatively easy course. The only bright spot was private housing in lakeside luxury, complete with a pontoon boat.

After missing the cut, Spalding flew to Jacksonville to attend a friend's wedding, then went home to Tampa for the first time since July to work with her coach and pack some warmer clothes.

Good thing, too. Saddled with two frosty 7:48 tee times last week at the JAL Big Apple (the field was re-paired by scores after the first day), Spalding shivered through teeth-chattering rounds while staying at a house with two small children "and a killer dog who tried to attack me every time he saw me." Swinging poorly and struggling with her short game, Spalding shot a second-round 84. "I felt like I was going to bogey every hole. I was hoping to break 90, it was so bad. I even thought about withdrawing and not playing in *this* tournament. I was very down, a very bad attitude."

Fortunately she brought her long johns to Kutztown. Teeing off on the 10th hole at 7:30 A.M., Spalding struggles through a cold, windy morning on soggy turf saturated by torrential rainstorms earlier in the week. The wide fairways of Berkleigh Country Club amble through hills adorned with cherry, birch, maple, and spruce trees. It's a pretty place, but now, with fat yellow and green and brown maple leaves plastering the wet grass and muddy pathways and rain-soaked bunkers, it's also depressing. This is the time of year when the ball feels like a rock at the moment of impact, stinging your hands, the time of year when the ball plugs in the fairway, turning 380-yard holes from cupcakes into bears, the time of year when all but the masochistic throw their sticks in the garage for the winter.

The gallery for Spalding, Alison Munt, and Leigh Ann Mills, numbers four people. One is Mark Klein, whose family is housing Spalding and Amy Fruhwirth this week. The atmosphere is subdued, the exact opposite of the excitement and hoopla and energy at the JAL Big Apple five days ago, when Caroline Pierce elevated herself into the ranks of the winners.

When Spalding jams in a 20-foot birdie putt from the fringe on the 492-yard 5th hole—the ball hits the back of the cup and pops up in the air before vanishing—Klein exclaims, "Yeah! Yeah!" Then he says quietly, "That could have been *way* past the hole."

At least Spalding has a fan cheering for her. "She's a doll," says the gray-haired Klein. "And she's concerned with what's going on outside her. Most professional athletes are just concerned with themselves."

Unfortunately, such personal references don't help. A good personality and character, plus the $2,000 application fee, will get you as far as Q-School. The winnowing process has begun, a sorting of the chosen from the outcasts, a process as cold as a dictionary definition: "Winnow—to reduce a large number of people (or things) to a much smaller number by judging their quality."

Some players have been winnowed in. Sue Thomas, touched by the angel/chiropractor in 1994, has worked her way up to 104th on the money list, with $44,047 in just 16 events. She's high enough on the eligibility list to secure a spot in the field in about 25 tournaments in 1997.

Spalding's pal Susan Veasey also has played her way into the top 125, ranking 120th, with $33,632. Perhaps the most impressive move up the ladder has been by Kim Saiki, who has jumped all the way from 115th in 1995 to 35th, with $169,652 this season, including a runner-up finish in Youngstown. Saiki credits a new sports psychologist. Previously she worked with Tiger Woods's mind doctor, Jay Brunza. "He tried to get inside my head," explains Saiki, but the Freud-like psychology didn't take. So she turned to Dr. David Wright, who sharpened Saiki's preshot routine. "Instead of aiming at a tree, he had me aim at a yellow leaf at the edge of the tree."

Others, even some who played extremely well this season, are on the wrong side of the tracks. Canadian Lorie Kane is 128th on the money list with $24,251, impressive numbers considering she has competed in only eight tournaments. LaRee Pearl Sugg, the Tour's only black golfer, also has played extremely well with $20,245 in just ten events. But when they miss the cut in Reading, they purchase one-way tickets back to Q-School.

Don't tell me how, say the golf gods. Don't tell me who. Just give me the number.

Spalding is wearing dark green rain pants, a pink turtleneck, and a dark green windbreaker with designs that resemble military fatigues, appropriate for a war of attrition.

A war she is losing. Spalding, a shadow of the golfer who played so well in Daytona Beach and Toledo, badly yanks a six-foot par putt on the 181-yard 6th hole, and scrambles for bogey on the 350-yard 7th hole after finding bunkers with both her drive and approach shot.

About 50 bundled-up fans sit in a small grandstand behind the green at the 330-yard 9th hole. Alison Munt knocks one stiff; the stiffs in the stands don't even notice. They all have their heads turned to watch Betsy King on the adjacent 1st tee. Leigh Ann Mills feathers a beautiful chip within inches of the cup. Two spectators clap. Like patrons of a noisy nightclub oblivious to the struggling entertainers on stage, they chatter and laugh as the golfers get ready to putt.

It's almost as if the players are phantoms. Spalding misses a ten-foot par putt—she's walking toward the ball in disgust before it stops rolling—and taps in for 79. She's steaming with anger as she disappears into the scorer's tent.

Spalding emerges drinking a Diet Coke.

"I'm so tired of this shit," she mutters under her breath.

"What?" asks a reporter.

"You heard me," she snaps. She blinks a few times, on the verge of tears, but quickly regains her composure, and heads for the sanctuary of the locker room, The Black Hole.

On Friday, October 4, the last day of her rookie season, Spalding recites her affirmations:

1. "I'm patient."
2. "I will win."
3. "I trust my abilities."
4. "I own each shot."
5. "I will hit each shot with conviction."
6. "I am a great putter."

Spalding realizes that the relentless pressures of the Tour have corroded her attitude.

"It's easy to get beat down out here. In the beginning, I appreciated what I was doing. I tried to smile at every volunteer. Instead of getting so down on myself, I should still be smiling because I'm so lucky to be out here."

She tees off at 12:45 and promptly bogeys the first three holes. Then she tells her caddie that her goal for the remainder of the day is to have fun.

There are some moments to enjoy. On the 495-yard 13th hole, she spins a wedge back to tap-in birdie distance, almost on top of Mills's ball. "The two best shots of the day," says a marshal. As a cool, almost blinding sun sinks over the trees, she birdies the 485-yard 16th hole with a nice ten-foot putt.

But she concludes the round with an 81-yard wedge shot to the 475-yard 18th hole that travels only about 60 yards, not even reaching the front bunker. After a nice pitch to three feet, Spalding blasts the putt five feet past the left edge, and misses coming back.

A three-whack from three feet for a double-bogey. A few fans in the crowded grandstand clap. To Spalding's ear, it probably sounds like they're mocking her. A more ignominious ending is hard to imagine.

"That was pretty ridiculous," she says a few minutes later after signing for 77 blows. She misses the cut by six strokes. Krumsville in Kutztown.

But she's already working on her attitude in preparation for Q-School. By Friday night Spalding is in an upbeat mood as she reminisces about the season.

"I can't believe it's over," says Spalding. "It went so fast." Spalding played in 25 tournaments. She earned $20,061 to rank 136th on the money list. She's $9,997 short of the magic 125th spot. One good week. Or a few cuts made instead of missed by one stroke.

Spalding muses about rookie mistakes—mental ("getting down on myself"), physical ("not working out enough"), and fiscal ("I wasn't very good with money"). She laughs at travel nightmares—a flight from Minnesota to Charlottesville to Rochester, when Spalding's clubs failed to accompany her and eventually arrived soaking wet. She marvels at the people she met—the McVickers in Toledo, for example, who cheered for her at three tournaments. She reminisces about wonderful experiences—boating and casino-shopping in Atlantic City, visiting the Grand Canyon, meeting Vince Gill and Amy Grant. "Every week was something memorable."

Her task next week is simple. "Play the kinks out and play my attitude out too." She'll be grinding on the range, trying to turn it around before Q-School.

It won't be easy. "It's more pressure for someone like Leslie," says Donna Andrews's caddie Chris Fitzpatrick. "She knows what she has to lose." Fitzpatrick plans to caddie at Q-School. He hopes to loop for a stranger; it's too wrenching to work for someone he knows.

"Too many tears," he says. "You feel so sorry for them. It's nothing I'd wish on my worst enemy."

Sun filters through a high haze on a mild late Sunday morning, highlighting the reds and rusts and plums and yellows and oranges streaking the trees.

Unable to change her plane reservation and leave town early, Spalding is on the range, hitting balls next to tournament leader Annika Sorenstam. On Thursday Sorenstam shot 66. The *total* length of her eight birdie putts was 30 feet, 3 inches. After adding rounds of 69 and 67, she holds a three-stroke lead over globe-trotting Laura Davies, who flew in from Japan on Monday, a nine-stroke lead over Juli Inkster, battling a cold and the flu, and a whopping 11-stroke margin over the rest of the field. Once again her foes are asking, "What course is *she* playing?"

It seems like ages ago that Sorenstam and Spalding were paired together in Wilmington. Since then Sorenstam has won another U.S. Open and adorned the cover of a new book published in Sweden (*Dare to Be the Best*) as well as a Swedish postage stamp.

Yet Sorenstam came to Kutztown in an angry mood after tying for thirtieth at Wykagyl, her worst finish of the year. Although the tight, tricky course suited her to a tee, she handled it poorly, allowing the winds to blow her off stride and quicken her tempo. Usually she doesn't practice on Monday. But she spent nine hours on the range and putting green at Berkleigh on Monday, at one point hitting wedges toward an unfolded, upside-down umbrella and sinking a sizable number.

Except at the Solheim Cup, Sorenstam has been a little off her feed for the last two months. Five weeks ago in Portland, after three-putting three times during the final round, she sullenly sat on her golf bag near the 18th tee, waiting for the preceding group to hit their drives. Fiancé David Esch crouched down next to her, trying to catch her eye.

Sorenstam wouldn't look at him. She cleaned her golf ball and cleaned her fingernails and plucked at the grass. As Esch said something to her, she crossed her arms and stared at the ground, like a pouting child, while a curious crowd milled around them.

She looked like a prisoner of fame, which is the headline of an article about Sorenstam in the next issue of *Golf Digest*.

But it's a false impression.

"It was just golf," Sorenstam said later, "not anything else."

Certainly there is a *price* for fame. When she leaves the range, signing autographs as she walks near the gallery rope, she's accompanied by two security guards. Yesterday a fan who had sent Sorenstam a birthday present (she turned 26 on Thursday), a "precious moments" figurine from an on-site Enesco booth (the company is providing financial backing for the tournament), refused to leave the course without her autograph and tried to find out where she was staying.

But a prisoner? Maybe in Sweden (the setting for the *Golf Digest* article), where Sorenstam is a national hero. But not in America, says Sorenstam, who sat for an interview earlier this week on a patio near Berkleigh's tarp-covered pool.

In a cheerful mood, Sorenstam said she's recognized on the average of once a day in the States. "They usually point and say, 'You're that golfer,' or 'You're from Sweden,'" Sorenstam said with amusement. And fame offers pleasure as well as problems. During the ShopRite in Atlantic City, she was absolutely delighted when *Sports Illustrated for Kids* called to ask for her favorite (pancakes with applesauce or jam) and least favorite (liver) school lunches.

Her real opponent these days is not fame but success. Sorenstam readily admits her motivation to practice has waned. She used to work on her game every day at home when she skipped a tournament. Recently she's only been practicing one or two days during an off-week. At the age of 26, Sorenstam has accomplished and exceeded her most ambitious goals. After grinding like crazy for almost half her life, years when she "ate, drank, and slept golf," she finds her interests and horizons expanding.

She's not obsessed with record books or the Hall of Fame. Asked how she'd like to be remembered, Sorenstam responds quickly. "As a fair player—somebody who loved sportsmanship. As one of many who helped more girls start playing golf and helped increase galleries. Somebody who enjoyed what she did out here."

Money doesn't drive her either. "I'm not a very materialistic person. I'm like . . . Uncle Scrooge?" she says with a smile. "I sit on my money." She and Esch have discussed the perils of wealth, particularly when the wife earns so much more than the husband, something that is considered a nonissue in Sweden.

"We agreed that it's our family's money, and that it's a positive thing. I know that *he* wants to take care of *me*. But I'd like to take care of him also. It's not like he has to buy me things to please me. Does that make sense?"

Eminently.

Sorenstam cherishes her time at home. (She and Esch split time between San Diego and Incline Village near Lake Tahoe.) She cooks dinner and bakes pies. The radio or CD player is almost always on. (Alanis Morissette and Celine Dion are current favorites.) She loves to garden and to ski. She's fascinated by computers and interested in business. She wants to have kids in the not-too-distant future.

Asked if she sees herself on tour in ten years, Sorenstam says, "No." Five years? "As long as I enjoy it. I will never give up golf. It's a matter of competing or not competing. Life is not just golf."

Sorenstam, in her own quiet, stubborn, perceptive way, is two up on fame. Nothing bothers her as she leaves the practice range en route to a final-round 68 and an eight-stroke victory over Davies. An enthusiastic, overflow, family gathering with lots of kids roars in delight when Sorenstam accepts a $90,000 check from Betsy King.

As Pia Nilsson predicted, Sorenstam has grown and blossomed. She's not just a star. She's "Annika-Star."

Left behind on the range are Leslie Spalding, Christa Teno, and Nancy Taylor, all preparing for Q-School. Spalding gets some help from Teno, who suggests tilting her right hip inward. "It lines up your spine correctly," says Teno. "That looks much better." Nancy Taylor offers the use of her video camera.

Spalding is hitting 6-irons, the balls floating softly to earth in a tight grouping. When she returned to Tampa last week, instructor Paul Enright found her swing had become very upright, with little body turn, leaving the club in a closed position at the top of her backswing.

She has a week to repair her swing and her attitude. Otherwise she won't be hitting brand new Titleist Tour 100s on a practice range next to Annika Sorenstam for at least one year, perhaps forever. Otherwise she is an ex-LPGA Tour professional. Otherwise she pounds the pavement in search of a job, although there is nothing else she wants to do.

The price of success?

Leslie Spalding is willing to pay it. But all the money in the world can't buy it. Not in professional golf, perhaps the purest meritocracy in America, a meritocracy that equitably but ruthlessly sorts out the haves from the have-nots.

CHAPTER 11

*J*apan: Snapshots

The bottom of the cup in America is composed of a hard plastic. When a golf ball drops into the hole, it makes a muted, deep-pitched sound—"PLUNK."

In Japan, the cups are metallic and appear to be deeper. When a putt falls in, it creates a sharp, high-pitched noise when it hits bottom—"CLANG!"

Ami Golf Club, located in a rural area in Ibaraki Prefecture, about 50 kilometers northeast of Tokyo, is the site of the $675,000 Nichirei International on October 25–27, a team competition pitting the U.S. LPGA Tour against the Japanese Tour (JLPGA).

It is sponsored by a major Japanese purveyor of snack foods and frozen foods. The first two days consist of team best-ball matches. The last day features singles competition.

The U.S. Tour has won the last 11 Nichirei Internationals. Last year the Japanese Tour took a seemingly unbeatable 12½ to 5½ lead into the singles matches, only to be blitzed by the U.S., which triumphed 19-17.

But even for the vanquished, the Nichirei is a sweet deal. The 18 players on the losing team will each pick up $13,500. The winners will receive $24,000. In addition, U.S. players are treated to a luxurious, all-expenses-paid trip to Japan, including first-class travel on JAL, hotels, meal chits, gifts such as CD players and jewelry, and lavish receptions and luncheons. Almost all the U.S. players will be staying in Japan next week as well to compete in the $750,000 Toray Japan Queen's Cup, an official LPGA event with a field composed of 46 LPGA players and 38 JLPGA players.

Still, it's not enough of an incentive to lure many of the LPGA stars. Sorenstam, a winner in Pennsylvania two weeks ago and a winner again last week in Korea at the $500,000 Samsung World Championship of Women's Golf, has flown home. So has Rosie Jones, who was also in the 16-player field. Others never left the States—Pepper, Mallon, Robbins, and Sheehan, all of whom were eligible to play in Korea and Japan (and earn a minimum of $25,500 just for teeing it up in the World Championship and the Nichirei) passed up the deal. All are vacationing, fried from the long season in general and the rigors of the Solheim Cup in particular.

Laura Davies, who skipped Korea to sew up the money title in Europe with a victory at the Italian Open in Sicily, is taking her only week off in the midst of a 22-week worldwide barnstorming tour. Davies, who represents the Japanese golf equipment company Maruman, is obligated to play several times in Japan during the season. It's not a burden. In fact, she enjoys the country so much she has expressed interest in spending an entire year on the Japanese circuit. She'll be here for the Toray Cup, as well as the Itoen Ladies Open the following week, before departing for the Australian Ladies Masters, followed by the ITT Tour Championship in Las Vegas, followed by year-ending unofficial events (the Diner's Cup, Wendy's Three-Tour Challenge, JC Penney Classic), followed by, perhaps, the member-guest Thursday afternoon nine-hole best-ball barbeque and beer blast at Obscure C.C. in Sioux City.

So although 18 of the JLPGA's top 19 money winners are on the Nichirei team, the U.S. team consists of players ranked thirty-fifth (Julie Piers) and thirty-sixth (Hiromi Kobayashi) on the U.S. money list.

But the U.S. Tour, featuring the best players in the world (including the best Japanese player, Kobayashi), still is an overwhelming favorite. The JLPGA is much more parochial, consisting almost solely of players from the Far East. Its Nichirei team is made up of golfers from Japan, China, and Korea, plus New Zealand's Marnie McGuire, one of only two Caucasian regulars on the circuit.

Team captains are appointed according to the money list; Karrie Webb and Aiko Hashimoto lead their respective squads. Webb, traveling almost as much as Davies, flew to Korea twice to play in tournaments recently. She's also locked in a fierce battle for leading money winner. Webb stands at $847,903, Davies at $827,483. (Sorenstam is still in the race at $792,311, although her absence from next week's Toray Cup field seriously compromises her chances.)

Webb's performance as captain opens on a shaky note, the equivalent of a shank out-of-bounds on the 1st tee.

"I pissed a few people off just by being me and not being organized. I didn't know exactly who was on the team. *That* was a big mistake. I thought I could wing it and get by."

No chance. Webb is responsible for pairings, speeches at ceremonial events, and daily sessions with the Japanese media.

She hopes the week goes more smoothly than did her two trips to Korea.

Five weeks ago Webb received the largest appearance fee of her young career to play in the Chief Rose Ladies' Open. (Golf is booming in Korea and a number of homegrown players, such as Seri Park, who placed third in the Samsung World Championship behind Sorenstam and Alfredsson, and Grace Park, the top-rated junior golfer in the U.S., are making their mark internationally.) The Korean media dubbed Webb "Cinderella."

The shoe definitely fit her. Or at least it would have. Webb didn't disappear at midnight; she vanished after the second round when she failed to sign her scorecard and was disqualified.

If it had been John Daly, who has taken the appearance money and run—or tanked—on occasion (he shot a second-round 89 at the Dutch Open in July to miss the cut by 23 strokes after banking a fee reported at around $100,000), critics would have howled. But Webb was just three strokes behind the leader when she was eliminated from the contest.

"I hadn't gotten over jet lag," explains Webb, who flew to Korea after registering her third victory of the season in Seattle. Exhausted after a second round that lasted five and a half hours, trying to avoid a reporter hot on her trail, she spaced out, deposited her card in a box without signing it, and split.

In her return visit to Korea for the Samsung World Championship last week, Webb tied for sixth. It was a strange trip for her and everyone else in the traveling party.

The tournament itself has little reason to exist, other than as a vanity project for Samsung and a marketing tool for IMG, which is a cosponsor. (That's why almost all of the eligible LPGA players who are represented by IMG, including Webb, Sorenstam, McGann, and Alfredsson, showed up.) This year it moved from a course on Cheiju Island, a beautiful setting popular with honeymooners, to one near Seoul, the DMZ, and the border between North and South Korea.

The event landed smack-dab in the middle of saber-rattling between the two countries in the wake of the landing of a North Korean submarine on a South Korean beach just a few weeks earlier.

"We could hear machine-gun fire all day," says Norman Hathaway, the HealthSouth therapist who accompanied the team.

The players were housed in a luxury Sheraton Hotel with all the amenities and then some—ten restaurants, a casino, a disco, a dinner-theater that featured Korean dance followed by a Las Vegas style revue. The golf course was nice, too, built into a mountain with lots of hills and elevational changes.

But the 30-mile bus rides to and from the hotel to the course were surreal. The morning excursions weren't bad, with travel time about one hour. But at night, on a two-lane road, with several military checkpoints to pass through and traffic congested to gridlock, the rides lasted from two to four hours. On a vehicle without a bathroom. Players hopped off the bus to squat in a ditch in the dark near the side of the road.

Then there was a near-international incident. One day, a Korean farmer driving a pickup truck cut off the bus, which swerved into some pylons. Bus and truck pulled off the road. The bus driver opened the door and began yelling at the farmer, who climbed on board. The bus driver kicked him in the chest.

The farmer began to choke the driver as players sitting nearby dove toward the rear of the bus. Caddie Jeff "Tree" Cable, a giant of a man, was sent to the rescue, carefully removing the farmer's hand from the throat of the driver.

By this time the farmer's wife was screaming. Everyone wound up at the police station. Diplomacy eventually prevailed.

The 45- to 60-minute bus rides in Japan from the small, bustling city of Tsukuba to Ami Golf Club are much more tranquil, although traffic in the city itself often is stop and go.

Signs of the Japanese enshrinement of American culture—often in its crappiest aspects—are everywhere. Noodle shops and markets with local produce coexist with Dunkin' Donuts, Coco's, and AM/PM minimarts.

But the countryside is lovely. Thick forests are painted with fall colors of orange, rust, red, and brown. Open fields cover much of the land, resembling the rice paddies of Vietnam.

Everything else is packed together. Roads are narrow. Bus drivers squeeze around garbage trucks with an inch to spare in the small villages. Compact, two-story houses rest on small plots of land. Many have small gardens of flowers and vegetables in the backyard and brand new autos, Cimas and Toyotas, in the driveway. Tiny cemeteries with hundreds of memorial markers are shoehorned into villages or near the edge of a greenhouse. In death as in life, the Japanese commune in close quarters.

Except at private country clubs. Ami Golf Course, named after the town it is located in, was built in 1992. Original memberships, sold mostly to corporations in Chiba and Tokyo, cost $480,000. The developers envisioned a membership roll of 700. Their dreams were crushed by the economic jolt that struck Japan a few years ago. The club went bankrupt in 1995.

Today it boasts 360 members, including a small number of women. Cost: $240,000. There are few takers at that price.

Not that Ami is a pig in a poke. It's a pleasant layout with nice greens and short, brownish rough dotted with stands of pine, oak, camphor, and zelkova trees. But the most distinguished feature of Ami is its clubhouse, an airy, ultramodern, two-story edifice of glass, stone, and marble, surrounded by perfectly trimmed shrubbery.

Everything at Ami is immaculate. It's commonplace to see 20 caddies and maintenance workers walking down a fairway late in the day, fixing divots and raking bunkers. Or a dozen people around a green, using wooden hoelike devices to brush the sand smooth in the same manner as one would sweep a kitchen floor.

The caddies for the Nichirei are the regular loopers at Ami, women who work full-time at the club. (Since Nichirei and Toray don't want to foot the bill to import the regular U.S. caddies, JLPGA players also are prohibited from using their Tour caddies. It's pot luck; club caddies are assigned to players through a blind draw.)

Except for their white gloves, caddies at Ami dress like golfers. They wear preppy blue plaid knickers, white turtlenecks, dark green sweater vests, perky navy hats, and white golf shoes. They push carts, sometimes running to keep up. (The carts are wide-wheeled and sturdy, vastly superior to U.S. models.) But the caddies don't do yardages, so players walk the course early in the week with yardage books, laser distance finders, and putters, scoping out the course and deciphering the greens.

Yoko Taguchi, 41, is in her second year as a caddie at Ami. She earns about $2,500 a month, more than she did in her former job as a nursery school teacher.

With the aid of a translator—Nichirei has supplied three translators to help players, caddies, officials, and reporters to communicate—Taguchi shyly says she is looking forward to caddying for Chris Johnson. It's an honor to participate in the Nichirei; caddies often become devoted to their players. Most prefer working for U.S. as opposed to Japanese Tour players.

"American players are more big-hearted," says Taguchi. "They seem to be enjoying the game of golf more."

Marnie McGuire, 27, graduated from Oklahoma State University in 1990 with a degree in marketing. But when the curly-haired redhead tried to sell herself to a sponsor to turn pro in America or Europe, she found little interest. So after playing amateur golf in New Zealand for a year, her father suggested Japan.

"I didn't even know there *was* a Tour here," says McGuire.

A very impressive one, actually: 38 events from March until November; prize money comparable with purses in the U.S. and far superior to the

European Tour; media coverage that makes the LPGA drool—every tournament is broadcast on network TV (as are a number of LPGA events from America, including several with Japanese sponsors).

In Japan, as in the Sandhills of North Carolina, it seems like its All Golf All the Time. One paper in Tokyo has *seven* full-time golf writers, who blanket not only the Japanese Tours, but the PGA, LPGA, and Senior Tour in America as well. Golf magazines proliferate: *Par Golf, Waggle, Niblick, Golf Digest Weekly, Albatross, Golf Digest Monthly,* which features Kevin Costner on the cover, promoting the opening of *Tin Cup* in Japan. The magazines feature reams of instruction and equipment information. Lengthy comic strips are regular highlights.

Calendars of golfers, particularly of blonde LPGA players—*Golf Digest Weekly* is advertising calendars of Vicki Goetze and Jill McGill—are hot sellers.

Japanese golfers are new-technology freaks, prime consumers in a worldwide golf equipment business, estimated at $2.2 billion annually. Putter manufacturer Bobby Grace sells 58 percent of his wares in Japan, including a number of $3,000 handmade putters at upscale department stores. He's hawking his newest blade, the HSM ("hole-seeking material") model, with a soft insert in the face of the putter composed of material used in golf balls, titanium, and "natural and synthetic material molded to a solid state," plus a pinch of eye of the newt.

So much for the high end of the golf business in Japan. When Marnie McGuire arrived, she found herself at the bottom of the heap, required to serve a lengthy apprenticeship.

"It was horrible," says McGuire. "It was the worst year of my life."

McGuire was sent by her sponsor, a golf course company, to Tomobe, a rural area 90 minutes north of Tokyo. From March through November, six days a week, nine in the morning to six at night, she practiced. No one spoke English. She wasn't allowed to play with the members. At night she painstakingly taught herself the language.

In August, 1991, she earned her Tour card—which she keeps for life—by playing three qualifying rounds in the required 12 over par or better. At the Japanese equivalent of Q-School, played in September, October, and November, she earned a spot in the field for 12 tournaments in the second half of the 1992 season. Along with four sponsor exemptions, she parlayed those 16 events into forty-seventh spot on the money list, acquiring the status of a ranked (exempt) player along with others in the top 50.

Still, says McGuire, "I was nobody. I was this foreign person. I hung out with my girlfriends, and there were only about two of them. To fit in is not very easy. The other players were very standoffish. You have to prove you can play."

She did, moving up steadily, winning one tournament in 1994, two in 1995, and one earlier in 1996. Currently she ranks twelfth on the money list with 34,653,000 yen (about $300,000). Her sponsors include Suntory (a major beverage and liquor company), MacGregor clubs (a subsidiary of Suntory), and Swan sunglasses.

"Year by year, it's gotten easier," says McGuire. "I speak the language better and understand the language better. The players are very competitive but very friendly and supportive of each other. There's no nastiness or any of that sort of thing. When you do well, players are genuinely happy for you."

Fans have supported McGuire, who is personable and attractive. But the media, she says, tend to focus on the stars. "You have to do really well to be on TV or in the paper. Second or third is not good enough." Overall McGuire says she's still "a novelty, kind of like a token foreigner."

When it comes to the operation of the Japanese Tour, all golfers are tokens, seen but not heard. While the LPGA is ultimately governed by the golfers, who comprise six of the 11 members of its Board of Directors, the Japanese Tour is an autocracy run by former players.

"They have no vision," says golf writer Junko Endo. "They want to protect their narrow world."

"We're allowed no say," says McGuire. "A lot of courses are set up ridiculously long with pin positions that are stupid. Laura Davies said, 'They're making you look like bunnies.'"

Hiromi Kobayashi, who won five times in Japan in 1989 before invading the U.S., agrees. "Sometimes it's ridiculous. There's reasonable hard versus stupid hard."

The lowest stroke average in 1996 is 72.73 by Akiko Fukushima, almost two and a half strokes higher than the best on the LPGA Tour. While LPGA players are better, they're not *that* much superior.

About 10 percent of Japanese Tour players are married. Several have children, but child care is nonexistent. Toshimi Kimura, a star, leaves her two children with her mother-in-law and sees them one day a week.

Jennifer Sevil from Australia, McGuire's best friend, drafts relatives to fly to Japan and look after 2-year-old Ryan at tournaments while Jennifer plays and husband Warren caddies.

However, Warren says there's one big advantage to competing in Japan— the longest trip is six hours by car, and the family is home every Sunday night.

The money is good. Sevil ranked 27th in 1995 with about $200,000 and will finish higher in 1996. [She winds up 20th.] Their apartment is gratis, furnished by a sponsor, Garden Golf Club. Tour players receive $500 a week to play in the Wednesday pro-am. Another sponsor, Bridgestone, which makes clubs and golf balls, pays her a salary plus bonus that run to about $50,000 a year.

So it's a very benign dictatorship.

Yet McGuire still dreams about the LPGA Tour, although she's torn between East and West. "People know me here and it's nice to be a novelty fish in a little pond. This is my comfort level now." But she may try America anyway, tempted by "the severe competition. Here I can relax and make cuts and make money. In the U.S. you can't let up."

For the moment, she'll settle for beating the U.S. Tour in the Nichirei. Last year, says Junko Endo, McGuire was "the engine. Players would say, 'Marnie gave me confidence.'"

Serving as subcaptain in 1995, McGuire stoked her teammates with motivational tactics she had absorbed from Ann Pitts, her coach at Oklahoma State. The Japanese players had never seen anything quite like it.

"This foreigner was yelling and screaming and going 'rah rah,'" says McGuire. "They thought, 'Oh, this is kind of fun.'"

But when the U.S. team cranked it up on the final day of singles matches, no amount of cheerleading could help. "They had champagne waiting in the locker room," says Julie Piers. "It wasn't there when they finished."

On the first day of the Nichirei matches, the Japanese team appears in jazzy white and black sweaters with phrases embroidered on them:

Sport Is Love
Sport Is Energy
Sport Is Life
We Are Family

The slogans are in English, not Japanese, which seems bizarre. Imagine a U.S. team showing up for an international competition in uniforms with slogans written in a foreign language.

Yet Japanese journalists don't find it the least bit odd. In fact, many Japanese, especially those who have lived or worked in the West, have English "names." Laura Davies's agent in Japan, Yumiko Ito, who works for IMG, is known to everyone as Betty. The Japanese are accustomed to the ubiquitous usage of English in all forms of commerce, from magazines (*Cutie: For Independent Women*) to food (Funky Egg Pizza), even when something is lost in the translation.

* * *

Despite the presence of the translators, communication problems run rampant, especially during play. U.S. players converse with their caddies, says Julie Piers, "by playing charades." A few Japanese Tour players speak English. Quite a few understand some English. But conversation often is limited to smiles and gestures.

Even when the words are clear, the intent sometimes is not. After the opening ceremonies, conducted in front of about 200 spectators under filtered sunshine on a warm, pleasant, late October morning, the best-ball matches commence.

Marianne Morris and Penny Hammel are competing against Ayako Okamoto and Akiko Fukushima. When Okamoto greets the Americans, she startles them by saying, "Let's play for money." Suggested stakes: $10 per hole.

Later some of Okamoto's friends, such as Jane Geddes, say she was just joking. But Morris begs to differ.

"I knew she was serious. Maybe I'm a prude, but I don't need any side bets. When I'm home playing with friends, fine."

It's not the first time Ayako Okamoto has proven difficult to decipher.

After starring as the best woman professional softball player in Japan, Okamoto took up golf at the age of 22. She served her apprenticeship practicing and caddying at a private club in Osaka. Her role model was Chako Higuchi, who dominated women's golf in Japan before winning the 1977 LPGA Championship, the only Japanese player to win a major in America.

Higuchi was a superstar—"Everyone knew her the way they knew the emperor," said Sandra Palmer. Yet Okamoto surpassed her. After soaring to the top at home, Okamoto, then 30, journeyed to America in 1981. She quickly moved into the ranks of the elite. She won 17 LPGA tournaments and topped the money list with $466,034 in 1987.

In terms of popularity in Japan, Okamoto was akin to a Michael Jordan or a Madonna. Jane Geddes, who has been visiting Japan for 13 years, stayed with Okamoto during her first trip to Tokyo, and hung out with the superstar on subsequent visits. Geddes says, "One time we took a train, and by the time we left there were a hundred older women pressed up against the window, crying and screaming just to see her." When they went to dinner or the beach or to play tennis, photographers would follow. "The press made her crazy," says Geddes. "They were just relentless. She lost her whole life to them."

For a while Okamoto lived in America, where she escaped from some of the frenzy. But the Japanese media continued to shadow her at LPGA tournament sites, and the burdens of representing the fervent hopes of her fans back home rested heavily on her shoulders.

Yet she radiated an implacable serenity inside the ropes, a marvelous professionalism. In contrast to Higuchi, who swayed off the ball, Okamoto's swing was almost picture-perfect, her tempo exquisite, her touch magnificent. "She has so much feel," says Inkster, who relished being paired with her.

And she was appealingly human to those who knew her well, such as Geddes and Sheehan, kindhearted and generous with a sharp sense of humor.

Plagued with back problems, she played sparingly on the LPGA Tour in 1994 and 1995 and returned to Japan to live. "Ayako's so Japanese," says Geddes. "She never really adjusted to the States. She likes the part of her life where she gets waited on."

The contradictions of Ayako. At 45 she can still play—she won her sixtieth JLPGA tournament this summer—but her appearances are infrequent. She's not even entered in the Toray Cup next week. Some of her Japanese friends believe she's embarrassed by her declining, although still formidable, skills.

Perhaps her quest for perfection waylaid her. Although her English is more than adequate, she has always used translators for interviews.

"I am not happy if I don't speak perfectly," she told Liz Kahn.

Certainly perfection was her objective as a golfer. For a while, she came as close as anyone to achieving it. In 1984 she placed third on the U.S. money list and captured the Women's British Open. She told Kahn, "With every single shot I felt I knew which way the ball would go. If there was one blade of grass between the ball and the club I knew how it would react . . . my moment of impact was so precise, it was a joy. It was what I had been searching for all my career."

Now she is an aging superstar, a hero in many quarters but also a curiosity. Single Japanese women over 35 are considered old maids; journalists called Okamoto "grandmother" behind her back.

There is a sense of the mystical surrounding her. She often feels a sense of destiny. Former caddie John Killeen said in 1992, just after Okamoto won the McDonald's Championship, "When she gets to a place where she feels good, she believes she's going to play well. And when she thinks it's her turn to win, she usually wins."

The contradictions of Ayako.

She has been the finest female athlete in Japan. Yet she describes herself as a klutz. "I embarrass myself constantly, even though I have an image of being cool and debonair," she told Kahn.

Asked what was her proudest accomplishment, Okamoto told both

Kahn and *Golf for Women* writer Debbie Allen it was her many close friendships. Yet friends say she often surrounds herself with a disposable, ever-changing cadre of yes-people.

There is a word in Japan—*kokoro*—that means both mind and heart. The Japanese see no distinction. But there is a sense that Okamoto cannot rationalize matters of the heart—friends, family, work, play—with her role as a superstar, particularly one whose fame is, inevitably, dimming.

Okamoto hasn't been out in public in Tokyo in six years. By necessity or by choice? She certainly is not swarmed upon at Ami. Perhaps it is simple politeness and courtesy on the part of the polite and courteous Japanese. Perhaps it is different in the streets of the city.

She is a prisoner of fame, a captive of past glories. The question is whether she has imprisoned herself. And, if so, whether she can untie the ropes that bind her.

(At the end of the year Okamoto and Chako Higuchi will be named vice chairman and chairman of the JLPGA, an inspired choice and perhaps the new challenge that Okamoto needs.)

"My life is peaceful now," Okamoto told Geddes recently. Perhaps so. Geddes says she looks much better now than she has in the last few years.

Yet she seems forlorn, weighted down. Contradictory, mysterious, appealing, unknowable: for a first-time visitor from America, Ayako Okamoto is as hard to fathom as Japan itself.

In the late 1980s in Japan, the golf boom, economic boom, and Okamoto's popularity combined to turn Japan into an all-you-can eat buffet line serving filet mignon and Dom Perignon, and LPGA players such as Neumann, Geddes, Amy Benz, Deborah Vidal, and Patty Rizzo, all of whom visited Japan regularly, feasted.

Endorsement deals with club manufacturers were worth $200,000 to $300,000 annually. Tournaments paid $25,000–$50,000 in appearance fees. A one-day exhibit could bring $10,000. Neumann, an instant star in Japan after her 1988 U.S. Open triumph, endorsed everything from textiles to coffee creamers to Pocari Sweat, an energy drink.

"It was a free-for-all," says Geddes, who represented Japanese equipment companies throughout her career (Bridgestone clubs and golf balls, Mizuno clubs) until signing with Callaway this year. "We just had piles of yen. We were laughing all the way to the bank."

The economic crash in Japan brought the golf market back to reality. But reality ain't too shabby. LPGA stars may not be laughing all the way to the bank in the mid-1990s, but they're still grinning from ear to ear.

How relaxed is the atmosphere among the U.S. team? Liselotte Neumann, waiting on the tee box for her foursome to be announced, dances a few steps of the macarena.

U.S. team players can be divided into two groups—the timid and the bold. The timid eat spaghetti at the hotel and avoid exotic delicacies at the numerous team receptions. The bold ride trains into Tokyo, and prowl the restaurants and bars and discos, including such establishments as Java Jive, Gas Panic, and the Motown Cafe, located in the neon-drenched Roppongi district.

Val Skinner has visited Japan about 20 times. But that didn't innoculate her from a case of food poisoning. Yesterday she was rushed to a hospital, where she spent six long, frightening hours.

Forced to play today or be replaced by an alternate for the entire competition, Skinner is on the tee, chatting with partner Brandie Burton, alternates Kim Saiki and Amy Fruhwirth, and Jim and Linda Ritts, who are sitting at the edge of the tee box. Judging from the conversation, she's feeling okay.

"Is my hair flat?" asks Skinner, who wears her black hair in something of a cloudlike beehive.

"Yeah," says Burton. "It's pretty flat today."

"You don't want to be out here with flat hair," jokes Skinner. "That's one of the things you think about on the first tee."

She has more pressing matters to think about after hitting her drive. As the ball lands, she turns to see her caddie, with a quizzical expression on her face, holding a 5-wood. Unbeknownst to Skinner, her caddie had picked up the 5-wood from Skinner's locker and stuck it in her bag. The caddie has just figured out—and Skinner knows as soon as she sees the club—that it's the fifteenth stick in her arsenal, one over the limit. The Skinner-Burton team is slapped with a two-stroke penalty. Skinner wonders if it's "caddie espionage"—Japanese caddies trying to assist the JLPGA by any possible means. But Japanese journalists dismiss the notion as unimaginable.

Later the caddies, embarrassed by the incident, gather to discuss it. But confusion continues to reign. The next day Geddes finds three extra clubs in her bag when she's warming up.

When the players complete their matches, they file up to a small grandstand behind the 18th green reserved for golfers, officials, and guests. The Japanese team munches on pastries. The U.S. team, locked in a 4½-4½ tie, is not particularly pleased.

"This has been a shitty day," grouses Barb Whitehead, as she joins her colleagues after she and Joan Pitcock lose to Akane Oshiro and Toshimi

Kimura, 67-69. Good thing she didn't hear a man behind the 6th green, who pointed to her name in the program, turned to his female companion, and said, "Barbo Whitoheado." Both started laughing as Whitoheado lined up her putto.

Actually, she would have gotten a kick out of it. Whitehead (formerly Thomas before her marriage to Phoenix businessman Trent Whitehead in 1995) can be ornery inside the ropes, but she's friendly and gracious on the outside, a devout Christian with a good sense of humor. After struggling in the fringe during most of her 13-year career, Whitehead, 35, broke through last year, winning her first tournament and placing 31st on the money list with $204,327. It wasn't a fluke—she's currently 30th with $182,602 in 1996.

After a conference with captain Webb, the Whitehead-Pitcock team is broken up. Tomorrow Webb will play with Pitcock and McGann with Whitehead.

"We're the weak-link team," Pitcock says sardonically. "We're so pathetic they have to put us with better players."

Marianne Morris trudges to the grandstand after she and Penny Hammel tie with Okamoto and Fukushima, 67-67. It's been a long day for Morris, battling a sinus headache and nonplussed by Okamoto's gambling proposition on the 1st tee. In a deep, droll voice, she says to her teammates, "[Penny] had a *huge* load to bear today. If I hadn't gone on a diet, she might be dead."

The final group, Geddes and Neumann, blister the course in 64 to defeat McGuire and Hashimoto by three shots.

"Nice pants," the U.S. players razz Geddes, referring to her balloonlike trousers. Unlike the classy, expensive, impeccably tailored, designer outfits at the Solheim Cup, Izod ("the official apparel of the LPGA") seems to have shipped its factory seconds to Japan. Players are either tripping over their pants legs or getting them hastily hemmed at the hotel. One U.S. golfer walked onto the 1st tee before noticing a bunch of dark threads sticking out of the crotch of her pants.

"Do you know what this looks like?" she said, joking but a little self-conscious too.

Rain begins falling as the first-round matches conclude. Val Skinner, one day out of the hospital, walks from the clubhouse toward the range with a bunch of clubs in her hand. The atmosphere may be looser at the Nichirei than anywhere else, but there's still a competition to be won. So food poisoning and flat, rain-drenched hair take a back seat to the job at hand.

"Ironhead," Skinner will say later. She's not describing her coiffure but her stubborn refusal to accept a less-than-stellar performance, regardless of the circumstances.

Is Japan sexist?

Do Japanese eat rice?

In a fascinating book published in 1991, *Learning to Bow: Inside the Heart of Japan*, Bruce Feilor, who spent a year teaching English in a rural school, wrote:

> Paradoxically, women were once venerated in Japan. . . . Confucian teachings adopted later dictated that a woman should obey her father in youth, her husband in maturity, and her son in old age. While women were restricted to the home, men were allowed more freedom—both social and sexual. . . . Men looked at women as just another part of their segregated public and private selves.
>
> This schism remains in force today. Even though occupying Americans included an equal-rights amendment in Japan's postwar constitution, equality never took hold. The Japanese school system for the last fifty years has essentially tried to produce girls who will serve as successful wives and mothers for workingmen. The results of this gender training are dramatic. In institutions of higher education, men outnumber women two to one, with the vast majority of the women in less prestigious two-year colleges. Fields of interest vary greatly as well. Ninety-nine percent of engineering majors in universities are men, as are 94 percent of law students, and almost 90 percent of scientists. Conversely, the most popular subjects for women are home economics and literature.

As Feilor points out, times are changing. Notions of equality are spreading to a younger generation of women, many of whom are mad as hell and unwilling to take it anymore.

But change is running up against powerful, entrenched societal bulwarks.

Case in point: Masaki Owada, a Harvard-educated diplomat in the Foreign Ministry before marrying Crown Prince Narahito three years ago. Although Narahito had to beg and plead and grovel at Owada's feet before she accepted, once they were hitched she was expected to do what all princesses in Japan are expected to do—walk two paces behind her husband, shut up (she was royally criticized for talking more than Narahito at a press conference), and conceive a male heir. Her inability to do the latter has tongues wagging throughout the country.

In Japan, equal employment opportunity laws relating to gender are voluntary—there are no sanctions for discrimination against women in the workplace. The media center at JLPGA tournaments is as male-dominated as the rest of society. More women are now working as writers and photographers. But JLPGA telecasts feature all-male casts of analysts, announcers, and reporters.

Sexism is as touchy a subject in Japan as in the U.S. After I asked a female writer about it, she muttered to another journalist, "Does he think we're still running around in kimonos?"

No, but I do think women athletes in Japan are placed on a pedestal with a hollow base. Ayako Okamoto is the object of adoration, on one hand, but put-downs, on the other, simply because she isn't married.

But Japan is hardly unique. If golf is a worldwide game, sexism in golf seems equally universal.

Even golf books written by such sophisticated journalists as George Plimpton and Dan Jenkins usually pigeonhole women as lively birds brightening up the galleries, or as dutiful wives tending to the home front while Daddy pursues fame and fortune (and often other women).

Or more bluntly, there's the 1980 remark of Seve Ballesteros to *El Pais*, a publication in Madrid: "You women want equality, but you'll never get it because women are inferior to men in all sorts of ways—physically, intellectually, and morally. There are exceptions, but on the whole women are inferior to men."

When women dared to venture onto the links, the boys in plaid pants banished them to the back of the golf cart. Jokes about women golfers became as ubiquitous as divots. Example: A golfer tells a buddy, "I just got a new set of clubs for my wife." His buddy replies, "Now that's what I call a real good trade."

The situation hasn't changed all that much. Marcia Chambers wrote an entire book, *The Unplayable Lie*, in 1995 about sexism in American golf. At many clubs, women are barred from membership. If their husband dies, or the couple divorces, the woman is cast away like an old Eskimo sent off on an ice floe.

How deeply rooted are the chauvinist attitudes? Consider the statement in the official program for the 1995 Portland LPGA tournament, which is organized and operated by Tournament Golf, Inc., a wonderful group founded in 1972 that runs the event with almost all volunteer help, which enables it to devote more money to charity—about $400,000 per year—than all but a few stops on the LPGA or PGA Tour.

"Tournament Golf, Inc., is a group of 45 Portland-area volunteer *busi-*

nessmen and their wives" (italics mine). The men sign up sponsors, sell pro-am spots to the business community, and set up the gallery ropes. The wives staff the hospitality area and pour coffee.

Other examples: This year a local tournament in Maryland featured an ice sculpture of a nude woman with "an anatomically correct vodka dispenser." The director of a Smith Barney office in New York was sued for sexual harassment for ordering female underlings to wear miniskirts and serve coffee to male employees at a golf outing. Marty Jenkins, son of Dan Jenkins, recently filed suit claiming he was improperly fired from The Golf Channel, in part because he reported allegations that Mike Whelan, vice president of production, exposed himself to two female subordinates in 1995. Next year the European Tour's orientation for rookies will advise them how to handle sexual advances from pro-am partners.

Much of the sexism in golf is simply a reflection of the wider culture.

But golf also reinforces and ratifies sexism, in ways most people don't even consider.

Take ladies' tees and women's clubs. Please. The concepts are, when you think about it, silly. Should the average 10-year-old boy play the "men's" tees. Should the average 80-year-old man? Should a strapping female high-school golf team member be directed to the ladies' tees? Or to the "women's section" to buy clubs with flexible shafts and a butterfly on the back of the clubface? Clubs and course lengths relate to individual ability and physique, not to gender.

One of my silly stereotypes involved Japanese golfers. I expected a bunch of athletes with swings as smooth as Okamoto's, and flawless, state-of-the-art techniques adopted from a classic such as *Ben Hogan's Five Fundamental Lessons.* In short, I figured golfers would roll off an assembly line like Sony TVs or Hitachi cameras.

Actually, instruction in Japan has been spotty. "It used to be more by feel than mechanics," says Hiromi Kobayashi. So golfers in Japan run the gamut in terms of swings, games, and backgrounds, just like LPGA players. The common link between East and West is that most women professional golfers are exceptional athletes.

Ikuro Shiotani, 34, currently fourth on the JLPGA money list, was a track star in her youth, holding the Japanese junior record in the broad jump.

Suzuko Maeda, 29, daughter of the proprietor of a noodle shop, is a big, strong woman who used to throw the javelin. She ranks seventh on the money list.

Mayumi Murai, 31, a kinetic bundle of energy, ranks sixth on the money list. She was an outstanding softball player.

As was Okamoto. As was Kobayashi, who won five times on the JLPGA circuit in 1989 and immediately bolted for Q-School. Although she originally failed her college entrance exams in Japan, she was a quick study in America, acing Q-School and adjusting to speedy U.S. greens. (Japanese greens, composed of korai grass, tend to be slower, forcing players, says Kobayashi, "to *hit* putts rather than stroke putts.") Kobayashi earned $66,325 in 1990 and edged Donna Andrews for Rookie of the Year honors. Three years later she captured the JAL Big Apple Classic, televised back to Japan, another tournament in Minnesota, and ranked eighth on the money list with $347,060. She also contended at the U.S. Open, finishing fourth and garnering lots of attention after admitting to the media, "I was so nervous I almost puked."

Although her success didn't elevate her to folk hero status, it did make her a star. She has lucrative endorsement deals with JAL, Hitachi, PRGR clubs, Dunlop, and an upcoming 1997 apparel deal with Ellesse.

Her growing popularity resulted in a freeze-out from Okamoto. Although Kobayashi diplomatically cites the 12-year difference in their ages to explain why they are "not really friends," Japanese journalists say Okamoto never speaks to Kobayashi.

(In contrast, Kobayashi has befriended Mayumi Hirase in her rookie season on the LPGA Tour. Hirase says everyone has helped her cope with a new language and country, even though she has been, at least geographically, "lost all the time." But she's closest to Kobayashi. "Whenever I have a problem, I ask Hiromi.")

Unlike Okamoto, Kobayashi has settled in America and insists on speaking English, which has progressed from fractured to first-rate. She lives in Atlanta, where the weather reminds her of Japan, in a house surrounded by trees.

Kobayashi radiates a sunny calmness; she's usually on the verge of a smile or a laugh. Her nickname is "Giggles." There is an openness and curiosity to Kobayashi that seems more Western than Eastern. Asked what she likes best about America, she says, "Everybody is equal." And worst? "Crime."

Although she feels the heat from the Japanese media, Kobayashi handles it exquisitely. "I try to be myself all the time," she says. One day after practicing at Ami, she talked and joked with eight journalists. Most weren't even taking notes; they were just shooting the breeze.

Her friendliness and good humor coexist with a fiercely competitive spirit. Her goal is to become the first Japanese woman since Chako Higuchi to win a major on the LPGA Tour. And her work ethic is unsurpassed. Good friend Missie Berteotti, who praises Kobayashi for her "genuineness," told *Golf for Women* in 1993, "Every night she eats dinner, every night she exercises, every night she goes to bed early. She's dedicated to what she is doing and to her success."

Kobayashi ranked nineteenth on the money list with $242,323 in 1994 and twenty-third with $233,125 in 1995. She's currently thirty-sixth with $169,501 in 1996.

Nice numbers. But she hasn't won since 1993, which means she's not content with her game. Not content with her putting—she discovered she was lining up with her eyes behind instead of over the ball. Not content with her ball-striking—she's changed graphite shafts six or seven times in the past two seasons, in search of the confidence and control she had three years ago.

Someday Kobayashi may return to play the Japanese circuit. Right now she's playing for the U.S. team. When she did so for the first time at the Nichirei in 1993, it was "so strange feeling. The gallery—it was confusing for them too. Now—it's okay," says the woman of two cultures.

Halfway across the globe, Leslie Spalding fights for her professional life.

Every morning at Ami, results from the previous day at Q-School are faxed from Daytona Beach. The scores on the sheets of paper illustrate just how cold the winnowing process, which started with 384 contestants at two sectional preliminaries, really is. The group was whittled to 70 golfers (low 30 plus ties at each site.) They joined 60 fringe dwellers, including Spalding, who held a Tour card in 1996 and received a bye into the 72-hole final. The hopes and dreams of the 130 players who teed it up at LPGA International are reduced to a number. The golf gods say, "Just the fax, ma'am."

As Cristie Kerr rises toward the top, Nichirei teammates gleefully exchange stories about her behavior. They shake their heads in disbelief at Kris Tschetter's experience with the youngster. Paired at the Sprint Title-holders Championship, Tschetter repeatedly flagged irons at the stick, but missed makable birdie putt after putt. Finally she stiffed one to three feet. Kerr brusquely asked her, "Are you gonna make that one?"

Spalding's first-round number is a disastrous 77. After starting play on the back nine, she four-whacked the 14th hole. She spent much of the evening "freaking out," contemplating alternative job possibilities for 1997 and drawing an utter blank.

Down and almost out, she thought about matches in high school and college, when she dug her way up from apparent defeat to rally and prevail. "I've always prided myself on my ability to come back. I thought if I could try to have fun I could still do it."

Spalding hit 16 greens and fired a second-round 71. "I got more and more comfortable with my game. I started hitting the ball on the clubface instead of on the toe."

A third-round 72—Spalding was four under par at one point before faltering—brought her in at 220. The cut fell at 223. She was tied for forty-fourth. An exempt spot, reserved for the top 20, was out of reach. She was right on the borderline (top 45 plus ties) to secure a conditional position and retain her card.

"I knew I had to play well to keep anything."

Spalding recited her affirmations before the final round:

1. "I am patient."
2. "I am the best."
3. "I always have fun."
4. "I can do anything."
5. "I always remain in the present."
6. "I am solid as a rock."

Forced to wait every shot, making her way through the creepiest Fun House of them all, Spalding was as solid as a rock. "I thought I had made it," she said after a final-round 72. "I didn't realize how close it was."

Spalding's total of 292 ties her for forty-third with six other golfers. She is the very last on the list of the conditional players for 1997. She is also the only golfer in the field to shoot a first-round 77 or higher and rally to place in the top 48. It is the comeback of her golfing life.

The sword falls without favor, knocking out familiar names such as Kay Cockerill, Suzy Green, Kelly Leadbetter (wife of instructional guru David Leadbetter), Connie Chillemi, Kim Shipman, Michelle Bell, Nina Foust, and Sue Ertl. (Most have permanent cards, granted to players who have been on Tour five consecutive years. But they're at the bottom of the heap on the priority list. Officially, they are LPGA Tour professionals. In reality, they have almost no chance to get into a single event, barring a sponsor's exemption or a Monday qualifier.)

Chris Greatrex, after a disasterous final-round 76, will only be able to get inside the ropes as a caddy next year. Page Dunlap, touted as an attractive contender on the rise just three years ago, hopes for more work as a fledgling TV golf reporter after shooting 297. Caroline Keggi, a former hot young star, won $180,197 in 1990, $208,534 in 1991, and $172,669 in 1992, before contracting an intestinal infection in 1993. She never fully recovered; she's out in the cold after finishing at 297. LaRee Pearl Sugg, also is on the outside looking in after a 297, her stellar play during the regular season all for naught.

How brutal is Q-School?

Alison Munt, who shot 293 to miss her conditional card by one stroke, was penalized two strokes for slow play during the third round.

How cruel is Q-School?

Seventeen-year-old Jenny Lee, who dropped out of the University of Texas to turn pro after her freshman year, stating, "My main goal is to be a professional and become famous," earned the worst sort of notoriety. After a one under par 287, followed by a victory in a playoff for one of the last exempt cards, she was told, as she walked off the green, that she was being disqualified from the tournament for taking an incorrect drop on the 71st hole.

Forty-eight players are much happier. Conditional cards for 1997 are awarded to Laura Baugh and Nancy Harvey, who has a job for her pal Chris Greatrex. Fully exempt players include Cristie Kerr, 23-year-old former NCAA champion Charlotta Sorenstam (who says her goal is to be number one, and bridles at questions comparing her game with that of her illustrious older sister), Denise Killeen, Kim Bauer, and European Solheim Cup members Dale Reid and Joanne Morley. Cards go to rookies from around the globe—Austria, England, Peru, Australia, India, Sweden—some of the 60 foreign players representing 16 countries who will compete in America next year, as the world continues to mass at the gates of the LPGA Tour.

Leslie Spalding slipped through just as the gates were slamming shut for the 1997 season. It will be a difficult year. An uncertain year—Spalding won't know until the last minute whether she will make the field for some events. A pressure-packed year—she'll need to score extremely well in Monday qualifiers and extremely well in her limited tournament appearances to contend for a top-125 spot on the money list. (The addition of four new tournaments to the LPGA schedule will help Spalding and other conditional players, opening up more positions in the field at many lesser events, as the stars pick and choose from a larger menu of tournaments.) An expensive year—Spalding must go back to her investors to try to raise enough cash to travel the circuit. A hat-in-hand year—Spalding will try to coax four sponsor's exemptions, the maximum, from tournament directors and bigwigs.

But she's undaunted. She overcame much greater odds and obstacles to make it to the Tour. And she believes—and tells herself every day when she recites her affirmations—that she belongs inside the ropes, competing against the best in the world.

"It's gonna be okay," says Spalding, from her home in Tampa. "I'm looking forward to next year."

The U.S. team cranks it up on Saturday and Sunday under sunny skies in front of crowds of several thousand people.

A group of six middle-aged women sit on a blanket near a bunker, buzzing and laughing as an approach shot from Kris Tschetter almost beans them. When they start to move, Tschetter smiles and says, "Oh, no, you're fine." After putting out, Tschetter tosses her ball toward them, but it falls short and lands in the trap. A gray-haired man dashes into the sand, trips and almost falls in his haste to secure his souvenir, as Tschetter puts her hand over her mouth and says, "Oops!"

It's all very pleasant, airy and serene. The Japanese fans are quiet but not surprised or depressed as the U.S. team romps to a 7-2 victory in best-ball matches on Saturday.

On Sunday the U.S. runs away with the early singles contests, removing any last trace of suspense. The final tally is 21½ to 14½, decisive but not humiliating to the hosts.

The Japanese players in the grandstand sing "Happy Birthday" to Kaori Harada, a tiny, adorable 30-year-old with an odd, swaying swing who ranks third on the money list.

Val Skinner, who cruises to victory over Akane Oshiro after Oshiro registered a 9 on an early hole en route to an 81, says, "I started making sympathy bogeys." Physically, Skinner is feeling fine. Mentally, she endured a strange day. Unable to converse with Oshiro or the caddies, she found her mind wandering during the blowout.

"Did you have anyone to talk to?" she asks her teammates as she joins them in the grandstand. "I had about fifteen voices going through my head. I felt like Sybil out there."

The U.S. players say farewell to their caddies. "It's hard," says Morris. "You spend five days with them." Chris Johnson gives Yoko Taguchi a beautiful handerchief, a thank-you card, and gifts for her two sons.

Through an interpreter a smiling Taguchi says, "I was very nervous. But Chris and Tracy [Kerdyk, who teamed with Johnson in the best-ball matches] are very good players and very kind."

If Webb was Cinderella in Korea, she's Wonder Woman in Japan. Undefeated for the week, she shoots 68 to defeat Okamoto by five shots, chatting cheerfully with the Japanese superstar throughout the round. It's the low score of the day, matched by Brandie Burton and JLPGA leading money winner Aiko Hashimoto.

Webb played brilliantly, handled the most nerve-wrecking part of the week—her speech-making duties—with panache (aided by some composing help from her teammates), and, once she found out who was on the team, got along famously with her mates, who gave her the same kind of good-natured shit they'd give a favorite younger sister. At the closing ceremonies, she makes a final speech and picks up almost all the goodies, including a pendant as the tournament's most valuable player and a kitchen load of Nichirei products.

By the next morning even some of her teammates think Webb is Wonder Woman.

Dressed up for a luncheon in Tokyo, U.S. players check out of the hotel in Tsukuba for a bus ride into the city. After lunch the traveling party will proceed to the luxurious Rigah Royal Hotel, located near the airport. The hotel will serve as headquarters for the Toray Cup, to be played at nearby Tone Golf Club.

A number of players celebrated in Toyko last night. They were impressed when Webb downed at least ten beers without a hint of inebriation. They also admired her slickness in leading on a pickup artist at the Motown Bar.

"Are you staying in Tokyo?" he asked.

"Yes," said Webb, toying with him.

"Where?"

"The Imperial Hotel." (It was the only hotel Webb knew.)

"That's where I stay. What room are you in?"

"1503," said Webb.

"Can I come to your room?"

"Okay."

"What time?"

"One o'clock."

Webb and the others are still laughing and wondering who might have opened the door of room 1503.

As she snoozes on the bus, Webb is at peace. She's simply having the time of her life. Except in Australia where she's famous, she's rarely recognized. The media haven't been overly burdensome, although Webb is weary of the question posed in every single interview: "Are you surprised by your success?" The second most frequent query—"What do you attribute your success to?"—she finds more amusing.

"Like it must be a secret formula that I have," she says with a grin.

She has weathered a broken engagement as well. Since she officially split with Haller during the week of the U.S. Open, she has spoken to him five or six times on the phone. Recently she called him on his birthday. But a reconciliation isn't in the cards.

Although it took a few weeks to adjust to traveling on her own, Webb soon discovered "a sense of freedom. I didn't have to tell anyone where I was going or what I was doing. It used to be my parents and then it was Todd. For the first time in my life I was free to make my own decisions."

Her biggest concern at the moment is with her golf game. "I've had good finishes, but I haven't played my best. But I've improved to where I can manufacture a score when I'm not playing well. I could have an unbelievable tournament if I played as well as I did at the start of the year."

After the Toray Cup, Webb returns to Australia for two weeks. Then it's on to Las Vegas and the grand finale, the ITT Tour Championship, where she and Davies (and perhaps Sorenstam) will conclude their season-long battle for the money title. It's pretty wonderous stuff for a youngster who sold her stereo and her car to raise part of the bankroll to turn pro less than two years ago.

WELCOME TO TORAY QUEEN'S CUP PRO-AM TOURNAMENT. HAVE A NICE DAY!

The big scoreboard near the pond by the 18th hole greets golfers at Tone Golf Club on October 31. Located in the countryside, Tone is a little like Pine Needles, with its hilly terrain, stands of pine trees (short as opposed to longleaf), pleasing variety of holes, and larks (the symbolic bird for the region) flitting through the trees.

But it's also distinctly Japanese-looking: the grass in the rough is brown and the landscape is dotted by humming silver electric-power stations shaped like shorter, broader Eiffel Towers.

The price of admission also is distinctly Japanese; most of Tone's 950 members paid an average of $1,600,000, although the economic crash has lowered the market price (private club memberships are traded like stocks in Japan) to about $700,000.

Last night's pro-am reception at the Rigah Royal Hotel was an Eastern version of the Nabisco Dinah Shore gala dinner. Several hundred business executives, including the captains of a number of Japanese corporations, sat at tables in a banquet room. Although it was a buffet, dozens of waitresses clad in black skirts and fancy white blouses hovered nearby, fetching plates and pouring drinks, often while kneeling geisha-style to refill glasses.

Toasts and speeches followed. It was something of an infomercial for Toray, a company that manufactures synthetic fabrics. Businessmen picked at their nails, thumbed through their programs, and checked their watches. A few closed their eyes and began to nod off.

But it was worth the wait for the food: sushi, noodles, Western dishes, desserts, platters of fruit and melon, a pricey treat in Japan. (The coffee shop at the hotel charges about $14 for a slice of melon.)

Today the Tone parking lot is jammed with gleaming Crowns and Mercedes and Cedric Broughams and Century Toyotas

Some of the pro-am contestants are accompanied by junior executives and secretaries, who lurk near the pine trees, dressed in dark suits, snapping photos and applauding when their bosses sink a putt. They are known as "clappers," a Japanese version of the Rent-A-Fan Club, although these salarymen seem to be owned. One female employee is observed pulling her fat boss up some of the hills by his golf club. Later the "clappers" stand in the parking lot like crows, waiting for their bosses to finish eating and drinking at the pro-am awards luncheon.

Female caddies at Tone appear to have descended from outer space, if not the set of a cheesy science fiction show. They wear velourlike powder blue knickers and shirts, with a wide yellow stripe down the pants leg and a yellow V on the shirt. An oversized, long-billed yellow and blue cap with yellow earflaps, white tennis shoes, and white gloves complete the ensemble.

But there aren't enough house caddies at Tone for the entire field of 84 golfers, so some male college students are imported for the 54-hole event.

The tournament begins under breezy skies and drizzle. Soon it deteriorates to a steady rain, sheets of water blowing sideways in the wind. Only handfuls of fans brave the elements to follow the first-round action.

In some ways it's business as usual, as the Thunder and Lightning Tour brings inclement weather to another continent. But in other ways, it's like golfing on an alien planet—near nonexistent galleries, outer-space caddies, and, in many cases, no one to talk to because of the language barrier.

As the rain pelts down, the college-kid caddies flunk the choreography test of umbrellas, towels, and rain gear. Many players are soaked to the skin. They squish off the final green and seek shelter under the eaves of the clubhouse, shaking off rainwater from hair and clothes like sheepdogs. A large contingent of media conduct interviews and shoot photos.

Emilee Klein is furious. "My caddie pulled the cup out of the ground on four." Her voice a fine whine, Klein continues, "He kept turning the umbrella upside down. Then he'd get dry towels and put them on the ground!" (Klein will shoot 78-76 and miss the cut. She'll leave her battered, black Callaway umbrella, stamped with her name, behind. It will be auctioned off after the final round to a fan for 10,000 yen, after a number of Japanese players autograph it.)

"I've never gotten that wet for that long in my history," says 21-year veteran Dale Eggling.

"Oh, my God, what was it like?" says Marnie McGuire, rain dripping off the tips of her red hair, unable to find words for the misery.

"Fun," says Liselotte Neumann with a wry smile.

Laura Davies, completely drenched, wordlessly slams her ball at a trash can and misses. She blistered the tougher back nine in 32, then hacked up the front side in 39. She's four strokes behind the 67 of first-round leader Hiromi Kobayashi. At 69 are Amy Benz, Ikuro Shiotani, and Maggie Will.

A persistent, cold rain half-submerges the rice fields near Tone on a dank Saturday morning. A small American flag at the gates of the club is blown almost stiff by the wind. The caddies from outer space have their carts and golf bags almost completely encased in plastic.

"She's got plastic bags coming out of her ears," jokes Vicki Fergon, standing near her caddie. "She's very good," Fergon adds.

It's a tense time for the caddies. The college kids were chewed out after the round yesterday by the caddie master. The house caddies, who, for the most part, were able to keep their players dry, are coping with their own nerves.

"She feels like *she's* playing," says a translator, after conversing with one of the loopers. "Her heart is almost like it's bursting. She feels insecure. She wants to say something to help her player feel better, but she doesn't want to upset her."

The caddie miscues have upset some of the Japanese Tour players, too, but for different reasons. Aki Takamura is particularly worried. She's been paired with Neumann two straight weeks, in the singles matches at the Nichirei (Takamura won 71-72) and yesterday in the first round of the Toray. Like many of the young Japanese players, Takamura, 24, is starstruck by Neumann, honored simply to be in her presence. Other players are envious and tell Takamura she's lucky. But Takamura fears the student caddies' screw-ups may be seen as a reflection upon her and the other Japanese professionals. She's afraid that Neumann hates her.

A journalist fluent in Japanese and English tries to explain Takamura's feelings to Neumann. But something is lost in the translation, and Neumann becomes alarmed.

"I didn't do anything wrong," she says, bewildered. If the rain persists much longer, we may have shamed and guilt-ridden players from Japan and Sweden, as well as dozens of caddies, committing ritual suicide with sharpened L-wedges.

Applause is subdued on the course, mainly because everyone is clutching umbrellas. But Maggie Will, paired with Mayumi Hirase and Michie Ohba, a sweet-swinging 23-year-old who used to be a speed skater, is in her element.

Despite her fragile appearance, the five-foot-four, 105-pound Will is a great mudder. In 1990 she won in bone-chilling cold and a 40-mph gale in

Las Vegas. In 1992 she prevailed at Nashville in wind, rain, and 45-degree temperatures. ("I had *everything* on that day.") After hitting her drive on the 368-yard 2nd hole, she sprints back to her caddie and a sheltering umbrella. Spotting some American acquaintances in the gallery, she smiles and rolls her eyes.

In the final group, a bundled-up Amy Benz blows on her hands and rubs them together, trying to stay warm. Kobayashi, with the customary half-smile she usually seems to wear, is sporting a white knit ski hat over her white golf cap. When she half-tops a fairway wood, some fans in the gallery actually laugh, a reaction that might earn a spectator a ritual murder with a sharpened L-wedge in the U.S.

Golf sounds a bit different in Japan. It looks a bit different as well. The 145-yard 4th hole has a green bordered by a semicircle of tall pines. About 200 fans stand beneath the trees on a hillside around the green, some in orange rainsuits, many clutching yellow umbrellas. With the caddies in their strange powder blue uniforms, it creates an almost otherworldly tableaux. Yet when a putt rolls over the green and clangs into the cup, it seems to blend East and West into a realm of its own, Planet Golf, where the language of the game transcends nationality.

Will and Hirase complete two rounds at four under par 140. Kobayashi stands at 141, Ohba at 143, and Geddes, Whitehead, Davies, and Susie Redman at 144. The cut falls at nine over par.

"I haven't practiced in two weeks," Will says cheerfully after the round. She's been busy with wedding arrangements—Will and Tom Halpin are getting hitched in a few weeks, on November 30. (Kris Tschetter, Vicki Goetze, Annika Sorenstam, and Missie Berteotti also are getting married in the next few months.) But she hopes to play in one more tournament prior to the big day. If she wins the Toray, she'll vault into the top 30 on the money list and qualify for the Tour Championship in Las Vegas. Since her three wins came in 1990, 1992, and 1994, she figures her number might be due.

"Last chance for romance," she says lightly, referring to tomorrow's final round. It's the last chance for a number of others on the bubble as well; the fight for top-30 spots has been a tournament-within-a-tournament all week.

It's the main goal for Kobayashi, who ranks thirty-sixth and probably needs to finish first, second, or third this week. Others are here trying to protect their positions—Joan Pitcock, Deb Richard, Chris Johnson, Tina Barrett, and Barb Whitehead cling to the twenty-sixth through thirtieth spots.

Before this year, the regular season concluded at the Toray to the sounds of no hands clapping, at least not American ones. Now there's a neon glow from The Strip that shines so brightly it beckons from 5,500 miles away.

Patches of turquoise on the horizon begin to erase the gray skies on Sunday morning. Players and caddies, tense and somber, gather by the bag room, quietly preparing their equipment for the upcoming struggle.

In both 1994 and 1995 Woo-Soon Ko won the Toray Cup in stunning upsets. She's buried in the pack this year. The rest of the Japanese Tour players quickly slip back as well, as Will, Kobayashi, and Hirase waltz around the top of the leader board.

Yesterday, after Laura Davies bogeyed two holes, her caddie told her, "You must try harder." It was unnecessary advice. If Davies can't win, she'll scrap and claw for whatever she can get.

Today she's playing steadily but making little headway on the leaders. Board watching as usual, she figures she's out of it.

"Just get third, just get third," she tells herself.

But after birdies on Nos. 11 and 12, and a drive and an iron to the 471-yard par-five finishing hole, Davies slam-dunks the eagle putt to finish at four under par. In a flash she vaults over Kobayashi, who misses a 12-foot par putt on No. 16, and Hirase, both at three under par. After clinging to the lead at the turn, Will has kissed her chances good-bye with five bogeys in six holes.

Going for the pin at the 168-yard 17th hole, Kobayashi airmails the green and eventually double-bogeys. Hirase, after a par, needs to birdie the last hole to force a playoff.

LPGA players, required to attend the closing ceremonies, gather behind the 18th green or on a stone bridge over the pond between the green and the clubhouse, sipping soft drinks or beers, watching the finish.

A shell-shocked Kobayashi, with victory seemingly in her grasp a few holes earlier, somehow snakes in an eagle putt from about 60 feet. As the ball nears the cup, playing partner Will raises both hands overhead to signal "touchdown." She gives Kobayashi an emphatic high-five and a beaming smile, almost as happy as if she had sunk the putt herself.

Fans packed in a towering grandstand above the green erupt in cheers but go silent as Hirase, after a brilliant wedge, lines up a three-foot birdie putt.

Hirase, 2nd on the money list in Japan last year, has fashioned an outstanding rookie season on the LPGA Tour, ranking 42nd with $137,871 coming into the Toray. She's done so without much fanfare, partly because Karrie

Webb has eclipsed the other rookies and partly because there aren't a lot of bells and whistles associated with her game. John Killeen, who caddied for Hirase earlier in the season, compares her with Meg Mallon, steady and solid.

She's rock solid on her putt, sighing deeply with relief when the ball drops.

The playoff commences on No. 18. Both reach the green in two and match birdies when Davies barely misses an eagle try from about 15 feet.

So it's back to the 360-yard 16th hole. Several hundred fans run across the hillsides to the tee, some slipping on the steep slopes, still slick from the rains.

Davies grimly prepares to hit. She's 0-5 in playoffs on the LPGA Tour, and desperately wanted to polish off the rookie on No. 18. She hacks at the turf to form a grass tee, then blasts a 2-iron about 230 yards into a mild head wind, the ball splitting the fairway.

Hirase buries her drive in deep grass in the right-hard rough. She does well to advance it within 50 yards of the green. Even when Davies, playing in such a rush she almost seems to be running along with the fans, skulls her short iron—it ends up just off the fringe to the right of the green—she holds the advantage.

And when Hirase's wedge checks up 20 feet short of the pin, and Davies hits an exquisite chip that rolls and rolls and rolls across the vast green to tap-in distance, it's game, set, and almost match.

Almost. If Davies had the same luck at the casinos as she does in LPGA playoffs, she'd be bankrupt. So it seems inevitable, if miraculous, when Hirase's last gasp clangs into the cup.

Onto the 168-yard 17th hole. Waiting her turn, Davies looks back at the small crowd behind the tee box, spots an acquaintance, smiles wryly and shakes her head back and forth in a "Can you *believe* it?" gesture that transcends language and nationality.

Both hit the green. Davies's 20-foot birdie putt slides two and a half feet past the hole. Although people are shuffling around in the grandstand behind her, she lines up the par putt quickly. But she comes off it badly, pushing it to the right. She nods a sarcastic "Thanks a lot" toward the grandstand, closes her eyes and grimaces.

She musters a nice smile and hug when Hirase taps in for victory. Then Davies, face frozen in anger, arms wrapped across her chest like she's bound in a straitjacket, is driven off in a cart by an LPGA official. An 0-6 playoff record is enough to induce madness in every sense of the word. Reverse those numbers, and Davies would be two thirds of the way to the Hall of Fame with 20 wins on the LPGA Tour.

Hirase walks off the green with her hands over her mouth in amazement. "*Ichi*" ("Number one") she blurts out in delight and disbelief.

Fans ringing the green applaud loudly, as do spectators along the way as she is driven back to the 18th green. A beaming smile on her face, Hirase waves and bows to her followers.

Ten days ago, on October 30, Hirase celebrated her twenty-seventh birthday. Players sang "Happy Birthday" to her at a reception.

Now she receives some belated but welcome gifts—a check for $112,500 and jewelry from a young woman in a kimono as the other golfers line up across the green and applaud. Then, as a Celine Dion song plays over a loudspeaker, a pack of photographers are joined by fans with pocket cameras to capture a shot of the newest Japanese star.

Kobayashi and Hirase knock Joan Pitcock and Chris Johnson out of the top 30. But it's only a consolation prize for Kobayashi, who could taste her first victory in three seasons. She smiles and says good-bye to several people as she walks through the clubhouse to the parking lot, but even a Western visitor can see she's crying on the inside.

By the time Davies leaves, almost all of the other players have departed on earlier buses for the hotel.

Davies is subdued but far from sad. Her second-place finish secures Player of the Year honors. Besides, she may have the best temperament in the world, male or female, for golf. She firmly believes that the bounce of the ball, which determines the winner and the runner-up, is a matter of fate.

"I'm a bit disappointed," she says. "But today it was not meant to be."

So the Laura Davies, worldwide catch-me-if-you-can, I'll-sleep-when-I'm-dead extravaganza rolls on. Davies has seemed dazed prior to some tournaments—eating breakfast in Sicily, and dinner in Reading, Pennsylvania, will do that to a person. And she readily admits her peripatetic globe-hopping is borderline crazy. But there's a method to her madness. Davies didn't set foot on the practice range all week except to warm up. Unless she's struggling with her swing, she never beats balls after she plays.

Almost every other pro grinds away on the assembly line following their round. To Davies it seems silly, particularly when a golfer is happy with her game and swing.

"I've never, ever to this day understood it. I know it looks to some people like I'm not caring enough, but I think it's a waste. That's the time to sit around and have a drink with your friends." As a result, Davies plays more competitive rounds than her colleagues, yet hits far fewer balls over the course of a season. It keeps her fresh and healthy.

Good thing too, since Davies is terrified of doctors. When she bought her dream house in 1994, she was required to undergo a physical to qualify for the mortgage.

"I must admit I nearly didn't buy the house," says Davies, who was relieved to hear she "was a hundred percent fit, maybe a bit heavy."

It was her first visit to a doctor since 1988, when she developed a nervous rash on one side of her face on the day before she was presented the prestigious MBE (Member of the British Empire) by Queen Elizabeth. "I tried to keep my face turned to the good side," Davies says with a smile. "I looked a little bit stupid at the Palace."

Even given her robust good health and sensible work habits, it's hard to fathom Davies's ability to travel constantly and remain competitive. Asked if she's ever felt disoriented during the last four-month stretch, when she played 14 out of 15 weeks, Davies says just once. Last week, during her only break, she woke up in a dark room and wondered, "Where the hell am I?" After an instant of panic she realized, "Good God, I'm home!"

To many people, Davies seems like a golfing savant. Never a lesson. Little practice. A swing so unorthodox—she repositions her left foot near impact, a move that would cause most people to fall down instead of hit 280-yard drives—it seems a fluke of nature.

It's highly misleading. As a youngster, she beat balls from dawn to dusk. In her early days as a pro, she hit shots too high to be a good wind player. But she diligently taught herself to punch wedges and short irons, learned so brilliantly she captured two majors this year in near gale-force conditions. Mickey Walker believes Davies is one of the great students of the game. She simply studies a curriculum of her own design. As Davies puts it in her new autobiography,

> To my mind, nothing is more calculated to interfere with the flow of the swing than dissecting it. If the set-up and alignment are correct [Davies thinks faulty alignment is the bane of most golfers], it's my belief that you are perfectly placed to imitate one of the many good swings you will see on your television. After all, if you wanted to learn a new song, you would do much better to listen to it than to be told that you needed to hop from C sharp to B flat, to E and to F, or whatever.

The concept is almost a Davies Mind Meld. She watches great players as intensely as an actress soaking up mannerisms of a person she is to portray.

When I look at top players such as Bernhard Langer and Seve Ballesteros, I am trying, first and foremost, to pick up their rhythm. Having watched them hit a few shots, I play those shots over and over in my head, almost as I would a song. Then, when I go to the practice ground, all I am trying to do is reproduce the timing and feel.

Riding back to the hotel, Davies carefully peruses the updated money list. She notes with satisfaction that she or Webb (who tied for thirty-fifth in the Toray Cup) can become the first player in the history of the LPGA to top the $1 million mark in official earnings with a victory at the Tour Championship. (Davies is back in the lead with $897,302; Webb is at $852,000. First prize in Las Vegas is worth $150,000.)

She's asked about a smaller sum—a recent report she was offered $5,000 (compared with Tiger Woods's $40 million deal) to endorse Nike. The amount is correct, although the offer was made in 1995.

"I wasn't insulted at all," Davies says with a straight face and a tone as dry as the desert. "I turned it down. I wouldn't know what to spend all that money on."

Five thousand dollars probably won't cover her gambling tab at the Tour Championship. Davies will be in Vegas for nine days, plenty of time to get into trouble at the roulette wheel and the blackjack tables.

"That's far too long," she says. "I'll stay at the golf course as late as I can every day." Then she says slyly, "I may even practice."

It is, of course, a joke.

CHAPTER 12

*L*as Vegas: *Playing Through*

A tiny 6-year-old girl named Alex is on the practice range at the Desert Inn Golf Course late in the afternoon on Monday, November 18. Alex and about 75 other kids are participating in the Crayola LPGA Tour Junior Golf Clinic Program, which is held at most tournament sites.

The Strip is just a block away. A number of pleasure palaces are visible from the practice range—Treasure Island, Harrah's, the Stardust, the Hilton, the Stratosphere. But the golf course is an island of tranquillity as the sun sinks toward the Spring Mountains and Red Rock Canyon.

Barb Mucha and Amy Fruhwirth, who will tee it up with the other 28 leading money winners of 1996 when the $700,000 ITT Tour Championship kicks off on Thursday, offer some pointers to the kids and their parents.

Then the youngsters get to whack balls. Alex is wearing a white sweatshirt tied around her waist. It has a picture of a kitten on it. Her blonde ponytail flows out from the back of her pink Crayola golf cap, in the style favored by the pros. With a solid swing and a nice follow-through, she smacks a few shots into the air and over the lush green grass.

After she hits her last ball, a clinic volunteer says, "Let's give Alex a nice hand." She rejoins some friends and another tot takes her place to hack away, receive some applause, and tote home a plastic bag full of gifts from Crayola, pink caps and crayons.

Future stars?

You never know.

Future CEOs of corporations which sponsor women's golf tournaments? A possibility.

Future recreational golfers and fans of the LPGA?

It's a good bet.

The stars come out at night in Las Vegas. They emerge in broad daylight for the pro-am on Tuesday, a Planet Hollywood/LPGA bash which benefits actor Jeff Bridges's End Hunger Network, promotes the Planet Hollywood Casino (a joint venture between ITT and Planet Hollywood), which will be built on property adjacent to the Sheraton Desert Inn, and produces the most impressive collection of celebrities that the LPGA has seen in decades.

Hordes of media flood the clubhouse area—*Entertainment Tonight, Extra, Pulse,* and other TV tabloids are filming the scene, as well as local news stations from Los Angeles to Las Vegas.

Rocky is here, displaying a blue-collar touch with white golf tee stuck behind his ear. Yesterday, as Alex and the kids happily hit balls, Stallone, father of a newborn daughter, did the same at the other end of the practice area before playing a casual nine holes with Kris Tschetter.

Batman's Robin (Chris O'Donnell) is here. So is Robocop (Peter Weller). So are other stars of the screen and tube (Richard Dreyfuss, two Baldwin brothers, Andrew Shue, Joe Pesci, Tom Arnold), the music biz (Rudy Gatlin, Stephen Stills, Frankie Avalon), and the sports world (Roger Clemens, Willie Gault, Joe Theisman).

The postround lunch and party in the clubhouse offers a glimpse into the lives of the rich and famous. A battalion of Desert Inn employees transform a pleasant dining area into an ornately decorated stage surrounded by a white picket fence (to keep out the riffraff), flowers, ice sculptures, bar, and buffet stations. (The Desert Inn is feeding the media lavishly as well.) If it seems incongruous to eat and drink like kings while raising some money to fight hunger, no one notices.

One might assume that would-be policewoman Marianne Morris, disturbed by Ayako Okamoto's gambling proposition in Japan, would be repelled by her pro-am partner, former Motley Crue lead singer Vince Neil, attired in shorts and leopard-print golf boots, which accentuates the large tattoo of abstract design covering one calf.

But they get along famously, finding common ground on the links.

It's not only Planet Hollywood that seems to be in alignment with the LPGA. The cosmos appears to be falling in place as well.

Four brand new tournaments have been announced for 1997. A record 43 events will offer a record $30 million in purses, an impressive increase of 20 percent over 1996.

LPGA players are in demand all over the globe. With the addition of a new tournament in Australia in February, the Tour will play official events in six countries (U.S., Canada, Australia, England, Korea, Japan) on four continents. The government of Peru, which is sponsoring the $100,000 Peruvian Championship in Lima in late January, has invited 18 LPGA players to compete. Soon the Tour may have an official event in South America.

The aces of the LPGA glittered all season long. The "Big Three"—Davies, Webb, and Sorenstam—elevated themselves from the pack with a panache seldom seen since the glory days of Palmer, Nicklaus, and Player. "The Great Eight"—Davis, Webb, Sorenstam, Pepper, McGann, Neumann, Mallon, and Klein—have won 25 events. Stars such as Sheehan, Lopez, and Robbins have had moments in the sun as well.

Five years ago SI's Jaime Diaz dismissed the LPGA with a blunt two words—"Who cares?" Now he believes it has never been healthier. Now it's the Senior Tour, with its dimming star power, that bores him.

IMG's Jay Burton believes 1996 was the best year in the history of the LPGA—"and I thought 1994 and 1995 were good." It's hard to find anyone to contradict him.

As the sports industry continues to spin out of control—Boston College football players, including two who bet against their own team, are busted for illegal gambling, Roberto Alomar spits in the face of an umpire—the contrast to the world of the LPGA Tour becomes more and more stark. Toledo columnist John Guggan writes:

"There is this other theory, mine, that people have become tired of overpaid, egotistical athletes with the maturity of a tomato seed. You do not find many people like that on the LPGA Tour."

Donna Lopiano, executive director of the Women's Sports Foundation, says the LPGA's image as caring athletes who give back to the community is "ideal. They're staying away from what has plagued big-time sports—the arrogance and the lawbreaking."

Perhaps most intriguingly, the condemnation of powerful strong women athletes is turning upside down in many circles. Ben Wright's cutting remarks about butch women beating courses to a pulp, uttered less than two years ago, seems completely out of touch. Now Bill Fields writes in *Golf World*:

"As the triple jump has come to figure skating, the powerful serve to tennis and even, on occasion, the dunk to basketball, power-hitting has come to women's golf, and there is nothing freakish about it."

Nothing freakish about it. Fields is onto something. Perhaps for the first time in American history, strong women athletes are not automatically suspect, condemned to crude assumptions about their sexuality. As more and more women and girls compete, as more and more couch potatoes marvel at the U.S. women's soccer team and basketball team, prejudice eases. The dads and moms who brought little Alex and the other girls and boys to the Crayola clinic on Monday know the score. So do the soccer dads and moms and the basketball dads and moms, and the softball dads and moms. Big league sports may be, for the most part, corrupt and disgusting, but sport itself is too enriching, too valuable, too much fun, to allow bigots or buffoons to restrict the playing field.

Golf writers suddenly are clamoring for a match between the Seniors and the LPGA, with everyone hitting from the same tees. The assumption is that it will be close. The assumption is that the women really can play.

(The newfound admiration of power golf is not an unalloyed blessing. The danger for the LPGA is that it will focus attention on strength, where men hold the edge, rather than skill. While it is an awesome sight to watch Laura Davies smash a drive 280 yards, it is just as fascinating to watch a Caroline Pierce shoot 67 at Wykagyl or a Patty Sheehan use all the tools in her illustrious arsenal to prevail in a major championship.)

Even major corporate muckety-mucks who, on a whole, have shunned the LPGA like it was a leper colony are beginning to see the light. Thanks to Dr Pepper, you may be seeing a lot more of Dottie Pepper. A press conference after the pro-am on Tuesday officially introduces the soft drink company's new spokeswoman.

Life-size grocery store cardboard cutouts of Pepper are propped up around the room. It's been a fine day for the golfer, whose beaming smile matches the expression on the cardboard cutouts. Earlier in the day Pepper won $25,000 for a hole-in-one in the pro-am. Now she says, correctly, that her endorsement deal "can only help us as an organization."

Both Pepper and McGann are about to enter negotiations with Cadillac, which has, until now, signed only male golfers. Lincoln Mercury, a strong presence on the PGA Tour, just became an LPGA licensee and soon will sign Annika Sorenstam. The barrier between the LPGA and the general public is wobbling.

On Wednesday, IMG confirms the rumors: Kelli Kuehne, 19, winner of the 1995 and 1996 U.S. Amateur titles, is turning pro. She will team with Tiger Woods in the upcoming JCPenney Mixed Team Classic in Florida. (They finish second, almost entirely due to Woods's outstanding play.)

Kuehne, a sophomore at the University of Texas, didn't attend Q-School. She can't quality for a Tour card until next fall. She can play, with a sponsor's exemptions, a maximum of four LPGA tournaments in 1997.

So why is she turning pro now?

Money. Nike money. Kuehne is an instant millionaire, a winner in the sports celebrity sweepstakes. The deal reportedly will pay her $250,000 a year for five years. (IMG also is negotiating with equipment companies, and expects an offer in the $200,000 to $400,000 per year range for a golf club and perhaps golf ball endorsement.)

The amount is unprecedented for a woman golfer. For Tiger Woods, who reportedly is receiving $40 million from Nike and $20 million from Titleist, it would be tip money. But in LPGA circles it's enough to raise hackles, even though the deal should help raise the bar for other pros in the future. For

Kuehne $1.25 million? After Nike offered Laura Davies $5,000? Sure, Kuehne is, on the surface, ideal Nike material. The five-foot-two star is young, talented, cute as a speckled pup, and ornerier than a junkyard dog.

"Every time I put the peg in the ground, I'm ready to play," Kuehne told *Golf World.* "You can't beat me, especially in match play."

But a great amateur career is no guarantee of success in the pros. Ask Kay Cockerill, who won back-to-back U.S. Amateurs in 1986–1987, signed a lucrative deal with Casio, and now is working primarily in television. Ask Vicki Goetze, winner of the U.S. Amateur in 1989 and 1992. She signed a six-figure deal with Yonex, but has labored in the pack, finishing eighty-second on the money list in 1994, seventy-seventh in 1995, and fifty-sixth in 1996. Not bad, but far short of what many people expected.

Kuehne has played in four professional events. She has missed the cut in every one. When she was paired with Sorenstam and Webb at the U.S. Open in Pine Needles, she quietly shot 78-78.

So players are buzzing about the deal. Val Skinner tells *Golf World:*

"I think Laura Davies deserves a half-million dollars. What about our really proven, great players. Where has Nike been for the women's tour for the last few years? . . . Why isn't Nike looking at Webb or Davies? That's the part I don't get. Do you make stars or do they become stars because they're great?"

Juli Inkster has worn Nike shoes for about eight years. She received $5,000 to 15,000 a year until Nike ended the arrangement after the 1995 season. She wore their shoes (Nike sent her six free pairs) without compensation this year. But she wasn't happy about it, especially after the company signed a number of male pros, including Nick Price, to big-money contracts.

"They put millions and millions into the men's tour, nothing for us," Inkster said back in January, around the time Nike decided not to sponsor an equivalent of its Nike Tour (a highly successful developmental circuit for pros who don't qualify for the major leagues) for women.

In September she talked to a Nike official at the Safeway Classic in Portland. He told her that Nike didn't have the appropriate product line to sign women pros.

So she's livid over the Kuehne deal. "They didn't tell me," says Inkster. "I've given them enough respect and backed them enough. I'm tired of them blowing smoke." Later she tells *USA Today,* "I'd rather go barefoot than wear Nikes."

The LPGA is too good for Nike. Literally. Women golf pros don't have the in-your-face, fist-pumping, show-me-the-money, bad-boy or -girl image that the company craves, the win-at-all-cost mentality that led to its memorable ad at the Summer Olympics—"You don't win silver, you lose gold"—the elevation of $100 sneakers into a twisted icon of the snarling, swaggering, self-reverential modern athlete, the hawking of athletic gear as something bordering on the quasi-religious (although hardly spiritual), a blend of hubris and chutzpah whipped into something resembling madness. Here's what Nike boss Phil Knight told *The New York Times* last February.

"We see a natural evolution . . . dividing the world into their athletes and ours. And we glory [*sic*] ours. When the U.S. played Brazil in the World Cup, I rooted for Brazil because it was a Nike team. America was Adidas."

Nike has been called many things; seldom has it been called dumb. The seven-figure signing of Kelli Kuehne is dumb.

Kuehne is the first to admit she is no Tiger Woods. She isn't in the same league with Webb, only two years her elder. Or, in all probability, with college rival and NCAA champ Marisa Baena. The five-foot-four and 116-pound Baena, a University of Arizona sophomore, stunned spectators and pros at the U.S. Open, launching drives almost into Laura Davies territory. She's truly the college equivalent of Tiger Woods. She's also very pretty, infectiously cheerful, and down-to-earth. Too nice for Nike?

Perhaps. Kuehne, on the other hand, seems to symbolize the harder edge the company relishes. Her brashness draws wildly diverse reactions. When an LPGA player from a Southern school talks to her former college coach about the Kuehne signing, the coach says, "Kuehne is a bitch." The player is shocked. She's never heard her coach swear before.

Yet Pete McDaniel, who covered Kuehne's 1996 U.S. Amateur triumph for *Golf World*, describes her as "endearing. She's very straightforward, honest to a fault. If that's perceived as cocky, it's because she wears her confidence like other people wear their fear."

She'll need all of that confidence after selling her sole to Nike. Unlike Cockerill and Goetze, popular with their colleagues, Kuehne can expect a very chilly reception from her competitors in the big leagues. She's getting lots of money. She'll earn every last dollar.

The Kuehne deal with Nike illustrates how far the LPGA has traveled. It also illustrates the gap between the women and the men.

Top PGA pros routinely receive six-figure club endorsement deals; stars get seven figures. Corey Pavin is ending his arrangement with Cleveland Golf to bolt to Japanese club maker PRGR for a reported $2 million a year. In comparison, Rosie Jones earned $426,957 in 1995 using Ram irons. Yet she says the company had previously offered her an endorsement contract that, had she accepted it, would have been worth, including bonuses, a paltry $7,000, chump change for such an outstanding season. Jones rejected the proposal and is now testing Callaway clubs. "Ram really [tried to] screw me," says Jones. "I want to work with a company putting money into women's golf and the LPGA."

This year the LPGA played for $25.4 million in official prize money. PGA pros carted home $68 million. The seniors hitched up their back braces to lug away $41 million. Michelle Dobek wound up 100th on the LPGA money list with $47,450. Olin Browne finished 100th on the PGA Tour with $223,703. Jim Ritts is at his most persuasive when he discusses the need to raise purses in order to give the LPGA's lesser lights—who are, after all, among the finest female golfers in the world—an opportunity to make a decent living in a profession that is so precarious and can be so fleeting.

Are the disparities in prize money unfair? Not really. Purse levels correlate to TV ratings and fan support. Last year the final round of the Memorial drew a 2.8 share of the market (about 2.6 million homes) in a head-to-head matchup with the Women's U.S. Open, which registered a 1.9 share (about 1.75 million homes). The final round of the Dinah Shore attracted a 2.0 rating; the Players' Championship, broadcast at the same time, registered 4.3.

For all its progress, the LPGA is unlikely ever to rival the PGA Tour. As Betsy Rawls puts it, "There's a limiting factor in women's sports, and that's simply strength. Men are more spectacular to watch. The U.S. Women's Open will never be quite on par with the men."

In many ways, the LPGA Tour is the Jane Austen of sports. The world it inhabits is small, intense, and absorbing. It is populated with women who, simply by pursuing their dreams, act to loosen "the constriction of female opportunity," as Martin Amis described Austen's characters in *The New Yorker*.

It may not corral the masses in the same manner as a $200 million Hollywood action flick featuring wall-to-wall "whammies"—Hollywood lingo for spectacular, explosive scenes of destruction. But quieter stories that offer sense and sensibility and beguile with persuasion are attracting a growing legion of fans.

Bigger is not always better. With the possible exception of the kids—Kelli Kuehne, Cristie Kerr, Jenny Lee, who may not know any better—few if any LPGA players want to be Just Like Mike or Arnold or Tiger. Karrie Webb and Annika Sorenstam and Laura Davies and Patty Sheehan and Liselotte Neumann are happy to shop in grocery stores and go to the movies and eat at restaurants with a minimum of fuss or disruption.

The glass may be half-full for the LPGA and its players. But the bubbles in the glass, which tasted like Alka-Seltzer for most of the 46-year history of the organization, now taste like champagne.

For the first time, the LPGA has the stability and strength to allow it to play through the vicissitudes of economic ups and downs, the slings and arrows of the chauvinistic media and corporate world, and the shifts in the cultural zeitgeist. (Nowhere is it preordained that golf will forever remain cool. In 20 years, the most popular entertainment in America may be Rollerball, with armchair parimutuel wagering via computer-driven remote controls.)

A large part of that stability and strength is psychological. Self-esteem, Charlie Mechem's priceless gift to the LPGA, may be as great an asset as the amazing talent on display between the ropes. No longer does the LPGA fret that there may not be a tomorrow. Instead, it confidently seeds a bright future with innovative, exemplary, grassroots programs for kids and a jazzy new high-tech, interactive Fan Village, both the brainchild of LPGA vice president Cindy Davis. (Next spring it will announce a partnership with the USGA and the Girl Scouts of America, which will link the LPGA's Girls Golf Club program with over 3 million Girl Scouts, backed by the USGA's financial assistance. It will soon be one of the biggest and best girls sports programs in the world.)

In fact, the visionary Mechem cautions that the challenge for the future may stem primarily from the LPGA's current success. When he retired last December, Mechem sent a letter to the players. It read, in part:

> The problem that troubles me in many respects is a perfectly natural result of the growth of women's amateur and professional golf in recent years. Players arrive on the Tour from increasingly protected backgrounds and this, combined with the significant financial rewards immediately available to them on Tour, can quite easily lead to an attitude of self-indulgence and a lack of understanding and appreciation for the "give-back" part of the equation. The problem is further complicated by the fact that, because of the higher profile which the Tour enjoys today, the demands on players from media, sponsors, licensees, etc., grow greater each year.

As long as it heeds Mechem's warning, the LPGA should flourish. It is riding—and helping to build—two powerful, surging, intersecting waves of popularity, one for golf and the other for women's sports, that may not crest for decades.

Yesterday, on the day the Kelli Kuehne deal with Nike was announced, Juli Inkster shot a 62 in the pro-am. It was the lowest round of her life. She joked to the media, "I do that all the time. I can't believe it's such big news." In some ways, it typifies her season. She's played extremely well, but not at the ideal times. "I hate to waste [a 62] in the pro-am."

Today she walks into the interview room after a first-round 68, carrying a plate of Mexican food from the media buffet table.

"If I get anything on me, guys, just let me know."

Although she's been working at her other full-time job, which she describes as "Miss Mom," since the tournament in Kutztown five weeks ago, Inkster's game is in superb form.

"She was just *creaming* it," says playing partner Caroline Pierce, who opens with a one under par 71, under drizzly skies that turn to steady rain in the afternoon. (It's the first measurable rain in Las Vegas in over 200 days.)

Last month in Kutztown, Inkster said, "If I can sneak in a win or another top-ten, I would say I had a good year. I'm playing better, more consistent."

Dog-sick, fighting a cold, chills, and stomach flu, and taking care of Cori, who accompanied her to Kutztown while Hayley stayed home, Inkster played great, at least for 67 holes. She was locked in a head-to-head final-day duel with Laura Davies for the runner-up spot behind Sorenstam before hitting a drive into a bush on the 14th hole and eventually stagger-ing off the green with a nine. She tied for tenth. Mission accomplished, although in a manner more bitter than sweet.

She's in high spirits in Las Vegas, apart from her pique at Nike. The fam-ily is fine. At least one of her daughters has accompanied her to all but three tournaments this year. This week she and Hayley are seeing the sights, including Siegfried & Roy and Circus Circus.

And her golf game is on the verge of its former glory. Inkster ranks twenty-second on the money list with $229,660. She's the Tour's leading "mommy" winner, just ahead of Lopez, the only other mom in the top 30. Including prize money, endorsement deals, and exhibition events, Inkster will earn over $500,000 in 1996.

"There's a light at the end of the tunnel," she says after her media inter-view. "Last year there was no light because my putting was so bad."

Inkster walks out in the rain to the practice green. As she putts, Hayley holds a big white and red Wilson umbrella over their heads, helping mom finish up her work for the day.

Laura Davies finally hits the wall. Davies spent about 20 hours traveling from Australia to Las Vegas on Monday. (She tied for second with Jane Geddes when Aussie Jane Crafter sank a 45-foot eagle putt on the final hole to win the Australian Ladies Masters by one stroke.) Davies went to bed last night at 11:00. She awoke at 7:00, opted for a little more shut-eye, and conked out until 10:40. Her tee time was at 11:14.

"It's the first time in eleven years on Tour I've overslept," says Davies, "and I never sleep for ten hours." Fortunately, she's staying at the Desert Inn, sharing a suite with her father, brother, and cousin. (Davies wanted to stay at Bally's, her favorite gambling emporium. But she was told there was no room at the inn, even for such a valued high-roller. Comdex, the largest convention of the year in Vegas, has brought over 200,000 computer industry geeks and entrepreneurs—gamblers of the first magnitude—to the desert and stuffed every hotel to the brim. If Davies had stayed at Bally's, her quest for the money title might have ended as she sat in a cab stalled in one of the traffic jams that have paralyzed The Strip all week.)

With no time to eat and barely time to dress, Davies arrives on the course at 11:02, rubbing sleep from her eyes. She hits twenty 6-irons and a few putts to warm up before shooting 69 in a steady rain on a course where she has struggled in the past.

"I played very well," she says after the round. "I'm very pleased with the way I hit it."

Caroline Pierce isn't at all pleased with the way she hit it, although she's happy with an opening 71. And she's thrilled with her breakthrough season.

After her triumph at the JAL Big Apple, Pierce tied for fifth in Kutztown, her second best finish of the year. She pocketed $23,398, and now ranks twenty-first on the money list with $240,544. Over half of that amount was earned in just two weeks in New York and Pennsylvania.

The spoils of victory, large and small, continue to accumulate. A new clothes deal—no cash but a spiffy wardrobe—with Ann Taylor. A congratulatory fax from college chum Colin Montgomerie, from whom she hadn't heard in ten years. A tape of the JAL Big Apple—Pierce fast-forwarded to the final few holes and watched her birdie barrage.

"I was grinning from ear to ear watching it. I looked okay. I looked happy. It was nice to see people rushing onto the green [to congratulate me], people you're competing against every week."

She has a new appreciation for the stars. "Someone like Dottie is so mentally strong. Any player out here can win—it's who can win regularly." And she feels better in their presence. "I'm a little more comfortable," she says, noting that she's played with the elite recently—Webb, Pepper, McGann, Mallon, Neumann—and more than held her own.

All in all, it has been a glorious autumn. Pierce bought photographs at an art gallery for her new house when she went to Monterey, California, for the annual LPGA's sponsors meeting after the tournament in Kutztown. She's dating a Taylor-Made representative to whom she was introduced by Tina

Barrett. (By February they will be engaged.) She picked up $10,000 by finishing third in the Mitsubishi pro-am near her home in Scottsdale last week. Her income in 1996, from all sources, will top $300,000. Not bad for someone who earned exactly $1,153 in 1988 when she joined the Tour.

Three years ago, when Pierce stared down the barrel of a handgun shakily pointed at her head, she thought she'd never see her mother again. Now Maureen is in town for a holiday. They're luxuriating in their complimentary room at the Desert Inn, going to shows (Dennis Miller, Cirque du Soleil), and gambling a little bit—"We're the slot machine queens," says Caroline.

It's a weird week in Vegas. Yeah, I know, every week is a weird week in Vegas.

You don't need to ingest anything more stimulating than a Starbucks grande latte to experience the hallucinatory effects of the exploding volcanoes, pirate ship battles, trapeze artists sailing over crap tables, and clockless casinos of Vegas. Forty stories above The Strip, real-life window washers clean the glass windows of the facades of the fake Big Apple skyscrapers at the soon-to-open New York, New York casino.

The Comdex convention has cranked up the bizarro factor to the max. Bill Gates addressed an overflow audience at the Aladdin two days ago. He told them that personal computers would become more and more powerful. He outlined a future where the computer will recognize the user and talk to him, much like, says Gates, the computer Hal in the movie *2001: A Space Odyssey.*

You remember Hal. The computer that killed or tried to kill every human it could get its megabytes on.

Thank God for the sanctity of the golf course. "It's a golden leader board," said Juli Inkster after the first round. It remains so all week. After the third round is completed on Saturday afternoon, Karrie Webb and Emilee Klein are tied at nine under par. Nancy Lopez, Michelle McGann, Brandie Burton, and Laura Davies are six under par. Juli Inkster, Pat Hurst, and Kelly Robbins are five under par.

Golfers stream through the interview room. Davies, who has struggled on the greens, is asked how she's doing at the casinos. "About as well as my putting." Fortunately, she limited herself to a $5,000 bank roll and left her credit cards at home.

Inkster, who shot 72 today and won $20 betting Michigan against Ohio State at the Desert Inn sports book, praises playing partner Klein. "Her fairway woods were right on line all day. Emilee hits those woods straighter than I hit my wedge."

Webb, who preceded Inkster in the interview room—"You whipped in front of me, you little rookie," Inkster kids her—would agree. Webb, like Inkster, hits the ball miles farther than Klein. After they were paired together yesterday, Webb said, "Emilee might be hitting a 7-wood while I'm hitting 8-iron. It just feels different. It doesn't feel like we're playing the same game." Klein shot a second-round 68 in cool, windy conditions. Webb fired a 70.

Today those numbers are reversed. Webb is at the top of her form after a lesson from coach Kelvin Haller, whom she saw last week for the first time in eight months. Instead of her customary straight shots or slight fades, Webb was hitting big hooks. Haller advised her to open up her stance and adjust her posture, and she began striking the ball squarely rather than from the inside-out.

Unlike Webb and Inkster, whose swings are the essence of athleticism, Klein appears to be Robogolfer. Her swing is stiff and mechanical. When she was 14, her father, Bob (whom Klein describes as "a golf nut—he plays and practices every day"), built her an extra-long 45-inch driver. Now she wields a 50-inch Callaway model.

"According to physics, the club shouldn't work," says Klein. According to the money list, she's ninth with $403,793.

In her youth, Klein rode hunter jumpers, but she gave up her horses to concentrate on golf at the age of 12. Her family has a putting green in the front yard. They used to have a sand trap, too. Even when she's home, Klein practices relentlessly.

"I love it too much," she says. Then she jokingly adds, "Golf's not important. It's just our religion."

After her interview, Klein hits the assembly line in the late afternoon as warm sunshine splashes down on the range. Despite a tendency to complain when things don't go her way, Klein is a likable young woman, friendly and utterly guileless. A reporter who has watched her Robogolf her way to stardom can't resist asking her about her athletic abilities.

Klein played a little basketball and ran track in junior high. But she readily admits, with a big smile, "I'm not very coordinated. Not coordinated at all. My arms and legs don't do what I want them to do."

She's a terrible swimmer and a terrible tennis player. At step aerobics she's always out of step. She's not very flexible. When Klein was about 13, she signed up for a ten-session jazz dance class.

"At the end of the first class they took me aside," she laughs. "The instructor said, 'We're going to give you your money back!' "

Then Klein says something you usually don't hear from a star golfer. "I have trouble when it comes to small balls."

"Can you catch a basketball?" she's asked.

Klein nods. "I can catch a basketball." A softball? Sometimes. A golf ball? In her dreams.

What a game golf is! Emilee Klein, at the age of 22, hits a golf ball better than almost any woman in the world.

Just don't try to toss her one.

Shadows lengthen across fairways and greens. The sun descends toward Treasure Island, its rays glinting off the red rock of the surrounding mountains, which are immaculately defined against a clear azure sky.

A few golfers are left on the putting green, an oval partially surrounded by a flower-strewn rock garden framed by a few small palm trees. Almost everyone else has departed.

Hayley Inkster sits on the green beside a cup and rolls balls back to Juli as she putts.

"That's really nice," says a security guard with a mellow smile. "That's the kind of thing that people don't see."

Suddenly Patty Sheehan and Rebecca Gaston, wearing white T-shirts and gray shorts, burst from a walkway beside the clubhouse and jog down the first fairway. Quincey and Sherlock, Sheehan's black and white poodles, scamper along beside them.

Sheehan is back in the pack after shooting 76-73-69, gradually shaking the rust off her clubs after a two-month vacation.

After the Solheim Cup, the Caddie Machine mentioned that Sheehan would play only six tournaments in the last six months of 1996. "Not a bad life," someone said to her. Sheehan cheerfully concurred.

It hasn't been all fun and games. Sheehan contracted bronchitis in Wales and spent three weeks getting back on her feet after the Solheim Cup.

But she was in fine fettle on October 27 when 85 relatives and friends, from as far away as Kansas City and Alabama, surprised her on her fortieth birthday. Sheehan spent three hours opening presents at a party in a suite of the Eldorado Hotel in Reno. She received a guitar, crystal, wine, and tons of gag gifts, including a bra. One cup read, "I've fallen." The other read, "I can't get up."

After the Tour Championship she'll cash in on her major success of a season with appearances in two lucrative postseason made-for-TV events, the Wendy's Three-Tour Challenge and the Diner's Cup Matches. Sheehan ranks 12th on the money list with $332,891 after playing in 15 events, fewer than anyone in the 30 player field. Her income for 1996, including her lucrative Callaway deal and the $100,000 appearance fee for her spring trip to Japan, will total about $750,000.

Sheehan and Gaston and the dogs jog back to the putting green and chat with Juli and Hayley Inkster, as Hayley picks up and pets Quincey. Ray Knight, in town this week to cheer for Lopez, walks over and slaps hands with Gaston.

A few days ago Lopez sat on a rock step beside the green. Despite her excellent play this season, she's still torn between her dual careers as a professional golfer and a wife and mother.

"Ideally, I'd retire for one year only, watch my husband manage in Cincinnati, and go back to playing golf. I miss him a lot."

So she'll balance her duties as best she can, playing about 15 events and working on her game at home while she cares for her kids. Even for Lopez, who can afford all the help she wants, it's a virtuoso juggling act on a treadmill that never stops. "I'm always so pulled and I get so tired of that feeling."

As twilight descends, Lopez, in a white jacket, and Knight, in a black sweatshirt, close up the putting green. Knight is a pretty good golf coach as well as baseball manager. He spotted Lopez decelerating on her putts earlier in the week. He stands behind his wife as she putts, studying her alignment.

A yellow-white full moon, fat and pale, hovers low over the horizon. A few high clouds, rose and white and gray, are brush-stroked against the deepening blue-black sky. The course is still and silent and peaceful. Eventually Knight sits on the clipped green grass in almost the same spot where Hayley Inkster sat a little while ago. As Lopez continues to practice, he rolls balls back to her.

Sometimes a golf course is the most wonderful place in the world.

On a crystalline morning under turquoise skies and a blinding white sun, Karrie Webb, 21, and Emilee Klein, 22, the final group of the 1996 season, arrive at the 480-yard 1st hole for their 11:10 tee time.

How bright is the future of the LPGA? Webb and Klein are not only the youngest players in the field; they are the two youngest players on the entire Tour.

The course has dried out and the wind has become a caressing breeze. The best women golfers in the world go to work, threading the narrow fairways and deciphering the small, undulating greens. Sorenstam and Geddes, back in the pack, open with birdie barrages and set the tone for the day.

As Webb and Klein stand on the tee, a sudden roar reverberates all the way back from the 1st green. Davies has eagled. She's now at eight under par, just one stroke from the lead. Webb glances at a nearby scoreboard. Later she'll say, "When Laura eagled the first, I was a little worried. I thought she'd go berserk today."

The game is on. Webb creases a drive down the left-center of the fairway.

It is a day of shooting stars. On the 362-yard 3rd hole, Brandie Burton, who has holed out from everywhere but the locker room this season, rifles an 8-iron from 135 yards that takes one bounce and rolls into the cup for an eagle. On the 155-yard 5th hole, playing partner Nancy Lopez flies an iron directly over the flag, then leaves a 15-foot putt teetering on the lip, as the gallery yells, "Get in! Get in!" A few seconds later, it bows to the wishes of the assembled masses and topples over the lip and into the cup.

Both birdie the 525-yard 5th hole, feeding off each other's fine play, as the happy crowd buzzes and shouts with glee. On the way to the 6th tee, an older woman, a Las Vegas resident named Pearl Duva, who scored for Lopez at a tournament about ten years ago, reintroduces herself.

It's not clear whether Lopez remembers her. But she offers a beaming smile, grasps Duva's hand, and says, "Thank you, thank you."

After nine holes Webb leads at 11 under par. Klein, Lopez, Burton, Davies, and Inkster are in hot pursuit at 9 under par.

As Webb prepares to attack the green with her second shot on the 471-yard 10th hole, a fan slams the door of a nearby Porta-John—"you know, the ones that have those signs on them that say, 'Please don't slam the door,'" Webb jokes later—just as her club is descending. Webb flinches, yanks the shot to the left, and spends the next few seconds in agony, heart jackhammering wildly, as the ball descends. Luck is on her side. The shot narrowly escapes a greenside water hazard.

It's her last close call. Webb gets up-and-down for birdie, and tacks on two more at Nos. 11 and 13 to soar to 14 under par as Juli Inkster, who birdies three consecutive holes, and Kelly Robbins, in the midst of a seven-birdie, no-bogey round that will take her to 12 under par, try to keep pace.

Webb's performance is eerily reminiscent of her near-flawless final-round 66 at the Sprint Titleholders Championship. In Daytona Beach she sealed the deal with a magnificent 3-iron from 200 yards to set up her winning birdie on the last hole. Seven months later, she rockets a 4-iron second shot from 195 yards ("I was pretty pumped up") to 12 feet of the stick on the 453-yard 15th hole.

Board watching all the way, Webb knows the eagle putt will give her a four-shot lead and slam the door on her foes. When she strokes it firmly into the cup, she pumps a fist in exultation.

A large gallery gathered around the 18th green welcomes the golfers. Patty Sheehan closes with a 69 and ties for sixteenth. She has accomplished all the goals that she could imagine when she took up the game in earnest as a

teenager. But she's not finished yet. A new goal, another trip to the Solheim Cup in 1998, will fuel her engines for the next two years.

Caroline Pierce, paired with Kelly Robbins, shoots 69 to finish twelfth.
Considering she skanked the ball all week, and today in particular, it's an
impressive showing, the kind of performance that great players are able to
pull out of the hat.

Even when she plays "crappy," Pierce is confident that she now has "the
ability to get it around and not shoot high numbers. I'm comfortable I have
the ability to compete every week rather than just make the cut."

Just as she did at Daytona Beach, Robbins chases Webb home. Her 65
ties for second with Lopez (66) and Klein (69). But she didn't expect to
catch the rookie. "Once you see Karrie get a couple of strokes ahead, you
know she's going to stay there."

After she emerges from the scorer's tent, a local reporter asks Robbins if
she knew she would shoot the lights out today.

"What kind of question is that?" she bursts out with an incredulous
laugh. Then she patiently explains that she, like every golfer, never knows
what the day will bring. Sometimes everything falls into place. Robbins had
"perfect numbers" today—she was never between clubs on her approach
shots to the greens.

Juli Inkster plays her heart out as she vainly chases the wondrous Webb.
Three down after parring the 16th hole, she walks onto the tee at No. 17,
greets a casino executive she knows, and says, "Gotta get two more birdies."
A few minutes later she barely misses a 15-footer and settles for par.

"Well, team, shall we make one [birdie] for the road?" Inkster says to
playing partner and fellow San Jose State alumna Pat Hurst.

They chatter cheerfully as they walk up the 18th fairway. Inkster pars
for a 67. She ties for fifth with Laura Davies (67) and Brandie Burton (67),
passed by Robbins, Lopez, and Klein down the stretch. On the relentlessly
and ever-increasingly competitive LPGA Tour, pars are rarely good enough
on the back nine on Sunday to get the big dough and the silver trophies.

But she's pleased with her performance and pumped up about 1997.
"I'm looking to have a great year. I need to get back in the winner's circle.
Until I do that, I don't think I've accomplished much."

She's accomplished plenty. And next month at the Diner's Cup Matches,
she'll be back in the winner's circle for the first time since 1992. It's an unofficial event, but her best-ball victory with Dottie Pepper over Kelly Robbins
and Tammie Green is worth $100,000, a sweet Christmas present.

On the 18th green, Karrie Webb lines up a 30-foot birdie putt. A storybook ending? Not quite. The putt burns the edge of the cup. Still, Webb's

year-long adventure is more amazing than any (Planet) Hollywood script writer could invent.

Webb is left with a one-foot putt to become the first woman in history to win $1 million in official money in a single season. When she taps it in, she raises both hands overhead, a beaming smile on her face.

"Luv ya, mate!" a voice calls out from the packed, cheering gallery. The tournament is being broadcast in Australia, and Webb is interviewed at greenside. The home folks are tuned in; cable was just installed in Ayr.

Last night Webb went to Siegfried & Roy and watched the white tigers vanish from the stage. Today she conjures up a bit of her own magic—a one-eagle, five-birdie, no-bogey performance with a 31 on the back nine that makes the opposition all but disappear.

"Awesome," says caddie Evan Minster. "One of the best rounds all year. She's just special."

Webb is typically gracious in victory. Earlier in the week, she discussed the Kelli Kuehne deal without a trace of rancor. "I can't have any bad feelings for her. It's great she can get an endorsement like that." Now she says, "Laura is number one in the world. I respect her a lot. I know it would have meant a lot to her to win the money title and win one million dollars."

(It wasn't in the cards for Davies this week, who won four times on the LPGA Tour, three times in Europe, and twice in Japan in 1996. But she and Sorenstam, according to a source at IMG, become the first women golf pros to amass over $2 million from all sources—official and unofficial money, appearance fees and endorsement deals—in a single year.)

Webb confesses she didn't sleep much last night, and says she was very nervous during the round. "I guess I didn't show it."

Guess not. She says, "Every time I looked up at my shot, it was going straight at the pin. . . . When you know you need to play well, and do everything you want to do, it's definitely a dream round."

One that began in the mind of a young girl on a scruffy golf course in a tiny sugarcane town on the other side of the world. "I dreamed about being in positions like this when I was a little kid."

Although she didn't know it at the time, Webb's dream was the American Dream. Often it's a cruel mirage, like the neon lights of Las Vegas, a tantalizing fantasyland of glitter, seductive and elusive, shimmering just beyond the grasp of eager fingertips.

Yet ambition and talent and hard work and good fortune nurture the Dream, which thrives on the emerald fairways of the LPGA Tour.

*   *   *

After all the interviews are over, Webb walks into the Desert Inn pro shop on the way to the locker room. A well-wisher offers congratulations. Starry eyed, Webb responds with a vigorous handshake and a happy smile. "Thanks a lot!" Next month, on her twenty-second birthday, Webb will parachute out of an airplane over the skies of Australia. But she'll never be as high as she is at this moment.

In 1976 Judy Rankin became the first woman golfer to win $100,000 in a season. Twenty years later, Webb secures a place in the history books by tallying $1 million. In 2016, a woman might earn $10 million on the links.

Maybe it will be a little girl like 6-year-old Alex, happily hitting balls with a club on a grassy field. Maybe it will be a little girl in Pakistan or China or Zaire.

Another season is over. But in less than two months, tournament winners from 1995 and 1996 and Hall of Famers will greet the new year by teeing it up at the $750,000 Chrysler-Plymouth Tournament of Champions in Ft. Lauderdale. One week later a full field of 144 golfers, including rookies fresh from Q-School, will vie at the HealthSouth Inaugural in Orlando.

A new season, filled with infinite possibilities, will begin.

Index